FRESH FROM FRANCE
DESSERT SENSATIONS

FRESH FROM FRANCE
DESSERT SENSATIONS

FAYE LEVY

ILLUSTRATIONS BY MAUREEN JENSEN
PHOTOGRAPHS BY GUS FRANCISCO

A DUTTON BOOK

DUTTON
Published by the Penguin Group
Penguin Books USA Inc., 375 Hudson Street,
New York, New York 10014, U.S.A.

Penguin Books Ltd, 27 Wrights Lane,
London W8 5TZ, England

Penguin Books Australia Ltd, Ringwood,
Victoria, Australia

Penguin Books Canada Ltd, 2801 John Street,
Markham, Ontario, Canada L3R 1B4

Penguin Books (N.Z.) Ltd, 182-190 Wairau Road,
Auckland 10, New Zealand

Penguin Books Ltd, Registered Offices:
Harmondsworth, Middlesex, England

First published by Dutton, an imprint of Penguin Books USA Inc.
Distributed in Canada by McClelland & Stewart Inc.

First printing, October, 1990
1 3 5 7 9 10 8 6 4 2

Copyright © Faye Levy, 1990
Illustrations © Maureen Jensen, 1990
Photographs © Gus Francisco, 1990
Food stylist: Andrea Swenson
Prop stylist: Laurie Jean Beck
All rights reserved

Library of Congress Cataloging-in-Publication Data

Levy, Faye.
Dessert sensations / Faye Levy. — 1st ed.
p. cm. — (Fresh from France)
ISBN 0-525-24893-5
1. Desserts.   I. Title.   II. Series: Levy, Faye.   Fresh from
France.
TX773.L463 1990
641.8′6—dc20   90-32164
                                                       CIP

Printed in the United States of America
Set in Garamond
Designed by Earl Tidwell

TO JULIA CHILD,

for inspiring me to master the art of French cooking

Contents

●

Eight pages of color plates follow page 168.

Acknowledgments

Although I have written the Fresh From France series for the home cook, and have presented mostly simple recipes, I feel that I couldn't have done it well without training with professional chefs. During the five years I spent at the Parisian cooking school La Varenne, I was fortunate to have had the chance to learn about desserts from some of the finest pastry chefs of France, and I am grateful to each of them. There is, however, one marvelous teacher and superb chef to whom I owe the most for my understanding of the basics of classic pastry- and cake-making: Albert Jorant, La Varenne's pastry chef.

To Denis Ruffel, one of France's most outstanding chefs and the author of several big, instructive cookbooks, I wish to express my sincere gratitude for teaching me the principles of modern pâtisserie. I appreciate his enabling me to do a "stage" at his excellent pastry shop, Millet, so I could learn and observe firsthand how his delicious treats are made.

In France there are two major categories of desserts: pastry shop desserts, or *entremets de pâtisserie,* and restaurant desserts, or *entremets de cuisine.* The second category includes soufflés, mousses, and other delicate, fragile desserts that usually demand last-minute attention. For educating me about these and about all types of desserts, I wish to thank chefs Fernand Chambrette and Claude Vauguet of La Varenne, with whom I studied every day during my years at the school.

Chefs Jorant, Ruffel, Chambrette, and Vauguet have been more than teachers; they have become my friends. And they taught me much more than recipes and techniques; they have communicated their love for their métier, their professionalism, and their sense of excitement in creating wonderful food.

Two other great chefs deserve special thanks: Maurice Ferré, the pastry chef of Maxim's in Paris, and Joël Bellouet, a Meilleur Ouvrier de France (MOF) and the author of impressive dessert books. Chef Ferré shared his knowledge in practical classes and numerous Saturday demonstrations; Chef Bellouet was my teacher in the "pâtisserie entrements" course for professional pastry chefs at Lenôtre's school for continuing culinary education near Paris.

I have also enjoyed learning how to make desserts, pastries, and other sweets from master pastry chef and MOF Jean Creveux; chocolatier Robert Linxe of La Maison du Chocolat; pastry chef Eric Saguez, MOF, of the Ecole de Gastronomie Française Ritz-Escoffier; Patrick Martin of the Paris Cordon Bleu; Chef Michel Comby, then of Lucas Carton and now of Chez Comby; Antoine Bouterin, at the time chef of Au Quai d'Orsay in Paris and now of Le Perigord in New York; Michel Marolleau, the first head chef of La Varenne; and chefs Gérard Besson, Jacques Cagna, Michel Pasquet, Pierre Vedel, John Desmond, Roger Baudry, Michel Ranvier of Jamin, and Michel Rostang.

My heartfelt thanks go to Anne Willan for giving me five years of training in writing recipes and cookbooks, and for making it possible for me to study with so many wonderful chefs.

I am grateful to Julia Child for encouraging me to study at La Varenne, in response to a letter I wrote to her in 1975 asking to become her assistant. Her books, as well as those of Jacques Pépin in the U.S. and of Yves Thuries in France, have provided me with continuous inspiration.

Thanks to Ruth Sirkis, my Israeli publisher, for publishing two books of mine on French desserts, thus giving me an opportunity to further explore this fascinating, sweet subject.

I truly value the contribution of my recipe testers, who worked alongside me to test recipes and who gave me new ideas. Most of all I am grateful to Annie Horenn, who helped me test the recipes for this book and is now a talented food stylist. Thanks also to Teri Appleton, now the creative pastry chef of Ocean Avenue Seafood in Santa Monica; and to chef Leona Fitzgerald and caterer Patsy Allen.

I sincerely appreciate the effort and dedication of my editor, Molly Allen, in helping this book get published in the best way possible. I will always be grateful to Carole DeSanti for making my Fresh From France series a reality. Thanks to food stylist Andrea Swenson and photographer Gus Francisco for producing such lovely photographs. I am also thankful to Maureen and Eric Lasher for their support.

Everyone who knows me knows what a significant role my husband and associate, Yakir Levy, plays in planning, writing, and publicizing each of my books. So, for the eleventh time, thanks!

Finally, thanks to my mother, Pauline Kahn Luria, for baking delicious cakes every Friday, and for never making me celebrate my birthday with a "bought" cake! I am sure all those lovingly baked cakes helped me learn at an early age the difference between a mediocre dessert and a fresh, fine-quality one.

Foreword

At La Varenne Ecole de Cuisine in Paris, Faye Levy has gone down in history as "Madame Mesure." For six happy years, Faye was with us as cookery editor, supervising the school's curriculum while researching and developing recipes for several major cookbooks. During the day she was at her desk, but in the evenings Faye would be found in class in the kitchens, observing, questioning, tasting. With a smile for her perfectionism and a sigh at her persistence, the chefs would expound on the dishes of the day until at last she was satisfied.

Faye Levy's recipes reflect this scrupulous attention. Reading them, you are at once transported into the kitchen with Faye at your side. "For sautéing, choose fruit that is not too soft," she cautions, and "To facilitate unmolding, choose plain molds or those with simple designs." Her text is a model of clarity and logic—indeed, Faye's graduate thesis at La Varenne was entitled "How to Write a Recipe." It still serves as required reading for our students.

During her stay in France, Faye acquired not only a mastery of the principles of French cooking, but also a grasp of the background—history, regional characteristics, national prejudices. (A Frenchman regards corn as cattle food, and chili pepper as devil's fire.) In this ongoing series of *Fresh from France,* Faye is quick to spot new trends. She points out that the current move toward reducing sugar in desserts has led to stronger flavors such as dark chocolate, and tart fruits like blackcurrant. She reiterates that the most sought-after quality in today's menu is freshness.

Faye Levy has written cookbooks in three languages but her first love is France, a preference shared by so many of us who enjoy good eating. For we gourmands, this book is destined to take pride of place on the kitchen bookshelf for many years to come, and we will revel often in its company.

ANNE WILLAN
Ecole de Cuisine La Varenne
Paris, France

FRESH FROM FRANCE
DESSERT SENSATIONS

Introduction

When we think of our favorite desserts—airy soufflés, rich mousses, and light sorbets, for example—we are thinking of French desserts, often without realizing it. Many of America's best desserts originated in France, yet have become part of our own culinary heritage and vocabulary. Moreover, French techniques and style are the basis for most of our new sweet creations. Culinary education acquired in France proves precious to many professionals. Five years of training there prepared and qualified me to develop many original desserts for our country's top cooking magazines and enabled me to win, in 1986, the IACP/Seagram Award for the best dessert and baking book of the year.

During the recent bicentennial of the French Revolution of 1789, I naturally reflected on another French revolution—the culinary revolution, which occurred nearly two centuries later and had a major effect on contemporary French desserts.

I was fortunate to be living in Paris when this chefs' revolt was taking place. In the seventies and early eighties I worked at La Varenne Cooking School, which decided to feature classes with chefs of trend-setting restaurants. Soon we noticed signs of a new style of cooking. These young French chefs were using cilantro and soy sauce in addition to the traditional chives, chervil, and tarragon; in their desserts they were experimenting with fresh ginger, mint, and other herbs in addition to the customary vanilla, chocolate, and coffee. This had been unheard of before. Chef after chef declared proudly, as he demonstrated his specialties, "I don't use flour at all in my kitchen, except to make dough," while dessert chefs boasted of their flourless soufflés and cakes. We were amazed! Clearly something was going on.

Without being aware of it at first, we were witnessing a dramatic transformation in the way the French cooked—"haute cuisine" was changing into the style that came to be known as "nouvelle cuisine." The sweet side of French cooking soon underwent a similar change and became "nouvelle pâtisserie."

There was a new attitude toward cooking, and the best chefs were gaining a special status as artists and as stars. The standard for judging a good chef was altered drastically—the goal was no longer the perfect duplication of a classic dish, but rather the invention of a new one. Chefs no longer were supposed to follow the culinary bible, Escoffier's *Guide Culinaire,* to the letter in order to be considered top professionals. Instead, after mastering the basics, each cook was free, and indeed expected, to put his own ideas into his cooking. Some chefs felt they were breaking ground and developing a new cuisine, while others, more modest but no less imaginative, insisted that they were simply updating the classics and adapting them to current tastes.

As in the historic French Revolution, the message was liberty—in this case, liberty to be creative in the kitchen.

But these rebellious chefs did not simply walk in and dethrone Escoffier without opposition. The "old guard" chefs resisted by criticizing, mocking, and even ridiculing them, finding their tastes for generous amounts of robust herbs and for boldly flavored dishes too aggressive. The classic style, after all, called for using flavorings with a delicate touch.

Parallel to nouvelle cuisine, with its growing use of assertive seasonings, a taste for more pronounced flavors in desserts evolved: chocolate desserts became more chocolaty, lemon ones more lemony, and vanilla bean desserts more intensely perfumed.

To a passionate student of French cooking like me, living in Paris during this period was very exciting. Everyone was discussing the new cuisine. The talk at school and around town was, "Did you hear about the chef who cooks lobster with vanilla beans? Or the restaurant featuring *petits pots de crème* with ginger? Or the chef who serves guava sorbet with fresh mango sauce?" We rushed to taste these novelties and to discover creations made with sea beans, tropical fruit, and other exotic ingredients.

There was no Reign of Terror in the culinary revolution, but there were wild excesses, in what could be called a Reign of the Absurd. The quest for originality was practically forced on chefs by restaurant reviewers and by the public. Even cooks who knew how to make fine food didn't necessarily know how to compose delicious new dishes. Chefs were often criticized for presenting ridiculously small servings of food on huge plates, for cooking some foods so briefly that they remained raw, and for adding silly decorations. Kiwi slices became the garnish de rigueur. These problems led certain writers to announce prematurely that the attempted revolution had failed, and that nouvelle cuisine was "dead."

Some even declared that French cooking has been in the midst of a counterrevolution, a backlash against innovation and lightness— that chefs have been returning to the classics, and to the substantial country- and grandmother-style cuisine of which the favorite elements are potatoes, leeks, hearty meats, and rice puddings.

I do not agree. In fact, I would go so far as to say that nouvelle cuisine is alive and well, only under different names, like "contemporary," "modern," "new classic," and "updated classic." Other labels in vogue beautifully illustrate the revolution's triumph in establishing the general climate of freedom and innovation. Successful French chefs now often describe their style of cooking as "personal," "improvised," or even "spontaneous."

Like the historic French Revolution, the recent revolution in the kitchens of the European culinary superpower had repercussions around the globe. It was imitated in many countries, including our own. In fact, in our country the influence was so strong, it even inspired the proclamations of elegant regional styles such as "new Southern cuisine," "new New England cuisine," and "California cuisine."

The most sought-after quality in all parts of today's menus, including desserts, is freshness. Contemporary desserts are characterized primarily by a greater presence of fresh fruit. Fruit gratins, fruit mousses, and fruit platters of artfully arranged fruit slices served with fruit sauce are now highlighted on fine menus. Even if a dessert is not made of fruit, fresh fruit is likely to accompany it, either as a sauce or sorbet, or simply sliced as a garnish.

Chocolate, too, has gained enormously in popularity. Bittersweet chocolate remains the uncontested favorite; however, white and milk chocolate, little used before, are now often made into desserts. Chocolate ganache, although mentioned in Darenne and Duval's *Traité de Pâtisserie Moderne,* the pastry chef's manual of classic desserts, was rarely used in desserts until recently. Now it is so fashionable it has overtaken chocolate buttercream as a basic chocolate filling and frosting in the best kitchens. Furthermore, it has been developed in a great variety of new forms, such as ganache glaze, whipped ganache, and ganache buttercream. Today, ganache is made with milk chocolate and white chocolate as well as bittersweet, and it is enhanced with numerous other flavors, such as orange, coffee, and cinnamon. Professional chefs even use it now as a basis for making chocolate sauces, mousses, and other desserts.

The emphasis on stronger flavors came with a decrease in sweetness. Many chefs use less sugar in desserts, just as they use less salt in the rest of the menu. Thus fondant, a very sweet frosting once used on many cakes, pastries, and petits fours, is less widespread, as in the Napoleon, for example. Rather than being glazed with fondant, it is often decorated with fresh fruit and whipped cream.

However, one type of flavoring that is used with a lighter hand than before is alcohol. Flambéed desserts doused with liquor are no longer in vogue. *Eau de vie* and other spirits are used mainly to complement other flavors.

Mousse cakes are the major dessert innovation of the last two decades. Pastry chefs strive for lightness in desserts as *chefs de cuisine* do in the rest of the menu, and thus many are preparing more mousse-filled cakes and fewer buttercream cakes. Mousse cakes are also well loved for their great variety and versatility, as the mousses can be prepared not only in many flavors, both familiar and inventive, but also in many forms. For example, a raspberry mousse filling can be prepared in any number of ways—by adding raspberry purée either to Bavarian cream, or to bombe mousse mixed with whipped cream, or to a mixture of Italian meringue and Chantilly cream, or to pastry cream mixed with gelatin and whipped cream. There are still more ways to prepare fruit mousse, and each will give a different texture and flavor. Add to this the opportunity to combine flavors in a single mousse, and to layer the mousses with different cakes, and the possibilities are endless. Many of these mousses are completely new as cake fillings.

Simplicity is an important attribute of many modern desserts, especially in their decoration; a subtle, natural garnish is à la mode rather than a complex decor. A few toasted nuts, sliced fresh fruit, or grated chocolate is often all that is used to give a dessert a festive appearance. Gaudy, heavily garnished cakes are much less popular now than they were before.

A glance at the fabulous new desserts of pastry chefs of starred restaurants and innovative pâtisseries, as well as those of fine cooking teachers and talented cookbook authors, shows immediately how much the sweet side of French cooking has evolved since the culinary revolution began. On the other hand, there are many pastry shops in France that give the impression that nothing has changed in the past twenty years—they display the same éclairs and gâteaux that they have always made. Even pastry shops that pride themselves in being at the forefront of nouvelle pâtisserie do present some traditional pastries. The French admire and enjoy novelty, but they have certain desserts that they love and want to continue enjoying unchanged. I have followed this approach by including not only new creations, but also classic favorites. In each chapter, I have pointed out what is new in that area of French desserts, as well as which traditional ones remain well-loved today.

This book, like the other volumes of my Fresh from France series, is for the home cook. Most of the desserts are fairly simple and require only a few minutes for garnishing. For me, a scoop of homemade caramel ice cream or a slice of fresh flavored almond cake is a real treat, and yet they are so easy to make. I'm not in favor of spending hours preparing extra mixtures that serve mainly as garnishes. However, I have included a few elaborate desserts, such as vacherins and certain mousse cakes, for those special occasions when you might want to prepare very impressive grand finales.

Enjoying desserts is an important element of the French *joie de vivre.* According to Christian Millau, the gastronomic guru of France, the consumption of desserts in France has tripled in the last twenty years, in spite of the obsession with *cuisine minceur,* or diet cooking. In this country, we also are nutrition conscious and try to find the ideal balance between our desire for a healthful diet and our need to pamper ourselves occasionally. My own approach toward desserts is similar to my attitude toward wine—I'm looking for quality, not quantity. Whenever I do treat myself to a dessert, I want it to be a very good one. And the best way to ensure this is to have a dessert only in a great restaurant or pâtisserie, or to make it yourself.

Hot Desserts

"Comfort food" desserts, from creamy rice puddings to warm vanilla-scented poached apples, are mostly family dinner fare. They make up an important part of this category of hot desserts, but you will also find grand finales, such as spectacular soufflés and soufflé-filled crêpes. In fact, soufflés are excellent for casual entertaining because they are easiest to bake and serve among friends in an informal setting.

One of the most memorable hot desserts I ever tasted was a citrus soufflé crêpe demonstrated by Parisian Chef Fernand Chambrette at La Varenne Cooking School. This was a new idea to all of us who were watching, and the result was as delicious as it was dramatic. It was the model for Orange Soufflé Crêpes.

Outside of a cooking school, there are many opportunities to enjoy warm desserts in France. Crêpes with a variety of sweet fillings are easy to find at outdoor stands and at the numerous crêperies found throughout the country. Soufflés are everywhere, too, from the menus of small restaurants with just a few tables to those of the most lavish three-star establishments. The contemporary favorites in the hot-dessert category seem to be fruit gratins glazed with rich sabayon sauces.

Hot-and-cold dessert combinations continue to be popular. When I dined at Troisgros restaurant in Roanne several years ago, I had a warm crêpe filled with lemon sorbet, as a prelude to their "grand dessert." This was like eating a "dessert appetizer" before the "dessert dinner" that came after the main course! A modern fashion in French restaurants is to serve a warm dessert, such as a fruit-filled crêpe or tart, topped with a sorbet of the same fruit. Although these are irresistible, I'm glad they have not displaced the best of the classics, such as delicious profiteroles filled with ice cream and cloaked in chocolate sauce.

Soufflés

A sweet soufflé is one of the lightest and most spectacular of desserts. What other dessert can match the drama of a glorious soufflé, risen high as if by magic, and richly flavored with chocolate, praline, or Grand Marnier?

The impressive appearance and unique delicate texture of these elegant desserts may lead to the conclusion that they must be complicated. Yet soufflés are actually simple to prepare. They are made of a thick, custardlike base, similar to the pastry cream filling of éclairs, mixed with whipped egg whites. Although some chefs gave in to the flour phobia of the seventies and stopped making soufflés with flour-thickened custards, I still like them because they have a creamier texture than flourless soufflés.

Flavorings can range from a few teaspoons of a favorite liqueur, a sprinkling of grated citrus rind, or a little instant espresso—to more exotic taste combinations, as in Coconut-Ginger Soufflé. The techniques required are familiar, since they are also used in making many cakes. Soufflés are quick desserts, too. The soufflé base cooks in minutes and can be prepared ahead, leaving only the beating of the whites and the brief baking to be done at the last moment.

Properly beaten egg whites folded gently into the base mixture are the key to successful soufflés. It is air bubbles caught in the egg whites that give soufflés their lightness by expanding in the oven and causing the soufflés to puff. Although many chefs insist that the egg whites for a soufflé must be whipped by hand in a copper bowl with a balloon whisk, I find that soufflés rise very well when the whites are beaten with the whip of a heavy-duty electric mixer. This method is certainly easier and more practical, especially for entertaining.

Soufflés rise best in soufflé dishes because the straight sides encourage the mixture to puff straight up. To give the dessert a pleasant sweet crust, the buttered dish is often coated with sugar.

A common question in my cooking classes is when to wrap a piece of paper around a soufflé dish to make a collar. Collars were devised for preparing cold soufflés, which are actually mock soufflés and just give the impression of having risen above the dish. In the case of hot soufflés, collars are required only for very thin soufflé mixtures and are rarely, if ever, used by French chefs. Collars are not needed for the soufflés included here, which have enough body to hold their shape as they rise.

Some cooks like to accompany their soufflés with sauces, such as custard sauce, softened ice cream, softly whipped cream, or fresh fruit sauce. In soufflés baked to the French taste, however, the center remains soft and moist and acts almost as a sauce for the firmer outer layer. All that is needed for a finishing touch on these delightful desserts is a light dusting of powdered sugar.

Hints

• If using a small oven, check whether there is plenty of room for the soufflé to rise without reaching its top; if there isn't, position the rack in the lower third of the oven instead of in the center.

• To be sure the oven reaches the proper temperature, preheat it for 15 to 20 minutes.

• To ensure even heat, do not bake other things at the same time as the soufflé.

• A 6-cup (1½-quart) soufflé dish is the ideal size for baking the soufflés in this chapter; a 7-cup dish is also fine. A 5-cup dish can be used, too; however, the soufflé rises very high and is a bit difficult to move from the oven to the table.

• Soufflés can be baked in other baking dishes of the same volume instead of soufflé dishes, although they will not rise as high and their baking times will be different.

• Generally it is most convenient to prepare the soufflé base ahead and bake the soufflé later. If you prefer to proceed immediately to baking and serving, preheat the oven and butter the dish before preparing the soufflé base.

• An egg is easiest to separate into white and yolk when it is cold, because the fat in the yolk is firmer and the yolk is less likely to break. The easiest working procedure for soufflés is to separate the eggs as soon as you remove them from the refrigerator, and then to let them come to room temperature while preparing the other ingredients for the recipe.

• If any yolk gets into the bowl of egg whites, use an eggshell half to scoop it out.

• A soufflé base with its flavoring should taste strong, because its flavor will become milder after the sweetened whipped egg whites are added.

• Beat the egg whites carefully: if overbeaten, they will be lumpy and will not blend into the base mixture; if underbeaten, they will not be firm enough to make the soufflé rise. Be sure to use a clean, dry bowl and clean beater. Begin beating the egg whites at medium speed and increase to medium-high, until they form soft peaks. With the mixer at high speed, gradually beat in the sugar and continue beating until the whites are just stiff and shiny but not dry, about 15 seconds.

• Beating a little sugar into whipped whites makes them smoother, prevents dryness, and thus makes it easier to fold the whites into the soufflé base.

• Fold the whites into the soufflé base as soon as they are beaten or they will deflate. One-quarter of the whites is first folded in to lighten the base and make folding in the remaining whites easier.

• To fold efficiently, with your right hand pull a medium or large rubber spatula through the center of the mixture to the bottom of the bowl, then toward the left side of the bowl and bring the mixture up over whites, while turning the bowl counterclockwise with your left hand at the same time. Repeat this motion several times until the batter is just blended. Reverse the directions if you are left-handed.

- Fold the egg whites into the soufflé base as quickly and as gently as possible, to avoid deflating their air bubbles. A few very small streaks of white may remain in the soufflé batter.
- To serve soufflés, use 2 spoons to pierce the crust, then scoop out some of the soft center and include some of the firmer outside for each portion.

SOUFFLÉ BASE
Crème pour soufflés

All that is needed is flavoring and whipped egg whites to turn this simple mixture, which is a version of pastry cream, into a splendid, high soufflé. This basic preparation is a component of some of the soufflés included in this section. MAKES ABOUT 1 CUP

1 cup milk
1 vanilla bean (see Note)
3 large egg yolks, room temperature

3 tablespoons sugar
1/4 cup all-purpose flour

Bring milk to a boil with vanilla bean in small heavy saucepan over medium-high heat. Remove from heat, cover, and let stand 30 minutes. Remove vanilla bean.

Return milk to a boil over medium-high heat. Remove from heat. Whisk egg yolks and sugar in medium, heavy bowl until well blended. Gently whisk in flour just until blended. Whisk in hot milk in a thin stream until mixture is smooth. Return mixture to saucepan and cook over medium-low heat, stirring constantly all over pan with whisk, until mixture is very thick and just falls heavily from whisk rather than flowing from it, about 2 or 3 minutes. Remove from heat. Use in soufflé recipes.

NOTE: For some recipes, vanilla bean is not needed. If omitting it, follow instructions beginning with the second paragraph.

HAZELNUT SURPRISE SOUFFLÉ
Soufflé aux noisettes en surprise

Toasted hazelnuts flavor this luscious soufflé. The "surprise" hidden inside is hazelnut liqueur–soaked ladyfingers, which reinforce the soufflé's taste.   MAKES 4 TO 5 SERVINGS

1/3 cup hazelnuts
Soufflé Base (page 11)
About 4 tablespoons granulated
*   sugar*
Powdered sugar for sprinkling

6 packaged ladyfinger halves
4 tablespoons hazelnut liqueur
5 large egg whites, room
*   temperature*
Pinch of cream of tartar

Preheat oven to 350°F. Toast and skin hazelnuts (see page 388). Cool completely. Grind in food processor, scraping inward often, until very fine.

Prepare soufflé base. Stir in hazelnuts. (If making soufflé base ahead, immediately cover with wax paper directly on its surface. It can be kept, covered with lid in addition to paper, 1 day in refrigerator. Before continuing, let stand about 30 minutes at room temperature.)

Position rack in center of oven and preheat to 400°F. Generously butter a 6- to 7-cup soufflé dish with soft butter, making sure rim is well buttered. Put about 2 tablespoons sugar in soufflé dish. Shake, turn, and tap dish until bottom and sides are evenly coated with sugar; remove excess. Have round heatproof platter ready near oven and a shaker of powdered sugar; or put a little powdered sugar in small strainer set over small bowl.

Break each ladyfinger half in 2 pieces crosswise. Put pieces, spongy side up, close together on small plate. Sprinkle them evenly with 2 tablespoons liqueur.

If soufflé base is still warm, whisk it briefly until smooth. If it is cold, heat it over low heat, whisking, until just warm and smooth, and remove from heat. Gradually whisk in remaining 2 tablespoons liqueur. Scrape down sides of pan.

Beat egg whites with cream of tartar in a large bowl until they form soft peaks. With mixer at high speed, gradually beat in remaining 2 tablespoons sugar and beat until whites are just stiff and shiny but not dry, about 15 seconds.

Immediately fold about one-quarter of whites into soufflé base to lighten. Gradually pour this mixture over remaining whites while folding. Use rubber spatula to transfer any remaining mixture from pan to bowl of whites. Continue folding together as gently but as quickly as possible. (Be careful not to deflate mixture; a few small streaks of white may remain.)

Transfer about half the batter to prepared soufflé dish, pouring it into center of dish. Set moistened ladyfingers on top in single layer without letting them touch sides of dish. Spoon remaining batter on top to cover ladyfingers. Smooth top gently but quickly with rubber spatula.

Bake until soufflé is puffed and brown, about 22 to 24 minutes; when you carefully move oven rack, soufflé should shake very gently. (Center will remain moist.) Set soufflé dish on round platter, quickly shake powdered sugar over soufflé, and serve immediately.

CREAMY CHOCOLATE SOUFFLÉ
Soufflé au chocolat

French soufflés are baked briefly so the creamy interior acts as a sauce. But recently my husband and I enjoyed a chocolate soufflé at Lucas Carton, one of the most elegant restaurants in Paris, and each serving was topped with soft pistachio ice cream. Homemade vanilla, coffee, or caramel ice cream (see recipes) is also delicious with this soufflé.   MAKES 4 SERVINGS

Soufflé Base (page 11)
4 ounces fine-quality bittersweet
    chocolate, chopped
About 4 tablespoons granulated
    sugar

Powdered sugar for sprinkling
5 large egg whites, room
    temperature
Pinch of cream of tartar

Prepare soufflé base. Melt chocolate in a small bowl above hot water over low heat. Stir until smooth. Cool to room temperature. Gradually whisk chocolate into soufflé base; blend in very thoroughly. (If making soufflé base ahead, immediately cover with wax paper directly on its surface to prevent skin from forming. Soufflé base can be kept up to 1 day, covered with lid in addition to paper, in refrigerator. Before continuing, let stand about 30 minutes at room temperature.)

Position rack in center of oven and preheat to 400°F. Generously butter a 6- to 7-cup soufflé dish with soft butter, making sure rim is well buttered. Put about 2 tablespoons sugar in soufflé dish. Shake, turn, and tap dish until bottom and sides are evenly coated with sugar; remove excess. Have round heatproof platter ready near oven and a shaker of powdered sugar; or put a little powdered sugar in small strainer set over small bowl.

If soufflé base is still warm, whisk it briefly until smooth. If it was prepared ahead, heat it over low heat, whisking, until just warm and smooth; remove from heat. Scrape down sides of pan.

Beat egg whites with cream of tartar in large bowl until they form soft peaks. With mixer at high speed, gradually beat in remaining 2 tablespoons sugar and beat until whites are just stiff and shiny but not dry, about 15 seconds.

Immediately fold about one-quarter of whites into soufflé base to lighten. Gradually pour this mixture over remaining whites while folding. Use rubber spatula to transfer any remaining mixture from pan to bowl of whites. Continue folding together as gently but as quickly as possible. (Be careful not to deflate mixture; a few small streaks of white may remain.)

Quickly transfer batter to prepared soufflé dish, pouring it into center of dish, and smooth top gently but quickly with rubber spatula.

Bake until soufflé is puffed and brown, about 20 to 22 minutes; when you carefully move oven rack, soufflé should shake very gently. (Center will remain moist.) Set soufflé dish on round platter, quickly shake powdered sugar over soufflé, and serve immediately.

COCONUT-GINGER SOUFFLÉ
Soufflé à la noix de coco au gingembre

Candied ginger, orange zest, and grated coconut impart an exciting taste to this creamy *nouvelle* soufflé.   MAKES 4 TO 5 SERVINGS

Soufflé Base (page 11), with
    vanilla bean omitted
1 1/2 teaspoons grated or finely
    chopped orange peel
About 4 tablespoons granulated
    sugar
Powdered sugar for sprinkling
1/4 cup chopped crystallized ginger

1/2 cup ground unsweetened coconut
    (see Note)
1 tablespoon strained fresh orange
    juice
5 large egg whites, room
    temperature
Pinch of cream of tartar

Prepare soufflé base without vanilla. Whisk in orange peel. (If making soufflé base ahead, immediately cover with wax paper directly on its surface. Soufflé base can be kept up to 1 day, covered with lid in addition to paper, in refrigerator. Before continuing, let stand about 30 minutes at room temperature.)

Position rack in center of oven and preheat to 400°F. Generously butter a 6- to 7-cup soufflé dish with soft butter, making sure rim is well buttered. Put about 2 tablespoons sugar in soufflé dish. Shake, turn, and tap dish until bottom and sides are evenly coated with sugar; remove excess. Have round heatproof platter ready near oven. Have ready a shaker of powdered sugar; or put a little powdered sugar in small strainer set over small bowl.

If soufflé base is still warm, whisk it briefly until smooth. If it was prepared ahead, heat it over low heat, whisking, until just warm and smooth, and remove from heat. Whisk in ginger, coconut, and orange juice. Scrape down sides of pan.

Beat egg whites with cream of tartar in large bowl until they form soft peaks. With mixer at high speed, gradually beat in remaining 2 tablespoons sugar and beat until whites are just stiff and shiny but not dry, about 15 seconds.

Immediately fold about one-quarter of whites into soufflé base to lighten. Gradually pour this mixture over remaining whites while folding. Use rubber spatula to transfer any remaining mixture from pan to bowl of whites. Continue folding together as gently but as quickly as possible. (Be careful not to deflate mixture; a few small streaks of white may remain.)

Quickly transfer batter to prepared soufflé dish, pouring it into center of dish, and smooth top gently but quickly with rubber spatula.

Bake until soufflé is puffed and brown, about 22 to 24 minutes;

when you carefully move oven rack, soufflé should shake very gently. (Center will remain moist.) Set soufflé dish on round platter, quickly shake powdered sugar over soufflé, and serve immediately.

NOTE: Unsweetened coconut is available at health-food stores and some supermarkets. It is sometimes called "macaroon coconut." (If using shredded unsweetened coconut, grind in food processor and measure ½ cup.)

COFFEE SOUFFLÉ
Soufflé au café

When you want a spectacular, easy-to-prepare dessert from ingredients likely to be in your kitchen, this soufflé is a good choice. Instant coffee gives a result very similar to that of the coffee extract frequently used by dessert chefs.   MAKES 4 SERVINGS

Soufflé Base (page 11)
4 teaspoons freeze-dried instant
*   coffee crystals*
2 tablespoons hot water
About 4 tablespoons sugar

Powdered sugar for sprinkling
5 large egg whites, room
*   temperature*
Pinch of cream of tartar

Prepare soufflé base. Dissolve instant coffee in hot water. Cool to room temperature. Gradually whisk coffee into soufflé base; blend in very thoroughly. (If making soufflé base ahead, immediately cover with wax paper directly on its surface to prevent skin from forming. Soufflé base can be kept up to 1 day, covered with lid in addition to paper, in refrigerator. Before continuing, let stand about 30 minutes at room temperature.)

Position rack in center of oven and preheat to 400°F. Generously butter a 6- to 7-cup soufflé dish with soft butter, making sure rim is well buttered. Put about 2 tablespoons sugar in soufflé dish. Shake, turn, and tap dish until bottom and sides are evenly coated with sugar; remove excess. Have round heatproof platter ready near oven. Have ready a shaker of powdered sugar; or put a little powdered sugar in small strainer set over small bowl.

If soufflé base is still warm, whisk it briefly until smooth. If it was prepared ahead, heat it over low heat, whisking, until just warm and smooth; remove from heat. Scrape down sides of pan.

Beat egg whites with cream of tartar in large bowl until they form soft peaks. With mixer at high speed, gradually beat in remaining 2 tablespoons sugar and beat until whites are just stiff and shiny but not dry, about 15 seconds.

Immediately fold about one-quarter of whites into soufflé base to lighten. Gradually pour this mixture over remaining whites while folding. Use rubber spatula to transfer any remaining mixture from pan to bowl of whites. Continue folding together as gently but as quickly as possible. (Be careful not to deflate mixture; a few small streaks of white may remain.)

Quickly transfer batter to prepared soufflé dish, pouring it into center of dish, and smooth top gently but quickly with rubber spatula.

Bake until soufflé is puffed and brown, about 20 to 22 minutes; when you carefully move oven rack, soufflé should shake very gently. (Center will remain moist.) Set soufflé dish on round platter, quickly shake powdered sugar over soufflé, and serve immediately.

SPIRITED SOUFFLÉ
Omit coffee and water. After reheating soufflé base, stir in 3 tablespoons fine-quality spirits, such as imported kirsch, pear brandy, clear raspberry brandy (framboise), or Grand Marnier.

🌿 FRESH LEMON SOUFFLÉ
Soufflé au citron

For many people this is the ideal dessert, with the tartness of the lemon balancing the creamy richness of the soufflé. It is a classic dessert that remains so popular that it is served at trend-setting Parisian restaurants such as Patrick Lenôtre, where I savored it as the finale of a tasting-menu feast.   MAKES 4 SERVINGS

Soufflé Base (page 11)
1 tablespoon grated or finely
  chopped lemon peel
3 tablespoons strained fresh lemon
  juice
1 tablespoon powdered sugar, plus
  additional for sprinkling

About 4 tablespoons granulated
  sugar
5 large egg whites, room
  temperature
Pinch of cream of tartar

Prepare soufflé base. Whisk in grated or chopped lemon peel. Mix lemon juice with 1 tablespoon powdered sugar, and gradually whisk into soufflé base. (If making soufflé base ahead, immediately cover with wax paper directly on its surface to prevent skin from forming. Soufflé base can be kept up to 1 day, covered with lid in addition to paper, in refrigerator. Before continuing, let stand about 30 minutes at room temperature.)

Position rack in center of oven and preheat to 400°F. Generously butter a 6- to 7-cup soufflé dish with soft butter, making sure rim is well buttered. Put about 2 tablespoons sugar in soufflé dish. Shake, turn, and tap dish until bottom and sides are evenly coated with sugar; remove excess. Have round heatproof platter ready near oven. Have ready a shaker of powdered sugar; or put a little powdered sugar in small strainer set over small bowl.

If soufflé base is still warm, whisk it briefly until smooth. If it was prepared ahead, heat it over low heat, whisking, until just warm and smooth; remove from heat. Scrape down sides of pan.

Beat egg whites with cream of tartar in large bowl until they form soft peaks. With mixer at high speed, gradually beat in remaining 2 tablespoons sugar and beat until whites are just stiff and shiny but not dry, about 15 seconds.

Immediately fold about one-quarter of whites into soufflé base to lighten. Gradually pour this mixture over remaining whites while folding. Use rubber spatula to transfer any remaining mixture from pan to bowl of whites. Continue folding together as gently but as quickly as possible. (Be careful not to deflate mixture; a few small streaks of white may remain.)

Quickly transfer batter to prepared soufflé dish, pouring it into center of dish, and smooth top gently but quickly with rubber spatula.

Bake until soufflé is puffed and brown, about 20 to 22 minutes; when you carefully move oven rack, soufflé should shake very gently. (Center will remain moist.) Set soufflé dish on round platter, quickly shake powdered sugar over soufflé, and serve immediately.

PECAN PRALINE SOUFFLÉ
Soufflé praliné aux noix de pacane

Praline is a favorite flavor for soufflés among French chefs, such as Michel Comby, the chef of Chez Comby in Paris, who taught me a hazelnut version of this recipe. I have made the praline for this soufflé with a popular American nut, which gives it an intriguing new taste.   MAKES 4 TO 6 SERVINGS

1 cup milk

3 large eggs, separated, plus 2 large whites

4 tablespoons sugar

¼ cup all-purpose flour

¾ cup pecan praline powder (page 374)

Pinch of cream of tartar

In small heavy saucepan, bring milk to a boil over medium-high heat. Remove from heat. Whisk egg yolks and 2 tablespoons sugar in medium, heavy bowl until well blended. Gently whisk in flour just until blended. Whisk in hot milk in a thin stream until mixture is smooth. Return mixture to saucepan and cook over medium-low heat, stirring constantly all over pan with whisk, until mixture is very thick and just falls heavily from whisk rather than flowing from it, about 2 or 3 minutes. Remove from heat. Cover with wax paper, then lid (to prevent skin from forming). Let stand at room temperature before continuing. (Soufflé base can be prepared 1 day ahead and re-frigerated, covered tightly.)

Position rack in center of oven and preheat to 400°F. Generously butter a 5-cup soufflé dish, making sure rim is well buttered. Have round heatproof platter ready near oven.

If soufflé base is cool, heat it over low heat, stirring, until just warm. Remove from heat. Stir in praline powder. In a large bowl, beat the 5 egg whites with cream of tartar until stiff but not dry. Gradually beat in remaining 2 tablespoons sugar at high speed and beat until whites are stiff and shiny but not dry, about 15 seconds.

Fold one-quarter of whites into praline mixture. Spoon this mixture over remaining whites and fold together as gently but as quickly as possible. (Be careful not to deflate mixture; a few streaks of white may remain.) Transfer batter to prepared soufflé dish and smooth top. Bake until soufflé is puffed and brown, about 18 minutes; when you carefully move dish, soufflé should shake very gently in center. (Center will remain moist.) Set soufflé dish on round platter and serve immediately.

INDIVIDUAL CAPPUCCINO SOUFFLÉS
Soufflés au café et au chocolat

The sensational soufflé of coffee and chocolate is sprinkled with a cinnamon-cocoa topping, a flavor combination inspired by the famous drink.   MAKES 5 OR 6 SERVINGS

2 tablespoons plus 1 teaspoon
    instant espresso powder
2 tablespoons plus 1 teaspoon very
    hot water
Soufflé Base (page 11)
1 ounce semisweet chocolate, very
    finely chopped
1/2 teaspoon cinnamon

1 teaspoon unsweetened cocoa
1 teaspoon powdered sugar
About 4 tablespoons granulated
    sugar
5 large egg whites, room
    temperature
Pinch of cream of tartar

Dissolve instant espresso in hot water. Prepare soufflé base. Upon removing it from heat, add chopped chocolate. Whisk until completely melted and blended into mixture. Gradually whisk in dissolved espresso. (If making soufflé base ahead, immediately cover with wax paper directly on its surface. Soufflé base can be kept up to 1 day, covered with lid in addition to paper, in refrigerator. Before continuing, let stand about 30 minutes at room temperature.)

Prepare topping by sifting together cinnamon, cocoa, and powdered sugar. Put in very small strainer above small bowl.

Position rack in center of oven and preheat to 400°F. Generously butter five 1¼-cup or six 1-cup soufflé dishes (see Note) and set them on baking sheet. Spoon about 1 teaspoon sugar into a dish. Shake, turn, and tap dish until bottom and sides are evenly coated with sugar; remove excess. Repeat with remaining dishes. Have ready 5 or 6 heatproof plates and topping mixture near oven.

If soufflé base is still warm, whisk it briefly until smooth. If it was prepared ahead, heat it over low heat, whisking, until just warm and smooth; remove from heat. Scrape down sides of pan.

Beat egg whites with cream of tartar in large bowl until they form soft peaks. With mixer at high speed, gradually beat in remaining 2 tablespoons sugar and beat until whites are just stiff and shiny but not dry, about 15 seconds.

Immediately fold about one-quarter of whites into soufflé base to lighten. Gradually pour this mixture over remaining whites while folding. Use rubber spatula to transfer any remaining mixture from pan to bowl of whites. Continue folding together as gently but as quickly as possible. (Be careful not to deflate mixture; a few small streaks of white may remain.)

Using a large spoon, transfer batter to prepared soufflé dishes, spooning it into center of dishes and filling to about ½ inch below top of dish. Smooth tops gently but quickly with rubber spatula.

Bake until soufflés are puffed and brown, about 15 minutes; when you carefully move baking sheet, soufflés should shake only slightly. (Centers will remain moist.) Quickly sift a little topping mixture in an even layer over each soufflé. Set soufflé dishes on plates and serve immediately. Serve any remaining topping mixture separately.

NOTE: Soufflés can also be baked in 8 or 9 ramekins of ⅔-cup volume for small servings. Bake them 12 minutes.

Crêpes

Cooks throughout France have long known that thin lacy crêpes make delicious and convenient wrappings for almost any sweet filling. With a batter that can be made in a minute, crêpes are one of the home cook's favorite standbys for a festive dessert or a more casual snack. With crêpes on hand, it is easy to have dessert ready at a moment's notice.

For a sweet snack or dessert, French cooks prefer delicate white flour crêpes, and reserve their heartier buckwheat crêpes for cheese, seafood, or vegetable fillings. Crêpes are delightful with just a pat of butter and a touch of sugar or honey or with a favorite fruit jam. They can enclose a simple filling of sautéed fruit, as in Pear-Filled Crêpes with Pear Brandy, or an airy soufflé that puffs as it bakes inside the gently folded crêpe. Ice cream makes a wonderful accompaniment for fruit-filled crêpes, as do fruit sauces or custard sauce.

In France, you can enjoy sweet crêpes at crêperies, or restaurants specializing in crêpes, where they might be flamed with Grand Marnier or Calvados, or filled with apple compote or fresh strawberries. Or, for a delightful spur-of-the-moment snack, you can buy them from street vendors, who heat them on a large griddle and fill them with melted chocolate and nuts, or with chestnut cream, then fold them in four. It is the custom to serve crêpes in France for Mardi Gras, when they are featured at numerous pastry shops as well.

Hints

- The filling is spread on the less attractive side of a crêpe, which is the side that was cooked second.
- Gratin dishes are perfect for baking crêpes. Either large or individual dishes can be used.
- Brush filled crêpes evenly with melted butter before baking them so they do not dry in oven.
- Filled crêpes should not be baked too long so they do not dry out.

Bake them only until the filling is hot. At 400°F. or 425°F., this should not take longer than 15 minutes.

 CRÊPES
Crêpes

These crêpes taste delicious on their own, simply served hot with butter and sugar, but they become special treats when filled with orange soufflé, page 26, or other fillings.

MAKES ABOUT 20 CRÊPES; 6 TO 8 SERVINGS

3 large eggs
1 1/4 cups milk, or a little more, if
  needed
3/4 cup all-purpose flour

3/4 teaspoon salt
5 tablespoons unsalted butter
Butter and sugar or preserves for
  serving (optional)

TO PREPARE BATTER IN FOOD PROCESSOR

Combine eggs, 1/4 cup milk, flour, and salt in work bowl and mix using several on/off turns; batter will be lumpy. Scrape down sides and bottom of work bowl. With machine running, pour remaining 1 cup milk through feed tube and process batter about 15 seconds. Scrape down sides and bottom of work bowl thoroughly. Blend batter about 15 seconds.

TO PREPARE BATTER IN BLENDER

Combine eggs, 1 1/4 cups milk, flour, and salt in blender. Blend on high speed until batter is smooth, about 1 minute.

TO PREPARE BATTER IN BOWL

Sift flour into medium bowl. Push flour to sides of bowl, leaving large well in center of flour. Add eggs, salt, and 1/4 cup milk to well and whisk ingredients in well briefly until blended. Using whisk, stir flour gently and gradually into egg mixture until mixture is smooth. Gradually whisk in 1 cup milk.

Strain batter if it is lumpy. Cover and let stand at room temperature about 1 hour. (Batter can be refrigerated, covered, up to 1 day. Bring to room temperature before continuing.)

Melt butter in small saucepan over low heat. Remove from heat and gradually whisk 3 tablespoons melted butter into crêpe batter. Pour remaining butter into a small cup and skim off foam to clarify. (Batter should have consistency of heavy cream. If it is too thick, gradually whisk in more milk, about 1 teaspoon at a time.)

Heat crêpe pan or skillet with 6- to 6½-inch base over medium-high heat. Sprinkle with few drops of water; if water immediately sizzles, pan is hot enough. Brush pan lightly with some of clarified butter; if using nonstick crêpe pan, no butter is needed. Remove pan from heat and hold it near bowl of batter. Working quickly, fill a ¼-cup measure half-full with batter (to easily measure 2 tablespoons) and add batter to one edge of pan, tilting and swirling pan until its base is covered with a thin layer of batter. Immediately pour any excess batter back into bowl.

Return pan to medium-high heat. Loosen edges of crêpe with metal spatula, discarding any pieces of crêpe clinging to sides of pan. Cook crêpe until its bottom browns lightly. Turn crêpe carefully over by sliding spatula under it and cook until second side browns lightly in spots. Slide crêpe out onto plate. Top with sheet of wax paper or foil, if desired. Reheat pan a few seconds. Continue making crêpes with remaining batter, stirring it occasionally with whisk. Adjust heat and add more clarified butter to pan as necessary. If batter thickens on standing, very gradually whisk in a little more milk, about 1 teaspoon at a time. Pile crêpes on plate as they are done. (Crêpes can be kept, wrapped tightly, up to 3 days in refrigerator; or they can be frozen. Bring them to room temperature before using, to avoid tearing them.)

If serving crêpes plain, reheat each on both sides in a little butter in medium skillet. Fold in two or four and serve hot, accompanied by butter and sugar or preserves.

NOTES

• To make larger crêpes, use a 7½- to 8-inch crêpe pan or skillet. Use about 3 tablespoons batter for each crêpe by filling a ¼-cup measure by three-fourths. Use slightly more filling for each of these larger crêpes.

• To season a cast iron or rolled steel crêpe pan, brush it with vegetable oil and bake it at 200°F. for 2 to 4 hours.

- Do not wash cast iron or rolled steel crêpe pans after use; to clean them, rub them well with paper towels while they are still warm.
- Before cooking crêpe batter, have all utensils ready near crêpe pan and burner: a plate for stacking them, a spatula for turning them, and a ¼-cup measure.
- If first crêpes are too thick, whisk a teaspoon of milk or water into batter to thin it.
- If too much liquid was added and crêpe batter is too thin, sift 2 or 3 tablespoons all-purpose flour into another bowl and gradually stir batter into it.
- A few small holes in a crêpe give a lacy effect and are fine; but if crêpes have many large holes, pan is probably too hot and heat should be reduced slightly.
- After melted butter is added, batter may become a bit lumpy on standing as butter cools, but this is nothing to worry about.

PEAR-FILLED CRÊPES WITH PEAR BRANDY
Crêpes aux poires

Pear *eau de vie* or brandy gives a spirited accent to the pears in the filling for these crêpes. Apple Compote (page 48) also makes a wonderful filling for crêpes and is loved throughout France. For a special occasion, serve the crêpes with Caramel or Vanilla Bean Ice Cream (see recipes) or crème anglaise (page 343).

MAKES 6 SERVINGS

Crêpes (page 23)

PEAR FILLING
2 pounds ripe pears
4 tablespoons butter
6 to 7 tablespoons sugar

¼ cup pear brandy or Grand
    Marnier

3 to 4 tablespoons butter

Prepare crêpes.

PEAR FILLING

Peel pears. Cut in half, core, and slice pears. Heat butter in a very large skillet (at least 12 inches). Add pears and turn slices over so both sides are coated with butter. Cook, uncovered, over low heat, stirring often, about 15 to 20 minutes, or until soft and some of pears have fallen apart. Continue cooking over medium heat to evaporate some of liquid. Add 6 tablespoons sugar and cook over medium-high heat, stirring, until mixture is thick and dry. (Filling can be kept, covered, 1 day in refrigerator; reheat before continuing.)

Remove filling from heat and stir in brandy or Grand Marnier. Taste and add more sugar, if desired.

Preheat oven to 450°F. Butter a shallow baking dish. Spoon 1 tablespoon filling onto less attractive side of each crêpe near one edge, and roll them like cigars. Arrange in one layer in baking dish. Cut remaining butter in small pieces and use them to dot crêpes. Bake about 5 minutes, or until very hot. Serve at once.

ORANGE SOUFFLÉ CRÊPES
Crêpes soufflées à l'orange

With the growing emphasis on lightness in cuisine, soufflé crêpes quickly gained popularity. This dramatic dessert is wonderful on its own, but it is sublime with raspberry sauce, or, as served at Taille-vent restaurant in Paris, with sabayon sauce.

MAKES 4 OR 5 SERVINGS

10 to 12 Crêpes (page 23)

ORANGE SOUFFLÉ FILLING

3 large eggs, separated, plus 1 large white
5 tablespoons sugar
1 cup milk

1/4 cup all-purpose flour
1/4 cup strained fresh orange juice
Zest of 1 orange

Prepare crêpes.

ORANGE SOUFFLÉ FILLING

In a medium bowl, whisk yolks lightly. Add 4 tablespoons sugar and 2 tablespoons milk and whisk until thick and smooth. Whisk in flour. Bring remaining milk to a boil in a small heavy saucepan. Gradually whisk half the hot milk into yolk mixture. Return mixture to pan, whisking. Cook over low heat, whisking, until mixture just comes to a boil. Remove from heat and whisk in orange juice. Grate in orange zest and whisk again. (If not using immediately, dab soufflé base with a small piece of butter or cover with plastic wrap directly on its surface to prevent a skin from forming; cool completely, cover, and refrigerate.)

A short time before serving, preheat oven to 400°F. Butter a heatproof platter or shallow baking dish. Transfer soufflé base to a saucepan and whisk until smooth. Heat over low heat, whisking, until just hot to touch. Remove from heat.

Beat the 4 egg whites until stiff. Add remaining tablespoon sugar and beat another 30 seconds until shiny. Fold one-quarter of whites into pastry cream mixture; then gently fold this mixture into remaining egg whites.

Spoon 2 or 3 tablespoons soufflé filling onto less attractive side of each crêpe. Fold crêpe in half and arrange in one layer on platter or baking dish. Bake about 10 minutes, or until filling puffs. Serve immediately.

PEACH CRÊPES WITH HONEY
Crêpes aux pêches et au miel

The goodness of fresh peaches is highlighted in this simple, natural-tasting dessert, for which they are sliced and cooked very briefly with butter and honey, then used to fill the crêpes. Crème fraîche or vanilla or peach ice cream go well with crêpes (see recipes).

MAKES 4 SERVINGS

8 Crêpes (page 23)   *2 tablespoons honey*
4 medium peaches (about 1 pound)   *2 teaspoons sugar*
3 1/2 tablespoons butter

Prepare crêpes.

Preheat oven to 425°F.

Put peaches in a saucepan of boiling water and heat for 30 seconds. Transfer peaches to a bowl of cold water and peel them with a paring knife. Cut them in thin wedges about ½ inch wide at widest point, cutting inward toward pit. Reserve 8 slices for garnish.

Melt 2 tablespoons butter in large skillet, add peaches and mix gently. Add honey and cook over medium heat 3 minutes, or until peaches are barely tender. Remove from heat.

Put 5 or 6 peach slices, with a little of their honey, near the edge of each crêpe. Roll them up and arrange in a buttered gratin dish or other baking dish. Dot crêpes with remaining butter and sprinkle with sugar. Bake about 5 minutes to heat through.

Serve on hot plates, with ice cream or crème fraîche. Garnish with peach slices.

CHOCOLATE SOUFFLÉ CRÊPES
Crêpes soufflées au chocolat

In these glorious treats, tender crêpes enclose a light-textured but rich chocolate filling. They bake very quickly and, like any soufflé, should be served immediately.

MAKES 5 GENEROUS OR 10 LIGHT SERVINGS

8-inch Crêpes (page 23), made 8
  inches in diameter

CHOCOLATE SOUFFLÉ FILLING

5 large eggs, separated, plus 3 large   *6 tablespoons all-purpose flour*
  whites   *8 ounces fine-quality semisweet*
½ cup granulated sugar   *chocolate, finely chopped*
1¾ cups milk   *Pinch of cream of tartar*

Powdered sugar for sprinkling
  (optional)

Prepare crêpes.

CHOCOLATE SOUFFLÉ FILLING

Whisk egg yolks with 6 tablespoons sugar and 2 tablespoons milk in a large bowl until blended. Lightly whisk in flour.

Bring remaining milk to a boil in a medium, heavy saucepan. Gradually whisk hot milk into yolk mixture. Return to saucepan and cook over medium heat, whisking constantly, until mixture becomes very thick and just begins to bubble. Remove from heat. Add chocolate and whisk until melted. If not using immediately, dab soufflé base with a small piece of butter to prevent a skin from forming. (Soufflé base can be kept, covered, up to 1 day in refrigerator.)

A short time before serving, position rack in center of oven and preheat to 450°F. Butter 2 large shallow baking dishes or heatproof platters.

Transfer soufflé base to a saucepan and whisk until smooth. Heat over low heat, whisking, until just warm to touch. Remove from heat.

Whip the 8 egg whites with cream of tartar in a large bowl at medium speed until soft peaks form. Gradually beat in remaining 2 tablespoons sugar at high speed and whip until whites are stiff and shiny but not dry. Quickly fold about one-quarter of whites into chocolate mixture. Spoon this mixture over remaining whites and fold in lightly but quickly, just until mixture is blended.

Spoon 1/2 cup soufflé mixture onto center of less attractive side of each crêpe. Spread gently to 1/2 inch of edges. Fold crêpe in half, without pressing on it, and gently arrange in one layer on platter or baking dish, without overlapping crêpes.

Bake about 8 minutes, or until filling puffs. Sprinkle quickly with powdered sugar, if desired. Serve immediately.

Simple Fruit Desserts

Although fruit plays a part in many types of warm desserts, from crêpes to puddings, this section focuses on simple desserts in which the fruit is clearly the star.

Poached fruit makes a lovely warm dessert, as does sautéed fruit. Lightly caramelized sautéed apples are one of the most popular hot fruit desserts, whether they are served on their own, topped with ice cream or crème fraîche, or used as a filling for crêpes or for a tart.

Fruit desserts are held in such esteem that many classic ones have been named for royalty. Take Pêches Eugénie, for example, in which the fruit is topped with champagne sabayon sauce and garnished with berries. This masterpiece was created for the Empress Eugénie, wife of Napoleon III of France.

The traditional pairing of fruit with a sabayon sauce is used in a new guise in fruit gratins, a relatively modern hot dessert. To prepare a fruit gratin, bite-size fruit pieces are set in a baking dish, usually an individual gratin dish, then coated with sabayon sauce and glazed in the broiler. The fruit can be poached or sautéed, or left uncooked if it is tender. The quick glazing gives the sauce an appetizing golden-brown crust but does not cook the fruit, and thus even delicate berries retain their texture. Cooks love the versatility of fruit gratins because they can be prepared with any seasonal fruit. The Winter Fruit Gratin of bananas and sautéed apples could serve as a model for other tempting compositions.

Hints

• Be sure to use good-quality, ripe fruit for all desserts. For sautéing, although the fruit should be ripe, try to choose fruit that is not too soft.

• Sauté delicate fruit such as nectarines or pears until just tende.. but not watery. If a large amount of juice collects in the pan, remove the fruit carefully with a slotted spoon, and boil the juice to reduce it before spooning it over the fruit.

SAUTÉED APPLES WITH CALVADOS AND VANILLA ICE CREAM
Pommes sautées au calvados, glace à la vanille

Warm, tender sautéed apple slices spiked with Norman apple brandy, Calvados, are superb with their traditional accompaniment of vanilla ice cream, but also make a terrific dessert when topped with homemade Caramel Ice Cream (see recipe) instead.

MAKES 4 SERVINGS

1 pound Golden Delicious apples
2 tablespoons butter
3 to 4 tablespoons sugar, according
  to sweetness of apples

2 to 3 tablespoons Calvados
1 quart Vanilla Bean Ice Cream
  (page 100) or packaged

Peel apples and cut in half. Core them and cut in thin wedges or slices.

Heat butter in a large skillet or sauté pan. When very hot, add apples and sauté over medium-high heat, turning pieces over from time to time, for about 2 minutes, or until they are coated with butter. Cover and cook over low heat for 10 minutes, or until apples are just tender. Try to keep pieces whole, but don't worry if some fall apart.

Raise heat to high and add 3 tablespoons sugar, turning apple wedges over so both sides are coated with sugar. Leave pan over high heat just until sugar dissolves. Add 2 tablespoons Calvados and heat briefly. Remove from heat. Taste and add more sugar if necessary; heat, tossing apples gently, just until sugar dissolves. Taste again and add more Calvados, if desired.

Serve hot or cold. To serve, scoop ice cream into deep dessert dishes and spoon apples over or around ice cream. Serve immediately.

SAUTÉED NECTARINES WITH GRAND MARNIER
Brugnons sautés au Grand Marnier

For most desserts nectarines are used like peaches, but nectarines are easier to sauté because they are firmer and hold their shape better. In addition, nectarines don't need peeling because their peel is not fuzzy, and thus are often more convenient for quick desserts. Serve these sautéed nectarines plain, over ice cream, or with whipped cream.

MAKES 4 SERVINGS

4 nectarines
1/4 cup butter
1/4 cup sugar

4 to 5 tablespoons Grand Marnier
  or peach brandy

Cut nectarines in medium-thick wedgelike slices, cutting inward toward the pits.

Melt butter in a large skillet. Add nectarine slices and sauté over medium-high heat, turning them over occasionally, about 2 minutes, or until lightly golden. Sprinkle with sugar and continue to sauté over high heat until sugar caramelizes lightly. Remove from heat and add 4 tablespoons Grand Marnier. Turn nectarine slices over so they are coated with Grand Marnier mixture. Let cool 1 minute. Taste and add more Grand Marnier, if desired. Serve hot or cold.

PEACHES WITH CHAMPAGNE SABAYON SAUCE
Pêches Eugénie

Sabayon sauce, the French version of the Italian zabaglione, is delicious and light when made with champagne and is a perfect partner for poached fruit. This classic dessert is the basis for a signature dessert of the fabulous Auberge de l'Ill restaurant in Alsace. Their specialty, *la pêche Haeberlin,* is composed of a poached peach and sabayon sauce served with pistachio ice cream. Besides peaches, champagne sabayon sauce is excellent with poached pears and with fresh berries.   MAKES 6 SERVINGS

CHAMPAGNE SABAYON SAUCE
1 cup dry champagne   *6 large egg yolks*
1/4 cup water   *1/2 cup sugar*

6 peaches   *2 tablespoons kirsch (optional)*
1 pint strawberries, hulled and cut
*   in half*

CHAMPAGNE SABAYON SAUCE
Combine ingredients in a saucepan or in the top of a double boiler. Whisk briefly. Set above hot but not boiling water over low heat and whisk constantly until sauce is frothy, about 5 minutes. Remove from heat and whisk until at room temperature.

Put peaches in a saucepan of boiling water and heat for 30 seconds. Transfer peaches to a bowl of cold water and peel them with a paring knife. Cut them in quarters and arrange them attractively in a deep serving dish with strawberry halves. Sprinkle with kirsch, cover, and let stand about 10 minutes.

Just before serving, whisk sauce until frothy. Spoon a little sauce over peaches, letting strawberries show. Serve remaining sauce alongside in a sauceboat or dish.

NOTE: This dessert is also good cold. Refrigerate sauce 30 minutes to 1 hour. After sprinkling peaches with kirsch, refrigerate about 10 minutes. Do not chill peeled peaches for too long, or they will turn brown. Just before serving, whisk chilled sauce until frothy. Serve as above.

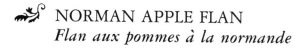 NORMAN APPLE FLAN
Flan aux pommes à la normande

For this simple dessert, sautéed apples are topped with a Calvados custard and baked in ramekins. This temptation was a favorite of the students of my fast French menu classes in California.

MAKES 4 SERVINGS

³/4 pound Golden Delicious apples   *1 ½ cups milk*
1 tablespoon butter   *2 large eggs plus 2 large yolks*
6 tablespoons sugar   *2 tablespoons Calvados*

Preheat oven to 350°F. Peel, core, and thinly slice apples. Heat butter in large sauté pan or skillet, add apples, and stir until coated with butter. Cover and cook over medium-low heat, stirring often, until apples are very tender, about 15 minutes. Add 2 tablespoons sugar and cook, uncovered, over medium-high heat, stirring often, until liquid that comes out of mixture evaporates.

Generously butter four ²/3-cup ramekins. Spoon apple mixture into ramekins.

Bring milk to a boil. Remove from heat and cool a few minutes.

Whisk eggs and egg yolks lightly in large bowl. Add remaining 4 tablespoons sugar and whisk just to blend. Gradually pour in about 1 cup milk in a thin stream, whisking constantly. Using a wooden spoon, gradually stir in remaining milk. Stir in Calvados. Pour mixture into measuring cup and skim foam from surface.

Set ramekins in roasting pan or large shallow baking dish. Pour custard mixture into ramekins, dividing it evenly among them. Place pan with ramekins in oven. Add enough very hot water to pan to come halfway up sides of ramekins. Set a sheet of foil on top to cover ramekins. Bake until cake tester or point of small thin-bladed knife inserted gently in center of each ramekin comes out clean, about 28 minutes. (During baking, if water in pan comes close to a boil, add a few tablespoons cold water to pan.)

Carefully remove ramekins from water bath and let cool on rack until warm or room temperature. Serve in ramekins. If you prefer to serve the flan cold, refrigerate at least 3 hours before serving. (Can be prepared up to 1 day ahead; keep covered.)

WINTER FRUIT GRATIN
Gratin de fruits d'hiver

Fruit gratins are popular modern French desserts. They are quick, easy, and elegant. Here fresh banana slices and sautéed apples are topped with a Grand Marnier sabayon sauce and glazed in the broiler. The luscious sauce, enriched with whipped cream so it coats the fruit better, gives a burst of Grand Marnier flavor. Berries, oranges, ripe peaches, and sautéed pears also make great gratins.

MAKES 4 SERVINGS

2 medium-size Granny Smith or
    Golden Delicious apples
2 tablespoons butter
2 large bananas, sliced

1/2 cup heavy cream, well chilled
4 large egg yolks
1/3 cup sugar
1/3 cup Grand Marnier

Peel and core apples and cut in eighths. Melt butter in a medium skillet over medium-low heat. Add apples and sauté, turning them over occasionally, about 9 minutes, or until tender. Transfer to individual gratin dishes or large ramekins. Add banana slices to dishes.

Whip cream in chilled bowl with chilled beater until stiff and reserve in refrigerator.

Preheat broiler. Combine egg yolks, sugar, and Grand Marnier in a large bowl. Set bowl in a pan of hot water over medium-low heat. Whip with a hand mixer at low speed about 7 minutes, or until mixture is lukewarm, lightens in color, becomes foamy, and increases in volume. Then whip 1 minute at high speed. Remove from heat. Fold in whipped cream.

Spoon sauce over fruit. Brown in broiler about 45 seconds. Serve immediately.

Puddings

Rice puddings are traditional desserts of many areas of France. In Normandy, for instance, a creamy rice pudding is prepared with apples, while in Brittany and the Loire Valley it might contain these regions' plump prunes. Chefs have transformed rice pudding into elegant desserts, often by topping it with seasonal fruit and pairing it with a sauce, as in Strawberries on a Bed of Creamy Rice.

For custard puddings with a moist, cakelike texture, a custard mixture of milk, eggs, and sugar is poured over ladyfinger halves or cake slices, which absorb it during baking, as in Custard Pudding with Raisins, Rum, and Ladyfingers. The pudding is then unmolded and garnished with whipped cream. French cooks also prepare bread puddings, which were originally designed to use up stale bread but have turned into a popular winter treat.

Perhaps the most festive of puddings is the light but rich soufflé pudding. Similar to a soufflé mixture, it is baked more slowly, in a water bath. Soufflé puddings can be made in all the familiar sweet flavors, such as orange, coffee, or vanilla, or can combine several, as in Chocolate Soufflé Pudding with Pears.

Hints

- Although short-grained rice is ideal for rice puddings, medium- or long-grain rice will also work.
- Rice and bread puddings are delicious accompanied by fresh or poached fruit or with crème anglaise or a fruit sauce.

CHOCOLATE SOUFFLÉ PUDDING WITH PEARS
Pudding soufflé au chocolat et aux poires

As its name suggests, a soufflé pudding is halfway between a pudding and a soufflé. Baked in a water bath like pudding, it rises more slowly than a soufflé but keeps its shape longer. Unlike a soufflé, it is served when baked until well-done instead of being briefly baked, so it is not as airy as a soufflé, yet it is very moist. This high, dark-chocolate dessert is dotted with sautéed pears and flavored with pear brandy.   MAKES 6 SERVINGS

2 large pears (1 pound)
8 tablespoons unsalted butter
4 ounces semisweet chocolate, chopped
1 cup milk
6 tablespoons sugar
Small pinch of salt

½ cup all-purpose flour
4 large eggs, separated, room temperature
3 tablespoons pear brandy (see Note)
Pinch of cream of tartar

Position rack in lower third of oven and preheat to 350°F. Butter a 5-cup soufflé dish.

Peel, core, and dice pears. Melt 2 tablespoons butter in a medium skillet. Add pears and sauté over medium heat, stirring often, about 10 minutes or until tender. Remove to a shallow bowl and cool. Put pears gently in a strainer above a small bowl to drain off excess liquid. (Reserve liquid if preparing variation in Note below.)

Melt chocolate in a heatproof medium bowl above hot water over low heat. Stir until smooth. Remove from pan of water and let cool.

Cut remaining 6 tablespoons butter in 6 pieces. Combine milk, butter, 1 tablespoon sugar, and pinch of salt in a small heavy saucepan and cook over low heat, stirring, until butter melts. Bring to a full boil over high heat. Remove from heat. Add flour all at once and mix vigorously with a wooden spoon until mixture comes away from sides of pan; it will look lumpy at first but keep beating and it will become smooth. Return to low heat and cook, stirring, 30 seconds. Cool 5 minutes.

Vigorously beat in egg yolks, 1 at a time. Gradually beat in chocolate. Beat in brandy, 1 tablespoon at a time.

Whip egg whites with cream of tartar in a large bowl until soft peaks form. Gradually beat in remaining 5 tablespoons sugar at high speed and whip until whites are stiff and shiny but not dry. Stir one-quarter of whites into chocolate mixture. Spoon this mixture over remaining whites and fold in lightly but quickly, just until blended. Fold in pears.

Transfer mixture to prepared dish. Set dish in a roasting pan and put in oven. Add enough very hot water to roasting pan to come halfway up sides of soufflé dish. Bake about 1 hour and 20 minutes, or until pudding is set and firm to touch and a cake tester inserted in it comes out clean. Serve immediately, or within 10 minutes.

NOTE: If you like, use up to 3 tablespoons of reserved pear liquid instead of pear brandy.

❧ CUSTARD PUDDING WITH RAISINS, RUM, AND LADYFINGERS
Pudding de cabinet

This moist loaf-shaped pudding is made of a baked custard studded with rum-soaked raisins and layered with ladyfingers. Cooks vary this classic dessert in many ways. Sometimes the raisins are mixed with candied fruits or with diced dried apricots. The rum can be omitted and the custard flavored instead with vanilla or lemon or orange peel. The dessert tastes great served on its own or accompanied by whipped cream or vanilla or rum crème anglaise. MAKES 6 TO 8 SERVINGS

1 cup dark raisins
3 tablespoons dark rum
3 1/3 cups milk
3 large eggs plus 5 large yolks

7 tablespoons sugar
4 1/2 ounces ladyfingers, split (about
    eighteen 3-inch ladyfingers)

GARNISH (OPTIONAL, IF SERVING COLD)
1/3 cup apricot preserves
1 teaspoon rum

2/3 cup heavy cream, well chilled

Rinse raisins and put in small jar or bowl. Pour rum over them, cover tightly, and shake to mix. Let stand at least 30 minutes, or up to 2 hours at room temperature.

Preheat oven to 400°F. Butter an 8-×-4-inch or an 8 1/2-×-4 1/2-inch loaf pan with nonstick surface. Bring milk just to a boil over medium heat. Remove from heat and let cool 5 minutes.

Whisk eggs with egg yolks lightly in large bowl. Add sugar and whisk just to blend. Gradually add about 1 1/2 cups hot milk, stirring with a whisk. Using a wooden spoon, gradually stir in remaining milk.

Arrange tight layer of ladyfinger halves crosswise in pan, spongy side facing up. Cut more ladyfingers and use to fill any spaces to make a complete layer. Drain raisins, reserving rum. Brush rum on ladyfingers in dish by dabbing lightly and evenly with a pastry brush. Sprinkle with one-third of raisins. Put another layer of ladyfingers on top, spongy side up, brush with rum, and sprinkle with another one-third of raisins. Top with third layer of ladyfingers, spongy side up, and brush with rum. Sprinkle with remaining raisins. Repeat with fourth layer of ladyfingers. Whisk any remaining rum into custard mixture.

Gradually ladle enough custard mixture over ladyfingers so it comes nearly to top of pan, reserving remaining mixture. Let stand 10 or 15 minutes before baking.

Set loaf pan in a roasting pan or large shallow baking dish and put in oven. Add enough of remaining custard to fill loaf pan just to top. Add enough very hot water to larger pan to come halfway up sides of loaf pan. Bake until cake tester or point of small thin-bladed knife inserted in center of mixture comes out completely clean and hot, about 50 minutes. During baking, if water in pan comes close to a boil, add a few tablespoons cold water to pan and reduce oven temperature to 325°F. Carefully remove loaf pan from water bath. If serving hot, let cool in pan on rack at least 10 minutes before turning out; otherwise cool to room temperature before turning out. (Dessert can be kept, covered, up to 2 days in refrigerator.)

To unmold, slide a metal spatula carefully around dessert and invert onto a platter. Serve warm, room temperature, or cold. If serving at room temperature or cold, decorate as below, if desired. Slice to serve.

OPTIONAL GARNISH

In a small saucepan, heat apricot preserves and rum over low heat until hot but not boiling. Strain into a small bowl, pressing on pieces. Using a pastry brush, brush preserves over top and sides of dessert. Wipe platter clean. Refrigerate 1 hour. If desired, bring dessert to room temperature for serving.

Whip cream in a chilled bowl until very stiff. Using a pastry bag and large star tip, pipe a ruffle of whipped cream around bottom edge of dessert.

⚜ BLACK-AND-WHITE RICE PUDDING
Pudding de riz noir et blanc

Many people long for comfort foods like a warm, creamy rice pudding. In this one, a rich chocolate rice layer is topped by a white rice layer studded with pecans and raisins. Walnuts or unsalted macadamia nuts can be substituted for the pecans and grated orange zest for the lemon zest.   MAKES 6 SERVINGS

3/4 cup medium-grain rice
3 cups milk
Pinch of salt
1/2 cup heavy cream
6 tablespoons sugar
5 tablespoons butter, room temperature
3 large eggs, separated, room temperature

1 1/2 teaspoons grated lemon zest
1/3 cup dark raisins
1/3 cup coarsely chopped pecans
4 ounces semisweet chocolate, chopped
Pinch of cream of tartar

Bring a large saucepan of water to a boil. Add rice and boil 3 minutes. Drain thoroughly.

Bring milk to a simmer in a large heavy saucepan. Add rice and salt. Cook over low heat, stirring often, about 40 minutes, or until rice absorbs milk.

Position rack in center of oven and preheat to 350°F. Generously butter a deep 2-quart baking dish.

Add cream to rice and cook, stirring often, about 2 minutes, or until rice is very tender and absorbs cream. Add 4 tablespoons sugar and stir over low heat until dissolved. Remove from heat, add butter, and stir until absorbed. Cool 5 minutes. Stir in egg yolks and grated lemon zest.

Spoon 2 cups of rice mixture into another bowl and stir in raisins and pecans.

Melt chocolate in a heatproof medium bowl over hot water over low heat. Stir until smooth, and cool slightly. Stir into plain rice mixture until blended.

Whip egg whites with cream of tartar in a large bowl until soft peaks form. Gradually beat in remaining 2 tablespoons sugar at high speed and whip until whites are stiff and shiny but not dry, about 15 seconds. Spoon half the whites onto raisin-rice mixture and remaining whites onto chocolate mixture. (To divide whites in half, use spatula to mark a line in center of whites in bowl.) Fold whites into each mixture lightly but quickly.

Transfer chocolate mixture to prepared dish and spread smooth. Carefully add raisin-rice mixture by spoonfuls; do not add too much mixture at a time so it will not sink into chocolate layer. Bake about 45 minutes, or until set and top is browned. Serve hot or warm.

ALSATIAN BREAD PUDDING WITH FRUIT
Pudding alsacien au pain et aux fruits

Bread puddings with fruit change with the seasons and vary from one region to another in France. In the winter, apples and pears are used; and in the warmer months, peaches, apricots, or cherries. When fresh fruit is not available, canned, dried, or candied fruit is used. The flavorings also can vary. In this version from Alsace, cinnamon and kirsch are preferred, but you can instead use vanilla or grated lemon rind.   MAKES 6 SERVINGS

4 ounces day-old good-quality white bread or egg bread
1 1/4 cups milk
1 pound apples
6 tablespoons sugar
2 large eggs, separated

1 1/2 teaspoons cinnamon
2 tablespoons kirsch
3 tablespoons chopped candied citrus peel (optional)
2 tablespoons butter, cut in small pieces

Preheat oven to 400°F. Generously butter a 5-cup baking dish. Remove crust from bread and cut in cubes. Bring milk to a simmer. Pour it over bread and let stand several minutes so bread softens.

Peel apples, cut in half, and core them. Slice them very thin.

Mash bread with a fork. Add 4 tablespoons sugar, egg yolks, 1 teaspoon cinnamon, and kirsch and mix well. Add apples and candied peel, if using, and mix to distribute evenly.

Whip egg whites until stiff. Gradually beat in remaining 2 tablespoons sugar and beat until stiff and shiny. Gently fold whites, in 2 batches, into bread mixture.

Transfer mixture to baking dish. Sprinkle with remaining ½ teaspoon cinnamon and scatter butter pieces on top. Bake 40 to 50 minutes, or until a thin knife inserted in pudding comes out dry. (Pudding can be kept warm in low oven for 15 minutes.)

Serve warm or cold, from baking dish. (Pudding is more attractive when hot, as it sinks when cool. If serving cold, pudding can be kept, covered, for 2 days in refrigerator.)

Cold Desserts

It is hard to resist the charm of a smooth crème caramel, a tangy lemon mousse, or a velvety kirsch Bavarian cream. All make use of the basic custard-cooking techniques to turn simple ingredients into sensational desserts that are rich yet light-textured. These cold desserts are perfect finales for a meal, because they are less filling than cakes or pastries.

What I find fascinating is that many of these delightful treats are now being utilized as elements to design new desserts. Joël Bellouet, my excellent teacher at Lenôtre's professional school for pastry chefs near Paris, recommended using chocolate mousse as a filling for Napoleons, or frozen as a layer in ice cream cakes. At the famous Moulin de Mougins restaurant in southern France, I tasted a delicious charlotte filled with coffee Bavarian cream topped by a layer of chocolate mousse. An apricot mousse I learned to prepare from Claude Vauguet, the head chef at La Varenne Cooking School, inspired my Apricot and White Chocolate Cold Soufflé. It's wonderful to realize

43

that once you can make these two types of desserts—Bavarian cream and mousse—you are able to transform them into many new, seemingly complex creations.

Simple Fruit Desserts

Fruit on its own is probably the most frequently served ending to a meal in France. After a rich dinner, many people want nothing more than a few slices of fresh fruit, or a very simple dessert that focuses on fruit.

An easy way favored by today's cooks to turn fruit into a light dessert, is to serve it with a sauce made from another fruit of a contrasting color and complementary flavor, as in Mangoes with Kiwi Sauce. When a slightly richer dessert is desired, the fruit and sauce are embellished with a creamy topping, like the one in Nectarines with Strawberry Sauce and Vanilla Cream.

Poached fruit, such as Vanilla-Scented Poached Apples, served with a few spoonfuls of its delicately flavored poaching syrup makes another light, refreshing, and simply prepared dessert. For a change of pace, wine can be used in the poaching liquid, as in Classic Cherries in Red Wine. Delicious by itself, poached fruit can also be topped by ice cream, sorbet, crème anglaise, or whipped cream, or it can be accompanied by homemade ladyfingers, cookies, or a slice of plain cake.

Hints

• Buy the best fruit possible and be sure to let it ripen properly. In simple desserts in which the fruit is the star, especially if it will be served uncooked, the quality of the fruit is the most important factor in the taste of the dessert.

• Hints on poaching fruit can be found on page 371.

NECTARINES WITH STRAWBERRY SAUCE AND VANILLA CREAM
Brugnons au coulis de fraises, crème vanille

For this fresh, simple dessert for summer, the nectarines do not require cooking, but are simply covered with strawberry sauce. For a low-calorie dessert, omit the accompanying vanilla cream, or prepare a light version by substituting plain yogurt for both types of cream. MAKES 4 SERVINGS

6 nectarines
3 tablespoons sugar
2 cups Strawberry Sauce (page 347)

½ cup heavy cream
½ cup sour cream
1 teaspoon pure vanilla extract
2 tablespoons slivered almonds

Cut nectarines in quarters. Put them in a gratin dish or other slightly deep serving dish and sprinkle with 2 tablespoons sugar. Refrigerate 10 minutes.

A short time before serving, pour strawberry sauce over nectarines. In a small bowl, whisk heavy cream into sour cream. Mix in remaining tablespoon sugar and vanilla. Keep nectarines and cream in separate dishes in refrigerator until ready to serve.

To serve, sprinkle fruit with almonds. Serve vanilla cream separately.

MANGOES WITH KIWI SAUCE
Mangues au coulis de kiwis

This modern dessert is light and colorful, and is a perfect conclusion to a rich dinner. It is composed of sliced mango presented on kiwi sauce. Be sure to use the best quality mangoes that can be sliced neatly. Ripe papayas or nectarines can be substituted for the mangoes.

MAKES 4 SERVINGS

2 ripe mangoes or papayas
Kiwi Sauce (page 349)

4 to 8 small strawberries or
  raspberries for garnish
  (optional)

Peel mangoes or papayas. Slice mangoes inward, toward pit. (If using papayas, remove seeds, then slice.) Spoon sauce over center of 4 dessert plates. Arrange mango or papaya slices attractively on each plate. Garnish with berries, if desired.

RASPBERRIES ROMANOFF
Framboises Romanoff

In the eighteenth and nineteenth centuries, French desserts with Russian names emerged, as French chefs were invited to cook for the Russian royalty. Strawberries Romanoff was named for a noble Russian family, but this princely dessert is, in fact, very simple to make. Here I present a luxurious twist. It is basically a spirited rendition of raspberries and cream, in which the raspberries are given a sprinkling of curaçao and fresh orange juice before being lavishly cloaked with whipped cream.

MAKES 4 SERVINGS

3 cups fresh raspberries (about 1
  pound)
1/4 cup sugar

1/4 cup strained fresh orange juice
1/4 cup curaçao or other orange
  liqueur

CHANTILLY CREAM
3/4 cup heavy cream, well chilled   *3/4 teaspoon pure vanilla extract*
1 tablespoon sugar

Put raspberries in a bowl and sprinkle with sugar, orange juice, and liqueur. Toss lightly. Cover and refrigerate 30 minutes. Spoon raspberries into wineglasses or dessert dishes.

CHANTILLY CREAM
In a chilled bowl, whip cream with sugar and vanilla until stiff. Using a pastry bag and medium star tip, pipe enough cream over berries to cover them almost completely. Serve immediately.

CLASSIC CHERRIES IN RED WINE
Cerises au vin rouge

This refreshing dessert goes beautifully with vanilla ice cream. The poaching liquid becomes the sauce for the ice cream, and a few cherries go on top. The preferred wines for this quick and easy dessert are red Bordeaux or Cabernet Sauvignon.   MAKES 4 SERVINGS

1 pound sweet cherries (about 2 1/2   *1/4 teaspoon cinnamon*
cups)   *1 tablespoon red currant jelly or*
1 1/2 cups dry red wine   *other red jelly*
3 tablespoons sugar

Cut off tips of cherry stems and leave rest of stems attached. Put cherries in a heatproof casserole that can also be used for serving. Pour wine over them and add sugar and cinnamon. Cover and cook over low heat for 10 minutes. Uncover and let cherries cool in wine for 30 minutes.

Drain wine into a saucepan. Boil it over medium-high heat until it reduces to about 1/2 cup. Add jelly and heat over low heat, stirring, until melted. Pour mixture over cherries. Chill thoroughly. Serve cold.

APPLE COMPOTE WITH CREAM AND GLAZED PECANS
Compote normande à la crème et aux noix de pacane caramelisées

This is a variation on the favorite Norman theme, apple compote with crème fraîche. The apples are flavored with the customary lemon juice, but you can use cinnamon instead, or add Calvados to the finished mixture for more zip. The cream topping is a quick substitute for crème fraîche, which is not so easy to find. The glazed pecans add a delightful crunch; to save time, though, simply sprinkle chopped pecans or walnuts over each serving instead. Apple compote also makes a good filling for tartlets and other pastries.

MAKES 6 SERVINGS

APPLE COMPOTE

2 pounds Golden Delicious, Pippin, or Granny Smith apples	1 teaspoon strained fresh lemon juice
1/4 cup butter	6 to 8 tablespoons sugar
1/4 cup pecans	1/3 cup sour cream
1 tablespoon plus 2 teaspoons sugar	1/3 cup heavy cream

APPLE COMPOTE

Peel apples, cut in half, and core them. Cut them in thin wedges or slices.

Heat butter in a large skillet or sauté pan. When it is very hot, add the apples and sauté over medium-high heat, turning pieces over from time to time, for about 2 minutes, or until they are coated with butter. Add lemon juice, cover, and cook over low heat for 5 minutes, or until liquid begins to come out of apples. Uncover and continue cooking over low heat, gently stirring from time to time, for 15 to 20 minutes, or until apples are tender. Try to keep pieces whole, but don't worry if some fall apart.

Raise heat to high and add 6 tablespoons sugar, turning apple wedges over so both sides are coated with sugar. Leave pan over high heat just until sugar dissolves. Remove from heat. Taste and add more sugar if necessary (amount needed varies with sweetness of apples); return to heat, tossing apples gently, just until sugar dissolves.

Transfer to a serving dish and let cool completely. (Compote can be kept, covered, 2 days in refrigerator.)

Oil a sheet of foil. Heat pecans and 1 tablespoon sugar in a small heavy saucepan over low heat, stirring constantly, until sugar melts, turns brown, and coats pecans. Transfer to sheet of foil. Let cool completely, and separate the pecans.

Whisk together sour cream, heavy cream, and remaining 2 teaspoons sugar just until mixed. Spoon topping over apple mixture, and decorate with the glazed pecans. Serve cold.

NOTE: For 2 cups apple compote, to use as filling or in Apple Mousse (see recipe), use 1 1/2 pounds apples, 3 tablespoons butter, 3/4 teaspoon lemon juice, and 4 to 6 tablespoons sugar.

STRAWBERRIES À LA RITZ
Fraises à la Ritz

What could be better than strawberries and cream? Strawberries à la Ritz, served under a bright pink cloud of berry-and-cream sauce. The creamy strawberry-raspberry sauce is also a classic accompaniment for fresh figs.   MAKES 4 SERVINGS

3 cups fresh strawberries   *2 teaspoons granulated sugar*

BERRY WHIPPED CREAM
1 cup fresh strawberries, hulled   *5 to 6 tablespoons powdered sugar*
1 cup fresh raspberries, or thawed   *1/2 cup heavy cream*
  and drained frozen raspberries   *1/2 teaspoon pure vanilla extract*

2 large strawberries, cut in half
  lengthwise, for garnish

Hull 3 cups strawberries and cut them in half; put them in shallow serving bowl in two layers, and sprinkle each layer with 1 teaspoon sugar. Chill about 30 minutes.

BERRY WHIPPED CREAM

Purée 1 cup strawberries in a blender or food processor until smooth. Transfer to a bowl. Purée raspberries in a blender or processor until smooth. Push through strainer to remove seeds. Mix with strawberry purée and add 4 tablespoons powdered sugar. Chill about 30 minutes.

A short time before serving, finish making sauce: In a chilled bowl, whip cream until nearly stiff. Add vanilla and 1 tablespoon powdered sugar and continue whipping until very stiff. Gradually fold berry purée into whipped cream. Taste sauce; fold in another tablespoon powdered sugar, if desired.

Spoon sauce over sweetened strawberry halves in bowl, and garnish each serving with a strawberry half. Serve immediately. (Dessert can be kept up to 30 minutes in refrigerator, but should not be kept for longer or berry purée will separate from cream.)

PEARS IN PORT WITH TOASTED ALMONDS
Poires au porto et aux amandes grillées

The pears in this classic dessert are poached in an orange-scented port syrup. If they are left overnight in their syrup, they will acquire a light pink color.   MAKES 6 SERVINGS

3 cups water   Zest of 1 orange
1 1/4 cups port wine   6 ripe but firm pears
3/4 cup granulated sugar

SWEET TOASTED ALMONDS
1/2 cup slivered almonds   2 tablespoons powdered sugar

Chantilly Cream (page 355)

Combine water, 1 cup port, and sugar in a medium saucepan. Grate in the orange zest. Bring to a boil, stirring. Remove from heat. Peel pears and cut in half lengthwise. With the point of the peeler, remove flower end and core of each pear, including long stringy section that continues to stem. Bring port syrup to a simmer and add pear halves. Cover with a small lid or plate to keep them submerged. Reduce heat to low and simmer 10 to 12 minutes, or until pears can be pierced easily with the point of a small knife. Let cool completely in syrup. (Pears can be kept in their syrup, covered, 2 days in refrigerator.)

With a slotted spoon, carefully transfer pears to a deep serving dish. Boil cooking liquid over medium heat, stirring it often, until reduced to about 1½ cups. Let it cool to room temperature. Add remaining ¼ cup port, pour the mixture over pears, and chill.

SWEET TOASTED ALMONDS

Preheat oven to 450°F. Mix almonds and powdered sugar in a small shallow metal baking pan. Toast in oven, stirring often, about 10 minutes, or until almonds brown lightly and sugar dissolves and browns. Be careful because mixture burns easily. Transfer to a plate and allow to cool completely. Grind in a food processor or nut grinder, but leave mixture slightly chunky.

Serve pears in port syrup with separate bowls of ground almonds and Chantilly Cream alongside.

VANILLA-SCENTED POACHED APPLES
Pommes pochées au sirop vanille

If you like baked apples, you will love poached apple quarters, served with a few spoonfuls of their vanilla poaching syrup. Their taste is pure and delicate, and the vanilla bean imparts a wonderful aroma to the poaching syrup. Cool poached apples make a light, refreshing dessert on their own, but they are superb served either warm or cold with vanilla ice cream. They can be prepared ahead and keep well.

MAKES 4 SERVINGS

3/4 cup sugar
3 cups water
1 vanilla bean

1 to 1¼ pounds Golden Delicious or Granny Smith apples (3 or 4 medium)
1 tablespoon strained fresh lemon juice

Combine sugar, water, and vanilla bean in a medium saucepan. Bring to a boil, stirring gently to dissolve sugar. Remove from heat.

Peel apples, cut in half, and remove cores. Cut each half in 2 pieces. Return syrup to a boil and add apple quarters and lemon juice. Reduce heat to low. Cover with a lid that is a bit too small for saucepan, to keep apples submerged. Cook 8 to 12 minutes, or until apples are very tender when pierced with the point of a knife. Let apples cool in their syrup. (Apples can be kept in their syrup about 4 days in refrigerator.) Serve cold, at room temperature, or warm. If desired, serve with vanilla ice cream.

STRAWBERRIES ON A BED OF CREAMY RICE
Fraises Condé

The French have always considered strawberries a noble fruit. Indeed, one of the oldest varieties of strawberries in France was known as *la princesse royale* or royal princess. This dessert, known as Strawberries Condé, was a tribute to the Condé family, which produced several French princes. In it, the rice simmers gently in milk so it becomes creamy, then is sweetened and flavored with citrus zests and vanilla. Next it is topped with strawberries and served with strawberry sauce. Actually, any fresh or poached fruit in season can be used. Peaches and apricots, for example, are wonderful in this dessert as well.   MAKES 6 SERVINGS

SWEET RICE
1/2 cup rice, preferably
   short-grained
2 cups milk, plus 2 or 3
   tablespoons more, if needed
Pinch of salt
1/4 cup sugar
Zest of 1 lemon

Zest of 1 orange
3 tablespoons chopped candied fruits
   (optional)
1 teaspoon pure vanilla extract
1 egg yolk
2 tablespoons butter

3 cups fresh strawberries
1 1/2 cups Strawberry Sauce,
   unstrained (page 347)
   (optional)

SWEET RICE

Bring a large pan of water to a boil and add rice. Boil 3 minutes; drain well. Bring milk to a boil in heavy saucepan. Add rice and salt and cook, uncovered, over low heat, stirring often, 45 to 50 minutes, or until rice is very soft and absorbs milk. If rice absorbs milk before becoming soft, gradually add a few more tablespoons milk and continue to cook. When rice is cooked, stir in sugar and grate in lemon and orange zests. Continue heating for 1 minute, stirring, until sugar dissolves. Remove from heat and stir in candied fruits, vanilla, egg yolk, and butter. Spread mixture in a round base about 1/2 inch high on a round platter. Cover and refrigerate until ready to serve.

To serve, arrange whole strawberries on rice. Serve sauce separately.

SUMMER FRUIT SOUP WITH RED WINE
Soupe de fruits d'été au vin rouge

Although called soup, the fruit is not cooked, but rather is macerated briefly in red wine so there is a flavor exchange. Fruit soups like this are a result of the modern quest for light desserts that are natural and do not require much sugar. This colorful dessert is a great choice for summer, especially after a rich dinner. It was a favorite in my classes on light French cooking. MAKES 6 SERVINGS

4 oranges
1 1/2 cups dry red wine, such as
Cabernet Sauvignon
1/4 cup water
4 tablespoons sugar

4 ripe peaches or nectarines
2 apricots (optional)
1 pint strawberries, hulled
A few mint sprigs

Combine juice of 2 oranges, wine, water, and sugar until sugar dissolves. Pour into a glass bowl.

To peel peaches, scald them in boiling water for 30 seconds, transfer to a bowl of cold water, and peel with a knife. There is no need to peel nectarines. Slice peaches or nectarines, and add them to bowl of wine mixture.

Slice apricots and add to bowl. Cut strawberries in half, and add them also.

Peel remaining oranges, removing as much as possible of white pith. Cut into segments, cutting on both sides of membranes between them in order to eliminate these membranes. Hold each orange over bowl while doing this to catch juice that escapes. Squeeze any juice remaining in oranges into bowl. Add the segments to bowl. Chill for 1 to 2 hours.

Decorate with mint sprigs, and serve cold.

NOTE: Other fruits, such as raspberries, blueberries, or tangerines, can also be used. Be sure to use a colorful combination of fruit.

Baked Custards

Baked custards are the *crème de la crème* of French restaurant desserts. Yet these silky, creamy desserts are simple to prepare at home, and the ingredients needed—milk, eggs, sugar, and flavorings—are usually at hand. Although these are the same ingredients of crème anglaise (custard sauce), the flavor and texture of baked custards are completely different because of their special cooking method.

There are two major groups of baked custards. Those of the creamier type, called *petits pots de crème* (little pots of cream), are baked and served in individual containers. It is possible to purchase elegant little dishes designed specifically for this purpose, but small ramekins or soufflé dishes work just as well. This type of custard is the richest because it contains a larger proportion of egg yolks and no egg whites. Desserts in the second category are baked in small or large dishes of various shapes and are turned out before serving. To make unmolding easy, the dish is either coated with caramel or generously buttered. The most famous example in this group is the French *crème caramel* (caramel custard), which is also popular in Italy, Spain, and Latin America. This type of custard contains both egg yolks for richness and whole eggs to make it firm enough to hold its shape when unmolded.

Custards can be flavored in the classic manner with vanilla, coffee, or chocolate, or with new combinations such as lemon and ginger. There are two techniques for adding the flavorings. Chocolate, coffee, and liqueur are stirred into the custard mixture. Vanilla beans, fresh ginger, and citrus zests are infused, that is, they are heated in the milk so they flavor it, then are removed. The dessert is smoother and more delicate than if, for example, the grated citrus peel were mixed into the custard. Pieces of candied ginger or other ingredients that are heavier than the basic mixture are added part way through the baking time so that they won't fall to the bottom. Tender fruit can be covered with the custard and baked, as in Norman Apple Flan (see recipe).

The French call custards *crèmes* for a good reason. Their texture should be smooth and creamy, and everything possible is done to keep it that way. Thus the mixture is usually strained before baking, and the custards are baked in a water bath, which is a large shallow pan of hot water. The water ensures that the desserts bake slowly and evenly and don't dry out in the oven. As the custards bake, the heat causes the eggs to thicken and the mixture to set.

The shiny surface of a *petit pot de crème* served in an attractive ramekin makes the dessert beautiful in itself, and so there is no need for a garnish. The caramel sauce that bakes with crème caramel forms its own decoration.

Hints

• When preparing the water bath, pull out the oven rack slightly, then add the hot water carefully to the pan containing the dishes of custard. Very carefully slide the rack back into the oven to avoid spilling water into the custards. One easy way is to gently push the rack in by slowly closing the oven door.

• If lifting a water bath with 5 or 6 ramekins is difficult, divide them among 2 pans to make 2 water baths.

• Cover custards by setting a piece of foil over their surface, but do not fold it around the edges of the pan, or the excess steam will not be able to escape and the water will boil.

• When baking custards, be sure the water in the water bath is hot but not boiling. If the water even begins to boil, the texture of the dessert becomes marred by small holes.

• If much of the water evaporates from the water bath during baking, especially with large desserts, add a little more hot water to maintain it approximately at the level of halfway up the sides of dishes.

- When using a cake tester to check baked custards, try to insert it straight down.

- Custards must be checked carefully. Overcooking produces rubbery rather than soft creamy desserts and may cause them to separate. Undercooked custards may fall apart when unmolded.

- When baking custards in several ramekins, check each one to see if it is done, because the temperature may not be uniform in the front and back of the oven.

- To test custards baked in ramekins or individual soufflé dishes, carefully insert a cake tester or the point of a small thin-bladed knife in the custard's center, which is the last part to set; if the tester comes out clean, the dessert is done. The exception is custards rich in chocolate, which are tested near their edge; the center is not yet set at this point, but the chocolate solidifies as it cools and causes the dessert to become firmer. A custard baked in a large dish is tested halfway between its edge and its center, because it continues to cook from the heat retained by the dish even after it is removed from the oven. The deeper and larger the dish used, the longer the time required for the mixture to set.

- Kitchen towels are easier to use than potholders for removing small ramekins from the water bath, because it is easier to get a grip on the ramekins.

- If baking custards in special *petits pots,* do not bake them with their lids. Put these on the custards before chilling them.

- If any dessert falls apart during unmolding, spoon it into dessert dishes and garnish it with whipped cream and fruit.

CREAMY COFFEE CUSTARDS
Petits pots de crème au café

These smooth custards are baked in dainty dishes that are also good for serving. The traditional dishes, called in French *pots à crème,* are small deep porcelain dishes with lids, but today pretty ramekins are most often used instead. The custards are delicately flavored with coffee extract, which is available at specialty shops. Purists prefer to serve them unadorned. For a festive look you might like to garnish them with rosettes of whipped cream and candied or chocolate coffee beans, grated chocolate, or candied violets.   MAKES 5 SERVINGS

2 cups milk   *⅓ cup sugar*
6 large egg yolks   *1 tablespoon sweetened coffee extract*

Preheat oven to 350°F. Bring milk just to a boil in small heavy saucepan over medium heat; remove from heat.

Whisk egg yolks lightly in large bowl. Add sugar and whisk just to blend. Gradually pour in about 1 cup milk in a thin stream, stirring constantly with whisk. Using a wooden spoon, gradually stir in remaining milk. Stir in coffee extract. Strain mixture into a large measuring cup. Skim foam from surface of mixture.

Set five ⅔-cup ramekins in roasting pan or large shallow baking dish. Pour custard mixture into ramekins, dividing it evenly among them. Skim any remaining foam from mixture in ramekins. Place pan with ramekins in oven. Add enough very hot water to pan to come halfway up sides of ramekins. Set sheet of foil on top to cover ramekins. Bake until top is set and does not move when pan is moved gently, or until cake tester or point of small thin-bladed knife inserted very gently in centers of ramekins comes out clean, about 28 minutes. During baking, if water in pan comes close to a boil, add a few tablespoons cold water to pan and reduce oven temperature to 325°F. Carefully remove ramekins from water bath and let cool on rack to room temperature. Refrigerate at least 3 hours before serving. (Can be prepared up to 1 day ahead; keep covered.) Serve cold, in ramekins.

NOTE: For a stronger coffee flavor, substitute 1 tablespoon dry instant coffee for coffee extract, and whisk it into hot milk. Increase sugar quantity to 7 tablespoons.

BITTERSWEET CHOCOLATE CUSTARDS
Crème au chocolat amer

Light, creamy, and very chocolaty, these elegant custards are easy to prepare and contain fewer eggs than most other custards; the chocolate is what makes them set.   MAKES 4 SERVINGS

3 ounces fine-quality bittersweet
    chocolate, chopped
1/2 cup heavy cream
1 cup milk

2 tablespoons unsweetened
    Dutch-process cocoa powder
1 large egg plus 2 large yolks, room
    temperature
1/4 cup sugar

Position rack in center of oven and preheat to 350°F. Set four ²/₃-cup ramekins in a roasting pan or large shallow baking dish.

Melt chocolate in a small bowl above hot water over low heat. Stir until smooth. Remove from pan of water and cool slightly.

Combine cream and milk in a medium saucepan and heat to lukewarm. Add cocoa and whisk until blended.

Whisk egg and egg yolks lightly in a large bowl. Add sugar and whisk just until blended. Gradually pour in cocoa mixture in a thin stream, stirring constantly with a whisk. Gradually stir in melted chocolate. Strain mixture into a large measuring cup. Skim foam from surface of mixture.

Pour custard mixture into ramekins, dividing it evenly among them. Skim any remaining foam from mixture in ramekins.

Place pan with ramekins in oven. Add enough nearly boiling water to pan to come halfway up sides of ramekins. Set sheet of foil gently on top to cover ramekins. Bake about 36 minutes, or until top is just set and does not shake when you move water bath gently. During baking, if water in pan comes close to a boil, add a few tablespoons cold water to it.

Carefully remove ramekins from water bath and cool on a rack to room temperature. Refrigerate 3 hours. (Custards can be kept, covered, up to 3 days in refrigerator.)

ᴥᵞ CLASSIC CRÈME CARAMEL
Crème caramel

This is a great rendition of one of the most fabulous of desserts that remains exceedingly popular on menus on both sides of the Atlantic. When the dessert is unmolded, the caramel forms a clear, shiny sauce on top of and around the custard. Perfectly cooked caramel has a slight, pleasant bitterness that balances the richness of the vanilla custard. MAKES 4 TO 6 SERVINGS

CARAMEL

1/2 cup sugar
1/4 cup cool water

1 tablespoon warm water

VANILLA CUSTARD

2 cups milk
1 vanilla bean
2 large eggs plus 3 large yolks,
* room temperature*

6 tablespoons sugar

CARAMEL

Heat sugar and cool water in medium, heavy saucepan over low heat, stirring gently, until sugar dissolves. Increase heat and bring to a boil. Boil syrup, without stirring, until it becomes light brown. Reduce heat to low and continue cooking until syrup is rich brown. Do not let it become too dark or caramel will be very bitter; if too light, however, caramel will be too sweet. Remove from heat. Add warm water *while standing at a distance* because caramel will bubble and splatter. Swirl pan gently to be sure water is mixed into caramel. Let stand until caramel stops bubbling. Carefully pour caramel into a 1-quart soufflé dish or charlotte mold. Holding dish with potholders, rotate and tilt it to evenly coat base and sides about three-quarters of way up to rim with caramel. Continue rotating dish until caramel stops flowing. Let stand at room temperature while preparing custard.

VANILLA CUSTARD

Preheat oven to 350°F. Combine milk and vanilla bean in medium, heavy saucepan and bring just to a boil over medium heat.

Remove from heat, cover, and let stand 15 minutes. Remove vanilla bean.

Whisk eggs with yolks lightly in large bowl. Add sugar and whisk just to blend. Gradually pour in about 1 cup milk, stirring constantly with whisk. Using a wooden spoon, gradually stir in remaining milk. Skim foam from surface of mixture. Pour mixture into caramel-coated dish.

Set dish in roasting pan or large shallow baking dish. Cover loosely with sheet of foil. Set pan with dish in oven. Add enough very hot water to larger pan to come about halfway up sides of soufflé dish. Bake until cake tester or point of small thin-bladed knife inserted in mixture halfway between center and edge comes out completely dry, about 60 to 70 minutes; do not pierce all the way to bottom of dish. During baking, if water in pan comes close to a boil, add a few tablespoons cold water to pan and reduce oven temperature to 325°F. Carefully remove from water bath and cool on rack to room temperature. Refrigerate at least 4 hours before serving. (Can be prepared up to 2 days ahead; keep covered.)

To unmold, slide thin-bladed flexible knife around edge of dessert, set a rimmed round platter on top and invert both. (Can be unmolded up to 2 hours ahead; keep uncovered in refrigerator.)

❧ BAKED GINGER-AND-LEMON CUSTARDS
Crème renversée au gingembre et au citron

Lemon zest and fresh ginger give this dessert an intriguing flavor. They are infused in the milk so that the custards stay smooth. Candied ginger is the tasty garnish.　　　　　　MAKES 4 SERVINGS

2 cups milk
1 teaspoon finely grated lemon zest
3 tablespoons finely grated peeled
　　fresh ginger (a 3-ounce or
　　2-inch piece)

1 large egg plus 6 large yolks
1/3 cup sugar
1 tablespoon very finely diced
　　crystallized ginger (see Note)

Preheat oven to 350°F. Generously butter four 3/4-cup ramekins (with slightly rounded bottoms, if possible). Bring milk just to a boil in medium, heavy saucepan over medium heat. Remove from heat and stir in lemon zest and fresh ginger. Cook, uncovered, over low heat 3 minutes, stirring occasionally. Remove from heat, cover, and let stand 20 minutes. Strain milk, pressing on mixture in strainer.

Whisk egg and yolks lightly in a large bowl. Add sugar and whisk just to blend. Gradually pour in about 1 cup strained milk in a thin stream, stirring constantly with whisk. Using a wooden spoon, gradually stir in remaining milk. Pour into measuring cup. Skim foam from surface of mixture.

Set ramekins in roasting pan or large shallow baking dish. Pour custard mixture into ramekins, dividing it evenly among them. Skim any remaining foam from mixture in ramekins. Place pan with ramekins in oven. Add enough very hot water to pan to come halfway up sides of ramekins. Set a sheet of foil on top to cover ramekins. Bake until cake tester or point of small thin-bladed knife inserted gently in center of each ramekin comes out clean, about 30 minutes. During baking, if water in pan comes close to a boil, add a few tablespoons cold water to pan and reduce oven temperature to 325°F. Carefully remove ramekins from water bath. Let cool on rack to room temperature. Refrigerate at least 3 hours before serving. (Can be prepared up to 1 day ahead; keep covered.)

To unmold, run thin-bladed flexible knife around each dessert and tilt ramekin slightly so dessert comes away from sides. Set plate on top and invert both. Shake once downward so dessert comes out onto plate. Sprinkle top of each custard evenly with diced crystallized ginger. Serve cold.

NOTE: Dark-colored candied ginger is best for garnish, because the golden brown pieces provide a pleasant color contrast to the creamy yellow custard. To dice candied ginger, use a very sharp thin-bladed knife. Cut ginger in very thin slices, then in thin strips, last in tiny dice. Set dice on plate so they don't stick together.

❧ ORANGE-SCENTED CHOCOLATE POTS DE CRÈME
Petits pots de crème au chocolat et à l'orange

The chocolate forms a dark, shiny topping on this super-rich dessert during baking. The custards can also be decorated with a flourish of whipped cream and a few pieces of Lightly Candied Orange Zest (see recipe).   MAKES 4 SERVINGS

Zest of 1 orange
1 1/3 cups milk
3 ounces fine-quality bittersweet or semisweet chocolate, chopped

4 large egg yolks
5 tablespoons sugar

Preheat oven to 350°F. Pare orange zest in strips and put in small heavy saucepan. Add 1 cup milk and bring just to a boil over medium heat. Remove from heat, cover, and let stand 10 minutes. Using slotted spoon, remove strips of peel.

Melt chocolate in remaining 1/3 cup milk in medium bowl above hot water over low heat. Remove from above water and stir gently with whisk until smooth. Gradually pour orange-flavored milk into chocolate, stirring with whisk; be sure to stir in any chocolate stuck on sides of bowl.

Whisk egg yolks lightly in large bowl. Add sugar and whisk just to blend. Gradually pour in about 2/3 cup chocolate mixture, stirring constantly with whisk. Using a wooden spoon, gradually stir in remaining chocolate mixture. Strain mixture into large measuring cup. Skim foam from surface.

Set four 2/3-cup ramekins in roasting pan or large shallow baking dish. Pour custard mixture into ramekins, dividing it evenly among them. Skim any remaining foam from mixture in ramekins. Place pan with ramekins in oven. Add enough very hot water to pan to come halfway up sides of ramekins. Set sheet of foil loosely on top to cover ramekins. Bake until top is nearly set and moves only very slightly when pan is moved gently, or until cake tester or point of small thin-bladed knife inserted very gently in mixture about 1/2 inch from edge of each ramekin comes out clean, about 30 minutes. During baking, if water in pan comes close to a boil, add a few tablespoons cold water to pan and reduce oven temperature to 325°F. Carefully remove ramekins from water bath and let cool on rack to room temperature. Refrigerate at least 3 hours before serving. (Can be prepared up to 1 day ahead; keep covered.) Serve cold, in ramekins.

Mousses

When made from a fine chocolate or from an aromatic ripe fruit in season, I find a chilled mousse to be one of the most irresistible of desserts. A few spoonfuls of a well-flavored mousse are, for me, the perfect treat.

Like so many other culinary terms, the word *mousse* came to us from French. It means foam and emphasizes the ethereal nature of these desserts. Whether lightened by beaten egg whites, whipped cream, or both, mousses have a smooth, gossamer texture. Unlike Bavarian creams, which follow a more or less set formula, mousses vary widely in their composition. Their base might be a fruit purée, a custard, a sabayon-type mixture, or a syrup-and-egg mixture known as *pâte à bombe,* such as the one I used in Two-Way Raspberry Mousse. Some mousses require a little gelatin to keep the mixture uniform or to permit it to be molded.

Mousse is often served in a wineglass, ramekin, or dessert dish, and occasionally in an edible container, such as a Tulip Cookie Cup (see recipe) or a meringue basket, as in Individual Black Forest Vacherins (see recipe). For a modern presentation, a spoonful of mousse can be served on top of fresh fruit salad, as in Light Lemon Mousse with Berries, or mousses of contrasting colors can be layered in a clear serving dish, as in Apricot and White Chocolate Cold Soufflé. They also make light and luscious fillings for cakes, charlottes, and tarts.

One of the most frequently prepared types of dessert by French home cooks, mousses are not only delicious but also practical. They are ideal for warm weather because they are served cold and require no baking. Menu planning is easy with these do-ahead desserts because they can wait in the refrigerator, and some can even be frozen.

Although mousses are among the most elegant of desserts, they do not involve many components or complicated procedures and are actually quite simple and often quick to prepare.

Hints

• Beat egg whites until stiff but not dry, and cream until fairly stiff, for folding into a mousse. Overbeaten whites or cream are difficult to fold into a mousse mixture.

• Fold in beaten whites or cream thoroughly; any whites or cream that have not blended in will be noticeable in the finished dessert.

• Molded mousses and Bavarian creams chill faster in a ring mold than in molds of other shapes, because a greater surface of the mousse is exposed to the cold.

• Mousses that do not contain pieces of fruit can be frozen.

• Instead of grating citrus peels, it is often more convenient to remove the peel with a lemon zester and chop it with a knife until very fine.

LIGHT MELON MOUSSE WITH RASPBERRY SAUCE
Mousse légère au melon, coulis de framboises

The color of this mousse may be light orange or pale green, depending on whether you use cantaloupe or honeydew. It is easy to serve, as no unmolding is required. The mousse is simply spooned into wineglasses, and served topped with a drizzle of raspberry sauce and a sprinkling of chopped walnuts. Strawberry Sauce or Melon Sauce (see recipes) can be substituted for the Raspberry Sauce.

MAKES 5 OR 6 SERVINGS

1 envelope unflavored gelatin (¹/₄ ounce)
¹/₄ cup water
7 tablespoons sugar
¹/₂ cup milk

1 small cantaloupe (1 ¹/₄ to 1 ¹/₂ pounds), seeds removed, and flesh cut in chunks
1 cup heavy cream, well chilled
Raspberry Sauce (page 345)
3 tablespoons coarsely chopped walnuts for garnish

Sprinkle gelatin over water and leave 5 minutes to soften.

In a small saucepan, heat sugar in milk over low heat, stirring, until sugar dissolves. Bring to a simmer. Remove from heat and add gelatin. Whisk thoroughly so gelatin dissolves. Pour mixture into a large bowl.

Purée melon in a food processor or blender until smooth. Mix it with milk mixture. (Mixture may appear separated, but will be fine when cream is added.) Chill, stirring occasionally, about 30 minutes, or until cold and beginning to thicken but not set.

In a large chilled bowl with chilled beater, whip cream until stiff. Fold cream into melon mixture. Divide mixture among dessert dishes or spoon it into a large bowl; refrigerate about 1 hour for individual dishes, or 3 hours for a large bowl until set. (The mousse can be kept, covered, 2 days in refrigerator.)

To serve, spoon a little raspberry sauce over center of each serving, and decorate with a few chopped nuts. Serve cold.

APPLE MOUSSE WITH CARAMEL SAUCE
Mousse aux pommes, sauce caramel

Flavorful apple compote forms the base for this mousse, which is enriched with whipped cream. Caramel is the apple's natural partner in French desserts, and here the two are paired again, with the caramel sauce balancing the mousse's richness.   MAKES 6 TO 8 SERVINGS

2 cups Apple Compote (see Note, page 49)
1/4 cup water
1 envelope unflavored gelatin (1/4 ounce)

1 cup heavy cream, well chilled
3 tablespoons sugar

CARAMEL SAUCE
1 cup sugar
1/2 cup room-temperature water
1/2 cup hot water

2 additional tablespoons cold water (optional)

6 to 8 red or green candied cherries, cut in half (optional)

Purée compote in a food processor or blender until smooth; leave in processor. Pour water into a small saucepan and sprinkle gelatin over it. Leave 5 minutes for gelatin to soften.

Set saucepan of gelatin in another pan of hot water over low heat. Heat, stirring, until gelatin is completely dissolved. Immediately pour hot gelatin mixture into food processor or blender and process to mix it thoroughly with apple compote. Let mixture cool to room temperature.

Lightly oil a 5-cup ring mold or other mold. Whip cream in chilled bowl with chilled beater until it begins to thicken. Add sugar and continue whipping until cream is fairly stiff. Fold apple mixture into cream. Spoon into mold and chill 2 hours, or until set. (Mousse can be kept, covered, 1 day in refrigerator.)

CARAMEL SAUCE

In a medium, heavy saucepan, dissolve sugar in ½ cup room-temperature water over low heat, stirring. Boil syrup over high heat without stirring, but skimming occasionally, until it becomes light brown in color. (Check color by looking under bubbles.) Reduce heat and continue cooking until color of caramel is rich brown, but don't let it become too dark or it will be bitter. Remove from heat.

Add hot water *gradually and standing at a distance* because sauce will bubble and splatter. Mix well. Return to low heat and heat, stirring, until sauce is smooth. Taste sauce; if it is too strong in flavor or too thick, stir in 2 tablespoons cold water. Refrigerate until ready to serve. (Sauce can be kept, covered, 1 day in refrigerator.)

Unmold dessert a short time before serving: Dip mold for about 10 seconds into enough warm water to come nearly to its top; pat dry. Run a thin-bladed flexible knife around edge of dessert, gently pushing dessert slightly from edge of mold to let in air. Set a serving platter on top of mold, hold tightly, and invert dessert and platter together. Shake mold downward once; dessert should come out onto platter. If dessert remains in mold, repeat procedure. Refrigerate until ready to serve.

If desired, decorate with halves of candied cherries. Serve sauce separately.

❧ CLASSIC CHOCOLATE MOUSSE WITH GRAND MARNIER
Mousse au chocolat au grand marnier

This fabulous French masterpiece is not only one of the world's favorite sweet finales, it is also one of the easiest desserts to make. During the five years I spent at La Varenne Cooking School in Paris, the chefs prepared this marvelous chocolate mousse many times. Most often they flavored it with Grand Marnier or rum, but sometimes they used brandy, coffee liqueur, or raspberry brandy. They served the mousse in glasses, ramekins, or deep dessert dishes. Occasionally they garnished it with a spoonful of softly whipped cream and a sprinkling of grated chocolate, or with a rosette of stiff whipped cream.

MAKES 4 SERVINGS

7 ounces semisweet or bittersweet chocolate, chopped
3 tablespoons Grand Marnier
1 tablespoon water

1 tablespoon unsalted butter
4 large eggs, separated
1 tablespoon sugar

In a medium bowl, melt chocolate with Grand Marnier and water above hot water over low heat. Remove from pan of water. Stir until smooth. Stir in the butter. Add egg yolks, 1 at a time, stirring vigorously after each addition.

Beat egg whites until stiff. Beat in sugar and continue beating about 30 seconds, or until whites are very shiny.

Quickly fold one-quarter of whites into chocolate mixture. Gently fold in the remaining whites. Spoon mousse into 4 dessert dishes, ramekins, or stemmed glasses. Cover and chill at least 2 hours, or until set. (The mousse can be kept, covered, 2 days in refrigerator.)

ꙮ LIGHT LEMON MOUSSE WITH BERRIES
Mousse au citron aux baies fraîches

This creamy, tangy mousse is served in contemporary fashion—a spoonful or two crown a colorful mixture of fresh fruit.

MAKES 6 SERVINGS

½ cup strained fresh lemon juice
1 envelope unflavored gelatin (¼ ounce)
Grated zest of 3 lemons
4 extra-large eggs, separated
1 cup sugar

1 cup heavy cream, well chilled
2 cups strawberries, hulled and cut in quarters lengthwise
½ cup blackberries
½ cup blueberries

Pour ¼ cup lemon juice into a small saucepan. Sprinkle gelatin over it and let stand 5 minutes to soften.

Combine lemon zest and egg yolks in a large bowl and beat with a hand-held mixer or whisk until smooth. Gradually beat in ¾ cup sugar. Beat in remaining ¼ cup lemon juice. Set bowl in a pan of hot water over low heat. Beat mixture for about 8 minutes, or until it is warm to touch, light in color, and thick enough to coat a spoon. Remove bowl from pan of water.

Heat gelatin mixture briefly over very low heat, stirring constantly, just until gelatin dissolves. Gradually beat dissolved gelatin into yolk mixture. Beat mixture until cool. Refrigerate mixture, stirring often, 20 to 30 minutes, or until cold and thick but not set. (For quicker chilling, set bowl in a larger bowl of ice cubes and water.)

Whip cream in a chilled bowl with chilled beater until fairly stiff. Fold into cold lemon mixture. In another bowl, with clean beater, whip egg whites until stiff. Beat in remaining ¼ cup sugar and continue beating until whites are very stiff and shiny. Gently fold whites into lemon mixture. Spoon mousse into a bowl or into individual dessert glasses or dishes. Refrigerate 1 hour, or until set. (It can be refrigerated overnight.)

Gently mix berries. Serve mousse topped with berries; or spoon berries into individual gratin dishes or other dishes, and top each with 1 or 2 spoonfuls of lemon mousse.

❧ STRAWBERRY MOUSSE WITH KIRSCH
Mousse de fraises au kirsch

This is one of the quickest fruit mousses to prepare. By spooning it into individual glasses and using the freezer to speed the cooling process, you can chill it just before serving dinner and it will be cool enough in time for dessert. The only garnish needed on top of each serving is a beautiful kirsch-scented strawberry.

MAKES 4 OR 5 SERVINGS

3/4 pound strawberries (one 12-ounce basket), hulled
1 envelope (1/4 ounce) plus 1 1/2 teaspoons unflavored gelatin (see Note)
1/2 cup water

2/3 cup plus 1 teaspoon sugar
1 cup heavy cream
5 to 6 teaspoons kirsch or cherry liqueur
4 or 5 whole strawberries for garnish

Purée strawberries in a food processor or blender until very smooth. Pour purée into a large bowl. In a small cup, sprinkle gelatin over 1/4 cup water and let stand about 5 minutes.

In a small saucepan, combine 2/3 cup sugar and remaining 1/4 cup water. Stir until thoroughly mixed. Heat over low heat, stirring, until sugar dissolves completely. Bring to a boil over medium heat. Simmer 30 seconds without stirring.

Remove from heat and immediately whisk in softened gelatin, in 2 portions. Let cool 3 minutes, stirring often. Gradually pour gelatin mixture into strawberry purée, whisking constantly. Chill mixture about 15 minutes, stirring often, until it is cold and beginning to thicken but is not set.

Whip cream in a chilled bowl with chilled beater until soft peaks form. Beat in 3 teaspoons kirsch. Gently fold cream into strawberry mixture. Taste and add 1 or 2 teaspoons more kirsch, if desired.

Ladle mixture into 4 to 5 dessert glasses, smoothing top. Chill in freezer about 20 minutes, then refrigerate until set, about 10 minutes more. Sprinkle the strawberries for garnish with 1 teaspoon sugar and 1 tablespoon kirsch, cover, and refrigerate until ready to serve. At serving time, set 1 strawberry on each portion.

NOTE: This amount of gelatin is designed to make the mousse set as quickly as possible. If you would like to prepare the mousse several hours or 1 day ahead, use only 1 envelope (1/4 oz.) gelatin.

🌿 PERSIMMON MOUSSE
Mousse au kaki

Persimmons are not very common in France, but I find they are perfect for making French-style mousses. Garnish the dessert with persimmon slices, if you like.   MAKES 6 SERVINGS

3 teaspoons unflavored gelatin
1/2 cup water
1/4 cup sugar
1 pound very ripe, soft persimmons
1 tablespoon strained fresh lemon
    juice

1 cup heavy cream, well chilled
Persimmon slices for garnish
Mint leaves for garnish (optional)

Sprinkle gelatin over 1/4 cup water in a small cup and let stand about 5 minutes.

In a small saucepan, combine sugar and remaining 1/4 cup water. Stir until thoroughly mixed. Heat over low heat, stirring, until sugar dissolves completely. Bring to a boil over medium heat. Remove from heat and immediately whisk in softened gelatin, in 2 portions. Pour into a bowl and cool to room temperature.

Cut persimmons in half. Using a spoon, remove all flesh from persimmons. Purée flesh in a food processor or blender until very smooth. Add to gelatin mixture and mix well. Stir in lemon juice.

Refrigerate mixture about 15 minutes, stirring often, until it is cold and beginning to thicken but is not set. Lightly oil a 5-cup mold.

Whip cream in a chilled bowl with a chilled beater until soft peaks form. Refrigerate until ready to use. When persimmon mixture is cold, fold in whipped cream. Spoon mousse into the mold. Cover with plastic wrap. Refrigerate until completely set, at least 2 hours. (Mousse can be kept, covered, 1 day in refrigerator.)

Unmold dessert a short time before serving: Dip mold for about 10 seconds into enough warm water to come nearly to its top; pat dry. Run a thin-bladed flexible knife around edge of dessert, gently pushing dessert slightly from edge of mold to let in air. Set a serving platter on top of mold, hold tightly, and invert dessert and platter together. Shake mold downward once; dessert should come out onto platter. If dessert remains in mold, repeat procedure. Refrigerate until ready to serve.

Serve cold, garnished with persimmon slices and mint leaves, if desired.

APRICOT AND WHITE CHOCOLATE COLD SOUFFLÉ
Soufflé froid aux abricots et au chocolat blanc

A ribbon of bright apricot mousse runs through the center of this soufflé, between two layers of white chocolate mousse. From the poached dried apricots used to make the mousse, you also get a zesty apricot sauce to accompany this lovely party dessert.

MAKES 8 TO 10 SERVINGS

APRICOT MOUSSE AND SAUCE

3/4 cup sugar

3 cups water

1 vanilla bean (optional)

2 1/2 cups dried apricots (about 12 ounces)

2 teaspoons unflavored gelatin

3 tablespoons water

WHITE CHOCOLATE MOUSSE

1 envelope (1/4 ounce) unflavored gelatin

1/4 cup plus 2 tablespoons water

8 ounces white chocolate, chopped

1 cup heavy cream, well chilled

6 tablespoons unsalted butter, cut in 8 pieces, room temperature

6 large eggs, separated, room temperature

About 2 tablespoons kirsch or water for sauce (optional)

APRICOT MOUSSE AND SAUCE

Combine sugar, 3 cups water, and vanilla bean in a medium saucepan. Bring to a boil, stirring. Reserve 5 or 6 small apricots for garnish. Add remaining apricots to syrup and bring to a simmer. Cover and poach them over low heat about 15 minutes, or until they are very tender. Let cool to room temperature in syrup. Remove vanilla bean.

Remove apricots from syrup, reserving syrup. Purée apricots in food processor with ½ cup reserved syrup. Reserve 2 cups purée for mousse, and the rest for sauce.

Sprinkle 2 teaspoons gelatin over 3 tablespoons water in a small cup and let stand 5 minutes. Set cup in a pan of hot water over low heat and stir until gelatin dissolves. Gradually pour it into apricot purée reserved for mousse, whisking constantly.

WHITE CHOCOLATE MOUSSE

Sprinkle gelatin over ¼ cup water in a small cup and let stand 5 minutes.

Combine white chocolate, butter, and 2 tablespoons water in a medium bowl and set it above hot water over low heat. Leave until melted, stirring occasionally. Whisk until smooth. Remove from pan of water.

Set cup of gelatin in a shallow pan of hot water over low heat and melt gelatin, stirring often, about 3 minutes. Whisk gelatin into white chocolate mixture. Add egg yolks, 1 at a time, stirring vigorously after each addition.

Whip egg whites in a medium bowl until soft peaks form. Whip at high speed until stiff but not dry. Stir one-quarter of whites into white chocolate mixture; fold in remaining whites in 2 batches.

Whip cream in large chilled bowl with chilled beater until fairly stiff. Gently fold ½ cup cream into white chocolate mixture. Fold remaining cream into apricot-gelatin mixture.

Pour 2 cups white chocolate mousse into a 1-quart soufflé dish. Cover and freeze 15 minutes. Keep remaining mousses at room temperature. Stir them occasionally.

Pour apricot mousse into soufflé dish on top of white chocolate mousse and gently spread smooth. Freeze 15 minutes.

Cut a 25-inch sheet of wax paper and fold it in half. Wrap wax paper around soufflé dish containing mousse so that it extends about 3 inches above rim to make a collar. Fasten tightly with tape. Gently ladle remaining white chocolate mousse over apricot mousse. Refrigerate 4 hours, or until completely set. (Dessert can be kept, covered, up to 3 days in refrigerator.)

To finish apricot sauce, stir remaining syrup into remaining apricot purée. If sauce is too thick, stir in 2 tablespoons kirsch or water, or enough to bring mixture to consistency of a thick, but pourable, sauce.

To serve, carefully peel off and discard wax paper. Set a ring of small dried apricots on top of soufflé. Serve sauce separately.

TWO-WAY RASPBERRY MOUSSE
Mousse aux framboises

My friend Maurice Ferré, the pastry chef of Maxim's in Paris, taught me how to make this creamy dessert, which can play two roles. As a mousse, it's lovely served in a glass and garnished with fresh raspberries. As a bright pink sauce, it's delicious with plain cakes such as French Angel Food Cake (see recipe) or with vanilla or fruit ice cream.

MAKES 4 TO 6 SERVINGS AS MOUSSE;
ABOUT 6 TO 8 SERVINGS AS SAUCE

3 1/2 cups fresh raspberries (see Note)
4 large egg yolks
1 cup sugar
1/2 cup water

2 cups heavy cream, well chilled
Fresh raspberries for garnish (optional)
Mint sprigs for garnish (optional)

Purée berries in food processor or blender until very smooth. Push through a strainer into a bowl, pressing on pulp in strainer; use rubber spatula to scrape mixture from underside of strainer. Measure 1 1/4 cups purée.

Put egg yolks in bowl of mixer fitted with whip.

Combine sugar and water in small heavy saucepan, preferably one with lip for pouring. Cook over low heat, stirring very gently from time to time, until sugar dissolves. Increase heat to medium-high and bring to a boil. Boil without stirring, but brush down sugar crystals from side of pan occasionally with pastry brush dipped in water, until candy thermometer registers 238°F. (soft-ball stage). To test without thermometer, remove pan from heat. Using teaspoon, take about ½ teaspoon hot syrup and dip spoon into cup of ice water, keeping spoon level. With your hands in ice water, remove syrup from spoon. *Caution: Do not touch syrup unless your hands are in ice water.* If syrup is ready, it will form a soft ball.

As soon as syrup is ready, gradually beat it into egg yolks in a thin stream; try to pour it between whip and sides of bowl so not too much gets caught in whip. Beat mixture at high speed until it is completely cool and thick, scraping down sides once or twice. Refrigerate about 1 hour, or until cold. Stir in raspberry purée.

To make mixture into mousse: Whip cream in a chilled bowl with chilled beater until fairly stiff. Fold it into raspberry mixture. Spoon into glasses and refrigerate 1 hour. Garnish, if desired, with fresh berries and mint.

To make mixture into sauce: Stir in unwhipped cream. Serve cold.

NOTE: You can substitute 12 ounces frozen unsweetened or very lightly sweetened raspberries for fresh.

Bavarian Creams

Bavarian cream deserves to be better known to American home cooks. It is creamy, silky, soft, and fabulous. Like French ice cream, it is made from a rich crème anglaise (custard sauce) and is flavored with vanilla, chocolate, coffee, caramel, liqueur, praline, citrus zest, or any flavoring that can be used for ice cream. The custard is thickened with a little gelatin and lightened with whipped cream, resulting in a glorious dessert resembling a mousse or luxurious pudding.

Once the custard has been removed from the heat and the gelatin has been added, the mixture is left to cool thoroughly before the cream can be folded in. The whipped cream would melt and lose body if added to a hot mixture. As the custard cools, it is stirred often to prevent it from sticking to the sides and bottom of the bowl, which become cold faster than the center of the mixture. When the custard is cold to the touch and quite thick but not yet set, the cream is folded in. Diced fruit can also be added, as in Fruit Bavarian Cream or Pineapple Bavarian Cream.

Bavarian cream is most dramatic when prepared in a decorative mold and turned out onto a pretty platter. Instead of being unmolded, these desserts can be prepared in a deep attractive dish and served directly from it. Bavarian creams also make a delectable filling for charlottes, such as Strawberry-Banana Charlotte (see recipe), and for cakes.

Classic fruit Bavarian creams are usually made without custard sauce, and consist simply of sweetened fruit purée, gelatin, and whipped cream. Today, most cooking professionals refer to these desserts as mousses, and so they are included in the mousse section.

There is no need for fancy garnishes for these desserts—rosettes of whipped cream are traditional. But since Bavarian creams are already creamy, I often like to serve them with sliced fresh fruit or a colorful fruit sauce, as in Pear Bavarian Cream with Raspberry Sauce.

Hints

• To cool the custard-and-gelatin mixture quickly, set the bowl of mixture in a larger bowl of ice cubes and water, instead of in the refrigerator; stir often so the mixture will not stick to the sides of the bowl.

• If the gelatin mixture sets before the cream has been folded in, whisk the mixture until smooth, then lightly fold in the whipped cream with the whisk.

• To facilitate unmolding, choose plain molds or those with simple designs.

• If the Bavarian cream does not contain pieces of fruit, it can be chilled in the freezer. Thaw the dessert in the refrigerator before serving.

• If some of the dessert sticks after unmolding, put it carefully in place and smooth it with a moistened spatula. If you like, use fresh fruit and/or rosettes of whipped cream to hide any faults.

✤ PINEAPPLE BAVARIAN CREAM
Bavarois à l'ananas

Although pineapple might seem like a "nouvelle" addition to French desserts, cooks in France have, in fact, been using it since the eighteenth century in a broad range of desserts. Poached fresh pineapple and its syrup give the Bavarian cream a superb fruit flavor. For a colorful presentation, spoon a little Strawberry Sauce (see recipe) around the dessert and set the garnishing pineapple slices on it.

MAKES 8 SERVINGS

Poached pineapple (page 373) (see Note)
1 cup milk
1 vanilla bean, split lengthwise, or 1 teaspoon pure vanilla extract
4 large egg yolks

5 tablespoons sugar
1/2 cup syrup reserved from poaching pineapple, strained
1 envelope unflavored gelatin (1/4 ounce)
1 cup heavy cream, well chilled

Cool pineapple completely. Bring milk and vanilla bean (but not extract) to a boil in a small heavy saucepan. Remove from heat, cover, and let stand 15 minutes.

Whisk egg yolks lightly in a large bowl. Add sugar and whisk until smooth. Reheat milk to a boil. Gradually whisk milk into yolk mixture. Return mixture to saucepan. Cook over medium-low heat, stirring and scraping bottom of pan constantly with a wooden spoon, until mixture thickens slightly and reaches 165°F. to 170°F. on an instant-read thermometer; begin checking after 5 minutes. (To check without thermometer, remove sauce from heat, dip a metal spoon in sauce and draw your finger across back of spoon—your finger should leave a clear trail in mixture that clings to spoon.) If necessary, cook another 30 seconds and check again. Do not overcook sauce or it will curdle. Strain immediately into a bowl and stir about 30 seconds to cool.

In small cup, cool 1/4 cup pineapple syrup to room temperature; sprinkle gelatin over this cool syrup, and let stand about 5 minutes. In a small saucepan, bring remaining 1/4 cup pineapple syrup to a boil over medium heat. Remove from heat, add softened gelatin, and whisk until completely dissolved. Gradually whisk gelatin mixture into custard. Cool to room temperature, stirring occasionally. If using vanilla extract, stir it into cool mixture. Lightly oil a 5- to 6-cup mold or bowl.

Drain pineapple well; reserve syrup for other uses, if desired. Set pineapple on paper towels. Cut out cores from slices with small sharp knife. Cut 7 rings in 1/2-inch dice; reserve remaining rings for garnish. Refrigerate all pineapple.

Refrigerate custard mixture about 20 minutes, stirring every 5 minutes, until it is cold and beginning to thicken but is not set. Stir in diced pineapple and refrigerate 15 minutes, stirring often, until mixture begins to set. Remove from refrigerator.

Whip cream in chilled bowl with chilled beater to soft peaks. Gently fold cream into pineapple mixture, blending thoroughly. Refrigerate 15 minutes, folding mixture occasionally. Pour mixture into prepared mold, smoothing top. Cover with plastic wrap and refrigerate 2 hours, or until completely set. (Dessert can be kept 1 day in refrigerator.)

Unmold dessert a short time before serving: Dip mold for about 10 seconds into enough warm water to come nearly to its top; pat dry. Run a thin-bladed flexible knife around edge of dessert, gently pushing dessert slightly from edge of mold to let in air. Set a serving platter on top of mold, hold tightly and invert dessert and platter together. Shake mold downward once; dessert should come out onto platter. If dessert remains in mold, repeat procedure. Cut reserved pineapple slices in thirds, and place around base of dessert. Refrigerate until ready to serve.

NOTE: A 20-ounce can of sliced pineapple in heavy syrup can be substituted for the poached pineapple and syrup.

COFFEE BAVARIAN CREAM
Bavarois au café

In my dessert classes, this is a favorite of my students. If you have never made Bavarian cream before, this is a good version to start with because there are no extra steps in preparing the flavorings—you simply use instant coffee. Rosettes of whipped cream and candied coffee beans make a delightful garnish.   MAKES 6 TO 8 SERVINGS

1/4 cup water
1 envelope (1/4 ounce) plus 1
    teaspoon unflavored gelatin
1 1/2 cups milk
1 tablespoon instant coffee powder
    or granules

5 large egg yolks
7 tablespoons sugar
1 cup heavy cream, well chilled

Pour water into a small cup, sprinkle gelatin over it, and let stand until ready to use.

In a medium, heavy saucepan, bring milk to a boil with coffee, whisking. Remove from heat.

Whisk egg yolks lightly in a large bowl. Add sugar and whisk until smooth. Gradually whisk hot milk into yolk mixture. Return mixture to saucepan. Cook over medium-low heat, stirring and scraping bottom of pan constantly with a wooden spoon, until mixture thickens slightly and reaches 165°F. to 170°F. on an instant-read thermometer; begin checking after 5 minutes. (To check without thermometer, remove sauce from heat, dip a metal spoon in sauce, and draw your finger across back of spoon—your finger should leave a clear trail in mixture that clings to spoon.) If necessary, cook another 30 seconds and check again. Do not overcook sauce or it will curdle.

Remove from heat and immediately add softened gelatin, whisking until completely dissolved. Pour mixture into a large bowl and cool to room temperature, stirring occasionally. Refrigerate until cold and beginning to thicken, about 15 to 20 minutes, stirring mixture every 5 minutes; do not allow custard mixture to set. Lightly oil a 4- to 5-cup mold.

Whip cream in chilled bowl with chilled beater until soft peaks form. Gently fold cream into custard. Spoon mixture into mold, cover with plastic wrap, and refrigerate until completely set, at least 2 hours. (Dessert can be kept, covered, 1 day in refrigerator.)

Unmold dessert a short time before serving: Dip mold for about 10 seconds into enough warm water to come nearly to top of mold; pat dry. Run a thin-bladed flexible knife around edge of dessert, gently pushing dessert slightly from edge of mold to let in air. Set a serving platter on top of mold, hold tightly, and invert the dessert and platter together. Shake mold downward once; dessert should come out onto platter. If dessert remains in mold, repeat procedure. Refrigerate until ready to serve.

PEAR BAVARIAN CREAM WITH RASPBERRY SAUCE
Bavarois aux poires au coulis de framboises

The pear has a split personality in the French kitchen. On the one hand, its flavor is so delicate, that cooks try to do everything to preserve it when making desserts. On the other hand, pears are often paired with strong-flavored ingredients such as caramel, chocolate, red wine, and even Roquefort cheese.

There's a reason for this treatment. Unlike many fruits, pears lack acidity. That's why their flavor is subtle, but also why they marry so well with most other flavors—there is no chance of a clash. The pale pear color leads chefs to match them with warm-colored sauces, such as chocolate or raspberry. When used judiciously, these assertive sauces provide a pleasant accent and prevent pear desserts from turning out bland.

MAKES 4 OR 5 SERVINGS

Poached Pears (page 373)
1 1/4 cups reserved syrup from
    poaching pears
1 cup milk
Vanilla bean from poaching pears,
    or 1 teaspoon pure vanilla
    extract

1 envelope unflavored gelatin (1/4
    ounce)
4 extra-large egg yolks
3 tablespoons granulated sugar
1 tablespoon pear brandy (optional)
1 cup heavy cream, well chilled

RASPBERRY SAUCE
1 pint fresh raspberries, or one
    12-ounce package frozen
    raspberries, thawed
3 tablespoons reserved syrup from
    poaching pears

3 tablespoons powdered sugar, or to
    taste

Drain 1 cup syrup from pears and simmer it in a saucepan over medium heat, until reduced to ½ cup. Reserve in saucepan.

In a small heavy saucepan, bring milk to a boil with vanilla bean (but not with vanilla extract). Cover and let stand 15 minutes. Pour remaining ¼ cup unreduced syrup into a bowl; sprinkle gelatin over it and allow it to soften.

Whisk egg yolks lightly in a large bowl. Add sugar and whisk until smooth. Remove vanilla bean from milk. Gradually whisk hot milk into yolk mixture. Return mixture to saucepan. Cook over medium-low heat, stirring and scraping bottom of pan constantly with a wooden spoon, until mixture thickens slightly and reaches 165°F. to 170°F. on an instant-read thermometer; begin checking after 5 minutes. (To check without thermometer, remove sauce from heat, dip a metal spoon in sauce, and draw your finger across back of spoon— your finger should leave a clear trail in mixture that clings to spoon.) If necessary, cook another 30 seconds and check again. Do not overcook sauce or it will curdle. Pour into a bowl.

Bring reduced syrup to boil over medium heat. Remove from heat, add softened gelatin, and whisk until completely dissolved. Gradually whisk this mixture into custard.

Cool to room temperature, stirring occasionally. If using vanilla extract, stir it into cool mixture. Stir in pear brandy, if using. Refrigerate mixture 20 to 30 minutes, stirring often to prevent it from setting at sides of bowl, until cold and thick but not set.

Cut 2 thin slices from base of each pear half; reserve slices in their poaching syrup for garnish. Dice remaining pears and refrigerate them.

When gelatin mixture is thick, whip cream in chilled bowl with chilled beater until stiff. Fold cream into gelatin mixture, in 2 portions. Refrigerate 10 minutes, gently folding mixture once in a while. Fold in diced pears. Chill another 5 minutes. Pour the mixture into a 5- or 6-cup mold or bowl. Refrigerate 2 hours, or until set.

RASPBERRY SAUCE

Purée raspberries with pear syrup in a blender or food processor. Strain, pressing hard on purée so only seeds remain in strainer. Sift powdered sugar into strained sauce and mix well. Taste, and add more powdered sugar, if desired. Refrigerate. (Dessert and sauce can be kept, covered, 1 day in refrigerator.)

Unmold dessert a short time before serving: Dip mold for about 10 seconds into enough warm water to come nearly to its top; pat dry. Run a thin-bladed flexible knife around edge of dessert, gently pushing dessert slightly from edge of mold to let in air. Set a serving platter on top of mold, hold tightly, and invert dessert and platter together. Shake mold downward once; dessert should come out onto platter. If dessert remains in mold, repeat procedure. Refrigerate until ready to serve.

To serve, carefully pour a ring of sauce around base of the dessert, and decorate with the pear slices. Serve cold.

CHOCOLATE BAVARIAN CREAM
Bavarois au chocolat

Try to get superior-quality chocolate for this fine dessert, and accompany each serving with fresh orange slices or raspberries. Serving fruit with creamy desserts might seem like a modern idea, but Escoffier's *Guide Culinaire,* the French chefs' manual published in 1921, already suggested accompanying Bavarian creams with fresh fruit salads.   MAKES 6 TO 8 SERVINGS

5 ounces semisweet or bittersweet chocolate, chopped
1 envelope (¼ ounce) unflavored gelatin
¼ cup water
3 large egg yolks
5 tablespoons sugar
1 cup milk

1 cup heavy cream, well chilled
Whipped cream for garnish (optional)
Grated chocolate for garnish (optional)
Raspberries or orange segments
Mint sprigs for garnish

Melt chocolate in a medium bowl above hot water over low heat. Remove from heat but leave above water. In a small cup, sprinkle gelatin over ¼ cup water. Let stand until ready to use.

Whisk egg yolks lightly in a large bowl. Add sugar and whisk until smooth. Bring milk to a boil in a small heavy saucepan. Gradually whisk hot milk into yolk mixture. Return mixture to saucepan. Cook over medium-low heat, stirring and scraping bottom of pan constantly with a wooden spoon, until mixture thickens slightly and reaches 165°F. to 170°F. on an instant-read thermometer; begin checking after 5 minutes. (To check without thermometer, remove sauce from heat, dip a metal spoon in sauce, and draw your finger across back of spoon—your finger should leave a clear trail in mixture that clings to spoon.) If necessary, cook another 30 seconds and check again. Do not overcook sauce or it will curdle.

Remove from heat and immediately add softened gelatin, whisking until completely dissolved.

Remove chocolate from over water and stir until smooth. Using a whisk, gradually stir custard into chocolate. Pour mixture into a large bowl and let cool to room temperature, stirring occasionally. Refrigerate until cold and beginning to thicken, about 15 to 20 minutes, stirring mixture every 5 minutes; do not allow custard mixture to set. Lightly oil a 4- to 5-cup mold.

Whip cream in a chilled bowl with chilled beater until soft peaks form. Gently fold cream into custard. Spoon mixture into mold, cover with plastic wrap, and refrigerate until completely set, at least 2 hours. (Dessert can be kept, covered, 1 day in refrigerator.)

Unmold dessert a short time before serving: Dip mold for about 10 seconds into enough warm water to come nearly to its top; pat dry. Run a thin-bladed flexible knife around edge of dessert, gently pushing dessert slightly from edge of mold to let in air. Set a serving platter on top of mold, hold tightly, and invert dessert and platter together. Shake mold downward once; dessert should come out onto platter. If dessert remains in mold, repeat procedure. Refrigerate until ready to serve.

Garnish, if desired, with rosettes or a ruffle of whipped cream and with grated chocolate. Serve with raspberries or orange segments and garnish with mint sprigs.

SEE PHOTOGRAPH.

◈ FRUIT BAVARIAN CREAM
Bavarois aux fruits

When the heady perfume of summer fruit greets us at the market, it reminds us to take advantage of these seasonal delights while they are at their peak. This Bavarian cream, studded with luscious fruit and kirsch-laced ladyfingers, is a wonderful way to do so. It is fun to vary the dessert according to what is best at your market—one time you can add fresh apricots, another day strawberries and nectarines, or, for an exotic touch, use ripe mangoes. For a striking presentation, prepare the dessert in a ring mold and, after unmolding it, garnish its center with sliced fresh fruit. If you like, give the dessert further sparkle by accompanying it with a fruit sauce made with fresh peaches, apricots, strawberries, kiwis, or mangoes (pages 347–352). MAKES 6 TO 8 SERVINGS

2 cups mixed thinly sliced fresh
fruit (strawberries, peeled
peaches, nectarines, apricots,
seedless grapes, mango, orange
or tangerine sections)

2 tablespoons sugar
2 tablespoons kirsch

KIRSCH BAVARIAN CREAM
1 cup milk
1 vanilla bean, split lengthwise
¼ cup water
1 envelope unflavored gelatin (¼
ounce)

3 large egg yolks
7 tablespoons sugar
2 tablespoons kirsch
1 cup heavy cream, well chilled

6 ladyfinger halves

Sprinkle fruit with sugar and kirsch and mix gently. Cover and refrigerate for 1 hour.

KIRSCH BAVARIAN CREAM

In a medium, heavy saucepan bring milk to a boil with vanilla bean. Remove from heat, cover, and let stand for 15 minutes. Remove vanilla bean.

Pour water into a small cup, sprinkle gelatin over it, and let stand until ready to use.

Whisk egg yolks lightly in a large bowl. Add sugar and whisk until smooth. Reheat milk to a boil. Gradually whisk hot milk into yolk mixture. Return mixture to saucepan. Cook over medium-low heat, stirring and scraping bottom of pan constantly with a wooden spoon, until mixture thickens slightly and reaches 165°F. to 170°F. on an instant-read thermometer; begin checking after 5 minutes. (To check without thermometer, remove sauce from heat, dip a metal spoon in sauce, and draw your finger across back of spoon—your finger should leave a clear trail in mixture that clings to spoon.) If necessary, cook another 30 seconds and check again. Do not overcook mixture or it will curdle. Remove from heat and immediately add softened gelatin, whisking until completely dissolved.

Pour mixture into a large bowl and let cool to room temperature, stirring occasionally. Lightly oil a 6-cup mold or bowl.

Stir kirsch into cooled custard. Refrigerate until cold and beginning to thicken, about 15 to 20 minutes, stirring mixture every 5 minutes; do not allow custard mixture to set.

Using slotted spoon, transfer marinated fruit to custard, reserving liquid. Stir fruit into custard. Refrigerate 2 minutes, stirring occasionally.

Whip cream in chilled bowl with chilled beater until soft peaks form. Gently fold cream into custard. Refrigerate, folding occasionally, about 5 minutes, or until beginning to set.

Spoon half the custard mixture into mold. Cut ladyfinger halves in half crosswise. Dip a ladyfinger quarter into reserved fruit liquid and set it on mixture. Repeat with 5 more ladyfinger pieces. Chill 2 minutes. Carefully spoon remaining custard mixture over ladyfingers in mold. Dip remaining ladyfinger quarters into fruit liquid and set them on top of mixture. Press them into mixture so top is level. Cover mold with plastic wrap. Refrigerate until completely set, at least 2 hours. (Dessert can be kept 1 day in refrigerator.)

Unmold a short time before serving: Dip mold for about 10 seconds into enough warm water to come nearly to top of mold; pat dry. Run a thin-bladed flexible knife around edge of dessert, gently pushing dessert slightly from edge of mold to let in air. Set a serving platter on top of mold, hold tightly, and invert the dessert and platter together. Shake mold downward once; dessert should come out onto platter. If dessert remains in mold, repeat procedure. Refrigerate until ready to serve.

SEE PHOTOGRAPH.

CARAMEL BAVARIAN CREAM
Bavarois au caramel

I learned the secret to making perfect caramel from Parisian pastry chef Albert Jorant. He taught me to pay strict attention to the caramel's color, so it is a deep warm brown. If it is merely golden, it will be too sweet, but if it is very dark, it will be too bitter. A good saucepan is important, too, because the caramel will burn if a thin, flimsy one is used. Even the saucepan's color matters—one with a dark interior distorts your perception of the caramel's hue, so choose a light-colored pan. For this terrific dessert, the caramel serves two purposes: some is used to flavor the dessert, and the rest becomes a superb caramel sauce. MAKES 6 TO 8 SERVINGS

CARAMEL
1 cup sugar
1/2 cup cold water plus 2
  tablespoons, if needed

1/2 cup hot water

BAVARIAN CREAM
1/4 cup water
1 envelope (1/4 ounce) plus 1
  teaspoon unflavored gelatin
1 cup milk

1/2 cup caramel (see above)
5 large egg yolks
5 tablespoons sugar
1 cup heavy cream, well chilled

CARAMEL
In a medium, heavy saucepan that does not have a black interior, dissolve sugar in 1/2 cup cold water over low heat, stirring. Boil the syrup over high heat without stirring, but skimming occasionally, until it becomes light brown in color. (Check color by looking under bubbles.) Reduce heat and continue cooking until color of caramel is rich

brown, but don't let it become too dark or it will be bitter. Remove from heat.

Add hot water *gradually and standing at a distance;* sauce will bubble and splatter. Mix well. Return to low heat and heat, stirring, until sauce is smooth. Remove from heat.

BAVARIAN CREAM

Pour ¼ cup water into a small cup, sprinkle the gelatin over water, and let stand until ready to use.

In a medium, heavy saucepan, bring milk to a boil with ½ cup caramel, whisking. Be careful because mixture tends to boil over.

In a large bowl, whisk yolks lightly. Add sugar and whisk until thick and smooth. Gradually whisk in half the hot milk mixture. Return mixture to pan of milk mixture, whisking. Cook over low heat, stirring constantly with a wooden spoon, about 4 minutes or until mixture thickens. To check whether it is thick enough, dip the spoon in mixture and draw your finger across back of spoon—your finger should leave a clear trail in mixture that clings to spoon. Be careful not to overcook mixture or it will curdle. Remove from heat and immediately add softened gelatin, whisking until completely dissolved.

Pour mixture into a large bowl and let cool to room temperature, stirring occasionally. Refrigerate until cold and beginning to thicken, about 15 to 20 minutes, stirring mixture every 5 minutes; do not allow custard mixture to set. Lightly oil a 4- to 5-cup mold.

Whip cream in chilled bowl with chilled beater until soft peaks form. Gently fold cream into custard. Spoon mixture into mold, cover with plastic wrap, and refrigerate until completely set, at least 2 hours. (Dessert can be kept, covered, 1 day in refrigerator.)

Taste remaining caramel mixture. If it is too thick or too strong in flavor, stir in 2 tablespoons cold water. Chill until ready to serve.

Unmold dessert a short time before serving: Dip mold for about 10 seconds into enough warm water to come nearly to top of mold; pat dry. Run a thin-bladed flexible knife around edge of dessert, gently pushing dessert slightly from edge of mold to let in air. Set a serving platter on top of mold, hold tightly, and invert the dessert and platter together. Shake mold downward once; dessert should come out onto platter. If dessert remains in mold, repeat procedure. Refrigerate until ready to serve. Serve caramel sauce separately.

Charlottes

Sensational charlottes are made of a ladyfinger case with a rich, creamy filling, most often a mousse or a Bavarian cream. The mousse can be studded with fruit, as in Charlotte Belle Hélène, or two layers of fillings can be used, as in Strawberry-Banana Charlotte. Frozen charlottes can be made with ice cream, sorbet, or a frozen mousse as the filling.

I remember how impressed I was when a chef showed me how to painstakingly cut fresh ladyfingers to fit precisely in a charlotte mold and to form a star pattern at the base. The result was beautiful, but it was so much work. Rather than constructing these traditional charlottes, I prefer to simply set the ladyfingers in a springform mold—there is no need to cut them to fit, nor even to unmold the charlotte. All you need to do is release the spring and remove the sides of the pan. These modern types of charlottes are easier to serve, too, because the springform pans are not as deep as charlotte molds, and it's therefore much simpler to cut the charlotte in portions. In fact, today many *pâtissiers* are preparing charlottes in this manner, sometimes with a thin band of sponge cake around the sides rather than ladyfingers.

Charlottes were the inspiration for the new mousse cakes. Their fillings are somewhat similar, but the cakes are assembled differently—in layers instead of as a cake frame with a mousse in the center.

Hints

- If using packaged ladyfingers that are attached, there is no need to separate each one before setting them in the springform pan.
- If using homemade ladyfingers, be sure to arrange them tightly in the pan, so that the mousse does not flow between them. If some mousse does come through, pipe decorative ruffles of whipped cream between the ladyfingers to hide it.

⚜ CHARLOTTE BELLE HÉLÈNE
Charlotte au chocolat et aux poires

For this luscious charlotte, which I developed for my article on French chocolate desserts in *Chocolatier* magazine, the filling is a chocolate Bavarian cream lightened with whipped egg whites and studded with vanilla-scented poached pears. The idea is based on the classic flavor combination in the French sundae, *poires belle Hélène,* of pears, chocolate, and vanilla. If you like, garnish the charlotte with whipped cream and serve it with crème anglaise or Chocolate Sauce (see recipe). MAKES 8 TO 10 SERVINGS

Poached Pears (page 373)
¾ cup reserved syrup from
  poaching pears
11 ounces bittersweet or semisweet
  chocolate, chopped
1 envelope (¼ ounce) plus 1¼
  teaspoons unflavored gelatin
⅓ cup cold water
5 large eggs, separated, plus 1 large
  yolk, room temperature

7½ tablespoons sugar
2 cups milk
3 to 4 ounces packaged split
  ladyfingers, or about 6 ounces
  homemade Ladyfingers (see
  recipe)
¾ cup heavy cream, well chilled

Cool poached pears completely in their syrup. Melt chocolate in a large bowl set in a pan of hot water over low heat, stirring until smooth. Remove from water. In a small bowl, sprinkle gelatin over the cold water and let stand until ready to use.

Whisk the 6 egg yolks lightly in a large bowl. Add 6 tablespoons sugar and whisk until smooth. Bring milk to a boil in a medium, heavy saucepan. Gradually whisk hot milk into yolk mixture. Return mixture to saucepan. Cook over medium-low heat, stirring and scraping bottom of pan constantly with a wooden spoon, until mixture thickens slightly and reaches 165°F. to 170°F. on an instant-read thermometer; begin checking after 5 minutes. (To check without thermometer, remove sauce from heat, dip a metal spoon in sauce, and draw your finger across back of spoon—your finger should leave a clear trail in mixture that clings to spoon.) If necessary, cook another 30 seconds and check again. Do not overcook sauce or it will curdle.

Gradually whisk custard mixture into melted chocolate.

Bring ¾ cup pear-poaching syrup to a boil and remove from heat. Add softened gelatin and stir until dissolved. Gradually whisk gelatin mixture into chocolate mixture. Cool to room temperature, stirring occasionally.

Stand ladyfinger halves up against sides of a 9- or 10-inch springform pan, forming a tight ring. Reserve 3 pear halves in syrup for decoration. Drain remaining pears and cut in small dice.

Chill chocolate mixture, stirring often, about 45 minutes, or until cold and beginning to thicken but not set. Whip cream in a chilled bowl with chilled beater until stiff. Refrigerate until ready to use. When chocolate mixture is cold, fold in whipped cream.

Beat egg whites in a large bowl until stiff. Add remaining 1½ tablespoons sugar and beat about 30 seconds until very shiny. Fold whites into chocolate mixture.

Carefully pour half of chocolate mixture into prepared pan. Refrigerate 10 minutes. Cover with diced pears, in one layer. Carefully pour remaining chocolate mixture over them. Chill about 3 hours, or until filling sets; to save time, the charlotte can be chilled in freezer for about 1½ hours. (It can be kept 3 days in refrigerator, or it can be frozen.)

Carefully run a thin-bladed flexible knife around charlotte and release sides of the pan. Drain reserved pear halves on paper towels. Cut pear halves in 4 or 5 lengthwise slices, and set them on top of charlotte, keeping each pear half together with its narrow end pointing inward. Serve cold.

❧ CITRUS CHARLOTTE
Charlotte aux agrumes

In modern cooking, Bavarian creams are often prepared with other liquids instead of the usual milk, as in this charlotte filling made with orange juice. To further intensify its citrus flavor, I add orange juice concentrate, a tip I learned from my Parisian friend, pastry chef *extraordinaire* Denis Ruffel.   MAKES 8 SERVINGS

1 ⅓ cups strained fresh orange juice (5 or 6 oranges)	2 tablespoons grated orange zest
4 teaspoons unflavored gelatin	1 teaspoon grated lemon zest
5 large egg yolks, room temperature	6 ounces packaged split ladyfingers, or 9 to 10 ounces homemade
6 tablespoons sugar	Ladyfingers (see recipe)
1 tablespoon strained fresh lemon juice	1 ⅔ cups heavy cream, well chilled
3 tablespoons frozen orange juice concentrate	1 or 2 seedless oranges for garnish

Pour ⅓ cup orange juice into a very small saucepan, sprinkle gelatin over it, and let stand while preparing custard.

Whisk egg yolks lightly in a large heatproof bowl. Add sugar and whisk until thick and smooth. Bring remaining 1 cup orange juice nearly to a simmer in a small heavy saucepan. Gradually whisk hot juice into yolks. Return mixture to saucepan, whisking. Cook over medium-low heat, stirring mixture and scraping bottom of pan constantly with a wooden spoon, about 10 minutes, or until mixture thickens slightly and is thick enough to coat a spoon. Do not overcook custard or it will curdle.

Pour into a large bowl and stir for about 30 seconds to cool. Heat gelatin mixture over very low heat, stirring, until dissolved. Gradually stir gelatin into orange custard. Stir in lemon juice, orange juice concentrate, and orange and lemon zests. Cool to room temperature, stirring occasionally.

Stand ladyfingers up against sides of a 9-inch springform pan, forming a tight ring. Arrange more ladyfingers on base, cutting some, if necessary, to form a tight layer.

Refrigerate citrus mixture about 10 minutes, stirring often, or chill mixture by setting bowl in a larger bowl of ice water for about 5 minutes, stirring very often, or until mixture is cold and beginning to thicken but is not set.

Whip cream in chilled bowl with chilled beater until nearly stiff. Gently fold cream into citrus mixture, blending thoroughly.

Pour 2½ cups of mixture into lined pan. Set another layer of ladyfingers on top (there's no need to make them tight). Add rest of mixture, spread evenly to sides, and smooth top. Refrigerate 10 minutes. Cover and refrigerate at least 4 hours, or until set. (Dessert can be kept, covered, up to 3 days in refrigerator.)

To unmold, gently release sides of springform.

To prepare garnish, cut peel from orange, removing any white pith. Cut orange in thin round slices. Reserve 1 attractive whole slice and cut remaining slices in half. Set whole slice on center of charlotte and arrange 8 half-slices around it, near edges.

STRAWBERRY-BANANA CHARLOTTE
Charlotte aux fraises et aux bananas

Two creamy layers form this light, fruity charlotte—one, a pink strawberry layer; and the other, a delicate banana layer. At serving time, the dessert is enhanced by a bright strawberry sauce. Using purchased ladyfingers and a springform pan instead of a traditional charlotte mold makes this new temptation easy to prepare, but you can use homemade ladyfingers if you like. MAKES 8 SERVINGS

1 envelope unflavored gelatin (¼ ounce)
¼ cup water
4 large egg yolks, room temperature
5 tablespoons sugar
1 cup milk
2 cups strawberries, hulled
1 large banana (about 7 ounces)
1 teaspoon strained fresh lemon juice

6 ounces packaged split ladyfingers, or 9 to 10 ounces homemade Ladyfingers (see recipe)
½ cups heavy cream, well chilled
Strawberry halves for garnish
2 cups Strawberry Sauce (page 347)
Banana slices (optional)

Sprinkle gelatin over water in a small cup and let stand while preparing custard.

Whisk egg yolks lightly in a large bowl. Add sugar and whisk until smooth.

Bring milk to a boil in a small heavy saucepan. Gradually whisk hot milk into yolk mixture. Return mixture to saucepan. Cook over medium-low heat, stirring and scraping bottom of pan constantly with a wooden spoon, until mixture thickens slightly and reaches 165°F. to 170°F. on an instant-read thermometer; begin checking after 3 minutes. (To check without thermometer, remove sauce from heat, dip a metal spoon in sauce and draw your finger across back of spoon—your finger should leave a clear trail in mixture that clings to spoon.) If necessary, cook another 30 seconds and check again. Do not overcook sauce or it will curdle.

Remove from heat and immediately add softened gelatin, whisking until it is completely dissolved. Pour mixture into a large bowl and stir about 30 seconds to cool. Pour ⅔ cup custard into another bowl.

Purée 2 cups strawberries. Measure 1 cup purée, add it to ⅔ cup custard, and stir with a whisk until blended. (Any remaining strawberry purée can be reserved for sauce.)

Purée peeled banana with lemon juice in a food processor until smooth. Measure ⅔ cup purée and whisk it into remaining (plain) custard. Cool both mixtures to room temperature, stirring occasionally.

Stand ladyfingers up against side of 9-inch springform pan, with their more attractive side facing outward, forming a tight ring. Arrange more ladyfingers on base of pan to form a layer. Cut more ladyfingers so they fit tightly on base and fill any holes.

Chill banana mixture by setting bowl in a larger bowl of ice water or in refrigerator about 10 minutes, stirring very often, or until mixture is cold and beginning to thicken but is not set.

Whip cream in a large chilled bowl with chilled beater until nearly stiff. Gently fold 1¾ cups whipped cream into banana mixture, blending thoroughly. Refrigerate remaining whipped cream.

Spoon banana mixture into ladyfinger case. Spread evenly. Freeze 10 minutes, leaving strawberry mixture at room temperature and stirring it occasionally.

Cover banana layer with another layer of remaining ladyfinger halves, spacing them evenly; there is no need to form a tight layer.

If strawberry mixture is not yet cold and beginning to thicken, set bowl of mixture in ice water or refrigerate briefly, stirring very often.

Fold remaining whipped cream into strawberry mixture. Gently spoon mixture into mold and spread smooth. Tap mold lightly on work surface so mixture settles. Refrigerate at least 4 hours, or until set. Cover when firm. (Dessert can be kept, covered, up to 2 days in refrigerator.)

To unmold dessert, release sides of pan. Leave dessert on base of pan and set on a round platter. Refrigerate until serving time.

When ready to serve, garnish top with strawberry halves. Serve with strawberry sauce separately, and, if desired, with sliced bananas.

SEE PHOTOGRAPH.

CHOCOLATE AND ALMOND-MACAROON CHARLOTTE
Charlotte bordelaise aux macarons

Unlike most charlottes, which have ladyfinger frames, this dessert from the Bordeaux area uses almond macaroons. Chocolate and butter enable it to set, and thus it does not require gelatin. Rich, dense, and fairly sweet, this charlotte is best served in small portions. It is a variation of a dessert I researched for the La Varenne book on French regional cooking.   MAKES 8 SERVINGS

CHOCOLATE FILLING

4 ounces semisweet or bittersweet chocolate, chopped
1/3 cup milk

1 large egg yolk
6 tablespoons unsalted butter
4 tablespoons sugar

4 to 5 tablespoons Cognac or brandy
4 to 5 tablespoons water

28 to 30 French Almond Macaroons (page 312)

CHOCOLATE GLAZE AND GARNISH

2 ounces semisweet or bittersweet chocolate, chopped

1 tablespoon unsalted butter
6 blanched almonds

CHOCOLATE FILLING

Melt chocolate in milk in a small saucepan or bowl set in a pan of hot water over low heat. Remove from heat. Very quickly whisk in egg yolk and leave to cool to room temperature. Beat butter with sugar until smooth and creamy. Gradually beat chocolate mixture into sugar mixture. Continue beating at high speed for 2 to 3 minutes to lighten.

Butter 1-quart charlotte mold or soufflé dish. Line base with a round of foil, and butter foil. Mix 4 tablespoons Cognac and 4 tablespoons water in a small bowl. Dip a macaroon briefly in mixture and place it in base of mold, flat side down. Dip and place enough macaroons on base of mold to form one layer. Dip more macaroons and arrange them in two rows up sides of mold, flat side in. Spoon about one-third of chocolate filling into mold. Dip more macaroons and arrange them in a layer on top of chocolate. Cut some macaroons in half to make a tighter layer. Repeat layering, using one-third of filling and a layer of macaroons each time; top layer of macaroons should be flat side up. If necessary, add the remaining Cognac and water to dipping mixture. Press macaroons in an even layer. Cover with a small plate, set a weight (such as a 1-pound can) on top, and chill at least 12 hours, or overnight.

To serve, run a thin-bladed, flexible knife around dessert several times and unmold it onto a platter. Carefully peel off paper.

CHOCOLATE GLAZE AND GARNISH

Melt chocolate and butter in a small saucepan set in a pan of hot water over low heat. Pour glaze over center of charlotte and spread very gently toward edges, letting it run down sides. Garnish with blanched almonds. (Dessert can be kept up to 2 days in refrigerator.) Let soften briefly before serving.

Ice Creams
and
Frozen Desserts

When I lived in France, my first trip outside Paris was to the Loire Valley. My husband and I enjoyed a relaxing drive in this beautiful area, which seemed to offer everything—the world-famous châteaux, the calm grandeur of the Loire River, the wineries along the way that offered tastings of the local wines, and the small pretty towns, where we sampled the specialties of the region. The dish I remember most of all is an ice cream dessert that we had in the town of Langeais. It was at a restaurant where we dined simply, except for dessert. In spite of its rather unassuming name of Frozen Orange Cake, it turned out to be a sumptuous creation—a base of almond meringue, topped with a generous layer of orange ice cream, frosted with Chantilly cream, and sprinkled with sliced toasted almonds.

From simple sundaes to impressive meringue vacherins decorated as lavishly as the spectacular Loire Valley château of Chambord, frozen desserts are the ideal treat for many occasions. They are not only delicious and refreshing, but also convenient, as they wait in the freezer rather than requiring last-minute preparation.

The recent proliferation of ice cream machines has contributed to a revolution in the preparation of homemade ice creams, sorbets, and other desserts. These machines give ice cream and sorbet their seductive smoothness and make it simple for us to turn a ripe fruit into a lovely, cooling, fresh-tasting sorbet.

Whether or not you make your own ice creams and sorbets, there are plenty of sensational desserts that can be prepared from commercial ice cream—"coupes" of ice cream and fruit, layered ice cream charlottes, and enticing ice cream cakes.

Ice Creams

Friends of mine are always arguing about where they have eaten the best ice cream, but for me the answer is clear—the most delicious ice cream is one that was just made out of a good crème anglaise—whether you are in your own kitchen or in a three-star restaurant in France.

It is quite amazing that the versatile custard mixture requires only a few common ingredients—milk or cream, egg yolks, sugar, and flavoring. For ice cream, the custard is made sweeter and usually richer in cream than for sauce. The custard can be made fairly quickly but does demand patience, as it must be stirred continually and watched carefully as it cooks. It thickens only slightly, from the gradual heating of the egg yolks. If the sauce is cooked too long or over too high heat and if it is not stirred constantly, the yolks will coagulate like scrambled eggs.

Next the custard is flavored. The time-honored favorites of vanilla, chocolate, and coffee are as popular as ever, but it is fun to try others as well. Fresh mint, smooth caramel, and chocolate-ginger are contemporary flavors for terrific ice creams that are fabulous on their own, as well as in sundaes or ice cream cakes.

In order to prevent ice crystals from forming, the ice cream mixture must be stirred as it is frozen. All ice cream machines work by this principle to achieve velvety smooth ice creams. The amount of time required to turn the custard mixture into ice cream varies with the machine, but it is best to allow the custard to cool before it is added to the machine.

Hints

- Have ready a strainer and bowl for the custard before you start to cook it.
- If the custard curdles slightly, gradually pour it into a blender or food processor with the motor running. This will save it.
- Have a bowl ready in the freezer for spooning the finished ice cream into it. You must work quickly because ice cream that has just come out of the machine is soft and melts easily.
- Pack down the ice cream firmly in the container for storing to prevent ice crystals from forming.

FRESH MINT ICE CREAM
Glace à la menthe fraîche

Fresh mint is one of the favorite ingredients of nouvelle pâtisserie. Mint sprigs seem to be the dessert chef's "parsley," appearing on many desserts as a garnish that adds freshness and color. To achieve an exuberant mint flavor, the best way is to infuse the mint leaves in milk in order to make custard, as for this ice cream, or in syrup to make sorbet (see Strawberry-Mint Sorbet).   MAKES ABOUT 1 QUART

4 ounces fresh mint	*8 large egg yolks*
2 cups milk	*1 cup sugar*
2 cups heavy cream	*Mint sprigs for garnish*

Remove mint leaves from stems (you will have about 5 cups leaves unpacked); coarsely chop them. Discard stems.

Bring milk to a boil in a medium, heavy saucepan. Add mint. Remove from heat and stir. Cover and let stand 1 hour. Strain, pressing on mint in strainer.

Return mint-flavored milk to a large heavy saucepan. Add cream and bring to a boil. Remove from heat.

Whisk egg yolks lightly in a large bowl. Add sugar and whisk until smooth. Gradually whisk hot cream mixture into yolk mixture. Return mixture to saucepan. Cook over medium-low heat, stirring and scraping bottom of pan constantly with a wooden spoon, until mixture thickens slightly and reaches 165°F. to 170°F. on an instant-read thermometer; begin checking after 7 minutes. (To check without thermometer, remove pan from heat, dip a metal spoon in sauce, and draw your finger across back of spoon—your finger should leave a clear trail in mixture that clings to spoon.) If necessary, cook another 30 seconds and check again. Do not overcook mixture or it will curdle. Strain immediately into a bowl and stir about 30 seconds to cool.

Cool completely, stirring occasionally. Pour mixture into ice cream machine and process until frozen. Meanwhile, chill bowl in freezer. Transfer ice cream quickly to chilled bowl, cover tightly, and keep in freezer until ready to serve. (Can be kept 2 weeks in freezer.)

Soften slightly before serving. Serve garnished with mint sprigs.

BLACKBERRY ICE CREAM
Glace aux mûres

This ice cream is a simple sorbet mixture to which cream is added. Prepared this way, the fruit flavor is intense and the ice cream is creamy, and there is no need to make a custard base.

MAKES ABOUT I QUART

1/2 cup sugar
1/3 cup water

1 pound fresh blackberries (about 3 2/3 cups) (see Note)
1 cup heavy cream

Combine sugar and water in small heavy saucepan. Heat over low heat, stirring gently, until sugar dissolves completely. Stop stirring. Bring to a full boil over medium-high heat and boil 30 seconds. Pour into medium heatproof bowl and cool completely. (Can be kept for several weeks in refrigerator.)

Reserve 12 blackberries for garnish, if desired. Purée remaining blackberries in food processor until smooth. Strain purée into a bowl, scraping purée from underside of strainer. Stir in cooled syrup, followed by cream.

Chill medium metal bowl and airtight container in freezer. Transfer mixture to ice cream machine and process until frozen. Transfer ice cream, as quickly as possible, to chilled bowl. Cover tightly and freeze until ready to serve. (Can be kept 1 week in freezer.) Soften slightly before serving. Serve in thoroughly chilled dessert dishes or wineglasses, garnished with blackberries, if desired.

NOTE: You can substitute 1 pound unsweetened or lightly sweetened frozen blackberries for fresh.

❧ CHOCOLATE ICE CREAM
Glace au chocolat

Although French chocolate ice cream can be made with all chocolate, I have found that a combination of chocolate and cocoa produces an ice cream with a creamier texture, because chocolate hardens when cold and a large proportion of it can make the ice cream too firm.

MAKES ABOUT 5 CUPS

2 cups milk
2 cups heavy cream
8 large egg yolks
1 cup sugar

6 ounces fine-quality bittersweet or semisweet chocolate, chopped
1/3 cup unsweetened Dutch-process cocoa, sifted

Bring milk and cream to a boil in a medium, heavy saucepan. Remove from heat.

Whisk egg yolks lightly in a large bowl. Add sugar and whisk until smooth. Gradually whisk hot milk-cream mixture into yolk mixture. Return mixture to saucepan. Cook over medium-low heat, stirring and scraping bottom of pan constantly with a wooden spoon, until mixture thickens slightly and reaches 165°F. to 170°F. on an instant-read thermometer; begin checking after 7 minutes. (To check without thermometer, remove pan from heat, dip a metal spoon in sauce, and draw your finger across back of spoon—your finger should leave a clear trail in mixture that clings to spoon.) If necessary, cook another 30 seconds and check again. Do not overcook mixture or it will curdle. Strain immediately into a bowl and stir about 30 seconds to cool. Cool 10 minutes.

Melt chocolate in large bowl above hot water over low heat. Stir until smooth. Remove from pan of water and cool briefly. Whisk custard into chocolate, about 1/2 cup at a time, whisking until blended after each addition. Thoroughly whisk in cocoa. Cool completely, stirring occasionally.

Pour mixture into ice cream machine and process until frozen. Meanwhile, chill bowl in freezer. Transfer ice cream quickly to chilled bowl, cover tightly, and keep in freezer until ready to serve. (Can be kept 2 weeks in freezer.) Soften slightly before serving.

CHOCOLATE-GINGER ICE CREAM
Stir 6 tablespoons finely chopped crystallized ginger into cool custard.

VANILLA BEAN ICE CREAM
Glace à la vanille

It is hard to find a dessert more delicious than homemade vanilla ice cream. If you would like to taste a smooth and velvety ice cream with a remarkable vanilla aroma, similar to the version prepared at the best restaurants in Paris today, try this recipe. It has more vanilla beans and fewer egg yolks than the classic recipe, and uses part milk and part cream rather than all milk as in the traditional formula. For greater flavor, the seeds are scraped from the vanilla bean and stirred into the custard. Serve the ice cream on its own, or with seasonal fruit, any fruit sauce, or chocolate sauce; or use it to fill profiteroles (page 242) or vacherins (page 151).   MAKES ABOUT 5 CUPS

2 to 4 vanilla beans, split	8 large egg yolks
2 cups milk	1 cup sugar
2 cups heavy cream	

Split vanilla beans and scrape out seeds. Put beans and seeds in large heavy saucepan and add milk and cream. Bring mixture to a simmer.

Remove from heat, cover, and let stand 30 minutes. Reheat to a boil and remove from heat.

Whisk egg yolks lightly in a large bowl. Add sugar and whisk until smooth. Gradually whisk hot milk-cream mixture into yolk mixture. Return mixture to saucepan and cook over medium-low heat, stirring and scraping bottom of pan constantly with a wooden spoon, until mixture thickens slightly and reaches 165°F. to 170°F. on an instant-read thermometer; begin checking after 7 minutes. (To check without thermometer, remove pan from heat, dip a metal spoon in sauce, and draw your finger across back of spoon—your finger should leave a clear trail in mixture that clings to spoon.) If necessary, cook another 30 seconds and check again. Do not overcook mixture or it will curdle. Pour immediately into a bowl and stir about 30 seconds to cool.

Cool mixture completely, stirring occasionally. Remove vanilla beans. Pour mixture into ice cream machine and process until frozen. Meanwhile, chill bowl in freezer. Transfer ice cream quickly to chilled bowl, cover tightly, and keep in freezer until ready to serve. (Can be kept 2 weeks in freezer.) Soften slightly before serving.

FRESH PEACH ICE CREAM
Glace aux pêches fraîches

Juicy, fragrant ripe peaches are needed to give this ice cream its refreshing taste. The peaches are not cooked, but are simply puréed with a little peach brandy and combined with a vanilla custard. Serve it garnished with fresh sliced peaches.   MAKES ABOUT 2 QUARTS

2 1/2 pounds peaches
5 tablespoons peach-flavored brandy

Vanilla ice cream mixture (page 100), room temperature

Put peaches in a saucepan of boiling water and heat 30 seconds. Transfer peaches to a bowl of cold water and peel them with a paring knife.

Cut peaches in pieces, discarding pits. Purée peaches with peach brandy in food processor; purée in batches, if necessary. Immediately stir purée into vanilla ice cream mixture.

Pour into ice cream machine and process until frozen. Meanwhile, chill bowl in freezer. Transfer ice cream quickly to chilled bowl, cover tightly, and keep in freezer until ready to serve. (Can be kept 1 week in freezer.) Soften slightly before serving.

CARAMEL ICE CREAM
Glace au caramel

Parisian chef Fernand Chambrette showed me how to make caramel ice cream. He used a special technique of transforming a creamy caramel sauce into a rich custard. The caramel gives this ice cream an appealing color similar to that of coffee ice cream and a bold flavor. Fresh berries or peaches are an ideal accompaniment.

MAKES ABOUT 4 CUPS

1 cup sugar
3/4 cup water
2 cups heavy cream

1 1/2 cups milk
8 large egg yolks

Combine sugar and 1/2 cup water in a medium, heavy saucepan that does not have a black interior. Have remaining 1/4 cup water ready near stove. Heat cream to scalding; remove from heat.

Heat sugar mixture over low heat until sugar dissolves, gently stirring occasionally. Increase heat to high and boil without stirring, but occasionally brushing down any sugar crystals from side of pan with a pastry brush dipped in water, until mixture begins to brown. Reduce heat to medium-low. Continue cooking, swirling pan gently, until mixture is a rich brown color (like color of maple syrup) and a trace of smoke begins to rise from pan. Do not let caramel get too dark or it will be bitter; but if too light, it will be too sweet. Immediately remove from heat, *stand back,* and add remaining 1/4 cup water; caramel will bubble *vigorously.* When caramel stops bubbling, add hot cream. Cool until mixture stops bubbling.

Stir milk into caramel mixture. Bring to a simmer, whisking. Remove from heat.

Whisk egg yolks lightly in a large bowl. Gradually whisk hot caramel mixture into yolk mixture. Return mixture to saucepan and cook over medium-low heat, stirring and scraping bottom of pan constantly with a wooden spoon, until mixture thickens slightly and reaches 165°F. to 170°F. on an instant-read thermometer; begin checking after 7 minutes. (To check without thermometer, remove pan from heat, dip a metal spoon in mixture, and draw your finger across back of spoon—your finger should leave a clear trail in mixture that clings to spoon.) If necessary, cook another 30 seconds and check again. Do not overcook mixture or it will curdle. Strain immediately into a bowl and stir about 30 seconds to cool.

Cool mixture completely, stirring occasionally. Pour into ice cream machine and process until frozen. Meanwhile, chill bowl in freezer. Transfer ice cream quickly to chilled bowl, cover tightly, and keep in freezer until ready to serve. (Can be kept 2 weeks in freezer.) Soften slightly before serving.

COFFEE BEAN ICE CREAM
Glace au café

This is the ice cream for coffee lovers. To give it a refined taste, coffee beans are gently infused in milk, which is then used to make a rich custard. French roast beans give the ice cream a strong coffee flavor and good coffee color, but you should use your favorite coffee beans.   MAKES ABOUT I QUART

1 1/2 cups coffee beans (about 3 1/2 ounces) (see Note)
2 cups milk
2 cups heavy cream

8 large egg yolks
1 cup sugar
Chocolate coffee beans for garnish (optional)

Put coffee beans in large plastic bag without closing bag. Coarsely crush beans with a rolling pin. Combine milk, cream, and coffee beans in heavy saucepan and heat over medium heat, stirring, until tiny bubbles begin to form around edge of pan; do not boil. Remove from heat, cover, and let stand 30 minutes. Strain through cheesecloth-lined strainer and squeeze to get out as much cream as possible. Return milk-cream mixture to cleaned pan and reheat to a simmer. Remove from heat.

Whisk egg yolks lightly in a large bowl. Add sugar and whisk until smooth. Gradually whisk hot milk-cream mixture into yolk mixture. Return mixture to saucepan and cook over medium-low heat, stirring and scraping bottom of pan constantly with a wooden spoon, until mixture thickens slightly and reaches 165°F. to 170°F. on an instant-read thermometer; begin checking after 7 minutes. (To check without thermometer, remove pan from heat, dip a metal spoon in sauce, and draw your finger across back of spoon—your finger should leave a clear trail in mixture that clings to spoon.) If necessary, cook another 30 seconds and check again. Do not overcook mixture or it will curdle. Strain immediately into a bowl and stir about 30 seconds to cool.

Cool mixture completely, stirring occasionally. Pour into ice cream machine and process until frozen. Meanwhile, chill bowl in freezer. Transfer ice cream quickly to chilled bowl, cover tightly, and keep in freezer until ready to serve. (Can be kept 2 weeks in freezer.) Soften slightly before serving. If desired, garnish with chocolate coffee beans.

NOTE: For a quicker mixture, bring milk and cream to boil and whisk in 2 tablespoons plus 2 teaspoons instant coffee powder. There is no need to strain this mixture.

CHOCOLATE-PRALINE ICE CREAM
Glace au chocolat pralinée

Praline and chocolate are a popular pairing in French truffles and buttercream. I love the combination of chocolate and caramelized toasted nuts in ice cream as well.   MAKES ABOUT 1 QUART

1 1/2 cups milk
1 1/2 cups heavy cream
6 large egg yolks, room temperature
1/2 cup sugar
6 ounces bittersweet or semisweet
chocolate, chopped
1 to 1 1/4 cups Almond, Hazelnut, or Brazil Nut Praline (page 374)

Bring milk and cream to a boil in a medium, heavy saucepan. Remove from heat.

Whisk egg yolks lightly in a large bowl. Add sugar and whisk until smooth. Gradually whisk hot milk-cream mixture into yolk mixture. Return mixture to saucepan and cook over medium-low heat, stirring and scraping bottom of pan constantly with a wooden spoon, until mixture thickens slightly and reaches 165°F. to 170°F. on an instant-read thermometer; begin checking after 7 minutes. (To check without thermometer, remove pan from heat, dip a metal spoon in sauce, and draw your finger across back of spoon—your finger should leave a clear trail in mixture that clings to spoon.) If necessary, cook another 30 seconds and check again. Do not overcook mixture or it will curdle. Strain immediately into a bowl and stir about 30 seconds to cool. Cool 10 minutes.

Melt chocolate in a double boiler or large bowl above hot water over low heat. Stir until smooth. Remove from pan of water and cool.

Whisk custard mixture into chocolate, about ½ cup at a time, whisking after each addition until blended. Whisk in 1 cup praline; taste and add more praline, if desired. Cool mixture completely, stirring occasionally.

Pour mixture into ice cream machine and process until frozen. Meanwhile, chill a medium bowl in freezer. Transfer ice cream to chilled bowl, cover tightly and keep in freezer until ready to serve. (Can be kept 2 weeks in freezer.) Soften slightly before serving.

Sorbets

Sorbet is the ultimate summer fruit dessert. Cool and refreshing, it captures the essence of the fruit and can be made in a rainbow of colors and a medley of flavors. Due to the emphasis of modern French cuisine on natural ingredients, simplicity, freshness, and lightness, sorbets have become one of the best-loved of finales to a meal and the symbol of the contemporary style of dessert making. And for good reason—sorbets are one of the easiest desserts to make and are virtually fat-free. French chefs are also using fruit sorbets instead of ice cream to top warm desserts, such as crêpes and some tarts.

Although sorbets are enjoying great popularity as a modern dessert, they can be traced back to ancient history. They were the first frozen desserts and appeared centuries before ice creams. In fact, in France an ice cream machine is still called a *sorbetière,* or sorbet machine. The ancestor of our sorbet was developed by the Chinese. They taught it to the Persians, and they in turn to the Arabs, who subsequently introduced it to Europe. The French word *sorbet,* now used in English as well, is derived from an Arabic word which means drink. At first sorbets resembled beverages and were made of fruit, honey, and snow. True sorbets developed only in the seventeenth century.

Sorbet is simply fruit juice or purée mixed with a basic syrup of sugar and water. The syrup that is mixed with the fruit not only adds a pleasing sweetness to the mixture, but also contributes to the sorbet's satiny texture, while lemon juice adds a touch of tanginess. The word *sherbet* is often used interchangeably with *sorbet,* but sherbet may include milk, cream, eggs, or gelatin; sorbet does not. There are versions of sorbet to which egg white or meringue is added for a fluffy texture, but today most cooks prefer not to add them because they diminish the intensity of the fruit flavor.

Since sorbet is made essentially of fruit, its flavor depends heavily on the quality of the fruit used. The fruit should be ripe, fragrant, and unblemished. Fresh fruit in season is ideal, but good-quality frozen fruit can be substituted. In some specialty shops, frozen fruit purées are sold especially for making sorbets, so that even the task of peeling the fruit is eliminated.

Generally, sorbet is made of one fruit to highlight its character, but sometimes it is composed of a mixture of berries or of tropical fruits, such as pineapple, mango, and banana. Orange juice, wine, or a small amount of liqueur or crème de cassis is occasionally added for a special accent.

The amounts of syrup and lemon juice are added according to the natural sweetness of the fruit, which often varies, and according to personal taste. When sorbets are served to clear the palate between courses in a sumptuous meal, they are made less sweet than for dessert.

Sorbets depend on being freshly made for perfect taste and texture, because they do not keep as well as ice cream. This is why they are best when made at home or in fine restaurants.

The ideal ending for a rich meal, sorbet is usually served in spoonfuls or scoops in dessert dishes or glasses, either alone or garnished with a few slices of the same fruit. A scoop of sorbet can be set on a slice of fruit or on a bed of fruit slices of a contrasting color and complementary flavor, such as strawberry sorbet on a slice of pineapple or mango sorbet on a bed of kiwi slices. A favorite presentation is to set spoonfuls of two or three sorbets of different colors on a plate. Sorbet is frequently accompanied by a fruit sauce, or sprinkled at serving time with a little of a matching liqueur, for example framboise (raspberry brandy) with raspberry sorbet or Grand Marnier with orange sorbet.

Sorbet can be part of other desserts, such as sundaes topped with whipped cream, frozen tarts, ice cream cakes, vacherins, and charlottes.

Hints

• If sorbet was stored several days and became too hard, soften it before serving: Chill the food processor bowl and blade in the refrigerator. Purée the sorbet, about 2 cups at a time, for a few seconds in the food processor. Softened sorbet can be returned to the freezer and will remain soft for 1 or 2 hours.

• If an ice cream machine is not available, freeze the sorbet mixture in metal trays or shallow cake pans. When it is almost completely frozen, purée the mixture in the chilled food processor until smooth. Return it to the pans and refreeze until firm. Transfer to an airtight container and cover tightly.

• Sorbets melt very quickly; before serving sorbet, it is best to chill the dishes and any serving utensils. When making desserts from sorbets, chill the measuring cup thoroughly before measuring sorbet.

• To spread sorbet when making layered desserts, spoon it in place in small pieces and then quickly spread it with short, quick movements of a flexible rubber spatula.

• See also Hints for making ice cream, page 97.

ORANGE SORBET
Sorbet à l'orange

A smooth orange sorbet is made here by infusing orange peel in a simple syrup, rather than adding grated peel. The orange syrup is then mixed with plenty of fresh orange juice.

MAKES ABOUT 3 CUPS; ABOUT 6 SERVINGS

3/4 cup sugar
1/2 cup water
Pared strips of peel of 1 medium
   orange

2 1/3 cups strained fresh orange
   juice
1 tablespoon strained fresh lemon
   juice, or to taste

Combine sugar, water, and orange-peel strips in small heavy saucepan. Heat over low heat, stirring gently, until sugar dissolves completely. Stop stirring. Bring to full boil over medium-high heat and boil 30 seconds. Pour syrup into heatproof bowl and cool completely. Cover and refrigerate at least 4 hours. (Can be kept for 1 week in refrigerator.)

Remove strips of peel from syrup with a slotted spoon. In large bowl, add 3/4 cup syrup to orange juice and mix thoroughly. Stir in lemon juice. Taste, and add more syrup or lemon juice if needed. Mixture should taste slightly too sweet, because sweetness of sorbet will be less apparent when it is frozen.

Chill medium metal bowl and airtight container in freezer. Transfer sorbet mixture to ice cream machine and process until mixture has consistency of soft ice cream; it should not be runny but will not become very firm. Transfer sorbet as quickly as possible to chilled bowl; sorbet melts very quickly. Cover tightly and freeze until ready to serve. If keeping sorbet longer than 3 hours, transfer it to airtight container when firm and cover tightly. (Sorbet is best served within 3 hours, but can be kept up to 4 days in freezer.)

If sorbet is frozen solid, soften it in food processor (see page 107). Serve in thoroughly chilled dessert dishes or wineglasses.

❧ LEMON SORBET
Sorbet au citron

Citrus sorbets like this one can be attractively displayed in the fruit; the top and a thin slice of the bottom are cut off, the pulp is scooped out, and the sorbet is piped in a decorative pattern into the fruit shell.   MAKES ABOUT 4 CUPS; ABOUT 6 TO 8 SERVINGS

1 1/2 cups sugar
1 cup water
Pared strips of peel of 1 medium
   lemon

1 1/3 cups strained fresh lemon juice
1 cup good-tasting water, such as
   uncarbonated bottled water

Combine sugar, 1 cup water, and lemon-peel strips in medium, heavy saucepan. Heat over low heat, stirring gently, until sugar dissolves completely. Stop stirring. Bring to full boil over medium-high heat and boil 30 seconds. Pour into heatproof bowl and cool completely. Cover and refrigerate at least 4 hours. (Can be kept for 1 week in refrigerator.) Remove strips of peel from syrup with a slotted spoon.

In large bowl, mix lemon juice with 1 cup good-tasting water. Add 1 2/3 cups syrup and mix thoroughly. Taste, and add more syrup if needed. Mixture should taste slightly too sweet because sweetness of sorbet will be less apparent when it is frozen.

Continue as in Orange Sorbet (page 108). Soften slightly before serving. Serve in thoroughly chilled dessert dishes or wineglasses or in prepared lemon shells.

GRAPEFRUIT SORBET
Sorbet au pamplemousse

If you think grapefruit can't be made into an exciting dessert, this one will come as a pleasant surprise. It makes a perfect ending to a rich dinner. Use ruby or pink grapefruit for a lovely color.

MAKES ABOUT 3 CUPS; ABOUT 6 SERVINGS

SYRUP FOR SORBET (see Note)
1 1/2 cups sugar   *1 cup water*

*2 1/3 cups strained fresh grapefruit
    juice*

SYRUP FOR SORBET

Combine sugar and water in medium, heavy saucepan. Heat over low heat, stirring gently, until sugar dissolves completely. Stop stirring. Bring to a full boil over medium-high heat and boil 30 seconds. Pour into heatproof medium bowl and cool completely. Cover and refrigerate 1 hour. (Can be kept for several weeks in refrigerator.)

Pour grapefruit juice into large bowl. Add 1 cup syrup and mix thoroughly. Taste, and add 1 to 3 tablespoons more syrup if needed. Mixture should taste slightly too sweet because sweetness of sorbet will be less apparent when it is frozen.

Continue as in Orange Sorbet (page 108). Soften slightly before serving. Serve in thoroughly chilled dessert dishes or wineglasses.

NOTE: Syrup makes about 1 3/4 cups.

RASPBERRY SORBET
Sorbet aux framboises

The intense fruit flavor and vibrant color make this sorbet a delight. For a wonderful summer dessert, serve a scoop of it alongside a scoop of vanilla ice cream, and garnish with fresh raspberries sprinkled with sugar and with *eau de vie de framboise,* clear raspberry brandy.

MAKES ABOUT 3 TO 4 CUPS; ABOUT 6 TO 8 SERVINGS

6 cups raspberries (about 1 1/2   *1 tablespoon fresh strained lemon*
pounds) (see Note)   *juice, or to taste (optional)*
1 2/3 cups Syrup for Sorbet (page
108)

Gently rinse berries and drain. Purée in food processor until very smooth. Pour purée into large bowl. Add syrup and mix thoroughly.

Strain mixture into a bowl, pressing on pulp in strainer. Use rubber spatula to scrape mixture from underside of strainer. Stir in lemon juice, if desired. Taste, and add more syrup or lemon juice, if needed. Mixture should taste slightly too sweet because sweetness of sorbet will be less apparent when it is frozen. Serve in thoroughly chilled dessert dishes or wineglasses.

NOTE: Two 12-ounce packages unsweetened frozen raspberries can be substituted for fresh berries.

BLACKBERRY SORBET
Substitute blackberries for raspberries. Use only 1 cup syrup.

STRAWBERRY-MINT SORBET
Sorbet aux fraises à la menthe

The tastes of strawberries and mint harmonize well, especially in this sorbet, which I serve garnished with strawberry slices and mint sprigs.   MAKES ABOUT 3 TO 4 CUPS; 6 TO 8 SERVINGS

1 cup plus 2 tablespoons sugar   *6 cups strawberries (about 1 1/2*
3/4 cup water   *pounds), rinsed and hulled*
1 cup medium-packed mint leaves,   *1 tablespoon strained fresh lemon*
coarsely chopped   *juice, or to taste*

Combine sugar and water in medium, heavy saucepan. Heat over low heat, stirring gently, until sugar dissolves completely. Stop stirring.

Bring to a full boil over medium-high heat. Add mint, return to a boil, cover, and let stand off heat 15 minutes. Uncover and cool completely. Strain syrup into a bowl, pressing on mint in strainer. Cover and refrigerate 1 hour, or up to several days.

Purée berries in food processor until very smooth. Pour purée into large bowl, add 1 1/4 cups cold syrup, and mix thoroughly. Strain mixture into a bowl, pressing on pulp in strainer. Use rubber spatula to scrape mixture from underside of strainer. Stir in lemon juice. Taste, and add more syrup or lemon juice, if needed. Mixture should taste slightly too sweet because sweetness of sorbet will be less apparent when it is frozen.

Continue as in Orange Sorbet (page 108).

STRAWBERRY SORBET
Omit mint. When preparing syrup, omit steps of letting pan of syrup stand off heat and of straining syrup.

MANGO SORBET
Sorbet aux mangues

Luscious, ripe mangoes produce a particularly rich-textured sorbet. To save time, instead of peeling and cutting mangoes, you can buy frozen mango pulp from some specialty stores; it, too, makes very good sorbet. MAKES ABOUT 3 CUPS; ABOUT 6 SERVINGS

3/4 cup sugar
1/2 cup water
3 1/2 pounds ripe mango (see Note)

1 tablespoon plus 1 teaspoon strained fresh lemon juice, or to taste

Combine sugar and water in small heavy saucepan. Heat over low heat, stirring gently, until sugar dissolves completely. Stop stirring. Bring to a full boil over medium-high heat and boil 30 seconds. Pour into heatproof bowl and cool completely. Cover and refrigerate 1 hour. (Can be kept for several weeks in refrigerator.)

Peel mango with a paring knife. Cut flesh from pit. Purée mango in food processor until very smooth. Pour purée into large bowl and add ½ cup plus 1 tablespoon syrup and mix thoroughly.

Strain mixture into a bowl, pressing on pulp in strainer. Use rubber spatula to scrape mixture from underside of strainer. Stir in lemon juice. Taste, and add more syrup or lemon juice, if needed. Mixture should taste slightly too sweet because sweetness of sorbet will be less apparent when it is frozen.

Continue as in Orange Sorbet (page 108). Soften slightly before serving. Serve in thoroughly chilled dessert dishes or wineglasses.

NOTE: 2⅓ cups frozen unsweetened mango purée can be substituted for fresh mango.

PAPAYA SORBET
Peel 3½ pounds fruit with a paring knife, cut in half, and scoop out seeds. Cut flesh in chunks. Purée fruit, and mix with ¾ cup syrup. There is no need to strain fruit. Stir in 5 tablespoons lemon juice, or to taste.

MELON SORBET
Sorbet au melon

For a pretty presentation, serve this sorbet in a melon half and garnish it with melon balls, fresh berries, and mint leaves.

MAKES ABOUT 3 TO 4 CUPS; 6 TO 8 SERVINGS

3 to 3½ pounds ripe cantaloupe or honeydew melon
Syrup for Sorbet (page 108), well chilled

2 tablespoons strained fresh lemon juice, or to taste

Cut melon in half and remove seeds with a spoon. Cut off rind and discard. Cut flesh in cubes. Purée melon in food processor until very smooth. Pour purée into large bowl. Add 1 cup syrup (for honeydew) or 1¼ cups syrup (for cantaloupe) and mix thoroughly. Stir in lemon juice. Taste, and add more syrup or lemon juice, if needed. Mixture should taste slightly too sweet because sweetness of sorbet will be less apparent when it is frozen.

Continue as in Orange Sorbet (page 108). Soften slightly before serving. Serve in thoroughly chilled dessert dishes or wineglasses.

KIWI SORBET
Sorbet au kiwi

The refreshing quality of kiwi is accentuated when it is made into sorbet. If you like, serve the sorbet atop a mixture of kiwi and peach slices and quartered strawberries.

MAKES ABOUT 3 TO 4 CUPS; 6 TO 8 SERVINGS

3 to 3 1/2 pounds ripe kiwis
Syrup for Sorbet (page 108), well
    chilled

1 tablespoon plus 2 teaspoons fresh
    strained lemon juice, or to
    taste

Peel kiwis with a paring knife. Cut flesh in chunks. Purée kiwis in food processor until very smooth. Sorbet can be left unstrained if texture of seeds is desired; most people like them. If a smoother sorbet is preferred, strain mixture without pressing, so that seeds will not go through strainer.

Pour purée into large bowl, add 1 2/3 cups syrup, and mix thoroughly. Stir in lemon juice. Taste, and add more syrup or lemon juice, if needed. Mixture should taste slightly too sweet because sweetness of sorbet will be less apparent when it is frozen.

Continue as in Orange Sorbet (page 108). Soften slightly before serving. Serve in thoroughly chilled dessert dishes or wineglasses.

TANGERINE GRANITA
Granité aux clémentines

Sparkling granita is made of jewellike frozen sweet crystals that instantly melt in your mouth. It is similar to sorbet, but works by the opposite principle—instead of trying to prevent crystals, for granita the goal is to promote them. Thus there is no need for an ice cream machine. Serve granita on its own, or accompany it with fresh or poached fruit. In a memorable dessert I had at Michel Guérard's marvelous restaurant in southwest France, a poached white peach was served atop a granita of a red Bordeaux wine. You can make granita out of any sorbet recipe in this book by stirring it as instructed below.

MAKES 6 TO 8 SERVINGS

1 cup sugar
3/4 cup water
2 pounds tangerines

3 tablespoons strained fresh lemon
juice
Fresh mint sprigs for garnish

Heat sugar in water in a heavy saucepan over low heat, stirring, until dissolved. Bring to a boil; remove from heat. Grate rind of 3 tangerines into syrup. Let cool completely.

Squeeze juice from tangerines and strain it. Add tangerine juice and lemon juice to cool syrup and mix thoroughly. Pour mixture into an ice cube tray without dividers or into another tray or very shallow bowl. Freeze until mixture begins to solidify; this takes between 1 and 2 hours, depending on depth of mixture and temperature of freezer.

Stir mixture with a fork; it will form small crystals. Return to freezer and freeze 30 minutes. Stir again with a fork. Cover and keep in freezer until ready to serve.

Serve in stemmed glasses or dessert dishes, and garnish each serving with a mint sprig.

Simple Ice Cream Desserts

Escoffier, the most famous chef of this century, is best known for a sundae—the familiar peach melba, made of poached peaches, raspberry sauce, and vanilla ice cream.

Known as *coupes* or cups by the French, sundaes can be as basic as a scoop of ice cream with a garnish of sliced fruit, or as elaborate as the fabulous dessert feasts served at some restaurants under poetic names such as "dessert symphony." The Troisgros restaurant in Roanne in central France started this fashion of very elegant sundaes; I was delighted with their splendid "grand dessert," which included a wonderful plate of fruit sorbet, a scoop of the finest vanilla bean ice cream, raspberry sauce, and sliced fresh seasonal fruit, accompanied by almond tile cookies, delicate palm-leaf cookies, and almond macaroons. It was actually an assortment of simple items, but the result was fantastic because each was perfect.

Whether served in a dish or a glass, coupes are inviting, refreshing, and are the easiest of desserts to prepare. There is no limit to the exciting desserts you can create by combining homemade or purchased ice creams or sorbets with any fresh fruit in season and with a colorful fruit sauce or a rich chocolate sauce. Try Fresh Mint Ice Cream (see recipe), for example, with strawberry sauce, sliced peaches or apricots, and a sprig of mint; or a scoop or spoonful each of cantaloupe sorbet and vanilla ice cream with kiwi sauce and a few cantaloupe balls and raspberries.

Rosettes of Chantilly cream, a little praline powder, toasted sliced almonds, grated chocolate, chopped crystallized ginger, or chocolate coffee beans are a few more possibilities for embellishing coupes.

Hints

- Assemble sundaes at the last minute. Do not keep them in the freezer, or the fruit will freeze.
- Be sure the ice cream or sorbet is not too hard.

BLACKBERRY VANILLA COUPE
Coupe de mûres et glace vanille

This sundae of blackberry sorbet and vanilla ice cream is based on a fresh black currant sundae I learned to prepare from Chef Patrick Martin at the Cordon Bleu in Paris, when I visited the school recently at its new location. The chef fashioned a cup of a firm almond-caramel mixture called *nougatine* and served the sundae inside, but you can make a simpler Tulip Cookie Cup (see recipe) instead, or, easiest of all, serve this sundae in dessert dishes or wineglasses.   MAKES 4 SERVINGS

1 pint Blackberry Sorbet or
   Blackberry Ice Cream (page
   111 or page 98)
1 pint Vanilla Bean Ice Cream
   (page 100) or packaged

1 cup Raspberry Sauce (page 345)
12 blackberries
4 sprigs fresh mint

Scoop blackberry sorbet or ice cream and vanilla ice cream into dessert dishes. Spoon a little sauce over each portion, and garnish with blackberries and mint sprigs. Serve remaining sauce separately.

FRENCH COFFEE SUNDAE
Café liégeois

A popular dessert at Paris cafés, this simple sundae is made of coffee ice cream and coffee served in a tall glass and topped with whipped cream. If you substitute chocolate ice cream and cocoa for the coffee ice cream and instant coffee, you will have another favorite, *chocolat liégeois.*
                            MAKES 4 TO 6 SERVINGS

COFFEE SAUCE
1 1/2 cups hot water
4 teaspoons instant coffee granules

4 teaspoons sugar

Chantilly Cream (page 355)
1 1/2 pints Coffee Bean Ice Cream
   (page 103) or packaged

4 to 6 chocolate coffee beans (see
   Note) or candied violets or a
   little grated chocolate for
   garnish

COFFEE SAUCE
   Pour hot water over coffee granules, add sugar, and mix thoroughly. Refrigerate until cold.

   Prepare Chantilly cream and spoon it into a pastry bag fitted with a star tip.
   To serve, spoon 2 to 3 tablespoons coffee sauce into each of 4 to 6 tall, preferably stemmed, glasses. Scoop ice cream into glasses. Using pastry bag, cover ice cream with a generous swirled mound of

Chantilly cream. Garnish with the chocolate coffee beans or candied violets, or sprinkle with grated chocolate. Serve immediately.

NOTE: Chocolate coffee beans are coffee-flavored chocolate candies shaped like coffee beans; they can be purchased at good candy shops.

PEARS WITH VANILLA ICE CREAM AND RICH CARAMEL SAUCE
Coupe de poires au caramel

This new caramel sauce, made by "deglazing" caramel by the addition of heavy cream, is absolutely heavenly with vanilla ice cream and fruit. I learned how to make it when I trained at the kitchen of the Parisian pastry shop, Millet.   MAKES 8 SERVINGS

RICH CARAMEL SAUCE

1 1/4 cups sugar

3/4 cup water

1 cup heavy cream

1 to 2 tablespoons milk (optional)

4 Poached Pears (page 373)

1 1/2 to 2 pints Vanilla Bean Ice Cream (page 100) or packaged

RICH CARAMEL SAUCE

In a medium, heavy saucepan that doesn't have a black bottom, dissolve sugar in water over low heat, stirring. Increase heat and bring to a boil. In another saucepan, heat cream over medium heat until it simmers. Keep cream warm over very low heat.

Boil syrup over high heat without stirring until it becomes light brown. (Check color by looking under bubbles.) Reduce heat and continue cooking until syrup is rich brown; do not let it become too dark or sauce will be bitter. Remove from heat.

Add hot cream *gradually and standing at a distance;* sauce will bubble and splatter. Mix well. Return to low heat and heat, stirring, until sauce is smooth. If it is too thick, add 1 to 2 tablespoons milk. Keep sauce warm in a saucepan set in shallow pan of hot water over low heat until ready to serve. (Sauce can be prepared up to 2 days ahead and refrigerated. Reheat gently over very low heat before serving.)

To serve, drain pears well. Put a scoop or spoonful of ice cream in each of 6 deep dessert dishes, and top with a pear half. Spoon a little hot sauce over the top. Serve remaining sauce separately.

RED FRUIT MEDLEY WITH ORANGE SORBET
Coupe de fruits rouges au sorbet à l'orange

Desserts of fruit and sorbet are becoming ever more popular in France, with the increasing desire for natural tastes and lighter cuisine. After a rich meal, this is one of the best desserts. Kiwi sorbet is also lovely served this way, with kiwi slices added to the red fruit.

MAKES 5 SERVINGS

1 pound cherries (about 2 1/2 cups)
1 pint strawberries
1 pint raspberries
3 tablespoons sugar
2 teaspoons strained fresh lemon
  juice

2 tablespoons Grand Marnier
About 3 cups Orange Sorbet (page 108) or packaged

Pit about a quarter of cherries, holding them over a large bowl to catch juice that escapes. Cut off ends of stems of remaining cherries, but leave rest of stem attached. Put all cherries, pitted and unpitted, in bowl. Hull strawberries, cut them in half, and add to bowl. Add raspberries, sugar, lemon juice, and Grand Marnier. Gently toss fruit in bowl to combine ingredients. Chill for about 1 hour.

Before serving, remove unpitted cherries from fruit mixture and set them aside. Divide mixture among 5 stemmed glasses. To serve, add 2 generous spoonfuls of sorbet to each glass. Top with unpitted cherries and serve immediately.

❦ EXOTIC FRUIT COUPE
Coupe aux fruits exotiques

The variety of exotic fruit in our markets makes possible many lovely and intriguing sundaes that change with the seasons. In this light dessert, the soft, rich texture of mango and guava contrasts with the crispness of Asian pears. A refreshing papaya or kiwi sorbet and a mango sauce complete the colorful picture. For a richer sundae, substitute vanilla or mint ice cream for the sorbet.

MAKES 4 SERVINGS

1 ripe mango or papaya
2 ripe kiwis
1 ripe feijoa, sapote, *or guava*
1 blood orange (optional)
1 small Asian pear

1 to 1 1/2 pints Kiwi or Papaya
Sorbet (pages 113, 114)
1 cup Mango Sauce (page 350)
4 thin slices ripe starfruit for
garnish (optional)
Fresh mint sprigs for garnish

Peel mango or papaya. Slice mango inward to pit. If using papaya, remove seeds with a spoon, then slice flesh. Peel kiwis, cut in half, and cut halves in thin slices.

Peel *feijoa* or *sapote.* Dice *feijoa.* Remove seeds from *sapote,* then dice flesh. Cut guava in half, remove seedy center, then dice flesh.

Peel orange and divide it in segments, removing any seeds. Slice or dice pear.

Gently combine all fruit. Divide it among 4 dessert dishes and top each with a scoop of sorbet or ice cream. Pour a little sauce over each serving, and garnish with starfruit and mint, if you wish. Serve remaining sauce separately.

❦ APRICOT AND RASPBERRY COUPE
Coupe d'abricots et framboises

For this picture-perfect, easy dessert, a brilliant red raspberry sauce and a bright apricot sauce cover half of each plate, and a scoop of vanilla ice cream marks their meeting point. Each sauce is topped with the contrasting fruit.   MAKES 4 SERVINGS

½ cup Raspberry Sauce (page 345)
½ cup Apricot Sauce (page 352)
12 raspberries
12 thin wedge-shaped slices fresh apricot

1 to 1½ pints Vanilla Bean or Fresh Mint ice cream (pages 97, 100) or packaged

Refrigerate sauces, covered, about 30 minutes.

To serve, spoon 2 tablespoons apricot sauce on one side of a dessert plate and 2 tablespoons raspberry sauce on other side. Tip plate slowly so each sauce covers half the plate and they just meet in the center. Do not let sauces mix. Repeat with 3 more plates.

On each plate, set 3 raspberries on apricot sauce and 3 apricot slices on raspberry sauce. Set scoop of ice cream in center of each plate. Serve immediately.

MELON MEDLEY
Coupe au melon

Cantaloupe sauce, melon sorbet, and melon balls of two colors make this a light and stylish summer dessert. If melon or lemon sorbet is not available or if you prefer a richer dessert, substitute vanilla or mint ice cream.   MAKES 4 SERVINGS

1 tablespoon Midori melon liqueur or kirsch
1 teaspoon sugar
1 teaspoon strained fresh lemon or lime juice
12 cantaloupe balls

12 honeydew balls
1 pint Melon or Lemon Sorbet (pages 109, 113)
Melon Sauce made with cantaloupe or honeydew (page 348), chilled

Mix liqueur, sugar, and lemon juice in a medium bowl. Add both types of melon balls and toss. Cover and refrigerate 15 minutes.

To serve, spoon or scoop sorbet into 4 dessert dishes. Spoon sauce around base of sorbet, letting sorbet show, and garnish with melon balls. Serve immediately.

PEACH-BLACKBERRY PARFAIT
Coupe de pêches et mûres

Layers of peach ice cream and blackberry sauce in a tall glass are embellished with fresh fruit and whipped cream in this easy, but glamorous, dessert. The French would call this a *coupe,* but in this country we refer to a layered ice cream dessert like this as a parfait. The word *parfait* is used by the French for a rich, frozen mousse, like the filling in Queen of Sheba Ice Cream Cake (see recipe).

MAKES 4 SERVINGS

1 cup Blackberry Sauce (page 346)
1 pint Fresh Peach Ice Cream (page 101) or packaged
1/2 cup heavy cream, well chilled
1 teaspoon sugar
4 thin wedge-shaped peach or nectarine slices
12 blackberries

Refrigerate sauce, covered, at least 30 minutes before using. Chill 4 parfait glasses or other relatively tall glasses of approximately 1 cup in volume for about 15 minutes. Fill each chilled glass by about one-third with peach ice cream. Spread top in an even layer to edges of glass. Whisk sauce to smooth it slightly, then add 2 tablespoons to each glass. Chill in freezer 10 minutes. Meanwhile, return remaining ice cream to freezer and remaining sauce to refrigerator.

Add enough peach ice cream to each glass to fill it by about two-thirds. Spread in an even layer to edges of glass. Top with another 2 tablespoons sauce. Chill in freezer 5 minutes.

Whip cream with sugar in chilled bowl with chilled beater until stiff. Using pastry bag with large star tip, pipe enough whipped cream into each glass to fill it, and top each portion with a large rosette of whipped cream. Top each rosette with a peach slice and 3 blackberries. Serve immediately.

❧ PERSIMMON COUPE
Coupe aux kakis

For the delicate, bright orange sauce in this sundae, be sure to use very ripe, soft, flavorful persimmons. Taste one to be sure it's sweet before making this dessert.　　MAKES 4 SERVINGS

PERSIMMON SAUCE

3/4 pounds soft, very ripe persimmons
1 tablespoon powdered sugar, sifted (optional)

1 teaspoon strained fresh lime or lemon juice (optional)

1 pint Vanilla Bean Ice Cream (page 100) or packaged
Mint leaves for garnish

1 ripe persimmon, cut in half, sliced, each slice cut in quarters

PERSIMMON SAUCE

Cut persimmons in half and remove pulp; discard peel. Purée fruit in food processor or blender. Process until very smooth. Taste sauce; often fresh natural taste of persimmons has right sweetness, but whisk in powdered sugar and/or lime or lemon juice, if desired. Cover and refrigerate 30 minutes. (Sauce can be kept, covered, 1 day in refrigerator.) Stir before serving. Serve cold.

Pour generous amount sauce into dessert dishes or ramekins. Put a scoop of ice cream on top, and place 2 mint leaves and a quarter persimmon slice on ice cream. Put more persimmon slices, if desired, in sauce around ice cream.

Frozen Desserts

One of the best desserts I have ever tasted was a rich chocolate iced soufflé served at Taillevent, which has been one of the most wonderful restaurants in Paris for years. The glorious treat was in fact a member of a large family of luscious frozen desserts made of special mousses that freeze smoothly without the need of an ice cream machine.

In addition to iced soufflés, a variety of other festive frozen desserts are included in this section. Some are made from ice creams or sorbets, some from frozen mousses, and some, like bombes, from a combination of ice cream and mousse.

Frozen charlottes, striped ice cream molds, and other desserts composed of layers of ice cream are beautiful and easy to make, whether with homemade or purchased ice cream. Of course, you can vary the flavors to your taste. In the Mango-Raspberry Charlotte, for example, you can substitute strawberry or kiwi sorbet or peach ice cream. Instead of a frozen fruit charlotte, you can prepare a richer ice cream charlotte with layers of coffee, vanilla, and chocolate or chocolate-praline ice creams. The same is true of the sorbets in Honeydew-Strawberry Sorbet Loaf. Just be sure to have a good choice of colors so the layers form an attractive pattern.

Most of these desserts are attractive on their own, but if you like, they will be even more impressive when served with a fresh fruit sauce, or, like Taillevent's iced soufflé, with crème anglaise.

Hints

• Work fast in layering and decorating, because ice cream melts quickly, especially if homemade.

• Return any frozen dessert to the freezer immediately after serving. It is better to take it out of freezer for second helpings than to let it melt.

• See also Hints for ice cream cakes (page 138).

ICED GRAND MARNIER MOUSSE
Mousse glacée au Grand Marnier

This mousse is a rich, ice cream–like dessert, made without an ice cream machine. Professional chefs call this type of mixture a bombe mousse, as it is classically paired with ice cream to form a bombe, but it makes a superb, easy-to-prepare treat on its own.

MAKES 6 TO 8 SERVINGS

1/2 cup water
7 tablespoons plus 2 teaspoons
* sugar*
4 large egg yolks
Grated zest of 1 orange

3 tablespoons Grand Marnier
1 cup heavy cream, well chilled
1/2 ounce semisweet chocolate
Lightly Candied Orange Zest for
* garnish (page 373) (optional)*

Chill a serving dish or container for freezing dessert.

In a small saucepan, heat water and 7 tablespoons sugar over low heat, stirring, until sugar dissolves. Bring to a boil and remove from heat.

Beat yolks in a medium bowl. Using a hand-held mixer or whisk, gradually beat hot syrup into yolks. Set bowl of yolk mixture in a pan of hot water over low heat. Continue beating mixture at medium speed 5 minutes, or until thick and warm to touch; do not let water boil.

Remove bowl from pan of water. Beat mixture until completely cool. Stir in grated orange zest and Grand Marnier.

Whip 1/2 cup cream in chilled bowl with chilled beater until fairly stiff. Fold cream into yolk mixture. Transfer to cold dish. Cover and freeze about 3 hours, or until firm. (Can keep 3 days in freezer.)

If desired, transfer dessert to individual serving dishes. A short time before serving, whip remaining 1/2 cup cream and 2 teaspoons sugar in a chilled bowl with chilled beater until stiff. Using a pastry bag and medium star tip, decorate dessert with a ring of rosettes of whipped cream. Grate chocolate over center, and garnish, if desired, with candied orange zest.

✻ HONEYDEW-STRAWBERRY SORBET LOAF
Gâteau de sorbets au melon et aux fraises

Two sorbets of contrasting colors layered with vanilla ice cream make an appealing summer dessert. I like to accompany the striped slices with strawberries and honeydew melon balls, or with Strawberry Sauce or Melon Sauce (see recipes).   MAKES 8 SERVINGS

*2 cups Vanilla Bean Ice Cream
   (page 100) or packaged
2 cups Strawberry Sorbet (see
   recipe) or packaged
2 cups Melon Sorbet made with
   honeydew (page 113)*

*8 strawberries for garnish
   (optional)
16 honeydew melon balls for
   garnish (optional)*

Lightly oil an 8-×-4-inch loaf pan and line with sheet of wax paper, folding corners of paper inward so it fits tightly and neatly and allowing paper to extend slightly above edges of pan. Lightly oil paper. Refrigerate lined pan 10 minutes. Chill medium bowl for softening ice cream.

    Soften ice cream in chilled bowl by stirring until spreadable. Add ice cream to prepared pan and press it down well so there are no holes. Spread with rubber spatula until smooth. Freeze 30 minutes. Again, chill medium bowl.

    Soften strawberry sorbet in chilled bowl by breaking sorbet apart with a spoon and stirring just until spreadable, although not completely smooth; do not let it melt. Carefully add small spoonfuls of strawberry sorbet to cover ice cream; do not add large chunks or they will force up vanilla layer when pressed down. Using rubber spatula, press sorbet down gently and spread to smooth even layer. Freeze 30 minutes. Again, chill medium bowl.

    Soften honeydew sorbet in chilled bowl. Carefully add small spoonfuls of honeydew sorbet to cover strawberry layer. Using rubber spatula, press down gently and spread to smooth even layer. Cover and freeze until firm, at least 6 hours. (Can be kept up to 4 days.)

    To unmold, run thin-bladed flexible knife around edges of paper, if necessary. Pull on paper to release it from sides of pan and turn dessert out onto board or rectangular platter. Peel off paper. Using a sturdy knife, cut loaf in slices about ¾ inch thick, wiping knife after each cut. Garnish plates, if desired, with strawberries and honeydew melon balls.

❧ FROZEN CHOCOLATE-ALMOND PUDDING
Pudding glacé au chocolat et aux amandes

When this elegant dessert is unmolded, the ladyfingers and delicate chocolate-almond filling form a sunburst pattern on top.

MAKES 10 TO 12 SERVINGS

¾ cup whole blanched almonds
  (about 3¾ ounces)
4 ounces semisweet chocolate,
  chopped
⅓ cup sugar
7 tablespoons unsalted butter
2 large eggs plus 3 large yolks
½ cup heavy cream, well chilled

About 2 ounces packaged
  ladyfingers (about 3 inches
  long)
2 tablespoons Cognac or brandy
1 tablespoon water
Chantilly Cream (page 355)
  (optional)

Preheat oven to 350°F. Toast almonds in a shallow baking pan in oven 10 minutes, or until lightly browned. Transfer to a plate and cool completely.

Melt chocolate in a small bowl above hot water over low heat. Stir until smooth. Remove from pan of water and cool.

Grind almonds with 1 tablespoon sugar in a food processor until as fine as possible, scraping inward occasionally.

Cream butter, add remaining sugar, and beat until smooth and fluffy. Beat in chocolate at low speed. Add eggs, 1 at a time, beating thoroughly after each addition. Beat in egg yolks, 1 at a time. Stir in almond mixture.

Whip cream in a chilled bowl with chilled beater until nearly stiff. Fold into chocolate mixture in 2 batches.

Packaged ladyfingers are usually split in half. If using whole ones, cut them carefully in half horizontally. Lightly oil a 5-cup ring mold. Line mold with ladyfinger halves, spongy side up, placing them crosswise in mold so they touch each other. Spaces will form between them near outer edge of mold; do not fill in spaces. Mix Cognac and water in a small bowl and brush ladyfingers with mixture. Spoon in chocolate mixture and smooth top. Cover and freeze about 4 hours, or until firm. (Dessert can be kept, covered, up to 1 week in freezer; Cognac flavor weakens by second day.)

To unmold dessert, rinse a thin-bladed flexible knife with hot water, dry it quickly, and run it around outer edge and center of ring. Dip mold in lukewarm water to come halfway up its sides for about 10 seconds. Dry base of mold. Set a round platter on top of mold. Holding firmly together, flip quickly so dessert is right-side up. Shake mold gently downward; dessert should slip from mold onto platter. If dessert remains in mold, put a hot damp towel on top of mold for a few seconds and tap platter on a folded towel set on work surface. Lift up mold carefully.

Let dessert stand 10 to 15 minutes at room temperature to soften before serving. Cut in thin slices with a sturdy knife. Serve with Chantilly cream, if desired.

ICE CREAM RING WITH FRESH BERRIES
Couronne de glace aux baies fraîches

For this no-fuss dessert, strawberry and peach ice creams are paired in a ring mold. All the decoration the finished dessert needs is a mixture of several types of berries in the center of the ring. If you wish, substitute lemon sorbet or mint or vanilla ice cream for the peach ice cream.   MAKES 6 TO 8 SERVINGS

1 pint Fresh Peach Ice Cream (page 101) or packaged
7 ladyfinger halves (nearly 1 ounce)
1 tablespoon kirsch
2 1/2 tablespoons strawberry preserves
1 tablespoon strained fresh lemon juice
1 pint strawberry ice cream
1 1/2 cups strawberries, hulled and cut in quarters
3/4 cup blueberries
3/4 cup blackberries

Lightly oil a 5-cup ring mold. Chill mold thoroughly. Soften peach ice cream in refrigerator until spreadable. Spoon into mold. Using rubber spatula, smooth top. Freeze until firm, about 30 minutes.

Arrange ladyfinger halves on ice cream in mold in 1 layer, spongy side up, so that ladyfingers form a ring on center of ice cream and do not touch sides of mold. Press to embed ladyfingers slightly in ice cream. Brush ladyfingers lightly with kirsch, dabbing it evenly over them. Cover and freeze 15 minutes.

Heat preserves and lemon juice in small saucepan, breaking up any large pieces in preserves with wooden spoon, until mixture just begins to bubble at edge of pan. Spoon preserves carefully over ladyfingers. Return immediately to freezer and freeze 15 minutes.

Soften strawberry ice cream in refrigerator until spreadable. Spoon ice cream gently in small portions above and around ladyfingers; be careful not to move ladyfingers and preserves. Using rubber spatula, smooth top. Cover and freeze overnight. (Dessert can be prepared up to 1 week ahead.)

To unmold and serve, run thin-bladed flexible knife carefully around outer and inner edge of dessert. Dip mold in room-temperature water for 5 seconds and pat dry; set platter atop mold, grip mold and platter tightly, and invert together. Shake mold downward once; dessert should release onto platter. If dessert remains in mold, redip in lukewarm water several seconds or surround with a towel that has been dipped in hot water and wrung dry. Carefully remove mold by lifting straight upward. Return dessert to freezer 5 minutes. Smooth top and edges with spatula. Gently mix berries and spoon into center of ring.

❧ MOCHA ICED SOUFFLÉS
Soufflés glacés au café et au chocolat

Iced soufflés are actually mock soufflés. They give the illusion of having risen because a removable paper collar enables the mixture to be spooned in above the level of the rim of the dish. Like hot soufflés, they gain lightness from beaten egg whites. Chocolate coffee beans provide an attractive and easy finishing touch for the soufflés and hint at the flavors inside.   MAKES 4 SERVINGS

5 large egg yolks, room temperature
8 tablespoons sugar
1 tablespoon plus 2 teaspoons
    instant espresso powder
3 tablespoons hot water

1 1/4 cups heavy cream, well chilled
2 egg whites, room temperature
3 ounces semisweet chocolate,
    coarsely grated

GARNISHES
1/3 cup heavy cream, well chilled   4 chocolate coffee beans

Wrap a strip of a double layer of waxed paper around a 2/3-cup ramekin so that it extends about 1 1/4 inches above rim of ramekin. Fasten tightly with tape. Repeat with 3 more ramekins.

Whisk egg yolks lightly in a heatproof medium bowl. Add 7 tablespoons sugar and whisk until blended. Set bowl in a pan of hot, not simmering, water over low heat. Heat egg yolk mixture, stirring constantly with whisk, about 10 minutes, or until it is just warm to touch (about 100°F. on an instant-read thermometer).

Remove yolk mixture from bowl of water and begin beating with mixer at high speed. Meanwhile, dissolve instant espresso in hot water, and pour gradually into yolk mixture, beating. Beat mixture at high speed until it is very thick and completely cool.

Whip 1 1/4 cups cream in a large chilled bowl with chilled beater until nearly stiff.

Whip egg whites in a small bowl at medium speed until soft peaks form. Gradually beat in remaining tablespoon sugar and whip at high speed until whites are stiff and shiny but not dry.

Gently fold whipped cream into coffee mixture. Fold in egg

whites in 2 batches. Fold in grated chocolate. Spoon mixture into ramekins, filling them nearly to tops of collars. Spread mixture smooth. Freeze at least 2 hours, or until firm. Cover if keeping for longer. (Soufflés can be kept, covered, up to 2 weeks.)

GARNISHES

A short time before serving, peel off and discard paper collars from desserts. Return to freezer until ready to serve.

Whip ⅓ cup cream in a small chilled bowl with chilled beater until very stiff. Using a pastry bag and medium star tip, pipe a large rosette of whipped cream onto each soufflé. Top with a chocolate coffee bean.

MOCHA ICED SOUFFLÉ

Double ingredients. Wrap a double layer of waxed paper around a 2-quart soufflé dish so that it extends about 3 inches above rim. Freeze mixture in dish, covering after 1 hour, about 8 hours or overnight. If desired, garnish with chocolate twigs and candied violets.

SEE PHOTOGRAPH.

MANGO-RASPBERRY CHARLOTTE
Charlotte aux mangues et aux framboises

Nobody will miss the calories in this light, low-fat dessert. Its fillings of fresh mango and raspberry sorbets make the charlotte sumptuous, stunning, and original.   MAKES 8 SERVINGS

5 ounces ladyfingers (about 3 inches long), split horizontally
2½ cups Raspberry Sorbet (page 110) or packaged
2½ cups Mango or Papaya Sorbet (pages 112, 113)
8 fresh raspberries for garnish

Lightly oil sides of an 8-inch springform pan. Stand ladyfinger halves up against sides of pan, with their spongy sides facing inward, forming tight ring. If ladyfinger halves are joined in a row, there is no need to separate them into individual ones. Arrange more ladyfinger halves on base of pan, spongy side up, to form a layer. Cut more ladyfingers so they fit as tightly as possible on base and fill any holes. Cover and refrigerate 15 minutes. Chill medium bowl for softening sorbet.

Soften raspberry sorbet in chilled bowl by breaking sorbet apart with spoon and stirring just until spreadable, although not completely smooth; do not let it melt. Carefully but quickly spoon raspberry sorbet into pan, without moving ladyfingers. Using rubber spatula, press sorbet down gently and spread to smooth even layer. Freeze 30 minutes. Again, chill medium bowl.

Soften mango or papaya sorbet in chilled bowl. Spoon into pan over raspberry sorbet. Pack down firmly. Spread smooth with rubber spatula. Cover and freeze until firm, at least 5 hours. (Can be kept up to 4 days in freezer.)

Before serving, run thin-bladed flexible knife carefully around edge of charlotte and release sides of pan. Arrange ring of raspberries on top and serve immediately. Slice with a sharp knife, wiping after each cut.

ALPINE WALNUT AND COGNAC CHARLOTTE
Charlotte aux noix et au cognac

Walnuts are an important product of the areas of France bordering the Alps and are often featured in the region's cakes and other desserts. In this frozen dessert, they are layered with a Cognac mousse and ladyfingers.   MAKES 10 TO 12 SERVINGS

COGNAC MOUSSE
1 cup sugar
3/4 cup water
6 large egg yolks

1/4 cup Cognac or brandy
1 cup heavy cream, well chilled

COGNAC SYRUP
1/4 cup sugar
1/4 cup water

2 tablespoons Cognac or brandy

5 ounces packaged ladyfingers, or
   about 9 ounces homemade
   Ladyfingers (page 379)
1/2 cup walnut pieces, coarsely
   chopped

1/2 cup heavy cream, well chilled
1 teaspoon sugar
7 to 10 walnut halves for garnish

COGNAC MOUSSE

Set freezer at coldest setting, if possible. Heat sugar and water in a medium saucepan over low heat, stirring until sugar dissolves. Bring to a boil. With a hand-held mixer or whisk, beat egg yolks thoroughly in large bowl. Gradually pour hot sugar mixture over yolks, beating constantly. Set bowl in a pan of hot water over low heat. Beat mixture at medium speed for 5 minutes, or until thick. Remove bowl from pan of water and beat until mixture is completely cool; if desired, set bowl in pan of ice water so mixture will cool faster.

When mixture is cool, beat in Cognac. In a large chilled bowl with chilled beater, whip cream until stiff. Fold about one-quarter of whipped cream into yolk mixture; then fold yolk mixture into remaining cream. Transfer to a container, cover, and freeze about 30 minutes.

COGNAC SYRUP

Combine sugar and water in a small saucepan. Heat over low heat, stirring, until sugar dissolves. Bring to a boil. Remove from heat and cool completely. Stir in Cognac.

In a 9-inch springform pan, stand up enough ladyfinger halves against sides, with their more attractive side facing outward, to form a very tight ring. If ladyfingers are much taller than height of pan, trim them; save trimmings. Put enough ladyfingers on base of pan to cover it completely; use trimmings or cut additional ladyfingers in small pieces to close up any holes. Using a pastry brush, dab ladyfingers on sides and base of pan evenly with Cognac syrup, using up all of syrup.

Carefully spoon about 4 cups mousse into springform pan, without moving ladyfingers. Sprinkle with chopped nuts. Freeze about 45 minutes; keep remaining mousse in refrigerator. Carefully spoon remaining mousse into pan, without moving walnuts. Freeze at least 4 hours, or until charlotte is firm; it will not be as hard as ice cream. (The charlotte can be kept, covered, 2 weeks in freezer.)

In a small chilled bowl with chilled beater, whip cream with sugar until stiff. Using a pastry bag with a medium star tip, pipe a circle of rosettes around top edge of charlotte and a large rosette in center. Top center rosette and every other rosette on border with a walnut half. Carefully slide a thin-bladed knife around edges of charlotte, then release sides of pan. Serve immediately.

STRIPED CHOCOLATE-VANILLA SLICES WITH RASPBERRY SAUCE
Tranches napolitaines au chocolat et à la vanille, coulis de framboises

This rich striped dessert features the best-loved pair of flavors—chocolate and vanilla. The alternating chocolate and white layers surrounded by the ruby-red sauce make a sensational-looking creation, which tastes even better than it looks!   MAKES 12 SERVINGS

10 ounces fine-quality bittersweet chocolate, chopped
7 tablespoons unsalted butter, room temperature
6 tablespoons granulated sugar
4 large egg yolks

2 moist vanilla beans, split lengthwise
2 cups heavy cream, well chilled
3 tablespoons powdered sugar, sifted
3 cups Raspberry Sauce (page 345)

Set freezer at coldest setting. Melt chocolate in a medium bowl above hot water over low heat. Stir until smooth. Remove bowl from pan of water and let cool.

Cream butter in a large bowl, add sugar, and beat until smooth and fluffy. Add egg yolks, 1 at a time, beating very thoroughly after each addition.

Transfer ⅔ cup butter mixture to a medium bowl and set aside for mixing with chocolate. Using point of a knife, scrape seeds from vanilla beans into remaining mixture, and mix well.

Whip cream in a large chilled bowl with chilled beater until nearly stiff.

Stir chocolate into reserved ⅔ cup butter mixture; mixture will stiffen. Remove 3 cups whipped cream and stir about ¾ cup of it quickly into chocolate mixture. Fold in rest of the 3 cups whipped cream in 2 batches.

Stir powdered sugar into remaining whipped cream until blended, then fold into vanilla mixture in 2 batches. (Mixture will appear slightly separated at this point but will be fine when frozen.)

Spoon 1½ cups chocolate mixture into an 8-inch springform pan. Smooth top with rubber spatula. Carefully spoon vanilla mixture on top and spread it smooth. Freeze 15 minutes.

Carefully top with remaining chocolate mixture in small spoonfuls and gently smooth top. Freeze dessert at least 6 hours, or until firm. Cover if keeping for longer. (Dessert can be kept, covered, up to 2 weeks in freezer.)

To unmold, gently release sides of springform pan. (Do not run a knife around dessert because it will mar striped pattern.) Slide a large knife under dessert to release it from base of pan, if desired, and set dessert on a platter. To serve, cut dessert in thin wedges like a cake, using a sharp knife. Wipe knife before each cut. Serve sauce separately.

FRESH APRICOT AND COCONUT BOMBE
Bombe à l'abricot et à la noix de coco

During the brief season for fresh apricots, treat yourself and your friends to this tempting new bombe. It is made of a quick version of coconut ice cream and has a fresh apricot mousse in the center.

MAKES 10 SERVINGS

COCONUT ICE CREAM

5 cups Vanilla Bean Ice Cream (see recipe) or packaged

1 cup finely grated dried unsweetened coconut

APRICOT MOUSSE

²/₃ cup sugar
¹/₂ cup water
2 large egg whites

5 ounces ripe apricots
³/₄ cup plus 2 tablespoons heavy cream, well chilled

¹/₂ cup shredded dried unsweetened coconut for garnish

2 ripe apricots, cut in thin slices for garnish

COCONUT ICE CREAM

Transfer vanilla ice cream to large bowl. Add coconut and mix quickly with cutting and stirring motion of wooden spoon. Return immediately to freezer and freeze until firm, about 30 minutes.

Lightly oil a 2½-quart bowl. Chill bowl thoroughly. Soften ice cream in refrigerator until spreadable. Spread ice cream in even layer on base and sides of bowl up to rim. Freeze until firm, about 30 minutes. If ice cream slides down sides of bowl, push back up sides with back of spoon and freeze another 15 minutes.

APRICOT MOUSSE

Combine sugar and water in small heavy saucepan. Place over low heat and swirl pan gently until sugar dissolves. Increase heat and bring to a boil. Boil, without stirring, 3 minutes, skimming off foam occasionally. Continue boiling syrup until candy thermometer registers 238°F. (soft-ball stage), about 4 minutes. (To test without a thermometer, take a little of hot syrup on teaspoon and dip spoon into cup of ice water, keeping spoon level. With your hands in water, remove syrup from teaspoon; if syrup is ready, it will form a soft ball. *Caution: Do not touch syrup unless your hands are in the water, because it is extremely hot.*)

Meanwhile, beat egg whites until stiff but not dry.

Gradually beat hot syrup into center of whites, with mixer at high speed; then continue beating until mixture is cool and shiny. Cut apricots in half and remove pits. Cut halves in pieces, then purée in a food processor fitted with a metal blade until very smooth. Measure ⅔ cup purée, and stir it into egg white mixture. Refrigerate 30 minutes.

Whip cream in chilled bowl with chilled beater until stiff. Fold cream into apricot mixture. Pour apricot mousse into ice cream–lined bowl. Cover and freeze 8 hours, or overnight. (Dessert can be kept 1 week.)

Preheat oven to 350°F. Toast coconut in shallow baking dish in oven, stirring occasionally, until golden brown, about 5 minutes. Transfer to plate and cool.

To unmold and serve, run thin-bladed flexible knife carefully around edges of dessert. Dip bowl in lukewarm water for 10 seconds and pat dry; set platter atop bowl, grip bowl and platter tightly, and invert together. Shake bowl downward once; dessert should release onto platter. If dessert remains in mold, put a hot damp towel on top of bowl for a few seconds until bombe comes out. Return dessert to freezer for 5 minutes, or until ready to serve. Smooth top and edges with a spatula. Sprinkle toasted coconut on top of dessert for garnish, and arrange apricot slices in ring at base.

SEE PHOTOGRAPH.

Ice Cream Cakes

Ice cream cakes are the perfect dessert. What other dessert is not only refreshing, beautiful, quick, and simple, but also can be made ahead and stored until needed? French pastry shops take advantage of their storage qualities and have ice cream cakes at hand, and this is a good idea for home cooks, too. Many ice cream cakes don't even require baking and don't heat up the kitchen, attributes that are much appreciated on hot summer days.

Ice cream and sorbet are the main ingredients of these creations. They are best when homemade, but commercial ice cream of fine quality will also produce delicious results. Even without an ice cream machine, you can prepare your own smooth fillings, such as the incredibly rich mocha parfait layered between rounds of walnut genoise in Mocha-Walnut "Ice Cream" Cake.

In many ice cream cakes, the rich filling is balanced by layers of a light cake. Another possibility is crisp meringues, which are frequently paired with ice cream in France, as in Chocolate-Mint Ice Cream Cake.

Instead of cake, a quicker base can be prepared from cookies, as in Café Liégeois Loaf, composed of crisp walnut cookies and coffee ice cream, then covered with rosettes of coffee whipped cream and garnished with chocolate coffee beans. A crunchy crust can be prepared from a combination of crumbled cookies and nuts. Amaretti cookies team up with toasted hazelnuts for an easy-to-make base for Caramel-Hazelnut Ice Cream Cake with Peaches, which is filled with caramel or vanilla ice cream and served with hot caramel sauce.

It is fun to develop new ice cream cakes because you can easily mix and match fillings and crusts. If, for instance, you substitute strawberry ice cream for peach in Nectarine and Ice Cream Tart and decorate the top with sliced strawberries, you'll have a delectable Strawberry Ice Cream Tart. Try coffee ice cream instead of chocolate in Pistachio Meringue Ice Cream Cake for a pleasing variation.

A simple garnish of colorful summer fruit or whipped cream makes an ice cream cake special. And, if you wish, you can dress up the whipped cream in a matter of seconds by flavoring it with chocolate, as in Queen of Sheba Ice Cream Cake, or with a small amount of a liqueur that harmonizes with the ingredients in the dessert.

Hints

- Try to judge amounts of ice cream by checking the package size and estimating, rather than using a measuring cup. If you must use a cup, chill it before measuring ice cream.
- If the ice cream starts melting at any point, stop and refreeze it before continuing.
- To spread ice cream, spoon it in small pieces over the cake, crust, or pan, and then quickly spread it with short quick movements of a flexible rubber spatula.
- Don't put layers of hard materials like whole cookies in the center of an ice cream cake, because they are hard to cut through and the ice cream oozes out.
- For desserts that require dipping in water before unmolding, the longer the dessert was frozen, the longer the dipping time. Desserts frozen in thick glass molds or bowls also require a longer dipping time.
- If you want to serve only a portion of an ice cream cake, don't decorate it with fresh fruit, because the fruit loses flavor and texture after freezing. Instead, garnish each portion with a little fruit when serving.

CARAMEL-HAZELNUT ICE CREAM CAKE WITH PEACHES
Gâteau glacé au caramel, aux noisettes et aux pêches

For this lively dessert, with its hazelnut crust and topping of hazelnut-liqueur Chantilly cream, I find that caramel and vanilla ice creams are ideal. But if you like, use only vanilla ice cream, and be sure to accompany the dessert with a warm caramel sauce.

MAKES 10 SERVINGS

HAZELNUT-AMARETTI CRUST

1/3 cup hazelnuts or filberts
3 ounces amaretti cookies (about 18 cookies, or 1 3/4 cups)

2 tablespoons unsalted butter, melted and cooled

3 cups Vanilla Bean Ice Cream (page 100) or packaged
3 cups Caramel Ice Cream (page 102)

Rich Caramel Sauce (page 118) (optional)

HAZELNUT-LIQUEUR WHIPPED CREAM

1 cup heavy cream, well chilled
2 teaspoons sugar

2 tablespoons hazelnut liqueur

2 ripe peaches

8 to 10 hazelnuts

HAZELNUT-AMARETTI CRUST

Preheat oven to 350°F. Toast and skin hazelnuts (see page 388). Cool nuts completely, then chop, leaving a few chunks.

Grind cookies in food processor to fairly fine crumbs; measure 2/3 cup. Mix crumbs with hazelnuts. Add melted butter and mix lightly with fork. Oil base of 9-inch springform pan. Lightly pat crumb mixture in even layer on base of pan. Freeze until firm, about 20 minutes.

Soften vanilla ice cream in refrigerator until spreadable. Spoon vanilla ice cream into pan, smooth top, and freeze about 30 minutes. Soften caramel ice cream in refrigerator. Spoon it above vanilla ice cream, smooth top, and freeze until firm, about 8 hours or overnight. (Cake can be prepared up to 2 weeks ahead.)

Prepare caramel sauce, if desired. Reheat gently over very low heat before serving.

HAZELNUT-LIQUEUR WHIPPED CREAM

Just before serving, whip cream with sugar and liqueur in chilled bowl with chilled beater until stiff.

Cut peaches in thin wedges. Set cake on platter. Run thin-bladed flexible knife around edges of cake, release spring, and remove sides of pan. Spread whipped cream over top and sides of cake, smoothing cream with long metal spatula held flat. Arrange peach wedges in ring on cake with 1 hazelnut between every 2 wedges. Press more peach wedges into cream on sides of cake, near base. Serve immediately. Serve sauce separately.

QUEEN OF SHEBA ICE CREAM CAKE
Gateau glacé reine de saba

Several versions of popular French chocolate cakes, usually made with almonds, are known as *Reine de saba* or Queen of Sheba. I used this theme to create a sumptuous ice cream cake, made of an almond-cocoa cake moistened with Grand Marnier syrup, then layered with an opulent chocolate parfait mixture that is even richer than ice cream, and garnished with chocolate whipped cream.

MAKES 10 TO 12 SERVINGS

Almond-Cocoa Cake (page 188)

GRAND MARNIER SYRUP

1/4 cup sugar

1/4 cup water

2 tablespoons Grand Marnier

CHOCOLATE PARFAIT

6 ounces semisweet chocolate, coarsely chopped

1/2 cup milk

4 large egg yolks

2/3 cup sugar

1 cup heavy cream, well chilled

CHOCOLATE WHIPPED CREAM

1 ounce semisweet chocolate, coarsely chopped

1/2 cup heavy cream, well chilled

2 teaspoons sugar

1/2 teaspoon pure vanilla extract

7 blanched almonds for garnish

Prepare cake and cool on a rack.

GRAND MARNIER SYRUP

Combine sugar and water in small saucepan. Place over low heat and stir gently until sugar dissolves. Increase heat and bring to a boil. Remove from heat and cool completely. Stir in liqueur.

CHOCOLATE PARFAIT

Melt chocolate in top of double boiler set over hot water over low heat. Stir until smooth and remove from pan of water. Bring milk to simmer in small heavy saucepan over low heat. Whisk yolks to blend in medium bowl. Whisk in sugar until smooth. Gradually pour hot milk into yolk mixture in a thin stream, whisking constantly. Pour mixture back into saucepan and whisk again. Cook over low heat, stirring constantly over entire bottom of pan with wooden spoon, until mixture is thick enough to coat back of spoon and finger leaves path on spoon when drawn across, about 1 to 2 minutes. Be especially careful because this custard is unusually rich in egg yolks and thickens quickly; do not boil or mixture will curdle. Remove immediately from heat.

Using whisk, gradually stir custard into melted chocolate until smooth. Pour mixture into large bowl and let cool to room temperature, stirring occasionally. Whip cream in chilled medium bowl with chilled beater until stiff. Fold cream into chocolate mixture in 3 batches.

Carefully cut cake in 2 even layers with a serrated knife. Set bottom layer, crust side down, in clean 9-inch springform pan. Brush with 2 or 3 tablespoons Grand Marnier syrup. Spoon in half of chocolate parfait (about 1 1/2 cups) and spread to edges of cake. Place second cake layer on top, crust side down. Brush with syrup. Spoon in remaining chocolate parfait and spread to edges. Cover and freeze until firm, at least 4 hours. (Cake can be kept 4 days in freezer.)

CHOCOLATE WHIPPED CREAM

Just before serving, melt chocolate in top of double boiler set over hot water over low heat. Stir until smooth, turn off heat but leave chocolate above hot water. Whip cream with sugar and vanilla in chilled medium bowl with chilled beater until stiff. Remove chocolate from above water and let cool for 30 seconds. Stir about 3 tablespoons whipped cream into chocolate. Quickly fold chocolate mixture into remaining whipped cream. Spoon whipped cream into pastry bag fitted with a medium star tip.

Set cake on platter. Run thin-bladed flexible knife around edges of cake, release spring, and remove sides of pan. Decorate cake by piping 12 rosettes of chocolate whipped cream near top edge. Set blanched almonds on alternate rosettes. Finish with a large rosette in the center, topped by a blanched almond. Serve immediately.

FROSTY MELON TART
Tarte glacée au melon

Fresh melon sorbet hides a layer of whipped cream in this easy tart, which makes use of a simple crust of amaretti cookie crumbs. Any fruit sorbet in this book is good presented this way.

MAKES 6 TO 8 SERVINGS

ALMOND CRUST
5 ounces amaretti cookies (about 3 cups) (see Note)
1/3 cup whole blanched almonds

1/4 cup unsalted butter, melted and cooled

FILLING
1/2 cup heavy cream, well chilled
2 teaspoons sugar

4 cups Melon Sorbet made with cantaloupe (page 113)

GARNISHES
1/2 cup heavy cream, well chilled
1 teaspoon sugar

6 to 8 cantaloupe balls

ALMOND CRUST
Grind cookies in food processor to fine crumbs; measure 1 cup and transfer to bowl. Remove any remaining crumbs from processor; there is no need to rinse processor bowl. Grind almonds in processor until very fine. Combine nuts thoroughly with measured cookie crumbs. Add melted butter gradually, stirring lightly with a fork until

thoroughly combined. Press crumb mixture with your fingers in a very even layer in a nonstick 9-inch pie pan. Refrigerate 10 minutes.

FILLING

Whip cream with sugar in chilled bowl with chilled beater until stiff. Cover sides of crust with small spoonfuls of whipped cream. Spoon remaining whipped cream over base so that crust is covered. Using a rubber spatula, gently spread cream in crust as evenly as possible so that it is level with top edge of crust. Freeze until cream is fairly firm but not frozen solid, about 30 minutes.

Meanwhile, chill measuring cup and food processor bowl and blade. When cream is sufficiently firm, soften 2 cups sorbet by puréeing a few seconds in food processor until spreadable. Transfer to medium bowl. Repeat with remaining sorbet. Spoon softened sorbet carefully into cream-lined shell. Using a rubber spatula, press sorbet down gently and spread to smooth layer, mounding sorbet slightly in center. Freeze until fairly firm, about 2 hours. (Can be kept up to 2 days; if keeping for longer than 4 hours, soften tart in refrigerator about 15 minutes before serving.)

GARNISHES

Whip cream in a chilled bowl with chilled beater until very stiff. Using a pastry bag fitted with medium star tip, pipe rosettes of whipped cream near edge of tart. Top rosettes with cantaloupe balls. Serve remaining whipped cream separately. Cut tart with sharp, sturdy knife. You will need forks and knives to eat this tart.

NOTE: Amaretti are sometimes called Italian macaroons. They are available in specialty shops, Italian groceries, and some supermarkets.

❧ CAFÉ LIÉGEOIS LOAF
Gateau glacé au café

This original, dazzling dessert, which I designed for a feature story I wrote on ice cream cakes, appeared on the cover of *Bon Appétit* magazine. Here I present a slightly simplified version. A takeoff on the French Coffee Sundae or Café Liégeois (see recipe), this loaf is composed of coffee ice cream layered with crisp walnut cookies and decorated with chocolate coffee bean candies.

MAKES 8 TO 10 SERVINGS

CRISP WALNUT COOKIES

1 cup all-purpose flour	*¼ cup firmly packed brown sugar*
½ teaspoon salt	*1 large egg*
½ teaspoon baking soda	*½ teaspoon vanilla*
½ cup unsalted butter	*1 ¼ cups walnuts, broken into*
¼ cup granulated sugar	*pieces*

2 pints Coffee Bean Ice Cream	*Coffee Whipped Cream (page 356)*
(page 103) or packaged	*12 chocolate coffee beans*

CRISP WALNUT COOKIES

Preheat oven to 350°F. Butter 2 baking sheets. Sift together flour, salt, and baking soda and set aside. Cream butter, add both types of sugar and beat until smooth; beat in egg and vanilla. Add flour mixture and stir until blended. Stir in nuts. Drop batter from a teaspoon, using about 1 ½ teaspoons batter for each cookie, placing them about 2 inches apart onto prepared sheets. Flatten each cookie by pressing it with the bottom of a fork dipped in water. Bake until lightly browned, about 7 minutes. Using a metal spatula, carefully transfer cookies to racks and let cool completely. Repeat shaping and baking with remaining batter. (Cookies can be kept up to 1 week in airtight container; or they can be frozen.)

Soften ice cream in refrigerator until spreadable.

Lightly oil an 8-×-4-inch loaf pan. Arrange one layer of about 8 cookies, flat sides down, on base of pan; fit them together as tightly as possible. Add 1 pint ice cream and press it down well so there are no cracks. Crumble 4 cookies and sprinkle evenly over ice cream. Carefully add remaining ice cream and press it down well. Smooth top with rubber spatula. Top with another layer of about 8 cookies, flat sides up, fitted tightly together. Cover and freeze for at least 1 day, so that cookies soften slightly and can be cut. (Cake can be prepared up to 2 weeks ahead.)

Just before serving, prepare Coffee Whipped Cream, and spoon it into pastry bag fitted with medium star tip.

To unmold loaf, run thin-bladed flexible knife around edges of dessert and turn out onto rectangular or oval platter. Pipe whipped cream in rows of rosettes touching each other, completely covering sides and top of cake. Pipe large rosette in center. Decorate top and sides with chocolate coffee beans. Return cake to freezer for 5 minutes to make cutting easier. Serve immediately, with remaining cookies on separate plate.

PISTACHIO MERINGUE ICE CREAM CAKE
Gâteau glacé aux meringues aux pistaches

You can make an astonishing variety of ice cream cakes using crisp nut meringues and luscious ice creams. They can be made in different shapes and sizes, and with either one or several flavors of ice cream. Try hazelnut meringues with chocolate and vanilla ice creams; walnut meringues with caramel or coffee ice cream; or almond meringues with strawberry or peach ice cream.   MAKES 8 SERVINGS

Two 8-inch Pistachio Meringues
(page 382)
1 pint pistachio, pistachio-almond,
or chocolate ice cream

1 pint vanilla ice cream
2 tablespoons shelled pistachios,
finely chopped for garnish

Using point of sharp paring knife with sawing motion, carefully trim meringue circles so that one just fits into an 8-inch springform pan and the other is about ¼ inch smaller than first all around (so there will be a small space between edge of this meringue and side of pan).

Set larger meringue round in springform pan with sides closed.

Soften pistachio ice cream briefly in refrigerator, just until spreadable. Top meringue in pan with pistachio ice cream in spoonfuls. Carefully but quickly spread smooth. Set second meringue on top, centering it so that sides do not touch pan. Freeze 10 minutes.

Soften vanilla ice cream in refrigerator just until spreadable. Spoon enough ice cream around edges of top meringue to cover generously. Gently push vanilla ice cream between edge of meringue and edge of pan so it meets pistachio ice cream layer. Spoon remaining vanilla ice cream over top of meringue. Gently smooth top. Cover and freeze 8 hours, or overnight. (Ice cream cake can be prepared up to 5 days ahead; if kept for longer, meringues soften.)

Set cake on platter. Run thin-bladed flexible knife around edge of cake. Release spring and remove sides of pan. Sprinkle top of cake with chopped pistachios and serve immediately.

MOCHA-WALNUT "ICE CREAM" CAKE
Gâteau glacé au café et aux noix

A smooth chocolate-coffee parfait is both the filling and topping for the layers of walnut génoise cake and makes this dessert look festive on its own. But if you are in a decorating mood, you can garnish it with rosettes of whipped cream and top them with walnuts, chocolate coffee beans, candied violets, or candied rose petals.

MAKES 10 TO 12 SERVINGS

Walnut Génoise (page 186)

KAHLÚA SYRUP

1/4 cup sugar

1/4 cup water

2 tablespoons Kahlúa or other coffee liqueur

MOCHA PARFAIT

5 ounces semisweet chocolate, chopped

4 large egg yolks, room temperature

2/3 cup sugar

1/2 cup milk

1 tablespoon plus 1 teaspoon instant coffee granules

1 cup heavy cream, well chilled

Bake génoise and let cool.

KAHLÚA SYRUP

Heat sugar and water in a small saucepan over low heat, stirring, until sugar dissolves. Bring to a boil over medium-high heat. Remove from heat and cool completely. Stir in Kahlúa.

MOCHA PARFAIT

Melt chocolate in a medium bowl over hot water over low heat. Stir until smooth. Remove from pan of water and set aside.

Whisk egg yolks lightly in a heatproof medium bowl. Add sugar and whisk until thick and smooth.

Bring milk to a boil in a small heavy saucepan. Gradually whisk hot milk into yolk mixture. Return mixture to saucepan. Cook over very low heat, stirring mixture and scraping bottom of pan constantly with a wooden spoon, about 4 minutes, or until thick enough to coat a spoon. (To check whether it is thick enough, remove sauce from heat, dip a metal spoon in sauce, and draw your finger across back of spoon—your finger should leave a clear trail in mixture that clings to spoon. If it does not, continue cooking another 30 seconds and check again.) Do not overcook mixture or it will curdle.

Remove immediately from heat and whisk in instant coffee. Pour immediately into a bowl and stir for about 30 seconds to cool. Cool 5 minutes, stirring occasionally.

Using whisk, gradually stir custard, about ⅔ cup at a time, into melted chocolate until smooth. Cool to room temperature, stirring occasionally.

Whip cream in a large chilled bowl with chilled beater until stiff. Fold cream into chocolate mixture in 3 batches.

Carefully cut cake into 2 layers with a large serrated knife. Set bottom layer, crust side down, in clean springform pan. Brush cake with 2 or 3 tablespoons syrup. Spoon in 1½ cups parfait mixture and spread smooth. Spread so filling flows into space between sides of pan and cake. Place second cake layer on top, crust side down, and brush with syrup. Spoon in remaining filling and smooth top. Cover and freeze at least 4 hours, or until firm. (Cake can be kept up to 4 days in freezer.)

Set cake in pan on platter. Carefully release spring and remove sides of pan. Serve immediately.

ꕔ NECTARINE AND ICE CREAM TART
Tarte glacée aux brugnons

As in a classic French fruit tart, this one is topped with sliced fruit and a shiny jam glaze. But here the resemblance ends. The filling in this original tart is fresh peach ice cream instead of the traditional pastry cream, and the base is an easy nut crust rather than pastry.

MAKES 6 TO 8 SERVINGS

PECAN CRUST

1 1/4 cups pecan halves (about 4 1/2 ounces)

2 tablespoons powdered sugar

Small pinch of salt

2 tablespoons unsalted butter, very soft

1 1/2 pints Fresh Peach or Vanilla Bean Ice Cream (pages 101, 100), or packaged

1 large or 2 small nectarines

GLAZE AND GARNISH

3 tablespoons apricot preserves

1 teaspoon strained fresh lemon juice

1 teaspoon granulated sugar

1 teaspoon water

Small sprig of fresh mint

PECAN CRUST

Preheat oven to 400°F. Using on/off motion of food processor, process pecans with powdered sugar and salt until finely chopped but still in small pieces; do not grind to a powder. Transfer to a bowl. Using a fork, lightly stir in butter until mixture is well blended. Lightly butter an 8-inch pie pan. Using a fork, press mixture into pie pan in a thin, even layer on base and sides. Bake until light brown, about 6 minutes. Cool completely. Freeze 10 minutes.

Soften ice cream in refrigerator until spreadable. Spoon ice cream into pie pan, mounding it slightly toward the center and spreading it as smooth as possible. Work quickly so ice cream doesn't melt. Freeze until firm, about 2 hours. Cover if not serving immediately. (Pie can be prepared up to 1 week ahead.)

Just before serving, cut nectarine in thin wedges. Arrange wedges on ice cream, radiating out from center in a pinwheel design.

GLAZE AND GARNISH

Heat preserves, lemon juice, sugar, and water over low heat, stirring often, until preserves melt. Strain mixture, then brush it over nectarine wedges. Decorate with small mint sprig in center. Serve immediately.

✎ CHOCOLATE-MINT ICE CREAM CAKE
Gâteau glacé au chocolat et à la menthe

Mint and vanilla ice creams layered with baked chocolate meringues make up this great-tasting modern dessert. If you serve it within a few days, the meringue retains its crunch and gives a pleasant contrast in texture to the smooth ice cream. If you like, you can use only one kind of ice cream, or replace the mint ice cream with rum-raisin or coffee ice cream. MAKES 10 TO 12 SERVINGS

COCOA MERINGUES

5 tablespoons unsweetened cocoa powder

¾ cup plus 3 tablespoons powdered sugar

5 large egg whites, room temperature

¼ teaspoon cream of tartar

½ cup plus 2 tablespoons granulated sugar

3 cups Fresh Mint Ice Cream (page 97)

3 cups Vanilla Bean Ice Cream (page 100) or packaged

½ cup heavy cream

1 teaspoon granulated sugar

COCOA MERINGUES

Position 1 rack in center of oven and another in lower part; preheat to 180°F. Line 3 baking sheets with foil or parchment paper. Lightly grease corners of baking sheets so paper adheres; butter and flour foil or paper, shaking off excess. Using a 9-inch springform pan as a guide, trace a 9-inch circle onto 2 baking sheets. Prepare spatula or slotted spoon for folding cocoa mixture into meringue, and pastry bag fitted with ½-inch plain tip. Using a clothespin or paper clip, close end of bag just above tip, so mixture won't run out while bag is being filled.

Sift cocoa powder with powdered sugar into medium bowl. Beat egg whites with cream of tartar in large bowl of electric mixer at medium speed until stiff. Switch speed to high. Pour ½ cup plus 2 tablespoons sugar into whites in a thin stream, beating constantly at high speed until meringue is very shiny. Gently fold in cocoa mixture as quickly as possible.

Immediately spoon meringue into pastry bag. Remove clothespin and begin piping meringue in center of circle marked on baking sheet, proceeding outward in tight spiral until circle is completely covered. Repeat with second circle.

Fit pastry bag with medium star tip. Pipe remaining mixture in very small kisses, or mounds with pointed tops, about ½ inch in diameter and 1 inch high. Place meringue circles in center of oven and kisses on shelf underneath. Bake until firm and dry, about 1½ hours for kisses and 3 hours for circles. To test meringue kisses for doneness, remove one and cool 2 minutes. Break apart; it should be dry and crumbly and not sticky. Using a large metal spatula, immediately remove meringue kisses from paper and cool on rack.

When meringue circles are done, gently release from paper with a large metal spatula. Peel off any remaining paper, if necessary. If meringue circles are sticky on bottom, set on parchment paper and bake 30 minutes more. Cool on rack. (Base and kisses can be kept 1 week in airtight containers.)

If necessary, carefully trim meringue circles with sharp knife so they fit into a 9-inch springform pan. Set 1 meringue circle in pan. Soften both types ice cream in refrigerator until spreadable. Spread mint ice cream over meringue circle in pan. Set second meringue on top. Spread with vanilla ice cream. Freeze 8 hours, or overnight. (Ice cream cake can be prepared up to 5 days ahead; if kept for longer, meringues soften.)

Just before serving, whip cream with 1 teaspoon sugar in chilled bowl with chilled beater until stiff.

Set cake on platter. Run thin-bladed flexible knife around edges of cake, release spring, and remove sides of pan.

Spread whipped cream in thin layer over top and sides of cake, using metal spatula. Holding spatula flat, spread cream as smooth as possible. Decorate top with ring of meringue kisses. Serve immediately.

Vacherins

One of the most stunning desserts is the vacherin, an elaborately decorated, almost baroque meringue case filled with ice cream, mousse, or whipped cream and fruit.

The classic way to construct the vacherin case involves stacking several fragile meringue rings on a baked meringue base and spreading meringue on the resulting sides. The modern, easier method I prefer consists of standing a border of baked meringue fingers on the edge of a meringue base and cementing together these components with "cooked meringue." Although this technique is less difficult, every step must be done with care.

To make entertaining easier, a vacherin can be prepared ahead, in several steps. Little last-minute decorating is required; unlike other cakes, here the splendid container dresses up the dessert. Colorful fruit, with perhaps a few rosettes of whipped cream, are all that is needed for the final touch.

Those who have never assembled a vacherin will find it an enjoyable experience. The cooked meringue that holds them in place is a pleasure to use. Like any meringue, it is made of egg whites and sugar, but they are whisked together above hot water until very thick and shiny. Cooked meringue is easy to pipe and holds a shape well. In contrast to the regular meringue used for the base and fingers, which requires working quickly, there is no need to rush when using cooked meringue. It holds the baked meringue fingers upright as if by magic.

After the case is put together, cooked meringue is used to decorate it, at the same time giving it further support. This is the time for anyone who enjoys using a pastry bag to go wild and pipe ruffles, points, rosettes, or any favorite design. There is nothing restrained about a vacherin; it should be lavishly decorated. The meringue can also be piped in small cases, for individual vacherins; each of these is piped in a single piece and does not require assembling.

Whipped cream is often an important filling element because its richness and smoothness perfectly complement the sweetness and crunchiness of the meringues. The tart flavor of fruit is another favorite balance for the meringue's sweet taste. Thus, the traditional interior of a vacherin is a mixture of Chantilly cream and fruit. Today, ice cream is a popular filling. Its advantage over whipped cream is that the vacherin cuts neatly like a cake, so if any is left, it can be kept in the freezer. High-quality commercial ice cream or sorbet can be used instead of homemade. Parfaits and mousses also make wonderful fillings.

Try mixing and matching different frozen or cold fillings to create new vacherins. The dark chocolate mousse, served cold in the Individual Black Forest Vacherins (see recipe), can be made without cherries and then will be perfect frozen; it can be layered with rich vanilla ice cream inside a large vacherin. The lemon parfait from Lemon Vacherin and the raspberry sorbet from Peach Melba Vacherin would also make a good pair. All the fillings are delectable desserts in their own right.

Hints

- Pipe the meringue bases and fingers quickly and put them in the oven immediately; the meringue softens the longer it waits.
- To prevent cooked meringue from drying, keep it covered until you are ready to use it.
- If a fruit sauce is served as an accompaniment, it should be spooned over individual servings and not over the whole vacherin, to avoid softening the meringues.
- Save the small pieces trimmed off the meringue fingers in an airtight container. For a simple tasty dessert, these crunchy bits can be mixed with whipped cream and fresh fruit and chilled, or mixed with softened ice cream and frozen.
- It is best not to bake meringues on a very damp day. Meringues will take much longer to dry; they might take twice as long or might not even dry at all.

🌿 VACHERIN CASE
Fond à vacherin

Prepare this meringue case for the following vacherin recipes, or serve it the classic way, filled with whipped cream and fresh fruit.

MAKES 1 CASE THAT HOLDS ABOUT 15 CUPS FILLING;

ABOUT 15 SERVINGS

BAKED MERINGUES
9 *large egg whites, room temperature*

1/2 teaspoon cream of tartar
2 1/4 cups sugar

COOKED MERINGUE
4 *large egg whites*

1 1/4 cups sugar

BAKED MERINGUES

Preheat oven to 180°F. Line 3 baking sheets with foil or parchment paper. Lightly grease corners of baking sheets so paper will stick. Butter and flour foil or paper, shaking off excess. Using a 9-inch cake pan or pan lid as a guide, mark a circle in flour on 1 baking sheet with your finger. On 2 baking sheets, mark crosswise lines 4 inches apart, as a guide for lengths of meringue fingers. Prepare spatula for folding sugar into whites, and pastry bag fitted with 5/8-inch or 1/2-inch plain tip (see Note). Close end of bag just above tip with a clothespin or paper clip, so mixture won't run out while bag is being filled.

Beat 9 egg whites and cream of tartar in large bowl of mixer, beginning at low speed and increasing to medium, until whites are stiff. With mixer at high speed, gradually add 1 1/4 cups sugar, pouring it into whites in a fine stream and beating constantly. Beat another 30 seconds until meringue is very shiny. Sprinkle about one-quarter of remaining sugar over whites and fold in as lightly and quickly as possible. Add remaining sugar in same way, in 3 batches. Fold lightly but thoroughly.

Immediately spoon meringue into pastry bag. Push it down toward tip so there are no air bubbles. Remove clothespin or clip.

Pipe a round of meringue on baking sheet, beginning in center of marked circle and piping a tight spiral going outward, until marked circle is completely covered with meringue.

With remaining meringue, pipe fingers 4 inches long and about 1¼ inches wide on remaining baking sheets. To end each one, stop pressing and turn tip sharply upward. (Don't worry about "tails" at end of fingers; they will be cut off later.)

Place meringue base and full baking sheet of meringue fingers in center of oven, if possible; put remaining baking sheet on rack underneath. Bake until firm and dry; meringue fingers require about 2½ hours and base about 3 hours. Do not open oven for first 2 hours. To test if meringues are done, remove a finger and let it cool a few minutes. Break it apart; it should be dry and crumbly and not sticky. Carefully remove meringue fingers from paper. To release meringue base from paper, use large metal spatula; if necessary, carefully peel off paper. If base of meringue is still sticky in center, bake another 30 minutes. Cool meringues on a rack. (Baked meringues can be kept up to 1 week in an airtight container in a dry place.)

COOKED MERINGUE

In a large heatproof bowl, combine 4 egg whites and 1¼ cups sugar. Set bowl in a pan of hot water over low heat. Beat with hand mixer at low speed about 5 minutes, then at medium speed for about 3 minutes, or until mixture is warm to touch. Beat at high speed for 2 minutes, or until very thick. Remove from pan of water and beat at high speed until completely cooled. Meringue will be very shiny and sticky. (It can be kept, covered tightly, 1 day in refrigerator.)

TO ASSEMBLE CASE

With sawing motion of small sharp knife, cut small piece from "tail" end of each meringue finger so finger is 3½ inches long and end is straight instead of rounded. If edge of meringue base is not of an even height, trim it carefully with sawing motion of sharp knife. Line a baking sheet with foil or parchment paper. Set meringue base on lined baking sheet.

Using a pastry bag with small star tip, pipe a border of cooked meringue on edge of baked meringue base. Stand 2 meringue fingers upright at edge of base, one next to and touching the other, by pressing their flat ends into the piped cooked meringue; their rounded side should face outward. Continue with remaining meringue fingers to form a round case. After every group of 4 or 5 meringue fingers, pipe a line of cooked meringue going upward between each pair of fingers, on both their outer and their inner edges, pressing hard to fill in cracks between fingers. Trim last meringue finger lengthwise, if necessary, in order to make it fit. Pipe border of cooked meringue at inner bases of fingers, on inside of case, pressing hard; border will help support meringue fingers.

Pipe a decorative line of cooked meringue to cover line that attaches each pair of meringue fingers, piping upward from base. Pipe a continuous decorative line of meringue along bases of fingers, all around bottom edge of case. Pipe a decorative line or continuous row of points of cooked meringue across top edges of meringue fingers. If desired, crown top with additional points or rosettes of meringue, above divisions between meringue fingers. Return case to 180°F. oven and bake 1 1/2 hours to dry cooked meringue. Cool completely before filling. (Baked unfilled case can be stored, uncovered, in a dry place up to 2 days.)

NOTE

• A larger tip produces smoother meringues but is more difficult to use because meringue tends to run from it. A smaller tip is easier to use but meringues may develop small cracks on sides during baking. Don't worry because these won't show in finished case.

PEACH MELBA VACHERIN
Vacherin aux pêches melba

This spectacular creation is a simplified version of a vacherin that I made up for my article on these showstoppers for *Bon Appétit* and that was featured as the cover of the magazine. The classic Peach Melba gains a new interpretation here—two layers of vanilla ice cream alternating with a ribbon of raspberry sorbet fill the meringue case, which is then garnished with peach slices and raspberry sauce. For a quicker dessert, instead of baking a vacherin, you can alternate the ice cream and sorbet as a charlotte filling, as in Mango-Raspberry Charlotte (see recipe).   MAKES 15 SERVINGS

1 baked Vacherin Case (see previous recipe)
10 or 11 cups Vanilla Bean Ice Cream (page 100) or packaged

4 or 5 cups Raspberry Sorbet (page 110) or packaged
3 to 4 peaches
2 cups Raspberry Sauce (page 345)

Prepare vacherin case and let cool.

Soften 5 cups vanilla ice cream briefly in refrigerator. Spoon ice cream into case. Using your fingers, press ice cream gently up to edges of case so filling is compact. Be careful not to press too hard so case won't crack. Spread with back of a ladle to smooth layer. Freeze vacherin 15 minutes. Soften sorbet, and add to case in same way. Freeze 15 minutes. Soften remaining vanilla ice cream and add to case in same way, adding enough to come to tops of meringue fingers. Smooth top, return to freezer, and freeze about 1 hour until firm. (Vacherin can be kept, covered, 2 weeks in freezer, but homemade ice cream tastes best when freshly made. Let soften slightly in refrigerator before serving.)

Just before serving, peel peaches: Heat them in boiling water 30 seconds, transfer them to a bowl of cold water, and peel with a paring knife. Slice peaches, and use them to garnish vacherin. Brush peaches lightly with raspberry sauce. Serve immediately, serving sauce separately.

᪥ LEMON VACHERIN
Vacherin au citron

A light and luscious lemon parfait is an excellent balance for the sweet meringue shell, but also makes a delicious dessert on its own or with a fruit sauce. For a fresh touch, instead of the strawberries, top the vacherin with blueberries just before serving; or accompany each portion with sliced nectarines, berries, and mangoes, or with Strawberry Sauce (see recipe).   MAKES 15 SERVINGS

1 baked Vacherin Case (page 153)

LEMON PARFAIT
3 2/3 cups sugar   *8 large egg whites*
2 cups water   *5 cups heavy cream, well chilled*
1 1/2 cups strained fresh lemon juice

Strawberry halves for garnish

Prepare vacherin case.

LEMON PARFAIT
Combine 2 2/3 cups sugar, water, and 1 cup lemon juice in heavy-bottomed medium saucepan. Cook over low heat, stirring occasionally, until sugar dissolves. Bring to boil and boil without stirring for 7 minutes; skim off foam occasionally. Begin whipping egg whites at low speed and continue whipping until stiff.

Meanwhile, boil lemon syrup until it reaches soft-ball stage (238°F.). (To test without a thermometer, take a little of hot syrup on a teaspoon and dip spoon into a cup of ice water, keeping spoon level. With your hands in water, remove syrup from spoon; syrup should form a soft ball. *Caution: Do not touch syrup unless your hands are in the water, because it is extremely hot.*)

Gradually pour hot syrup onto stiff egg whites, beating constantly at high speed. Continue beating until mixture is cool and very shiny.

Gradually beat remaining 1/2 cup lemon juice into cool meringue. Whip half the cream in large chilled bowl with chilled beater until it thickens. Gradually beat in ½ cup sugar and continue beating until stiff. Remove cream, clean bowl, rinse with cool water, and dry. Whip remaining cream in same way, and beat in remaining ½ cup sugar. Fold all of cream into lemon mixture in a few batches. Cover and freeze at least 2 hours, or until firm. (Can be prepared 2 to 3 days ahead and kept covered in freezer.)

Spoon lemon parfait into vacherin case. Smooth top with back of a spoon dipped in warm water and dried. Freeze 1 hour. (Vacherin can be kept, covered, 2 weeks in freezer. Let soften slightly in refrigerator before serving.) Just before serving, garnish with strawberry halves. Use a knife and spoon to serve.

MELON-VANILLA VACHERIN
Vacherin au melon et à la vanille

For this sensational summer dessert, a rich melon mousse and vanilla ice cream are the refreshing fillings for the vacherin, which is accompanied by a lemon-accented melon sauce. The melon mousse also makes a great dessert on its own.   MAKES 15 SERVINGS

1 baked Vacherin Case (page 153)

FROZEN MELON MOUSSE
5 pounds cantaloupes   *¾ cup granulated sugar*
10 large egg yolks   *1½ cups heavy cream, well chilled*

MELON SAUCE AND GARNISH
2 pounds cantaloupes   *¼ cup powdered sugar*
*2 tablespoons strained fresh lemon
    juice*

9 cups Vanilla Bean Ice Cream   *½ cup heavy cream, well chilled*
*   (page 100) or packaged*   *1 teaspoon granulated sugar*

Prepare vacherin case.

FROZEN MELON MOUSSE

Cut cantaloupes in half, discard seeds, and scoop out flesh. Purée melon flesh. Spoon ¾ cup melon purée into heavy-bottomed small saucepan. Simmer over medium heat until thick and reduced to ⅜ cup. Cool completely.

Combine egg yolks, 6 tablespoons unreduced melon purée, and sugar in large heatproof bowl and set it in a pan of hot water over low heat. Using a hand-held mixer, beat at slow speed 5 minutes, then at medium speed 5 minutes more, or until mixture is warm. Remove from pan of water and beat until cool.

Gradually beat in reduced melon purée, then 1½ cups unreduced melon purée. Freeze 30 minutes, stirring often, until mixture begins to thicken.

Whip cream in a large chilled bowl with chilled beater until stiff. Fold cream into melon mixture. Freeze 4 hours, folding often, until very thick and beginning to become firm.

MELON SAUCE AND GARNISH

Make 15 melon balls for garnish. Purée remaining melon flesh in food processor until very smooth. Whisk in lemon juice and powdered sugar. Strain if smoother texture is desired. Chill sauce until ready to serve. (Can be prepared 1 day ahead and kept covered in refrigerator.)

Soften vanilla ice cream briefly in refrigerator. Spoon vanilla ice cream into case. Using your fingers, press ice cream gently up to edges of case so filling is compact. Be careful not to press too hard so case won't crack. Spread with back of a ladle to smooth layer. Freeze vacherin 15 minutes. Spoon melon mousse on top of ice cream. Smooth top with back of a spoon dipped in warm water and dried. Freeze 1 hour. (Vacherin can be prepared up to 2 weeks ahead and kept covered in freezer. Let soften slightly in refrigerator before serving.)

A short time before serving, whip ½ cup cream in chilled bowl with chilled beater until it thickens. Add sugar and whip until stiff. Spoon whipped cream into pastry bag fitted with small star tip. Pipe a decorative border of whipped cream around top edge of vacherin, then a decorative line across center. Garnish with melon balls, and serve immediately using a knife and spoon to cut and serve vacherin. Serve sauce separately.

INDIVIDUAL COFFEE VACHERINS
Vacherins au café

Individual vacherins are much quicker and easier to make than large ones and also make elegant desserts. Instead of the coffee ice cream, you can fill the meringue cases with Chocolate-Ginger Ice Cream or with Mango or Raspberry Sorbet (see recipes). An extra bowl of Chantilly cream is a welcome accompaniment to the meringues.   MAKES 8 SERVINGS

INDIVIDUAL VACHERIN CASES

4 large egg whites, room   *1 1/4 cups sugar*
*   temperature*

2 pints Coffee Bean Ice Cream   *1 teaspoon sugar*
*   (page 103) or packaged*   *8 chocolate coffee beans or candied*
1/2 cup heavy cream, well chilled   *violets for garnish (optional)*

INDIVIDUAL VACHERIN CASES

Position rack in center of oven and preheat to 200°F. Lightly butter corners of 2 baking sheets and line them with foil. Butter and flour foil, tapping to remove excess flour. Using a 3-inch cookie cutter as a guide, mark 8 circles 1 1/2 inches apart onto baking sheets.

In a large heatproof bowl, combine egg whites and sugar. Set bowl in a pan of hot water over low heat. Beat with a hand-held mixer at low speed about 5 minutes, then at medium speed for about 3 minutes, or until mixture is warm to touch. Beat at high speed for 2 minutes, or until very thick. Remove from pan of water and beat at high speed until completely cooled. Meringue will be very shiny and sticky.

Spoon meringue into a pastry bag fitted with small or medium star tip. Pipe meringue in a tight spiral, beginning in center of 1 marked circle on baking sheet, until marked circle is completely covered with meringue. Without stopping, continue piping a second layer of meringue on rim of circle, then a third layer, so that rim is higher than base and forms a case. Repeat for each circle.

Bake about 1 hour, or until meringues feel firm and dry to touch and not sticky at bottom. Transfer meringues carefully to a rack with a slotted metal spatula and let cool. (Meringues can be kept in an airtight container up to 1 week in dry weather.)

Soften ice cream slightly in refrigerator. Spoon enough ice cream into each meringue case to fill it. (Dessert can be kept, covered, up to 1 week in freezer.)

Just before serving, whip ½ cup cream with 1 teaspoon sugar until stiff. Using a pastry bag and medium star tip, pipe a rosette of whipped cream on each serving, and garnish with chocolate coffee beans or candied violets, if desired. Serve additional ice cream and remaining whipped cream separately.

Cakes

During the years that I studied with Parisian master pastry chef Albert Jorant, I always found it fascinating to watch him demonstrate classic French cakes. Before the demonstration was over he had filled the kitchen with such a splendid assortment of cakes, that it appeared he had created a pastry-shop display before our eyes. What was incredible was what he could make with one basic cake—either génoise or meringue—and one basic buttercream recipe. From them he would create *gâteau Singapour* filled with vanilla buttercream and poached pineapple; *gâteau Grand Marnier* with chopped candied orange peel soaked in the liqueur that also flavored the syrup and the frosting; *gâteau moka* with coffee buttercream, rum syrup, and chopped toasted almonds; *gâteau fraisier* with kirsch buttercream and fresh strawberries; and *gâteau succès* with almond meringue and praline buttercream. The selection was always different, according to the season, the fruit available, and his fancy. And the cakes were always wonderful.

Our excellent teachers at La Varenne Cooking School made it very clear that all we, the students, had to do was learn how to make génoise, meringue, buttercream, and syrup, and then we, too, could easily prepare many fabulous cakes. They explained that the cake mixtures are actually quite simple to make; and that the techniques required, of beating eggs or egg whites and folding ingredients together, are basic and are the same procedures used for making mousses and most familiar desserts.

Although some of the classic decorating techniques demand a good deal of practice, today a simple garnish of fresh fruit is fashionable and, in many cases, more appropriate.

To the French taste, good cakes have a certain balance of richness. Light cakes are matched with buttery frostings, while rich cakes are served on their own, or perhaps with a thin glaze or a light frosting. Lately lightness has become such a modern virtue that a light frosting such as whipped cream can also be paired with an airy sponge cake. When it comes to desserts, the French are not in favor of the idea that "bigger is better," and they always serve small portions. In fact, most French cakes are much smaller than American ones.

The French differentiate between cakes for coffee or teatime and cakes for dessert. Mousse and meringue cakes are more likely to be served at the end of a meal, simple cakes are generally an afternoon snack with tea or coffee, and layer cakes suit either occasion. When a plain cake is dressed up with fruit sauce, crème anglaise, or perhaps whipped cream and sliced fresh or poached fruit, it is perfect for any time.

When I returned to the United States after living in France, I found that many pastry shops had attractive-looking desserts that were disappointing to taste. It appeared that the chefs concentrated on decorating, but skimped and used shortening and artificial ingredients and flavorings instead of butter, real cream, and natural flavorings. After a number of such let-downs, it's rare that I even bother to taste these cakes anymore. I much prefer to make my own.

Simple Cakes

The French repertoire of cakes and cookies includes many sweets that make great gifts. A whole category of French cakes is known as *gâteaux de voyage* or "traveling cakes" because they keep well. These include butter cakes, pound cakes, fruit cakes, and nut cakes. What makes them stay moist and fresh-tasting is their relatively high proportion of nuts, butter, liqueur, or some combination of these. Their richness makes fillings and frostings unnecessary, and so they are much easier to transport.

These cakes appear in this chapter, as do others, like French Angel Food Cake, that are light and delicate and are also served without filling. A few are frosted with a quick glaze or, in the case of some of the lighter cakes, with whipped cream. All are simple to prepare because they are not split into layers and are rarely garnished.

In spite of the enthusiasm these days for new culinary creations, few can match the popularity of the old-fashioned, simple pound cake and other butter cakes. Their special dense texture, buttery flavor, and attractively browned crust have obviously contributed to their broad appeal. But there are also practical reasons—the cakes keep well and the batter is quick and easy to make. No wonder pound cake and butter cakes have long been a staple of home cooking in the Old World and the New. A sweet reminder of more leisurely days, they still hold a place of honor even in the displays of the elegant pastry shops in France.

In traditional pound cake, as its name suggests, there is a pound of each of its major ingredients—butter, sugar, eggs, and flour. In France, the cake is called *quatre quarts,* which mean four quarters, to indicate the equal weights of the four ingredients. To obtain a moister, more tender pound cake, some contemporary cooks prefer to alter the formula slightly and add a small amount of liquid, which may be milk, cream, or half-and-half, and a little more sugar. This works especially well for deep cakes baked in loaf pans, such as Lemon Pound Cake.

Pound cake is a special type of butter cake or "creamed cake," which also includes other rich cakes, such as French Fruit Cake with Rum and Chocolate Coffee-Bean Cake. When the butter is "creamed," or beaten until creamy with sugar, it entraps air. During baking, air in the butter expands and moisture in the eggs turns to steam. Together they cause the cake to rise.

Besides the usual vanilla and citrus rinds, pound cakes and other butter cakes can be flavored with cinnamon and other "sweet" spices, cocoa, chocolate, or ground or chopped nuts. Pound cake batter is thick enough to support fruit without letting it sink during baking. For an extra touch, dried or candied fruit can first be macerated in a small amount of liqueur and added with its spirit to the cake batter. The liqueur adds flavor and also helps prevent pieces of candied fruit from sticking together so they can be mixed more evenly into the batter.

Fresh fruit, such as plums, peaches, apricots, cherries, berries, pears, and apples, can be paired with these rich cake batters in several ways. It can be layered with pound cake batter to form a juicy filling, as in Pear Pound Cake. Or the fruit can be set on top of the batter before baking, as in Lorraine Plum Cake. Another possibility, especially good for dried fruit, is to arrange the fruit in the pan, spoon a pound cake batter over it, and turn it over after baking to make an upside-down cake, as in Pound Cake with Prunes and Walnuts.

Butter cakes are usually served alone or sprinkled with powdered sugar. They are also delicious accompanied by crème anglaise, fruit sauce, whipped cream, ice cream, or fresh or poached fruit. Heavy frostings are too rich for pound cakes, although a very light glaze can be brushed on top.

Hints

• For nut cakes or any dessert containing nuts, be sure to use fresh nuts. Do not keep nuts for too long. Walnuts especially turn rancid very easily and are best kept in the refrigerator.

• The ingredients of butter cakes blend best when they are at room temperature. If they are too cold, the mixture separates. The butter should not be close to melting, however.

• To measure flour, use measuring cups designed for dry measuring. Dip the cup into the container of flour, mounding the flour slightly, and level off the flour even with the rim of the cup with the edge of a metal spatula. Do not pack down the flour.

- Break each egg into a bowl before adding it to a cake batter to prevent getting any pieces of shell in batter.
- When making a batter or dough, never leave egg yolks and sugar in contact without mixing them, or the sugar will cause a dry crust to form on the egg yolks.
- Butter cake batter can be baked in other cake pans besides those specified; it should fill the pans by about two-thirds.
- When filling the pan, spoon the batter into the center of the pan in order to avoid getting any batter on the pan's upper edges.
- When baking a pound cake that contains fruit, or when using a pan that does not have a nonstick surface, line the pan with parchment paper, foil, or wax paper to prevent sticking.
- If a cake contains fruit, do not tap the pan on the working surface before baking, or the fruit may fall to the bottom.
- If cakes are attractively browned but not yet done, cover them with foil during the rest of the baking time.
- Unfrosted cakes are best served at room temperature.

PISTACHIO CAKE WITH FRESH FRUIT
Gâteau au pistaches et aux fruits frais

In this colorful, summery dessert, nectarine and kiwi slices add a refreshing flavor and an attractive garnish. Other fresh fruits, especially berries, can be substituted when they are in season. A sprinkling of grated chocolate accents both the light pistachio cake and the whipped cream frosting.   MAKES 8 TO 10 SERVINGS

PISTACHIO CAKE
2 ounces semisweet chocolate,
    coarsely chopped
1 cup shelled unsalted pistachios
    (about 4 ounces) (see Note)
2/3 cup sugar
1/3 cup all-purpose flour
1/4 teaspoon baking powder

3 large eggs, separated, room
    temperature
1 teaspoon pure vanilla extract
1/4 teaspoon cream of tartar
1/4 cup unsalted butter, melted and
    cooled

CHOCOLATE-FLECKED CHANTILLY CREAM

¾ cup heavy cream, well chilled
2 teaspoons sugar
¾ teaspoon pure vanilla extract

1 ounce semisweet chocolate, finely
grated (see Note)

GARNISHES

1 kiwi
1 nectarine

About 1 tablespoon shelled
pistachios, coarsely chopped

PISTACHIO CAKE

Position rack in center of oven and preheat to 350°F. Lightly butter a round 9-inch layer cake pan, line its base with parchment paper or foil, and butter paper or foil. Flour sides of pan and lined base, tapping pan to remove excess.

Chop chocolate in a food processor in tiny pieces, scraping inward occasionally, or grate chocolate finely and transfer to a medium bowl. Grind pistachios with 3 tablespoons sugar in processor until as fine as possible. Transfer nuts to bowl of chocolate. Sift flour and baking powder onto nut mixture. Using fork, stir gently until thoroughly blended.

Beat egg yolks lightly in a large bowl; beat in ¼ cup sugar and continue beating at high speed about 5 minutes, or until mixture is pale and very thick. Beat in vanilla.

Whip egg whites with cream of tartar in a large bowl until soft peaks form. Gradually beat in remaining 3⅔ tablespoons sugar at high speed and beat until whites are stiff and shiny but not dry.

Gently fold about one-third of whites into yolk mixture until nearly incorporated. Sprinkle about one-third of nut mixture over yolk mixture and fold in gently. Repeat in 2 batches with remaining whites and nut mixture. When batter is nearly blended, gradually pour in cool melted butter while folding. Continue folding lightly but quickly, just until batter is blended.

Transfer batter to prepared pan and spread evenly. Bake about 30 minutes, or until a cake tester inserted in center of cake comes out clean.

Cool in pan on a rack 5 minutes. Run a thin-bladed flexible knife or metal spatula carefully around sides of cake. Invert cake onto rack and carefully remove paper. Invert onto another rack and cool completely; cake will settle in center. Invert cake onto a platter so that smoother side of cake faces up. (Cake can be kept, wrapped, up to 1 day at room temperature.)

CHOCOLATE-FLECKED CHANTILLY CREAM

Whip cream with sugar and vanilla in chilled bowl with chilled beater until stiff. Gently fold in grated chocolate. Using a long metal spatula, spread cream on side and top of cake, mounding cream slightly in center. Smooth top, spreading lightly and quickly to avoid melting chocolate. (Frosted cake can be kept, covered with a cake cover or large bowl, up to 1 day in refrigerator.)

GARNISHES

Peel kiwi with a small paring knife. Cut in thin slices, and cut each slice in half lengthwise. Put 10 to 12 half-slices of kiwi in a ring around outer top edge of cake, with their rounded ends resting on edge of cake.

Slice nectarine in thin wedges, inward toward pit. Cut off a thin diagonal piece from 8 to 10 slices where peel is reddest, forming a wedge shape.

Put chopped pistachios in center of cake. Arrange nectarine wedges radiating out from center like spokes of a wheel, with their peel side facing up.

NOTES

• About ½ pound unshelled pistachios are needed to give 1 cup of shelled nuts.

• A nut grinder can be used to grind nuts instead of a food processor; grind the nuts without sugar, and add the 3 tablespoons sugar to the amount beaten with egg yolks.

• On a warm day, chill both chocolate and grater before grating chocolate, and chill food processor about 15 minutes before chopping chocolate.

Orange Layer Cake
with Grand Marnier
*Gâteau à l'orange
et au Grand Marnier*

Fruit Bavarian Cream
Bavarois aux fruits

Chocolate Bavarian Cream
Bavarois au chocolat

Peach Tart with Cinnamon Cream
Tarte aux pêches, crème à la cannelle

Nectarine Napoleon
*Mille feuille
aux brugnons*

Strawberry and Cream Puffs
Choux aux fraises

Mocha Iced Soufflé
Soufflé glacé au café et au chocolat

Fresh Apricot and Coconut Bombe
Bombe à l'abricot et à la noix de coco

Strawberry-Banana Charlotte
*Charlotte aux fraises
et aux bananes*

❧ LIGHT ALMOND CAKE WITH COFFEE WHIPPED CREAM
Gâteau aux amandes à la crème au café

Instead of being iced with coffee whipped cream, this delicate cake is also good with vanilla whipped cream, or unfrosted and accompanied by Vanilla Custard Sauce (see recipe) and fresh fruit or by Coffee Custard Sauce (page 344).　　MAKES 8 SERVINGS

LIGHT ALMOND CAKE

1/2 cup blanched almonds
5 large eggs
3/4 cup powdered sugar
6 tablespoons granulated sugar

1/2 cup potato starch
3 tablespoons unsalted butter,
　melted and cooled

COFFEE WHIPPED CREAM AND GARNISH

1/2 cup heavy cream, well chilled
4 teaspoons granulated sugar
1 teaspoon instant coffee powder

8 chocolate coffee beans for garnish
　(optional)

DELICATE ALMOND CAKE

Butter and flour a 9-inch cake pan, 2 or 3 inches deep. Preheat oven to 350°F. Grind almonds in food processor or nut grinder to a fine powder. Separate 4 eggs.

Beat remaining whole egg with powdered sugar and ground almonds until mixture is well blended. Beat in egg yolks, 1 at a time.

Whip egg whites until stiff. With mixer at high speed, beat in granulated sugar and whip until whites are stiff and dry, about 15 seconds.

Sift potato starch over egg yolk mixture. Add about one-quarter of whites and begin folding together. Continue folding, adding remaining whites in 2 batches. Last, pour in melted butter in a thin stream while folding, and fold together lightly and quickly.

Transfer batter immediately to prepared pan and bake 25 to 30 minutes, or until cake pulls away from sides of pan; when pressed in center, cake should spring back. Carefully run a knife around cake. Invert cake onto a rack and cool completely. (Cake can be wrapped and kept 2 days in refrigerator; or it can be frozen.)

COFFEE WHIPPED CREAM AND GARNISH

Whip cream with sugar and coffee in a chilled bowl with chilled beater until stiff. Refrigerate until ready to use.

Before serving spread whipped cream over top and sides of cake. If desired, garnish with chocolate coffee beans. (Frosted cake can be kept overnight in refrigerator.)

POUND CAKE WITH PRUNES AND WALNUTS
Quatre quarts aux pruneaux et aux noix

Inspired by Breton prune pound cake, which is usually made with a plain butter cake batter, this version uses an orange-and-walnut-flavored batter to cover the prunes. It is a form of upside-down cake, with the prunes coming out on top when the cake is turned over. Serve this hearty cake with tea or coffee.   MAKES 16 SERVINGS

16 moist pitted prunes (about 6 ounces or 1 1/4 cups)
3/4 cup walnuts
1 1/2 cups all-purpose flour
1 1/2 teaspoons baking powder
3/4 cup unsalted butter, room temperature

1 cup plus 2 tablespoons sugar
3 large eggs, room temperature
2 teaspoons finely chopped or grated orange peel
6 tablespoons heavy cream or milk

Put prunes in bowl and cover with hot tap water. Let stand 30 minutes until softened. Remove prunes from water, set them on paper towels, and cover with more paper towels. Thoroughly pat dry.

Position rack in center of oven and preheat to 350°F. Butter a 9- to 9 1/2-inch square pan. Line its base with parchment or foil. Generously butter paper or foil. Flour pan, tapping it to remove excess.

Set prunes on paper in pan at equal intervals, with their more attractive sides downward. Chop walnuts with a knife into fairly small but even pieces.

Sift together the flour and baking powder. Cut butter in 6 pieces and put in large bowl; cream it with paddle beater of mixer, if possible, at medium speed until butter is soft, smooth, and most of it clings to side of bowl. Gradually beat in sugar. Beat mixture at medium speed, scraping down twice, until it is very pale, smooth, and fluffy, about 4 minutes. Beat in 2 eggs, 1 at a time, at medium speed, beating thoroughly after addition and scraping mixture down occasionally. Beat third egg in small bowl. Add it to mixture gradually, beating very thoroughly after each addition. With last few additions, batter may look like it is beginning to separate, but it will come together when flour is added.

With mixer at low speed, add about one-quarter of flour mixture to batter. Blend in orange peel and about 1 tablespoon cream. Blend in remaining flour in 3 batches, alternating with remaining cream. Beat at low speed just until ingredients are blended. Stir in walnuts.

Spoon batter carefully into pan without moving prunes. Spread smooth with rubber spatula. Tap pan once on work surface to level batter. Bake until cake comes away from sides of pan and cake tester inserted in center comes out clean, about 40 to 45 minutes.

Cool cake in pan on rack 5 minutes. Turn cake out onto rack, carefully remove paper, and cool completely. (Cake can be kept, wrapped in plastic wrap or foil, up to 3 days at cool room temperature, or up to 1 week in refrigerator.) Serve at room temperature. To serve, cut in squares around prunes.

FRENCH POUND CAKE WITH VANILLA SAUCE
Quatre quarts, sauce à la vanille

Perfect on its own for teatime, pound cake becomes an elegant dessert when served with classic crème anglaise flavored with a vanilla bean. Fresh fruit of the season makes a lovely accompaniment.

MAKES 6 SERVINGS

3/4 cup unsalted butter
3 large eggs
1 1/3 cups cake flour
Pinch of salt
3/4 cup plus 2 tablespoons
  granulated sugar

1 1/2 teaspoons pure vanilla extract
Powdered sugar for sprinkling
  (optional)
Vanilla Custard Sauce (page 343)

Remove butter and eggs from refrigerator about 1 hour before making batter so they come to approximately room temperature. Egg shells should feel just slightly cool to touch. Butter should be fairly firm but easy to press with your finger.

Position rack in center of oven and preheat to 350°F. Butter an 8- to 9-inch round cake pan, line it with parchment paper or foil, and butter paper or foil. Flour pan, tapping pan to remove excess. Sift together cake flour and salt.

Cream butter in large bowl with paddle beater of mixer, if possible, at medium speed until butter is soft, smooth, and most of it clings to sides of bowl. Gradually beat in sugar. Beat mixture at medium speed, scraping down twice, until it is very pale, smooth, and fluffy, about 4 minutes. Beat in eggs, 1 at a time, at medium speed, beating thoroughly after each addition and scraping down mixture occasionally. With last egg, batter will look like it is beginning to separate, but it will come together when flour is added.

Sprinkle about one-quarter of flour over batter and stir it in with a rubber spatula. Stir in vanilla. Stir in remaining flour in 3 batches. Mix well; be sure there are no lumps.

Spoon batter carefully into pan. Smooth top with spatula. Tap pan a few times on work surface to level batter. Bake until cake pulls away from sides of pan and a tester inserted in center of cake comes out completely clean, about 30 to 35 minutes.

Run thin-bladed flexible knife around edges of cake. Turn cake out onto rack and cool it completely. (Cake can be kept, wrapped in plastic wrap or foil, up to 3 days at cool room temperature or in refrigerator; or it can be frozen about 2 months.)

Serve cake at room temperature. Sift powdered sugar over it, if desired. Cut cake into 1/2- to 3/4-inch-thick slices with a serrated knife. Serve sauce separately.

CHOCOLATE POUND CAKE
Quatre quarts au chocolat

Do not be deceived by the modest appearance of this cake—it is very rich and has an intense bittersweet chocolate flavor. The reason is simple—while traditional French pound cakes have equal weights of butter, sugar, eggs, and flour, this one includes an equal weight of chocolate as well! For a quick, easy dessert, place a slice of Chocolate Pound Cake on an individual plate and cover with whipped cream and whole raspberries, then top with another slice of cake, more cream, and raspberries. Spoon a ribbon of Raspberry Sauce (see recipe) around each "sandwich." MAKES 10 TO 12 SERVINGS

6 ounces bittersweet chocolate, chopped
1 1/2 cups cake flour
1/2 teaspoon baking powder
3/4 cup unsalted butter

1/2 cup firmly packed dark brown sugar
3 large eggs, separated, room temperature
1/4 teaspoon cream of tartar
1/4 cup granulated sugar

Position rack in center of oven and preheat to 350°F. Lightly butter an 8 1/2-×-4 1/2-inch loaf pan, line pan entirely with a single piece of parchment paper or wax paper, letting paper extend about 1 inch above edge of pan, and butter paper.

Melt chocolate in a medium bowl above hot water over low heat. Stir until smooth. Remove from pan of water and cool. Sift together cake flour and baking powder into a large bowl.

Cream butter in another large bowl, add brown sugar and beat until smooth and fluffy. Add egg yolks, 1 at a time, and beat very thoroughly after each addition. Stir in melted chocolate with a wooden spoon.

Whip egg whites with cream of tartar in a large bowl until soft peaks form. Gradually beat in 1/4 cup sugar at high speed, and beat until whites are stiff and shiny but not dry.

Gently fold about one-third of whites into chocolate mixture until nearly incorporated. Sprinkle about one-third of flour mixture over chocolate mixture and fold in gently. Repeat with remaining whites and flour mixture in 2 batches, and fold until batter is completely blended; be sure there are no lumps.

Transfer batter to prepared pan and spread evenly with spatula. Bake 45 minutes. Reduce oven temperature to 300°F. and bake about 20 minutes, or until a cake tester inserted in center of cake comes out clean.

Cool in pan on a rack 30 minutes. Invert onto rack and remove paper. Turn cake over and cool to room temperature. (Cake can be kept, wrapped, up to 3 days at room temperature.) Serve cake in thin slices.

PEAR POUND CAKE
Quatre quarts aux poires

Fresh pear slices, dried pears, and clear pear brandy give this cake a three-way pear flavor and keep it moist. It is inspired by a delicious pound cake with sautéed pears that I tasted at one of Burgundy's best restaurants, La Côte Saint-Jacques in Joigny.

MAKES 10 TO 12 SERVINGS

5 dried pear halves, finely chopped
    (about ½ cup chopped)
3 tablespoons pear brandy
1 cup unsalted butter
4 large eggs
1 cup plus 2 tablespoons granulated
    sugar

1¾ cups cake flour
Pinch of salt (optional)
1½ teaspoons finely chopped or
    grated lemon peel
2 small ripe juicy pears (about
    10½ ounces total)

GLAZE (OPTIONAL)
1¼ cups powdered sugar, sifted   ¼ cup pear brandy

Combine dried pears and pear brandy in a small jar or bowl. Stir, cover tightly, and leave to macerate at least 4 hours or overnight.

Remove butter and eggs from refrigerator about 1 hour before making batter so they approximately come to room temperature. Egg shells should feel just slightly cool to touch. Butter should be fairly firm but easy to press with your finger.

Position rack in center of oven and preheat to 325°F. Line a 9-×-5-inch loaf pan completely with parchment or wax paper, folding paper at corners of pan so it will fit neatly and allowing edges of paper to extend slightly beyond edges of pan. Butter paper.

Sift together cake flour and salt. Cut butter in 8 pieces and put in large bowl; cream butter with paddle beater of mixer, if possible, at medium speed until butter is soft, smooth, and most of it clings to sides of bowl. Gradually beat in sugar. Beat mixture at medium speed, scraping down twice, until it is very pale, smooth, and fluffy, about 4 minutes. Beat in 3 eggs, 1 at a time, at medium speed, beating thoroughly after each addition and scraping down mixture occasionally. Beat fourth egg in small bowl. Add it to mixture, a scant tablespoon at a time, beating very thoroughly after each addition. With last few additions, batter will look like it is beginning to separate but it will come together when flour is added.

Sprinkle about one-quarter of flour over batter and stir it in, using a rubber spatula. Stir in remaining flour in 3 batches. Mix well; be sure there are no lumps. Stir in lemon peel and dried pears with their brandy.

Peel fresh pears, cut them in half, and core them. Cut them in ¼-inch slices crosswise. Spoon 1½ cups cake batter into pan. Spread smooth with rubber spatula. Arrange about half the pear slices on batter in 1 layer without allowing them to touch sides of pan. Carefully spoon another 1½ cups batter over pears without moving them. Gently spread it smooth. Arrange another layer of pears; a few extra slices may be left over. Carefully spoon remaining batter over pears. Gently spread it smooth.

Set pan on a baking sheet and put in oven with a short side of loaf pan facing back of oven. Bake until a cake tester inserted in center of cake comes out completely clean, about 1 hour and 10 minutes.

Cool cake in pan on rack 5 minutes. Invert cake onto rack. Carefully remove paper. Carefully turn cake back over and set on rack. Put tray or sheet of foil under rack.

GLAZE

Combine powdered sugar and brandy in small saucepan and mix well. Heat over medium heat, stirring, until sugar just dissolves; mixture will become slightly paler but will not be clear. Do not boil. Brush glaze over top and sides of hot cake, brushing each area only once. Let cake stand on rack until cool. (Cake can be kept, wrapped in plastic wrap or foil, up to 2 days at cool room temperature, or up to 4 days in refrigerator.)

🌿 LEMON POUND CAKE
Quatre quarts au citron

Some cooks add cream to the traditional pound cake batter to make it especially moist, as in this tangy cake.

MAKES 10 TO 12 SERVINGS

3/4 cup unsalted butter
3 large eggs
1 1/2 cups all-purpose flour
1 1/2 teaspoons baking powder
1 cup plus 2 tablespoons granulated
  sugar

3 tablespoons finely grated or
  chopped lemon peel
6 tablespoons heavy cream,
  half-and-half, or milk
Powdered sugar for sprinkling
  (optional)

Remove butter and eggs from refrigerator about 1 hour before making batter so they approximately come to room temperature. Egg shells should feel just slightly cool to touch. Butter should be fairly firm but easy to press with your finger.

Position rack in center of oven and preheat to 350°F. Butter and flour a nonstick 9-×-5-inch loaf pan, tapping pan to remove excess flour. Sift flour with baking powder.

Cut butter in 6 pieces and put in large bowl; cream butter with paddle beater of mixer, if possible, at medium speed until butter is soft, smooth, and most of it clings to sides of bowl. Gradually beat in sugar. Beat mixture at medium speed, scraping down twice, until it is very pale, smooth, and fluffy, about 4 minutes. Beat in 2 eggs, 1 at a time, at medium speed, beating thoroughly after each addition and scraping mixture down occasionally. Beat third egg in small bowl. Add it to mixture gradually, beating very thoroughly after each addition. With last few additions, batter may look like it is beginning to separate, but it will come together when flour is added.

With mixer at low speed, add about one-quarter of flour mixture to batter. Blend in lemon peel and about 1 tablespoon cream. Blend in remaining flour in 3 batches, alternating with remaining cream. Beat at low speed just until ingredients are blended.

Spoon batter carefully into pan. Smooth top with spatula. Tap pan a few times on work surface to level batter. Set pan in oven with short side of loaf pan facing back of oven. Bake until cake tester inserted in center of cake comes out completely clean, about 1 hour. Cake will rise to a peak in center and the peak will split, showing light-colored interior.

Cool cake in pan on rack 10 minutes. Run thin-bladed flexible knife around edges of cake. Turn cake out onto rack. Carefully turn cake back over and cool it completely. (Cake can be kept, wrapped in plastic wrap or foil, up to 3 days at cool room temperature, or up to 1 week in refrigerator; or it can be frozen about 2 months.)

Serve cake at room temperature. Sift powdered sugar over it, if desired. Cut cake into ½- to ¾-inch slices with serrated knife.

GENOA ALMOND CAKE
Pain de gênes

The French name actually means "Genoese bread," but this is a light and luscious almond cake. It is served on its own, without frosting, because the almonds and butter provide enough richness. They also help it to keep well, and thus it is a favorite example of a *gâteau de voyage,* or "traveling cake." For the best flavor, blanch and peel the almonds yourself. At the wonderful Moulin de Mougins restaurant in Provence this cake was baked in tiny tartlet molds and served to us as petits fours, each topped with a banana slice and a pistachio.

MAKES 6 TO 8 SERVINGS

5 tablespoons unsalted butter
¾ cup whole blanched almonds
½ cup plus 1 tablespoon
*   granulated sugar*
2 tablespoons cornstarch

2 tablespoons all-purpose flour
½ teaspoon baking powder
3 large eggs
2 tablespoons Grand Marnier
Powdered sugar for sprinkling

Butter an 8-inch round cake pan, about 2 inches deep. Line base with a round of parchment paper, wax paper, or foil, and butter paper or foil. Preheat oven to 375°F.

Melt butter in a small saucepan over low heat and let cool to room temperature. Grind almonds with sugar to a fine powder in a food processor. Sift cornstarch with flour and baking powder.

In a mixer bowl, beat 1 egg with almond mixture at low speed until blended, then at high speed for about 2 minutes, or until mixture is thick and smooth. Add remaining eggs, 1 at a time, and beat at high speed about 3 or 4 minutes after each addition. Scrape down mixture occasionally. Beat in Grand Marnier. Sprinkle cornstarch mixture over egg mixture and fold it in gently. Gently fold in melted butter in a fine stream. Transfer immediately to cake pan and bake 28 to 30 minutes, or until cake comes away from sides of pan and a cake tester inserted into center of cake comes out clean.

Carefully turn cake out onto a rack. Gently remove paper. Turn cake over again so its smooth side is down. Leave to cool. (Cake can be kept, wrapped, at room temperature or in refrigerator for 3 days, or it can be frozen.)

Serve cake, smooth side up, at room temperature. Just before serving, sprinkle it with powdered sugar from a shaker or through a strainer.

SPICED CHOCOLATE CAKE
Gâteau au chocolat et aux épices

Cinnamon became a fashionable flavor in French nouvelle pâtisserie, but it has long been popular in Alsace, the region bordering Germany. Together with other spices it flavors both the whipped cream topping and the dark butterless chocolate cake. Unlike many "chocolate" sponge cakes that are actually flavored with cocoa, this one contains melted chocolate, which makes it exceptionally moist.

MAKES 8 SERVINGS

SPICED CHOCOLATE CAKE
5 ounces semisweet chocolate,
    chopped
3 tablespoons water
1/2 cup all-purpose flour
1 teaspoon ground cinnamon
Pinch of freshly grated nutmeg

Pinch of ground cloves
6 large eggs, separated, room
    temperature
6 tablespoons sugar
1/4 teaspoon cream of tartar

SPICED WHIPPED CREAM

3/4 cup heavy cream, well chilled
1 tablespoon plus 1 teaspoon sugar
1 1/2 teaspoons unsweetened cocoa
 powder

1/4 teaspoon ground cinnamon
Pinch of ground cloves

Quick Chocolate Curls (page 389),
 or grated chocolate

SPICED CHOCOLATE CAKE

Position rack in center of oven and preheat to 350°F. Lightly butter a 9-×-2 1/2-inch springform pan, line its base with parchment paper or foil, and butter paper or foil. Flour sides of pan and lined base, tapping pan to remove excess.

Combine chocolate and water in a medium bowl above hot water over low heat. Leave until chocolate is melted. Stir until smooth, remove from pan of water, and let cool.

Sift together flour, cinnamon, nutmeg, and cloves into a medium bowl and stir to blend.

Beat egg yolks lightly in a large bowl. Beat in 4 tablespoons sugar and continue beating at high speed about 5 minutes, or until mixture is pale and very thick. Fold in chocolate mixture in 2 batches, until just blended.

Whip egg whites with cream of tartar in a large bowl at medium speed until soft peaks form. Gradually beat in remaining 2 tablespoons sugar and continue whipping at high speed until whites are stiff and shiny but not dry.

Gently fold about one-third of whites into chocolate mixture until nearly incorporated. Sprinkle about one-half the flour mixture over chocolate mixture and fold in gently. Fold in another third of whites, then remaining flour mixture, last remaining whites, adding each batch before previous one is completely blended in. Continue folding lightly but quickly, just until batter is blended. Transfer to prepared pan and spread evenly. Bake about 30 minutes, or until a cake tester inserted in center of cake comes out clean.

Cool in pan on a rack 5 minutes. Run a thin-bladed flexible knife or metal spatula around sides of pan, release spring, and remove sides of pan. Set wax paper and rack on top of cake and invert so that cake is on wax paper–lined rack; wax paper prevents sticking. Carefully remove base of pan. Peel off foil or parchment. Cool cake completely; cake will settle in center. Invert cake onto a platter, so that smooth side faces up. Remove wax paper.

SPICED WHIPPED CREAM

Whip cream with sugar in chilled bowl with chilled beater until nearly stiff. Sift cocoa, cinnamon, and cloves into cream and beat at low speed, scraping down sides occasionally, just until blended and cream is stiff.

Using a long metal spatula, spread cream evenly on sides and top of cake. Swirl top. Garnish with chocolate curls or grated chocolate. Refrigerate at least 1 hour before serving. (Frosted cake can be kept, covered with a cake cover or large bowl, up to 1 day in refrigerator.)

FRENCH FRUIT CAKE WITH RUM
Cake aux fruits

Rather than being dense with fruit like English fruit cakes and many American fruit cakes, French fruit cakes are relatively light and have a higher proportion of cake, which is made from a butter-cake batter. Our expression "nutty as a fruit cake" would not make sense in France, because French fruit cakes rarely contain nuts!

MAKES 10 TO 12 SERVINGS

½ cup mixed candied fruits and citrus peels (about 2 ounces), chopped
¾ cup raisins (about 4 ounces)
¼ cup rum
1¾ cups all-purpose flour
½ teaspoon baking powder
¾ cup unsalted butter

¾ cup sugar
3 large eggs
Grated rind of ½ orange
Grated rind of ½ lemon
¼ cup apricot preserves
6 to 8 candied cherries, cut in half, for garnish

Put chopped candied fruits and raisins in a container, add rum, and mix well. Cover tightly and refrigerate at least 8 hours or overnight.

Preheat oven to 350°F. Butter an 8½-×-4½-inch loaf pan, line with parchment paper or wax paper, and butter paper.

Drain fruits, reserving rum in a covered container. Pat fruits dry with paper towels. Toss fruits with ¼ cup flour with your fingers, carefully coating each piece. Sift remaining 1 ½ cups flour with baking powder.

Cream butter, add sugar, and beat until smooth. Add eggs, 1 at a time, beating very thoroughly after each addition. Stir in flour mixture. Stir in the grated rinds, then candied fruit mixture. Stir until no trace of flour remains.

Transfer to prepared pan and bake about 1 hour, or until a cake tester inserted in center comes out clean. Cool cake in pan about 15 minutes. Turn out onto a rack and cool completely. The cake can be wrapped in foil and kept at room temperature; or it can be frozen.

To finish, heat apricot preserves with 2 tablespoons of reserved rum until warm. Strain, pressing on mixture. Brush mixture over top and sides of cake. Decorate top with candied cherries, brushing them lightly with preserves mixture to stick them on. Serve at room temperature.

CHOCOLATE-WALNUT CAKE
Gâteau au chocolat et aux noix

A cloud of delicate chocolate whipped cream coats the cake and complements its nutty flavor. Only a small amount of butter and flour are needed in this rich, cocoa-flavored nut cake, since the walnuts provide both richness and body.   MAKES 8 TO 10 SERVINGS

1 cup walnut halves (about 3 ½ ounces)
¾ cup sugar
3 tablespoons plus 1 teaspoon all-purpose flour
2 tablespoons unsweetened cocoa powder, preferably Dutch-process

½ teaspoon baking powder
3 large eggs, separated, room temperature
3 tablespoons unsalted butter, melted and cooled
Chocolate Whipped Cream (page 356)
8 to 10 walnut halves for garnish

Position rack in center of oven and preheat to 350°F. Lightly butter a round 9-×-2-inch baking pan, line its base with parchment paper or foil, and butter paper or foil. Flour sides of pan and lined base, tapping pan to remove excess.

Grind walnuts with ¼ cup sugar in a food processor until as fine as possible, scraping inward occasionally. Transfer to a medium bowl. Sift flour, cocoa, and baking powder onto nut mixture and stir gently until thoroughly blended.

Beat egg yolks lightly in a large bowl; beat in ¼ cup sugar and continue beating at high speed about 5 minutes, or until mixture is pale and very thick.

Whip egg whites with cream of tartar in a medium bowl at medium speed until soft peaks form. Gradually beat in remaining ¼ cup sugar at high speed and beat until whites are stiff and shiny but not dry.

Sprinkle about one-third of walnut mixture over yolk mixture and fold gently until nearly incorporated. Gently fold in one-third of whites. Repeat with remaining walnut mixture and whites in 2 batches. When batter is nearly blended, gradually pour in cool melted butter while folding. Continue folding lightly but quickly, just until batter is blended. Pour into prepared pan and bake about 25 minutes, or until a cake tester inserted in center of cake comes out clean.

Cool cake in pan on a rack 10 minutes. Without releasing cake, set rack on pan, turn both over and leave upside down for 10 minutes. Turn upright and run a thin-bladed flexible knife or metal spatula carefully around sides of cake. Invert cake onto rack, carefully remove paper, and cool cake completely. Invert cake onto a platter so that smoother side of cake faces up.

Prepare chocolate whipped cream. Using a long metal spatula, spread it evenly on sides and top of cake. Swirl top slightly. Garnish with walnut halves. Refrigerate at least 1 hour before serving. (Frosted cake can be kept, covered with a cake cover or large bowl, up to 1 day in refrigerator.)

LORRAINE PLUM CAKE
Gâteau lorrain aux prunes

In Lorraine in eastern France, the origin of this country cake, cooks sometimes use whole plums without pitting them. You can follow this custom, but warn your guests! Relatively small plums, such as prune plums, are best. The plums bake in a rich batter scented with plum brandy or kirsch. The cheese in the batter adds moistness, but this is not a cheesecake. In France the cake is made with soft cream cheese; our cream cheese mixed with sour cream is a good substitute.

MAKES 6 TO 8 SERVINGS

3/4 pound small fresh plums, such as prune plums
1 1/2 cups cake flour
1 teaspoon baking powder
4 ounces cream cheese, softened
1/3 cup sour cream

4 large eggs, separated
3/4 cup granulated sugar
2 tablespoons plum brandy, kirsch, or brandy
1/4 teaspoon cream of tartar
Powdered sugar for sprinkling

Thoroughly butter a 9-inch springform pan. Heat oven to 350°F. Cut plums in half lengthwise and pit them. Sift together cake flour and baking powder.

Cream the cheese until soft. Add sour cream and beat until blended. Remove to a small bowl. Whip egg yolks with 1/2 cup sugar until thick and light. Beat in cheese mixture. Stir in brandy.

Beat whites with cream of tartar to form soft peaks. Gradually beat in remaining 1/4 cup sugar. Beat another 30 seconds at high speed until stiff and shiny.

Fold about half the flour into cheese mixture, followed by half the whites. Repeat with remaining flour and whites, working lightly but quickly.

Transfer batter to prepared pan, smooth lightly, and set plum halves on top, cut side up, nearly touching. Bake about 45 minutes, or until a cake tester inserted in cake comes out dry and dough browns lightly. Let stand 5 minutes. Run knife around cake and release spring. Cool slightly on a rack.

Serve warm or at room temperature. Before serving, sprinkle with powdered sugar. (Cake can be kept, covered, 1 or 2 days in refrigerator.)

FRENCH ANGEL FOOD CAKE
Gâteau de neige

This quick, easy-to-prepare cake is similar to our traditional American angel food cake, but is richer because it contains butter and is smaller. It is flavored with a touch of lemon and embellished with walnuts. It is great with a cup of coffee, or for dessert with vanilla or hazelnut liqueur crème anglaise (pages 343–344) or with raspberry mousse sauce (page 73) and a garnish of fresh raspberries.

MAKES 8 SERVINGS

7 tablespoons unsalted butter
12 walnut halves
1/2 cup all-purpose flour
6 tablespoons cornstarch

Grated rind of 1 lemon (about 2
    teaspoons)
6 large egg whites
3/4 cup plus 2 tablespoons sugar

Preheat oven to 350°F. Melt butter in small saucepan over low heat. Let cool but do not let it harden.

Butter and flour an 8-inch cake pan, about 2 inches deep, with nonstick surface; if using pan with regular surface, lightly butter base, line with a round of foil or parchment paper, then butter and flour foil and sides of pan. Put walnuts in pan at equal intervals. Sift flour with cornstarch into bowl. Add grated lemon.

Beat whites to soft peaks. Gradually add sugar while beating, then beat at high speed about 30 seconds, or until whites are stiff and shiny. Fold in flour mixture in 2 batches. Before mixture is entirely blended, lightly fold in melted butter.

Spoon some batter carefully over nuts without moving them. Then spoon remaining batter into pan. Gently smooth top. Bake about 35 minutes, or until cake tester inserted in cake comes out dry. Run knife around cake. Turn out onto rack and cool. (Cake can be kept, wrapped, 3 days in refrigerator; or it can be frozen.)

CHOCOLATE COFFEE-BEAN CAKE
Gâteau aux grains de café en chocolat

Coffee-flavored chocolate candies shaped like coffee beans are a favorite garnish on chocolate and coffee desserts, but here are used inside the cake as well. Lovers of a strong coffee taste can use chocolate-coated real coffee beans instead, which add a crunchy texture. Both types of confections are available in specialty candy shops and gourmet shops and by mail order.   MAKES 8 SERVINGS

BUTTER CAKE WITH CHOCOLATE COFFEE BEANS

1/2 teaspoon instant coffee powder or
   freeze-dried granules
1/2 teaspoon hot water
1/2 cup chocolate coffee-bean candies
   (about 3 1/2 ounces)
3/4 cup all-purpose flour

1/2 cup cornstarch
1 1/2 teaspoons baking powder
1/2 cup unsalted butter
3/4 cup sugar
3 large eggs
Pinch of salt

KAHLÚA WHIPPED CREAM

3/4 cup heavy cream, well chilled
1 1/2 teaspoons sugar

1 tablespoon plus 3/4 teaspoon
   Kahlúa or other coffee liqueur

8 chocolate coffee-bean candies for
   garnish

BUTTER CAKE WITH CHOCOLATE COFFEE BEANS

Position rack in center of oven and preheat to 350°F. Generously butter a 5- to 6-cup ring mold. Dissolve coffee powder or granules in hot water. Cool completely. Using a heavy knife, cut each coffee bean candy in half, except those reserved for garnish. Sift flour, cornstarch, and baking powder into a medium bowl.

Cream butter in another medium or large bowl, add sugar, and beat until smooth and fluffy. Add eggs, 1 at a time, beating very thoroughly after each addition. Stir in coffee mixture and salt; batter may separate slightly but this will not affect cake. Gently stir in one-quarter of flour mixture with a wooden spoon. Stir in remaining flour mixture in 3 batches. Stir in halved candies.

Transfer batter to prepared mold and spread evenly. Bake about 30 minutes, or until a cake tester inserted in cake comes out clean.

Run a thin-bladed flexible knife very carefully around outer and inner edges of cake. Invert cake onto a rack and cool completely. Transfer cake to a platter. (Cake can be kept, wrapped, up to 1 day at room temperature.)

KAHLÚA WHIPPED CREAM
Whip cream with sugar in chilled bowl with chilled beater until nearly stiff. Gradually beat in Kahlúa.

Using a metal spatula, spread whipped cream evenly on cake, including inner surface. Decorate top with reserved coffee-bean candies. (Frosted cake can be kept, covered with a cake cover or large bowl, up to 4 hours in refrigerator.)

WALNUT GÉNOISE
Génoise aux noix

Serve this light nut cake with whipped cream and fresh fruit, or glazed with ganache (chocolate cream frosting); or use it to make Mocha Walnut Ice Cream Cake (see recipe).   MAKES 8 SERVINGS

1 cup walnuts (about 3 1/2 ounces)	*4 large eggs, room temperature*
2/3 cup sugar	*5 tablespoons unsalted butter,*
1/2 cup all-purpose flour	*melted and cooled*
1/2 teaspoon baking powder	*Ganache (page 362) (optional)*

Position rack in center of oven and preheat to 350°F. Lightly butter a 9-inch springform pan. Line base of pan with parchment paper or foil and butter paper or foil. Flour sides of pan and lined base, tapping pan to remove excess.

Grind nuts with 2 tablespoons sugar in a food processor until as fine as possible, scraping inward occasionally. Transfer to a medium bowl. Sift flour and baking powder onto walnut mixture and mix thoroughly.

Beat eggs lightly in a large heatproof bowl. Whisk in remaining sugar. Set bowl in a pan of hot water over very low heat. Whisk about 3 minutes, or until mixture is barely lukewarm to touch. Remove from water and beat mixture at high speed about 5 minutes, or until very thick.

Sprinkle about one-third of nut mixture over egg mixture and fold it in as gently as possible. Repeat with remaining nut mixture in 2 batches. When batter is nearly blended, gradually pour in cooled melted butter while folding. Continue folding lightly but quickly, just until batter is blended.

Transfer batter to prepared pan and spread evenly. Bake about 25 minutes, or until a cake tester inserted into center of cake comes out clean.

Cool cake in pan on rack about 5 minutes. Run a thin-bladed flexible knife around edges of cake and release sides of pan. Turn cake out onto rack, carefully remove base of pan, and peel off paper or foil. Cool cake completely.

To frost cake, cool ganache, preferably at room temperature, until it is thick enough to spread. On a warm day or to save time, cool ganache by setting bowl of mixture in larger bowl of ice water or in refrigerator, gently stirring often from sides of bowl to center. It will take about 20 to 30 minutes to cool in refrigerator. Ganache is ready to spread when it has thickened and drops or flows slowly rather than running from spoon. Do not let it get too thick or it will be difficult to spread. Spread ganache quickly on top and sides of cake so it does not thicken too much on standing. If ganache becomes too thick, set bowl of mixture briefly above saucepan of hot water to soften it. (Frosted cake can be kept 2 or 3 days in refrigerator. Let it stand at room temperature about 30 minutes before serving so that ganache softens.)

ALMOND-COCOA CAKE
Biscuit aux amandes et au cacao

This light-textured cake is perfect for ice cream cakes, like Queen of Sheba Ice Cream Cake (see recipe), in which it is layered with a rich chocolate parfait. For a quicker dessert, it can be layered with good-quality packaged vanilla or chocolate ice cream.

MAKES 8 SERVINGS

1/4 cup unsalted butter
*1/2 cup blanched almonds (about
    2 1/2 ounces)*
8 tablespoons sugar
1/4 cup all-purpose flour

1/2 teaspoon baking powder
*2 tablespoons unsweetened cocoa
    powder*
3 large eggs, separated

Position rack in center of oven and preheat to 350°F. Butter 9-inch springform pan. Line base of pan with foil by putting sheet of foil on base, then attaching sides of pan so they hold foil tightly in place; butter foil. Flour sides of pan and foil-lined base, shaking off excess. Melt butter and let stand until cooled but not congealed. Finely grind almonds with 2 tablespoons sugar in food processor. Sift flour with baking powder and cocoa into small bowl. Add almond mixture and mix well.

Beat egg yolks in large bowl until blended. Gradually beat in 4 tablespoons sugar. Continue beating until thick and light in color, about 5 minutes. With clean, dry beater, beat egg whites in large bowl until stiff but not dry. Gradually beat in remaining 2 tablespoons sugar at high speed and continue beating until very shiny, about 30 seconds.

Gently fold about one-third of almond-cocoa mixture into egg yolk mixture, followed by about one-third of egg whites. Fold in half the remaining almond-cocoa mixture, then half the remaining egg whites. Fold in remaining almond-cocoa mixture, then remaining egg whites as lightly as possible; when whites are nearly blended in, fold in cooled butter in a thin stream just until blended. Spoon batter into prepared pan and smooth top with rubber spatula. Bake until cake tester inserted into center of cake comes out dry, about 20 minutes. Cool cake in pan on rack about 5 minutes. Run thin-bladed flexible knife around edges of cake and release sides of pan. Turn cake out onto rack, carefully remove base of pan, and peel off foil. Cool cake completely before serving or using to make desserts. (Cake can be stored for 2 days, wrapped, at room temperature or in refrigerator. It can also be frozen.)

Layer Cakes

The visitor to a quality pâtisserie cannot help being tempted by the splendid array of fine cakes with luscious frostings. From the great variety of colors and flavors, it appears that the pastry chefs make numerous cakes, frostings, and fillings. Yet many of the gâteaux are made from génoise cake layered with buttercream frosting. The chefs create cakes in a myriad of tastes and colors by using different flavors in the frosting or in the syrup used to moisten the cake layers, and by adding fruit or sprinkling chopped nuts on the layers.

Génoise is a special type of sponge cake that is often enriched with a little butter. Light in texture and delicate in flavor, it is easier to prepare than other sponge cakes because the eggs are whipped whole rather than being separated into yolks and whites. French chefs most often bake génoise in a rather deep pan and split the cake in two layers, but it can also be baked in separate layer pans like American layer cakes. Before frosting the layers, many cooks like to brush them with a simple sugar syrup, frequently flavored with a liqueur to reinforce or complement the taste of the filling.

Layer cakes can also be made from the familiar type of sponge cake, which the French call *biscuit.* For these sponge cakes, the egg yolks and whites are beaten separately to incorporate air into both. They are then combined with the other ingredients gently and quickly, so the batter loses as little air as possible and rises properly. The best of these cakes are flavored with ground nuts. Little or no butter is needed in these cakes because the oil in the nuts imparts richness. Only a small amount of flour, cornstarch, or bread crumbs is added to give them a little extra body so they won't collapse.

Sugar plays several important roles in génoise and other sponge cakes. It is sugar beaten with the whole eggs in the case of génoise, or with egg yolks in the case of other sponge cakes, that enables them to become very thick and to trap air to lighten the cake. A little sugar beaten into the whipped egg whites gives them stability and smoothness and helps prevent dry, lumpy whites, so that folding them into the remaining ingredients is easier and less air is lost.

In all these cakes, folding the ingredients together properly is essential. The flour or dry-ingredient mixture is folded into the egg mixture in several batches. In the case of sponge cakes, the stiffly beaten egg whites and the dry ingredients are folded alternately in batches into the whipped yolks so that the consistency of the batter remains light during the whole process. If the flour or nut mixture were added all at once, their weight would make the batter fall.

Chocolate is a delightful addition to many layer cakes. Semisweet or bittersweet chocolate is the best-loved flavoring for the richest chocolate cakes. Because of the special properties of chocolate, the procedure for making batters containing it is slightly different from that of other sponge cakes. For a lighter cake, cocoa is often used instead of chocolate. Other popular flavorings for sponge cake batters are vanilla extract and lemon and orange zests.

The most frequently used filling and frosting for French layer cakes is buttercream. Silky buttercream prepared the French way is infinitely superior in flavor to the cloyingly sweet powdered-sugar icings that are sometimes given this name in certain American cookbooks. Made of butter, sugar syrup, and usually egg yolks, buttercream takes little time to prepare and keeps well in the refrigerator or freezer. Buttercream's smooth, creamy texture makes it easy to spread and to pipe. As a filling and frosting, it is popular not only for layer cakes, but also for petits fours and for the sumptuous holiday rolled cake, *bûche de Noël.* A lighter version, popular for summer, is made with egg whites, as in Walnut Cake with Rum Meringue Buttercream, and an easy version, that does not require syrup, can be made with whole eggs, as in Coffee Layer Cake with Toasted Almonds.

In addition to classic favorites like liqueur, coffee, chocolate, and vanilla buttercreams, today's repertoire includes buttercreams flavored with nuts, fruit purées, and sweet spices like cinnamon. Two or more harmonious flavors can also be used, such as white chocolate and lemon, hazelnut and orange, or bittersweet chocolate, fresh raspberry purée, and raspberry brandy.

The technique pastry chefs use to easily create several different frostings from a single mixture is very simple and a good trick to know when making desserts at home. It is illustrated in Vanilla-Chocolate-Hazelnut Layer Cake, in which the cake layers alternate with hazelnut and chocolate fillings and the finished dessert is coated with vanilla frosting and crowned with chocolate rosettes.

Chantilly cream, or slightly sweetened whipped cream, is a popular frosting for layer cakes, especially those made with nuts, because its lightness and smoothness are a perfect complement to their nutty texture. However, cakes frosted with buttercream keep longer.

The most fashionable chocolate frosting and filling is a fairly recent arrival in the French repertoire. It is a satiny, intensely flavored mixture called *ganache,* made of chocolate and cream. Adding butter turns it into ganache buttercream, as in Cinnamon Ganache Gâteau. For a lighter effect, ganache can be whipped to a fluffy texture. Whipped ganache can be spread as a frosting and filling on all types of cakes, especially sponge cakes and other light cakes.

Layer cakes can also be made with mousse fillings (see the next section, Mousse Cakes), or with a meringue base (see Meringue Cakes).

For a simple garnish for a cake, use fresh fruit, grated chocolate, or small candies to match the flavor of the frosting; for example, use fresh raspberries or blackberries on a cake frosted with raspberry brandy buttercream. An easy but effective garnish for nut cakes is whole or halved nuts of the type in the cake, so that they act not only as a decoration but also give a hint of the flavors to expect.

Hints

• Organization is very important when making génoise and sponge cakes. Before beating the whole eggs, yolks, or whites, preheat the oven, prepare the cake pan, and get out all tools, so there will be no need to look for anything after the batter is ready.
• To prevent sticking, it is best to line the base of the cake pan with parchment paper or foil. The pan is lightly buttered first in order to allow the paper to stick.
• Grind nuts for nut cakes until very fine, using an on/off motion of the food processor, but be careful not to grind them for too long

because they will start to cake and lose their light texture. For most recipes, a small amount of sugar ground with the nuts helps prevent this from happening. If using a large quantity of nuts, it is best to grind them in batches; if the processor container is too full, the nuts won't grind evenly. Scrape them inward toward the blade occasionally to further ensure even grinding. Instead of a food processor, an electric nut grinder or a hand rotary grater can be used.

• If possible, when making sponge cakes beat the yolks in one bowl and the whites in another, so the yolks don't lose air when transferred to another bowl.

• For whipping egg whites, always use clean dry beaters and a clean dry bowl. Beating the whites should always be the last step in the preparation of cake batter. They cannot wait, or they will lose air. Fold them into the other ingredients as soon as they are beaten, and put the cake in the oven immediately.

• See also the hint on folding, in "Soufflés" (page 10).

• When folding ingredients, add each batch of dry mixture or egg whites before the previous addition is completely mixed in.

• Before turning a cake out of the pan, carefully run a knife around the edges of the cake, unless using a pan with a removable bottom. For this type of pan, the bottom slides down when the cake is turned over, so the sides of the pan are very easy to remove. To release the cake from the base of this type of pan or from a springform pan, use a metal spatula.

• Cakes containing a high proportion of nuts and little or no flour are quite fragile. Often the top of a nut cake settles down a little when cooling, but this is normal and nothing to worry about. The technique designed to help these cakes keep their shape is to let them cool with their smoothest side against the rack so that this side remains flat. The cake is then turned back over before it is frosted so that the smoothest side becomes the top of the cake.

• Cakes frosted with whipped cream should be served cold.

• Chill cakes frosted with buttercream about 1 hour to make cutting easier. To enjoy them to their fullest, serve them at cool room temperature, so that the buttercream softens slightly; if served straight from the refrigerator, the buttercream is usually a little too firm.

• Cakes spread with buttercream flavored with spirits are most flavorful if served within one day; the taste of the spirits weakens if the cake is kept for longer.

- Because buttercream is rich, cakes frosted and filled with it are best at teatime or after light meals.

MACADAMIA NUT CAKE
Gâteau aux noix de macadam

Macadamia nuts, popular in America but rare in France, are here used in a traditional French almond cream filling. When combined with the macadamia nut cake and the chocolate whipped cream, the result is a magnificent creation that would be loved on both sides of the Atlantic. If unsalted nuts are available, use them. If only salted nuts are available, desalt them as on page 389 and they will be fine in this cake. MAKES 10 TO 12 SERVINGS

MACADAMIA NUT CAKE

2 1/3 cups macadamia nuts (about 10 ounces)

3/4 cup plus 2 tablespoons granulated sugar

1/4 cup all-purpose flour

5 large eggs, separated, room temperature

3/4 teaspoon vanilla

1/4 teaspoon cream of tartar

MACADAMIA NUT FILLING

6 tablespoons unsalted butter, softened

5 tablespoons powdered sugar, sifted

1 large egg yolk

1 tablespoon hazelnut liqueur

1/2 cup macadamia nuts (about 2 ounces)

SPIRITED CHOCOLATE CREAM

1 ounce semisweet chocolate, cut into bits

1 tablespoon plus 1 1/2 teaspoons hazelnut liqueur

3/4 cup heavy cream, well chilled

2 teaspoons sugar

12 whole macadamia nuts for garnish

MACADAMIA NUT CAKE

Position rack in center of oven and preheat to 325°F. Butter a 9-inch springform cake pan, about 3 inches deep. Line base of pan with parchment or foil; butter parchment or foil. Flour sides of pan and lined base, shaking out excess. In food processor, grind as fine as possible 1 cup nuts with 3 tablespoons sugar and transfer to bowl. Repeat with remaining nuts and another 3 tablespoons sugar. Sift in flour and stir until thoroughly blended.

Beat egg yolks with ¼ cup sugar in large bowl of mixer about 5 minutes, or until pale yellow and thick enough to form ribbon when beaters are lifted. Add vanilla and beat until blended. In another large bowl, beat egg whites with cream of tartar until fairly stiff. Gradually beat in remaining ¼ cup sugar at high speed and continue beating until whites are very stiff and shiny but not dry, about 30 seconds. Sprinkle one-third of nut mixture over yolks and fold gently. Spoon one-third of whites on top and fold gently. Repeat until all nut mixture and whites are added. Continue folding just until blended and no white streaks remain.

Pour batter into prepared pan and quickly spread as evenly as possible. Bake until cake tester inserted in center of cake comes out clean, about 55 minutes. Cool in pan on rack for about 10 minutes. Cake will settle in center during cooling, but this won't show in finished cake. Run a thin-bladed flexible knife around sides of cake, turn over onto rack, and remove sides and base of pan. Carefully peel off paper. Invert cake again onto another rack so its smooth side is against rack and let cool completely. (Cake can be kept, wrapped, 2 days in refrigerator.)

MACADAMIA NUT FILLING

Beat butter and 4 tablespoons powdered sugar until very smooth. Add egg yolk and beat until smooth. Gradually beat in liqueur. In food processor, grind nuts until fine with remaining 1 tablespoon powdered sugar. Stir nuts into butter mixture.

Turn cake back over so smooth side is up. Using long serrated knife, split cake horizontally into 2 layers. Spread bottom layer with filling. Set other layer on top, smooth side up. Refrigerate 1 hour.

SPIRITED CHOCOLATE CREAM

Melt chocolate in a double boiler set over hot water over low heat. Stir chocolate until smooth, add liqueur, and remove mixture from heat, leaving it above hot water. In a chilled bowl, beat cream with sugar until it holds stiff peaks. Remove chocolate from above water and let it cool for 30 seconds. Quickly stir about ⅓ cup whipped cream into chocolate mixture. Quickly fold chocolate mixture into remaining whipped cream.

Spread chocolate cream on sides and top of cake. Garnish top of cake with whole macadamia nuts. Chill for 1 hour before serving. (Frosted cake can be kept, covered when frosting is firm, 1 day in refrigerator.)

HAZELNUT PRALINE CAKE
Gâteau praliné aux noisettes

Praline flavors this hazelnut génoise-based gâteau in three ways: in the hazelnut praline filling; in the praline-liqueur whipped cream; and coarsely chopped, as a topping.   MAKES 8 TO 10 SERVINGS

HAZELNUT GÉNOISE
½ cup hazelnuts
⅔ cup sugar
⅔ cup all-purpose flour

4 extra-large eggs
¼ cup unsalted butter, melted and
*   cooled slightly*

PRALINE WHIPPED CREAM
1 cup heavy cream, well chilled
1 teaspoon sugar
2 teaspoons praline liqueur or
*   hazelnut liqueur*

7 tablespoons hazelnut praline
*   powder (page 374)*

¼ cup coarsely chopped hazelnut
*   praline for garnish (page*
*   374)*

HAZELNUT GÉNOISE
Position rack in center of oven and preheat to 350°F. Toast and skin hazelnuts (see page 388). Cool completely.

Butter a 9-×-2-inch round cake pan. Line base with parchment or foil. Butter paper. Dust pans with flour and shake out excess. Grind toasted nuts with 1 tablespoon sugar as finely as possible in processor. Transfer to medium bowl. Sift flour onto nut mixture and stir to blend well.

If using a heavy-duty mixer, beat eggs and remaining sugar at high speed 10 minutes, until very thick.

If using portable electric mixer, beat eggs and remaining sugar to blend in large bowl. Set bowl in pan of hot (but not boiling) water over low heat. Beat at medium speed until mixture is lukewarm and thick, about 7 minutes. Remove from pan of water. Beat at high speed until completely cool and very thick.

Sprinkle about one-third of nut mixture over egg mixture and fold it in as gently as possible. Repeat with remaining nut mixture in 2 batches, folding just until blended and drizzling in melted butter just before final addition of nuts is completely blended.

Immediately pour batter into prepared pan. Bake until tester inserted in center comes out clean, about 35 minutes. Run a thin-bladed flexible knife carefully around sides of cake; turn out onto rack and remove paper. Cool completely. Invert cake again onto another rack, then onto platter. Using long serrated knife, cut cake in half horizontally.

PRALINE WHIPPED CREAM

Beat cream with sugar in a chilled bowl with chilled beater until soft peaks form. Add liqueur and beat until stiff.

Transfer 1 cup whipped cream to small bowl. Add praline powder and fold together lightly. Spread mixture over bottom cake layer. Place second layer on top, smooth side up.

Spread remaining (white) whipped cream on sides and top of cake. Chill 1 hour. (Can be frosted 4 hours ahead and refrigerated.) Just before serving, sprinkle top of cake lightly and evenly with coarsely chopped praline. Serve cold.

❦ RASPBERRY LAYER CAKE
Gâteau aux framboises

Wonderfully fragrant *eau de vie de framboise* (clear raspberry brandy) flavors both the syrup that moistens the cake layers and the luscious buttercream, then the cake is topped with fresh berries. Use either all red raspberries, or alternate them with blackberries or golden raspberries. Instead of vanilla génoise, you can use chocolate. You can also bake the cake in 2 separate layers (as on page 189), rather than splitting the cake in two, and omit the syrup.

MAKES 8 SERVINGS

Génoise or Cocoa Génoise (page 377)

RASPBERRY BRANDY SYRUP (OPTIONAL)
¼ cup sugar
¼ cup water

2 tablespoons clear raspberry brandy (framboise)

RASPBERRY BRANDY BUTTERCREAM
Buttercream (page 356)
3 tablespoons clear raspberry brandy

1 ¼ pounds raspberries, or 12 ounces raspberries and 12 ounces blackberries for garnish

Prepare cake batter and bake in 9-inch pan. Cool on rack.

RASPBERRY BRANDY SYRUP
Combine sugar and water in small saucepan. Place over low heat and swirl pan gently until sugar dissolves. Increase heat and bring to a boil. Remove from heat and cool completely. Stir in brandy.

RASPBERRY BRANDY BUTTERCREAM
Prepare buttercream. Measure raspberry brandy into small cup. Using wooden spoon, very gradually beat brandy into Buttercream.

Using a long serrated knife, split cake horizontally into 2 layers. Brush bottom layer with syrup. Spread about one-third of buttercream on bottom layer. Brush cut side of top layer with syrup, then flip it over to set it on cake, crust side up. Spread sides and top of cake with remaining buttercream and smooth with long metal spatula. Decorate top of cake with raspberries, or with circles of raspberries alternating with circles of blackberries.

Chill 1 or 2 hours before serving. (The cake can be prepared up to 4 hours ahead and kept in refrigerator. It can be kept 1 day without berries; they should be put on a short time before serving, before cream is completely set. If cream has set, let cake stand outside refrigerator 15 to 30 minutes to soften cream, then top with berries.)

If any berries remain, alternate them on cake plate around base of cake, or serve them as an accompaniment.

BRAZIL NUT AND ORANGE LAYER CAKE
Gâteau aux noix de brésil à l'orange

Brazil nuts impart an exotic flavor to this cake. Their assertive taste harmonizes well with the easy orange filling and the chocolate glaze.   MAKES 12 SERVINGS

BRAZIL NUT CAKE

2 1/8 cups Brazil nuts (about 10 ounces)

3/4 cup plus 2 tablespoons granulated sugar

1/4 cup all-purpose flour

5 large eggs, separated, room temperature

1 teaspoon grated orange zest

1 tablespoon strained fresh orange juice

1/4 teaspoon cream of tartar

ORANGE FILLING AND FROSTING

3/4 cup unsalted butter, softened

1/2 cup superfine sugar

1 teaspoon grated orange peel

5 tablespoons strained fresh orange juice

CHOCOLATE GLAZE

4 ounces semisweet chocolate, chopped

3 tablespoons unsalted butter

BRAZIL NUT CAKE

Position rack in center of oven and preheat to 350°F. Toast nuts in shallow baking dish in oven 10 minutes. Transfer one-third of nuts to large strainer. Turn off oven and leave in remaining nuts. While nuts are hot, remove skins by rubbing them energetically with towel against strainer; some of skins will stay on. Lift nuts from strainer and remove to bowl. Repeat with remaining nuts. Cool nuts completely.

Turn oven down to 325°F. Butter a 9-inch springform cake pan, about 3 inches deep. Line base of pan with parchment or foil, and butter parchment or foil. Flour sides of pan and lined base, shaking out excess. In food processor, grind 1 cup nuts with 3 tablespoons sugar as fine as possible. Transfer to bowl. Repeat with remaining nuts and 3 more tablespoons sugar. Sift in flour and stir until thoroughly blended.

Beat egg yolks with ¼ cup sugar in large bowl of mixer about 5 minutes, or until pale yellow and thick enough to form a ribbon when beaters are lifted. Beat in grated zest and orange juice. Beat egg whites with cream of tartar in another large bowl until stiff. Gradually add remaining ¼ cup sugar and continue beating at high speed until whites are very stiff and shiny but not dry, about 30 seconds. Sprinkle one-third of nut mixture over yolks and fold gently. Spoon one-third of whites on top and fold gently. Repeat until all nut mixture and whites are added. Continue folding just until blended and no white streaks remain.

Pour batter into prepared pan and quickly spread as evenly as possible. Bake until cake tester inserted in center of cake comes out clean, about 48 minutes. Cool in pan on rack for 10 minutes. Cake will settle in center during cooling, but this won't show in finished cake. Run thin-bladed flexible knife around sides of cake, turn over onto rack, and remove sides and base of pan. Carefully peel off paper.

Invert cake again onto another rack so its smooth side is against rack, and let cool completely. (Cake can be wrapped and kept 2 days in refrigerator.)

ORANGE FILLING AND FROSTING

Beat butter and superfine sugar until smooth. Beat in orange peel. Gradually beat in orange juice.

Turn cake back over so smooth side is up. Using a long serrated knife, split cake horizontally into 2 layers. Spread half the filling on bottom layer. Set other layer on top, smooth side up. Spread remaining orange mixture on sides but not on top of cake. Refrigerate until frosting is firm, about 3 hours. (Cake can be frosted 1 day ahead and kept, uncovered, in refrigerator.)

CHOCOLATE GLAZE

Melt chocolate in small saucepan set in pan of hot water over low heat. Add butter and stir until melted. Remove from pan of hot water and cool 2 minutes, stirring. Pour glaze over center of cake. Spread glaze very gently toward edges and let it trickle down sides of cake at intervals. Refrigerate until just set, about 1 hour. Serve at cool room temperature.

WALNUT CAKE WITH RUM MERINGUE BUTTERCREAM
Gâteau aux noix à la crème au rhum

This type of flourless nut cake with bread crumbs is favored in Alsace in eastern France, which has a substantial German influence on its desserts. The rich walnut cake layers are sandwiched with a thin layer of rum-spiked apricot preserves, then frosted with a light but luscious meringue buttercream.   MAKES 12 SERVINGS

WALNUT CAKE

3 cups walnuts (about 10 ounces)
1 cup sugar
6 tablespoons unflavored bread
    crumbs

6 large eggs, separated, room
    temperature
1 1/2 teaspoons grated lemon peel
1/4 teaspoon cream of tartar

APRICOT FILLING

1/3 cup apricot preserves
4 to 5 teaspoons dark rum (see
    Note)

RUM MERINGUE BUTTERCREAM

Meringue Buttercream with 2 Egg
    Whites (page 360)

3 to 4 teaspoons dark rum (see
    Note)

WALNUT CAKE

Position rack in center of oven and preheat to 350°F. Butter two 9-inch round cake pans, about 1 1/2 inches deep. Line base of each with parchment or foil, and butter parchment or foil. Flour sides of pans and lined bases, shaking out excess. In food processor, grind 1 1/2 cups walnuts with 2 tablespoons sugar to a fine powder, and transfer to a bowl. Repeat with remaining walnuts and another 2 tablespoons sugar. Add bread crumbs and stir until well blended.

Beat egg yolks with 1/2 cup sugar in large bowl of electric mixer until pale yellow and slowly dissolving ribbon forms when beaters are lifted, about 5 minutes. Beat in grated peel. Beat egg whites with cream of tartar in another large bowl with clean beater until stiff. Gradually add remaining 1/4 cup sugar and continue beating at high speed until whites are very stiff and shiny but not dry, about 30 seconds. Sprinkle one-third of walnut mixture over yolks and fold gently. Spoon one-third of whites on top and fold gently. Repeat until all walnut mixture and whites are added. Continue folding just until blended and no white streaks remain.

Pour batter into prepared pans and quickly spread as evenly as possible. Bake until cake tester inserted in center of layers comes out clean, about 25 minutes. Without releasing cakes, set rack on top of each pan, turn over, and leave upside down for 10 minutes, with pan still on cake. Turn back over. Run a thin-bladed flexible knife around sides of each cake. Turn out onto racks, carefully peel off paper, and let cool completely. (Cakes can be prepared 2 days ahead and kept wrapped in refrigerator.)

APRICOT FILLING

In small saucepan, heat preserves, stirring and breaking up large pieces with spoon, just until melted. Stir in rum. Spread over 1 cake in thin layer. Set other cake on top, smooth side up.

RUM MERINGUE BUTTERCREAM

Prepare buttercream. Using wooden spoon, gradually beat in rum, 1 teaspoon at a time.

Spread sides and top of cake with buttercream and smooth with long metal spatula. Spoon remaining buttercream into pastry bag fitted with medium star tip. Pipe row of rosettes of buttercream along top edge of cake. Refrigerate until buttercream is firm, about 2 hours. (Cake can be frosted 2 days ahead and kept, uncovered, in refrigerator.)

NOTE: Use smaller quantity of rum if serving cake on same day it is filled and frosted; use larger quantity if keeping cake for more than 1 day as flavor weakens after a day.

CINNAMON GANACHE GÂTEAU
Gâteau glacé au chocolat à la cannelle

For this layer cake, a smooth cinnamon ganache is made by gently infusing cinnamon sticks in cream before pouring it over chopped chocolate. Use 2 cinnamon sticks for a delicate taste, or 3 for a more pronounced one. With the addition of butter, the new flavored ganache becomes a smooth, rich, easy-to-make ganache buttercream.

MAKES 8 SERVINGS

Two 9-inch Génoise Layers (page 378)

CINNAMON GANACHE

3/4 cup heavy cream
2 or 3 cinnamon sticks (3 inches long)
8 ounces fine-quality semisweet chocolate, very finely chopped

1/2 cup unsalted butter, cut in pieces

8 pecans or blanched almonds for garnish

Bake génoise in two 9-inch layer pans. Let cool completely.

CINNAMON GANACHE

Scald cream with cinnamon sticks in small heavy saucepan over medium-high heat until bubbling at edges. Remove from heat, cover, and let stand 30 minutes.

Remove cinnamon sticks. Put chocolate in heatproof medium bowl. Heat cinnamon-flavored cream in small heavy saucepan over medium-high heat, stirring with whisk, until it comes to a full boil. Pour boiling cream over chocolate all at once. Stir with whisk until chocolate is completely melted and mixture is smooth. Cool to room temperature, occasionally stirring gently.

Whisk ganache briefly until smooth. Cream butter in large bowl, using paddle beater, if available, until very soft and smooth. Add ganache in 3 batches, beating constantly at low speed until mixture is smooth.

Spread about one-third of frosting on bottom cake layer. Set second layer on top and frost sides and top with remaining frosting. Swirl frosting at top, from edge inward, forming small curves. Garnish with pecans or almonds.

On a cool day, let cake stand at room temperature for a shiny glaze; otherwise, refrigerate until ganache sets, about 1 hour. If cake has been refrigerated for more than 1 hour, let it stand at room temperature about 30 minutes before serving, so that frosting softens.

COFFEE LAYER CAKE WITH TOASTED ALMONDS
Gâteau moka

Made of génoise cake and a coffee buttercream, this is the standard gâteau always referred to by French pastry chefs when discussing cakes. This version makes use of an easy type of buttercream that does not require boiling a sugar syrup. The gâteau is decorated in the classic manner, with chopped toasted almonds on the sides of the cake and rosettes of the coffee buttercream on the top. For a simpler decor, Parisian pastry chef Jean Creveux recommends covering the frosted cake completely with the almonds.　　MAKES 8 SERVINGS

Génoise (page 377)　　　　　　*1 1/4 cups slivered almonds*

SIMPLE COFFEE BUTTERCREAM
2 teaspoons instant freeze-dried　　*3/4 cup sugar*
　　coffee granules　　　　　　*1 cup plus 2 tablespoons unsalted*
2 tablespoons boiling water　　　　　*butter, room temperature*
3 large eggs

Bake génoise and cool.
　　Preheat oven to 350°F. Chop almonds into small cubes with a knife. Toast almonds on a baking sheet in oven, stirring often, for about 5 minutes, or until lightly browned. Transfer to a bowl and cool completely.

SIMPLE COFFEE BUTTERCREAM
　　Dissolve coffee in boiling water and cool completely. Beat eggs slightly in a large heatproof bowl. Beat in sugar, then dissolved coffee. Set bowl in a pan of hot water over low heat. Using a hand-held electric mixer, beat at medium speed 5 minutes, then at high speed until a thin, slowly dissolving ribbon forms when beaters are lifted, about 3 minutes. Do not heat mixture for too long or eggs may curdle. Remove from pan of water and beat until cool.
　　Cream butter in large bowl until very soft and smooth. Beat in 1/2 cup egg mixture. Gradually beat in remaining egg mixture, beating constantly and stopping occasionally to scrape down mixture.

Using a long serrated knife, split cake horizontally into 2 layers. Spread about one-third of buttercream on bottom layer. Set other layer on top. Spread sides and top of cake with more buttercream and smooth with a long metal spatula. If desired, swirl buttercream on top. Stick toasted almonds by handfuls onto sides of cake. Spoon remaining buttercream into a pastry bag fitted with medium star tip. Pipe row of small rosettes of buttercream at top edge of cake and one larger rosette in center. Refrigerate 2 hours before serving. (Cake can be kept, covered, 2 days in refrigerator.) Serve at cool room temperature.

VANILLA-CHOCOLATE-HAZELNUT LAYER CAKE
Gâteau fourré à la vanille, au chocolat et aux noisettes

Here is an easy way to have a delightful dessert with complex flavors from one basic cake and a batch of buttercream. Simply divide the buttercream into three portions, and flavor each differently; here I have used vanilla, chocolate, and toasted hazelnuts. Or try the flavors used in a delectable gâteau I enjoyed at l'Auberge du Père Bise on the beautiful lake of Annecy near the Alps—kirsch, chocolate, and praline. MAKES 12 SERVINGS

Three 8-inch Génoise Layers (page 378)
Buttercream (page 356)
1/4 cup hazelnuts

2 1/2 ounces bittersweet or semisweet chocolate, chopped
1 1/2 teaspoons pure vanilla extract

Prepare cake layers and buttercream. Preheat oven to 350°F. Toast hazelnuts on small baking sheet until lightly browned and skins begin to split, about 7 minutes. Transfer them to large strainer and rub vigorously with towel to remove most of skins. Cool completely. Grind in food processor with on/off motion until very fine.

Melt chocolate in very small heatproof bowl over hot, not simmering, water over low heat, stirring occasionally. Remove from pan of water and cool to body temperature.

Spoon 1/2 cup unflavored buttercream into a small bowl. Stir in hazelnuts. Spoon 1/2 cup unflavored buttercream into second small bowl and stir in chocolate. Using a wooden spoon, gradually stir vanilla into remaining buttercream.

Reserve ¼ cup chocolate buttercream for garnish. Spread remaining chocolate buttercream on bottom cake layer. Set second cake layer on top and spread with hazelnut buttercream. Set top layer in place. Frost top and sides of cake with vanilla buttercream. Using a pastry bag and small star tip, pipe rosettes of chocolate buttercream in ring on top of cake for garnish. Refrigerate at least 2 hours before serving. (Cake can be kept, covered, 2 days ahead in refrigerator.) Serve at cool room temperature.

ORANGE LAYER CAKE WITH GRAND MARNIER
Gâteau à l'orange et au Grand Marnier

In this classic gâteau, génoise layers are moistened with Grand Marnier syrup and spread with orange buttercream. The decoration is simple but lovely: a circle of buttercream is piped near the center of the gâteau, then filled with chopped toasted almonds. The gâteau is also wonderful when made with Cocoa Génoise (page 378). You can use the other flavor variations of buttercream in this way to create other cakes. Choose a complementary liqueur for the syrup, or use Vanilla Syrup (page 215).   MAKES 8 SERVINGS

Génoise (page 377)
About ¼ cup chopped almonds for garnish

GRAND MARNIER SYRUP
¼ cup sugar
¼ cup water
2 tablespoons Grand Marnier

EASY ORANGE BUTTERCREAM
3 large eggs
¾ cup sugar
2 tablespoons strained fresh orange juice
Grated zest of 1 large orange
1 cup plus 2 tablespoons unsalted butter, room temperature

Chocolate-Dipped Orange Sections (page 376) (optional)

Bake cake and cool completely.

Preheat oven to 350°F. Put almonds in a baking dish and toast in oven, stirring often, for about 5 minutes, or until lightly browned. Transfer to a bowl and cool completely.

GRAND MARNIER SYRUP

Combine sugar and water in small saucepan. Place over low heat and swirl pan gently until sugar dissolves. Increase heat and bring to a boil. Remove from heat and cool completely. Stir in Grand Marnier.

EASY ORANGE BUTTERCREAM

Beat eggs lightly in a large heatproof bowl. Beat in sugar, then 2 tablespoons orange juice. Set bowl in a pan of hot water over low heat. Using a hand-held electric mixer, beat at medium speed 5 minutes, then at high speed until a thin, slowly dissolving ribbon forms when beaters are lifted, about 3 minutes. Do not heat mixture for too long or eggs may curdle. Remove from pan of water and beat until cool. Add grated orange zest.

Cream butter in large bowl until very soft and smooth. Beat in ½ cup egg mixture. Gradually beat in remaining egg mixture, beating constantly and stopping occasionally to scrape down mixture.

Using a long serrated knife, split cake horizontally into 2 layers. Brush bottom layer with Grand Marnier syrup. Spread about one-third of buttercream on bottom layer. Brush cut side of top layer with syrup, then flip it over to set it on cake, crust side up. Set aside about ¼ cup buttercream for garnishing. Spread sides and top of cake with remaining buttercream and smooth with a long metal spatula. Swirl buttercream at top, from edge inward, forming small curves.

Spoon reserved buttercream into a pastry bag fitted with a small star tip. Pipe a ring of rosettes of buttercream about halfway between edge and center of cake. Fill center of ring with chopped nuts. Press gently so they adhere to frosting. Refrigerate at least 2 hours before serving. (Cake can be kept, covered, 2 days ahead in refrigerator.) Serve at cool room temperature. Serve orange sections separately.

SEE PHOTOGRAPH.

WHITE CHOCOLATE WALNUT CAKE WITH NECTARINES
Gâteau au chocolat blanc, aux noix et aux brugnons

This summery dessert consists of an unusual combination: a light walnut cake, a white chocolate whipped cream filling and a topping of glazed nectarines. Other soft fruit, especially berries, can be substituted for the nectarines.   MAKES 8 SERVINGS

LIGHT WALNUT CAKE
1 cup walnuts (about 3 1/4 ounces)
3/4 cup plus 2 tablespoons sugar
6 tablespoons all-purpose flour
4 large whole eggs plus 4 large egg
   whites, room temperature

1/4 teaspoon cream of tartar
2 tablespoons unsalted butter,
   melted and cooled

WHITE CHOCOLATE WHIPPED CREAM
4 ounces fine-quality white
   chocolate, chopped

1 cup heavy cream, well chilled

NECTARINE TOPPING
2 nectarines
1/4 cup apricot preserves

1 teaspoon peach or apricot brandy
   or kirsch

LIGHT WALNUT CAKE
Preheat oven to 375°F. Lightly butter corners of a 17-×-11-inch rimmed baking sheet. Line with foil or parchment paper. Butter foil or paper.

Grind nuts with 1/4 cup sugar in a food processor until as fine as possible, scraping inward occasionally. Transfer to a medium bowl. Sift flour onto nut mixture and stir until blended.

Beat whole eggs lightly in a large bowl, beat in 1/2 cup sugar and continue beating at high speed about 5 minutes, or until mixture is pale and very thick.

Whip egg whites with cream of tartar in a large bowl until soft peaks form. Gradually beat in remaining 2 tablespoons sugar at high speed and beat until whites are stiff and shiny but not dry.

Sprinkle about one-third of walnut mixture over whole-egg mixture and gently fold it in. Repeat with remaining walnut mixture in 2 batches. When batter is nearly blended, gradually pour in cool melted butter while folding. Fold in egg whites in 3 batches. Continue folding lightly but quickly, just until batter is blended.

Transfer batter to prepared baking sheet and spread evenly but lightly. Bake about 15 minutes, or until cake is light brown on top and golden brown at edges. Cool in pan on a rack.

WHITE CHOCOLATE WHIPPED CREAM

Melt chocolate in a small bowl set above a pan of hot water over low heat. Whisk until smooth. Turn off heat but leave bowl of chocolate above hot water.

Whip cream in a large chilled bowl with chilled beater until stiff. Remove chocolate from above water and cool for 30 seconds. Quickly stir about ½ cup whipped cream into chocolate. Quickly fold mixture into remaining whipped cream until smooth. Cover and refrigerate 1 hour.

Cut cake in half crosswise; each half will be about 8¼ inches long. Remove one half carefully from paper and put on a platter. Spread ¾ cup white chocolate cream on cake layer.

Unstick second half of cake very carefully from foil and lift very gently with both hands; it is fragile. Set it in place on cake, positioning it so cut sides of both layers are even with each other. Spread remaining white chocolate cream on top. Trim edges. Refrigerate at least 2 hours. (Cake can be kept, covered, up to 2 days in refrigerator.)

NECTARINE TOPPING

Up to 4 hours before serving, slice nectarines into thin wedge-shaped slices. Cover top of cake with 3 crosswise rows of nectarine slices. Heat apricot preserves in a small saucepan over low heat until hot but not boiling. Strain into a small bowl, pressing on pieces. Stir in brandy. Brush glaze gently on nectarines without dripping it on frosting. Refrigerate 10 minutes, or up to 4 hours before serving.

✿ LEMON HAZELNUT CAKE
Gâteau au citron et aux noisettes

An intensely flavored, almost flourless, hazelnut sponge cake is paired here with a refreshing lemon buttercream. Nut cakes of this type can play a variety of roles—as dessert after a special dinner, as the highlight of the sweet table at a buffet, as a festive partner for a cup of coffee, or as a delightful change-of-pace birthday cake.

MAKES 8 TO 10 SERVINGS

1 1/2 cups hazelnuts (about 6 1/2 ounces)
3/4 cup plus 3 tablespoons sugar
3 tablespoons plus 2 teaspoons all-purpose flour, sifted
5 large eggs, separated, room temperature
1 teaspoon finely grated lemon zest (optional)
1/4 teaspoon cream of tartar
3 tablespoons unsalted butter, melted and cooled
Lemon Buttercream (page 359)
8 to 10 hazelnuts for garnish

Position rack in center of oven and preheat to 350°F. Toast and skin hazelnuts (see page 388). Cool completely.

Butter two 9-inch round cake pans, 1 1/2 to 2 inches deep. Line bases of pans with parchment paper or foil and butter paper or foil. Flour pans, shaking out excess. In a food processor, grind nuts with 1/4 cup sugar to a fine powder. Transfer to a bowl and mix thoroughly with flour.

Beat egg yolks with 1/2 cup sugar in large bowl of mixer about 5 minutes, or until pale yellow and thick enough to form a ribbon when beaters are lifted. Beat in lemon zest. Beat egg whites with cream of tartar in another large bowl until stiff. Gradually add remaining 3 tablespoons sugar and continue beating at high speed until whites are very stiff and shiny but not dry, about 30 seconds. Sprinkle one-third of hazelnut mixture over yolks and fold gently. Spoon one-third of whites on top and fold gently. Repeat until hazelnut mixture and whites are folded in. Before mixture is completely smooth, drizzle melted butter over it and gently fold in. Continue folding just until blended and no white streaks remain.

Pour batter into prepared pans and quickly spread as evenly as possible. Bake until cake tester inserted in center of cakes comes out clean, about 17 minutes. Run a thin-bladed flexible knife around sides of each cake. Turn out onto racks and let cool.

Prepare buttercream. Spread about one-third of buttercream on one cake layer. Set other layer on top. Spread sides and top of cake with more buttercream and smooth with a long metal spatula. If desired, swirl buttercream on top. Spoon remaining buttercream into pastry bag fitted with medium star tip. Pipe row of small rosettes of buttercream at top edge of cake and a larger rosette in center. Top a few of the rosettes with hazelnuts and put 1 in center. Refrigerate 2 hours before serving. (Cake can be kept, covered, 2 days in refrigerator.) Serve at cool room temperature.

Mousse Cakes

On my latest visits to France, whenever I discussed the important developments in modern dessert making with leading chefs and cooking-school directors in Paris, mousse cakes immediately came up in the conversation. It is only in the last few years that these desserts of cake layers and mousse filling have appeared as a whole new category of cakes.

These luscious French desserts have become favorites at the finest restaurants and pastry shops throughout France, and, indeed, in good French restaurants all over the world. At certain innovative pâtisseries, mousse cakes have, to a considerable extent, displaced cakes made with buttercream. I first learned about mousse cakes when a talented young chef, Denis Ruffel, introduced them to the students at La Varenne Cooking School in Paris. He layered almond meringues with chestnut mousse for one cake, and génoise with a refreshing orange mousse for another. The results were absolutely delicious. I was very pleased to later have a chance to work in the kitchen of his pastry shop, Millet, and to learn to make many more mousse cakes, which were the inspiration for several desserts in this chapter.

A few months ago I went to France to do further research for this book. Mousse cakes seemed to be everywhere. My husband and I revisited our friend Denis Ruffel and savored a sublime gâteau at Millet that was filled with a mousse of exotic fruit. At the famous Parisian pastry shop, Fauchon, we tasted a pistachio cake with almond mousse and a delicious chocolate gâteau topped with a mint mousse.

Fillings for mousse cakes are lighter and more creamy than those for traditional cakes because most of them are based on cream instead of butter or are lightened by meringue. Some fillings are mousses, while others are actually Bavarian creams or a related mixture called *crème diplomate,* which is known by several names and appears here in Papaya-Vanilla Cake and in Nouvelle Chocolate Yule Log. These are not only delicious, but many are also easier to make than traditional buttercream.

The cake component of these desserts is in thin layers, and the favorites are the lighter cakes: génoise, sponge cake, and meringues. Because these fillings are lighter, there is usually a higher proportion of filling to cake than in a buttercream-filled cake. And since mousse fillings are usually soft, they are not usually spread on the cake like buttercream. Rather, they are spooned over the cake in a mold, allowed to set, and then unmolded. At home it's easy to make these desserts in a springform pan. Pastry chefs use a deep ring that doesn't have a spring, and so they usually unmold their desserts by briefly heating the ring with a small blowtorch.

These spectacular desserts are perfect for entertaining. They are practical because most can be made ahead and kept in the freezer. In fact, dessert chefs in France take advantage of the freezer, both for chilling the mousse cakes quickly and for keeping them.

Hints

• If the sides of a mousse cake are not smooth enough after unmolding, the mousse can be carefully smoothed with a spatula. If necessary, warm the spatula slightly by rinsing it in hot water, then drying it.

• Mousse cakes that do not contain fruit can be frozen.

• Any mousse or Bavarian cream that is firm enough to be unmolded (see chapter on "Cold Desserts") can be the filling of a mousse cake. To make a very easy mousse cake, instead of alternating the mousse and cake layers, the mousse can be spooned onto a single cake layer inside a springform pan.

NOUVELLE CHOCOLATE YULE LOG
Bûche de noël nouvelle

This splendid new rendition of the French yule log is my favorite. I used a creamier, lighter-textured chocolate filling than the classic buttercream, and a version of génoise that is flexible and easier to roll than the traditional génoise. MAKES 12 SERVINGS

CHOCOLATE CRÈME DIPLOMATE

1 envelope unflavored gelatin (¼ ounce)
¼ cup water
8 ounces semisweet chocolate, chopped

2 cups milk
5 large egg yolks
⅔ cup sugar
¼ cup cornstarch
1 cup heavy cream, well chilled

RICH GÉNOISE

¼ cup all-purpose flour
¼ cup cornstarch
4 large eggs plus 3 large yolks

7 tablespoons sugar
1 teaspoon vanilla

GARNISHES

¼ cup heavy cream, well chilled
Cocoa for sprinkling (optional)

Chocolate coffee beans or grated chocolate (optional)

CHOCOLATE CRÈME DIPLOMATE

Sprinkle gelatin over water and let stand 5 minutes. Melt chocolate in a medium bowl above hot water over low heat. Stir until smooth. Remove from pan of water.

In a medium, heavy saucepan, bring milk to a boil. Whisk yolks and sugar in a bowl until smooth. Gently stir in cornstarch with a whisk. Gradually add hot milk to yolk mixture, whisking quickly. Transfer mixture to saucepan and whisk well. Cook over medium-low heat, whisking constantly, until mixture comes just to a boil; it will be very thick. Continue cooking over low heat, whisking constantly, for 1 minute. Do not cook too long or the yolks will curdle. Remove from heat. Whisk in softened gelatin. Transfer to a bowl. Whisk in melted chocolate. Cool to room temperature, stirring often to prevent a skin from forming.

Whip cream in a chilled bowl with chilled beater until stiff. Gently fold about one-quarter of whipped cream into pastry cream. Return this mixture to bowl of whipped cream and fold gently until blended. Refrigerate while making cake.

RICH GÉNOISE

Position rack in center of oven and preheat to 400°F. Lightly butter corners of a 17-×-11-inch rimmed baking sheet. Line with foil or parchment paper. Butter foil or paper. Sift together flour and cornstarch into a small bowl.

Beat eggs and yolks lightly in large bowl. Beat in sugar and whip mixture at high speed about 5 minutes, or until very thick. Beat in vanilla. Sift one-third of flour mixture over batter and fold in as gently as possible. Repeat with remaining flour in 2 batches.

Spread batter evenly but lightly on prepared baking sheet. Bake about 6 minutes, or until cake is just firm, slightly springy to touch, and beginning to brown lightly.

Transfer cake with its paper to a rack. Pull foil from sides of cake. Cool to room temperature. Fill cake as soon as possible, so it will not be dry.

Spread 2 cups chocolate filling over cake. Beginning with a long side, roll up cake carefully, releasing paper. Use paper to help roll cake. At end, use edge of paper to roll cake toward you. Cover and refrigerate 30 minutes. Cut off a slice from each end of cake and set it askew on cake (like bumps on a log). Frost cake generously with remaining chocolate cream. (Cake can be kept up to 1 day in refrigerator.)

GARNISHES

Decorate cake by making lengthwise lines in frosting with a fork, if desired. Whip cream in a chilled bowl with chilled beater until stiff. Using a pastry bag and medium-sized plain tip, pipe a little whipped cream onto cake in the shape of 3 or 4 mushrooms, first piping long stems, then rounded caps. Sprinkle cocoa on mushroom caps. *Or,* use a star tip and pipe a ruffle of whipped cream lengthwise on center of cake; set a few chocolate coffee beans on top of ruffle, or garnish it with grated chocolate. Serve cold or at a cool room temperature.

PAPAYA-VANILLA CAKE
Gâteau aux papayes à la crème vanille

The luscious vanilla cream filling for this gâteau is based on a new filling that I learned at Lenôtre's school for pastry chefs near Paris, where the chef used the filling between layers of chocolate génoise. The filling is made of vanilla bean pastry cream enriched with whipped cream and held together with a touch of gelatin. Here it is a perfect partner for the slices of ripe papaya and golden génoise cake. Other fruit, such as slices of mango or of poached peaches or pears, would also be delicious in this modern dessert.

MAKES 8 SERVINGS

Génoise (page 377)

VANILLA SYRUP
¹/₄ cup sugar
¹/₄ cup water

1 teaspoon pure vanilla extract

VANILLA CRÈME DIPLOMATE
2 cups milk
1 vanilla bean
1 envelope unflavored gelatin (¹/₄ ounce)
¹/₄ cup water

5 large egg yolks
²/₃ cup sugar
¹/₄ cup cornstarch
2 cups heavy cream, well chilled
1 teaspoon pure vanilla extract

1 ripe papaya (about 1 pound)

Bake génoise in a 9-inch pan and cool completely on a rack.

VANILLA SYRUP

In small saucepan, dissolve sugar in water over low heat, stirring. Bring to a boil. Pour into a small bowl and cool completely. Stir in vanilla extract and set aside.

VANILLA CRÈME DIPLOMATE

In a medium, heavy saucepan, scald milk with vanilla bean. Cover and let stand 30 minutes. Remove bean. Sprinkle gelatin over water and let stand 5 minutes.

Return milk to a boil. Whisk egg yolks and sugar in a bowl until smooth. Gently stir in cornstarch with a whisk. Gradually add hot milk, whisking quickly. Transfer mixture to saucepan and whisk well. Cook over medium-low heat, whisking constantly, until mixture comes just to a boil. Continue cooking over low heat, whisking constantly, for 1 minute. Remove from heat. Whisk in softened gelatin and transfer to a bowl. Cool to room temperature, stirring often to prevent a skin from forming.

Whip cream with vanilla extract in a chilled bowl until stiff. Gently fold cream, in 4 batches, into thick custard mixture.

Peel papaya and cut in thin slices lengthwise, about ¼ inch thick. Reserve most attractive slices for top.

Split cake in 2 layers with a long serrated knife. Lightly oil sides of a 9-inch springform pan, 3 inches deep. Put bottom cake layer in pan, spongy side up. Brush top with syrup to moisten. Spoon 3 cups vanilla cream over cake. Push cream between sides of cake and mold with spatula. Top cream with about half the papaya slices, pressing them into cream.

Brush spongy side of second cake layer with syrup. Turn over and set in pan, crust side up. Add enough of remaining vanilla cream to come to top of pan. Again push cream between sides of cake and mold with spatula. Garnish with attractive papaya slices. Refrigerate 4 hours, or until set. Refrigerate any extra cream. (Cake can be kept, covered, 2 days in refrigerator.)

To serve, run a thin bladed flexible knife around edges of cake. Release spring and remove sides of pan. Spread extra cream on sides to smooth them, if necessary. Serve cold or at a cool room temperature.

🌿 MACADAMIA MOUSSE CAKE
Gâteau à la mousse de noix de macadam

The delicate flavor of macadamia nuts makes them ideal for today's modern, light-textured French mousse cakes. I developed this new dessert of macadamia meringue and macadamia praline mousse for my article on this richest of nuts for *Gourmet* magazine. Although there are several steps, much of the preparation can be done ahead. The garnish is simply a few whole caramelized nuts reserved during the making of the praline.   MAKES 10 SERVINGS

MACADAMIA MERINGUE
1 cup (about 4 1/2 ounces) raw or unsalted dry-roasted macadamia nuts (see Note)
2/3 cup sugar

3 tablespoons all-purpose flour
5 large egg whites, room temperature
1/4 teaspoon cream of tartar

MACADAMIA PRALINE MOUSSE
Macadamia Nut Praline (page 374)
1 envelope unflavored gelatin (1/4 ounce)
1/4 cup water
1 1/4 cups milk

5 large egg yolks
6 tablespoons sugar
1 cup heavy cream, well chilled
2 large egg whites, room temperature

MACADAMIA MERINGUE
Preheat oven to 225°F.

Lightly butter corners of 2 baking sheets; line them with foil, shiny side down; and butter and flour foil. Using a 9-inch springform pan rim as a guide, trace a circle onto each baking sheet, drawing it inside rim. In a food processor, grind nuts with 6 tablespoons sugar until fine, stopping often to scrape inward. Transfer nut mixture to a bowl, sift flour over mixture, and stir lightly with a fork.

In a large bowl of an electric mixer, beat egg whites at moderate speed until they are frothy, add cream of tartar, and beat whites until they hold soft peaks. Gradually beat in remaining sugar at high speed, and beat whites until they hold stiff peaks. Fold in nut mixture gently but thoroughly.

Immediately transfer mixture to a pastry bag fitted with a ½-inch plain tip. Beginning at center of a marked circle, pipe meringue onto baking sheet in a tight spiral, until circle is completely covered. Repeat with second circle. Pipe remaining meringue in mounds about 1 inch high and 1½ inches wide.

Bake meringues in middle of preheated oven for 1½ hours, or until they are firm, dry, and light beige in color. Gently release meringues from foil with a large metal spatula. Carefully peel off any remaining foil, if necessary. Transfer meringues to a rack and let them cool completely. (Meringues can be kept 5 days in an airtight container in dry weather. Save small meringue mounds for another recipe or as an accompaniment for ice cream.)

MACADAMIA PRALINE MOUSSE

Make praline but do not grind it. While it is still hot, use a fork to quickly separate 6 attractive caramel-coated nuts from rest of the mass for garnish, so they do not touch rest of praline. Let praline cool completely.

To store nuts reserved for garnish, place a paper towel in an airtight container and put a piece of wax paper over it. Arrange nuts on wax paper, keeping them separate, and close container.

Break praline into small chunks and grind it fine in a food processor, scraping mixture down occasionally.

In a small cup, sprinkle gelatin over water and let stand about 5 minutes. In a medium, heavy saucepan bring milk to a boil. In a large bowl, whisk yolks lightly, add 5 tablespoons sugar, and whisk until thick and smooth. Add milk in a stream, whisking. Return the custard to a saucepan and cook it over medium-low heat, stirring constantly with a wooden spoon, for about 4 minutes, or until it reaches 165°F. on a thermometer or is thick enough to coat the back of a spoon. Do not boil or overcook custard or it will curdle. Remove from heat and immediately add softened gelatin, whisking until it is completely dissolved. Transfer custard to a large bowl, set bowl in a larger bowl of ice, and let custard stand, stirring very often, about 10 minutes, or until it is cool and thick; do not let it set.

In a chilled bowl with chilled beater, beat cream until it holds soft peaks. In a small bowl, beat egg whites until they hold soft peaks, then beat in remaining tablespoon sugar and beat until stiff. Fold cream, then egg whites, into custard gently but thoroughly. Fold in praline.

If necessary, carefully trim meringue circles with a sharp knife so they fit into the 9-inch springform pan with about ¼ inch of space between edge of each meringue and rim of pan. Set 1 meringue circle in pan. Spoon 3 cups mousse into pan. Spread it gently to edges of pan. Set remaining meringue gently on top so that it does not touch sides of pan, and spoon remaining mousse over it. Cover and chill dessert at least 6 hours before serving. (Dessert can be kept, covered, 1 day in refrigerator.)

To serve, run a metal spatula slowly around edges of dessert, moving it carefully up and down. Release springform rim and lift it up carefully. Decorate top of dessert with reserved whole caramelized macadamia nuts. Serve cold or at a cool room temperature.

NOTE: Unsalted macadamia nuts are easiest to use, but if only salted nuts are available, they can be desalted (see page 389) and used in the recipe.

CHOCOLATE MOUSSE CAKE WITH CANDIED GINGER
Gâteau à la mousse au chocolat et au gingembre

Chef Albert Jorant, the pastry chef of La Varenne Cooking School, taught me that chocolate mousse used as a cake filling should be richer in butter than mousse served on its own, so that it will be easy to spread. For this dessert the rich chocolate mousse fills a light cocoa génoise cake and gains zip from diced crystallized ginger. A lavish decoration of rosettes of Chantilly cream completes the exquisite picture.   MAKES 8 SERVINGS

Cocoa Génoise (page 378)
Vanilla Syrup (page 215),
    (optional)

CHOCOLATE MOUSSE AND GINGER FILLING
6 1/2 ounces semisweet or bittersweet   *4 large eggs, separated*
    chocolate, chopped   *4 teaspoons sugar*
1/2 cup unsalted butter, cut in   *2 tablespoons finely diced*
    pieces, room temperature   *crystallized ginger*

CHANTILLY CREAM AND GARNISH
3/4 cup heavy cream, well chilled   *1 tablespoon finely diced crystallized*
1 1/2 teaspoons sugar   *ginger*
1/2 teaspoon pure vanilla extract

Bake génoise and cool completely. Make vanilla syrup, if desired, and let cool.

CHOCOLATE MOUSSE AND GINGER FILLING
Melt chocolate in a medium saucepan set in a pan of hot water over low heat and stir until smooth. Add butter, stir quickly, and remove the pan of chocolate from pan of water. Stir until butter is combined. Add egg yolks, 1 at a time, stirring vigorously after each addition. Beat egg whites until stiff. Beat in sugar and continue beat-

ing about 30 seconds, or until whites are very shiny. Quickly fold one-quarter of whites into chocolate mixture. Gently fold in the remaining whites.

Using a long serrated knife, split cake horizontally into 2 layers. If using vanilla syrup, brush it on cut sides of both cake layers. Spread about half the mousse on bottom layer. Sprinkle evenly with 2 tablespoons diced ginger. Set other layer on top. Spread remaining mousse on sides, and if any is left, spread it on top (it will be covered with cream); work quickly because mousse sets rapidly. Chill thoroughly about 1 hour, or until mousse sets.

CHANTILLY CREAM AND GARNISH

Beat cream with sugar and vanilla in chilled bowl with chilled beater until stiff. Spoon cream into a pastry bag fitted with medium star tip. Beginning with center, cover top of cake with rosettes of Chantilly cream. Sprinkle top of cake with diced crystallized ginger. If any cream remains, pipe a row of rosettes at lower edge of cake. (Cake can be frosted 8 hours ahead and kept, uncovered, in refrigerator.) Serve cold.

🌿 STRAWBERRY MIRROR
Miroir aux fraises

This professional-looking gâteau, which resembles those in the best French pastry shops, is named for its shiny strawberry topping. Underneath are layers of light almond cake and strawberry mousse filling. For maximum strawberry flavor, the custard base for the mousse is made with strawberry purée instead of milk and is enriched with strawberry whipped cream. This is a large dessert, perfect for a party, but "mirrors" are also prepared as individual cakes. At the graduation reception of the new École de Gastronomie Ritz-Escoffier in Paris, which I attended recently, the students used the mirror idea in a creative way—they prepared a square raspberry mirror cake and cut it into lovely petits fours.   MAKES 10 TO 12 SERVINGS

Delicate Almond Cake batter (page 169)

1 1/2 pounds strawberries, hulled

STRAWBERRY SYRUP
1/4 cup sugar
1/4 cup water
1 tablespoon strawberry brandy or liqueur or kirsch

1/4 cup strawberry purée (from berries above)

STRAWBERRY MOUSSE
1 envelope (1/4 ounce) plus 1 teaspoon gelatin
1/2 cup water
1 1/2 cups strawberry purée (from berries above)
5 large egg yolks

3/4 cup sugar
1 tablespoon strawberry brandy or liqueur or kirsch
2 large egg whites
1 cup heavy cream, well chilled

STRAWBERRY GLAZE
1 tablespoon water
1 teaspoon gelatin
1/4 cup strawberry purée (from berries above)

2 1/2 tablespoons sugar
1 teaspoon strawberry brandy or liqueur or kirsch

Butter and flour a 10-inch springform pan. Preheat oven to 350°F. Prepare batter for almond cake. Bake in prepared pan about 25 minutes, or until a cake tester inserted in cake comes out dry. Carefully run a knife around cake, release spring, and allow cake to cool on a rack.

Purée all the strawberries in a food processor or blender until very smooth. Reserve purée.

STRAWBERRY SYRUP

In small saucepan, dissolve sugar in water over low heat, stirring. Bring to a boil, remove from heat, pour into bowl, and cool completely. Stir in brandy and ¼ cup strawberry purée.

STRAWBERRY MOUSSE

Sprinkle gelatin over ¼ cup water and let stand about 5 minutes to soften.

Heat 1¼ cups strawberry purée until hot but not boiling. Whisk egg yolks with ¼ cup sugar in a large bowl. Gradually pour hot strawberry purée into mixture, whisking constantly.

Return to saucepan and heat over low heat, stirring constantly with a wooden spoon, until mixture is thick enough to coat back of a spoon. Do not boil or overcook custard or it will curdle. Immediately remove from heat and add softened gelatin. Stir quickly to dissolve gelatin in mixture. Pour mixture into a bowl and cool to room temperature, stirring occasionally. Stir in brandy.

In a small heavy saucepan, heat remaining ½ cup sugar and ¼ cup water over low heat, stirring, until sugar dissolves. Bring to a boil over medium-high heat and boil 3 minutes. Watch mixture; it tends to boil over.

Whip egg whites until stiff. Meanwhile, continue boiling syrup to soft-ball stage. To test, remove from heat, take a little of hot syrup on a teaspoon and dip spoon into a cup of ice water, keeping spoon level. With your hands in ice water, remove syrup from teaspoon; if syrup is ready, it will form a soft ball. *Caution: Do not touch syrup unless your hands are in the water, because it is extremely hot.* Remove syrup immediately from heat.

Gradually pour hot syrup into egg whites while beating. Beat at high speed until whites are cool and shiny.

Whip cream in a chilled bowl with chilled beater until fairly stiff.

Add ¼ cup strawberry purée and whip just until blended. Fold meringue mixture into whipped cream, then fold this into strawberry custard.

Clean springform pan. Cut crust off sides of cake. With a long serrated knife, cut cake into 2 layers. Set bottom layer in springform pan and close sides of pan around it. Brush layer with half the strawberry syrup.

Set aside 1 cup mousse. Spoon remaining mousse over cake.

Brush remaining strawberry syrup on cut side of top half of cake. Flip it over and set in pan with crust side up. Spread remaining 1 cup mousse over cake in an even layer. Freeze cake 3 hours, or refrigerate 8 hours or until set. (Cake can be kept 1 day in refrigerator.) If using a stainless-steel pan, cake can be kept 1 week in freezer. If pan is not of stainless steel but you wish to make cake ahead, remove sides of pan when cake is set and return cake to freezer. Before glazing cake, carefully put springform ring back in place.

STRAWBERRY GLAZE

Prepare glaze on day cake will be served. Sprinkle gelatin over water in a small bowl and let stand 5 minutes.

In another small saucepan, combine ¼ cup strawberry purée with sugar and bring almost to a boil, stirring gently. Remove from heat.

Set bowl of gelatin in a pan of hot water over low heat and stir until melted. Stir gelatin into strawberry mixture and mix very well. Strain into a bowl and cool completely but do not let glaze set. Stir in brandy. Pour glaze over cake and gently spread it, if necessary, in an even layer. Refrigerate a few minutes, or until glaze sets. To serve, carefully run a knife around cake and remove springform ring. Serve cake cold.

MOCHA MOUSSE CAKE
Gâteau à la mousse au café et au chocolat

The French often name their desserts for the key ingredient's place of origin. Mocha is the name of a port city in Yemen from which much coffee was exported to France at one time and is the name of some fine French coffee desserts. I have followed this custom in naming my new dessert of delicately crisp nut meringues layered with a soft, creamy mousse. The mousse is actually a coffee-bean and chocolate Bavarian cream lightened with whipped egg whites. Chocolate coffee beans and whipped cream provide the simple but lovely decoration. MAKES 10 TO 12 SERVINGS

Cocoa-Pecan Dacquoise (page 382)

MOCHA MOUSSE

3/4 cup coffee beans, preferably
  Mocha Java or French Roast
  (about 2 1/4 ounces)
About 2 cups milk
3 ounces semisweet chocolate,
  chopped
1 envelope (1/4 ounce) plus 1
  teaspoon unflavored gelatin

5 tablespoons water
5 large egg yolks, room temperature
7 tablespoons sugar
1 1/4 cups heavy cream, well chilled
2 egg whites, room temperature
1/3 cup heavy cream, well chilled
10 to 12 small chocolate coffee
  beans

Bake dacquoise layers and let cool.

MOCHA MOUSSE

Place coffee beans in a plastic bag and coarsely crush them with a rolling pin. Scald 1 1/2 cups milk with coffee beans in a medium, heavy saucepan. Cover and let stand 30 minutes. Strain milk through cheesecloth, squeezing hard so as much milk as possible comes through. Measure strained milk and add enough milk to make 1 1/4 cups.

Melt chocolate in a medium bowl above hot water over low heat. Turn off heat but leave chocolate above water. Sprinkle gelatin over 5 tablespoons water in a small cup and let stand while preparing custard.

Bring milk to a boil in a medium, heavy saucepan.

Whisk egg yolks lightly in a large heatproof bowl. Add 6 tablespoons sugar and whisk until thick and smooth. Gradually whisk in hot milk. Return mixture to saucepan, whisking. Cook over medium-low heat, stirring mixture and scraping bottom of pan constantly with a wooden spoon, until mixture thickens slightly and reaches 165°F. to

170°F. on an instant-read thermometer; begin checking after 4 minutes. (To check whether it is thick enough without a thermometer, remove sauce from heat, dip a metal spoon in sauce, and draw your finger across back of spoon—your finger should leave a clear trail in mixture that clings to spoon. If it does not, continue cooking another 30 seconds and check again.) Do not overcook mixture or it will curdle.

Remove from heat and immediately add softened gelatin, whisking until it is completely dissolved. Pour mixture into a large bowl and stir about 30 seconds to cool.

Remove chocolate from pan of water and stir until smooth. Using a whisk, gradually whisk chocolate into custard mixture. Refrigerate mixture about 20 minutes, stirring often, or chill mixture by setting bowl in a larger bowl of iced water about 10 minutes, stirring very often, or until mixture is cold and beginning to thicken but is not set.

Whip cream in a large chilled bowl with chilled beater until nearly stiff. (Refrigerate cream if custard mixture is not yet ready.)

Whip egg whites in a small bowl to soft peaks. Beat in remaining 1 tablespoon sugar and beat whites until stiff but not dry. Fold cream into custard mixture gently but thoroughly. Fold in egg whites.

Set 1 dacquoise circle in a round 9-inch springform pan. Spoon 2¾ cups mousse into pan and spread it gently to edges of pan. Set remaining dacquoise circle gently on top and spoon remaining mousse over it. Cover and refrigerate dessert at least 6 hours before serving. (Cake can be kept up to 3 days in refrigerator.)

When ready to serve, run a metal spatula slowly around edges of dessert, moving it carefully up and down. Release springform rim and lift it up carefully. Return dessert to refrigerator.

Whip cream in a small chilled bowl with chilled beater until stiff. Using a pastry bag and medium star tip, pipe 10 to 12 rosettes of cream on dessert to garnish. Set chocolate coffee beans on rosettes.

🌿 CHOCOLATE-CHESTNUT MOUSSE CAKE
Gâteau à la mousse au chocolat aux marrons

The classic pairing of chocolate and chestnuts is used here in a spectacular contemporary presentation. This lovely creation is composed of a flourless chocolate-chestnut-almond cake layered with a luscious chocolate-chestnut mousse.　　　MAKES 12 SERVINGS

CHOCOLATE-CHESTNUT CAKE

3 ounces bittersweet or semisweet chocolate, coarsely chopped
2 tablespoons unsalted butter
1 cup whole blanched almonds (about 5 ounces)
6 tablespoons sugar

2 teaspoons unsweetened cocoa powder
4 large eggs, separated, room temperature
One 8¾-ounce can sweetened chestnut purée (¾ cup) (see Note)

CHOCOLATE-CHESTNUT MOUSSE

4 ounces bittersweet or semisweet chocolate, coarsely chopped
7 tablespoons unsalted butter, cut in 7 pieces, room temperature

4 large eggs, separated, room temperature
One 8¾-ounce can sweetened chestnut purée (¾ cup) (see Note)

CHANTILLY CREAM

½ cup heavy cream, well chilled
1 teaspoon sugar

¼ teaspoon pure vanilla extract

CHOCOLATE-CHESTNUT CAKE

Preheat oven to 350°F. Generously butter two 9-inch springform pans. Line the base of each with parchment paper or foil; generously butter paper or foil.

Melt chocolate and butter in small heatproof bowl above hot water over low heat, stirring until smooth. Remove from pan of water and cool.

Grind almonds with 2 tablespoons sugar in a food processor until as fine as possible, scraping inward occasionally. Transfer to a medium bowl. Sift cocoa onto almond mixture and mix well.

Beat egg yolks in a large bowl with 2 tablespoons sugar until blended. Add chestnut purée and beat at high speed about 3 minutes, or until mixture is pale and very thick. Beat in chocolate mixture. Gently stir in almond mixture.

Whip egg whites in a large bowl until soft peaks form. Gradually beat in remaining 2 tablespoons sugar at high speed and beat until whites are stiff and shiny but not dry. Fold about one-third of whites into chocolate mixture. Spoon this mixture over remaining whites and fold lightly but quickly, just until batter is blended.

Immediately pour batter into prepared pans, dividing it as equally as possible. Spread evenly and bake about 25 minutes, or until cake begins to pull away from sides of pans and a cake tester inserted in centers of cakes comes out clean. Cool cakes completely in pans on rack.

Run knife around sides of cakes and remove sides of springform pans. Invert each cake onto a rack so that base of springform faces up. Very carefully remove base of each pan by sliding a metal spatula between base and paper. Carefully remove paper from cake. Cake is fragile and breaks if not handled with care; but even if it breaks, it will not be seen once mousse sets.

CHOCOLATE-CHESTNUT MOUSSE

Melt chocolate in medium bowl above hot water over low heat, stirring until smooth. Stir in butter all at once until blended. Remove from pan of water. Cool slightly.

Beat egg yolks in a large bowl until blended. Add chestnut purée and beat about 3 minutes, or until thick and light. Beat in chocolate mixture in 4 batches.

Beat egg whites until stiff but not dry. Fold about one-third of whites into chocolate mixture. Spoon this mixture over remaining whites and fold lightly but quickly, just until mixture is well blended.

Set 1 cake layer on base of springform pan. Using a thin sharp knife, carefully cut off 1/4 inch from edge of cake all around; work carefully because cake tends to crumble. Repeat with second layer and base of other pan. Brush off any crumbs.

Close springform side around 1 springform base, leaving cake on it. Spoon 2 1/2 cups mousse over cake layer in pan and spread gently with a rubber spatula so mousse flows into space between edges of cake and sides of pan. Freeze mousse-coated cake layer 10 minutes, leaving remaining mousse and cake at room temperature.

Carefully slide metal spatula under second cake layer to free it. Slide cake carefully on top of mousse in pan, with aid of springform base. If cake breaks, push it inward with rubber spatula so it does not touch sides of pan. Spoon remaining mousse over cake and spread gently with a rubber spatula so mousse flows into space between edges of cake and sides of pan. Shake pan gently so mousse is evenly distributed. Refrigerate at least 6 hours. (Cake can be kept, covered, 3 days in refrigerator.)

To unmold, run a hot dry knife around dessert, release spring, and carefully remove sides of pan. Heat a metal spatula by running hot water over it and drying it. Use hot spatula to gently smooth mousse on sides of cake. Refrigerate cake.

CHANTILLY CREAM
Whip cream with sugar and vanilla in chilled bowl with chilled beater until very stiff. Using a pastry bag and large star tip, pipe a ruffle of whipped cream at top edge of cake. Serve cold.

NOTE: Sweetened chestnut purée is often labeled "chestnut spread" or *"crème de marrons."*

Meringue Cakes

Airy, crunchy meringue layers are the base for many elegant contemporary desserts. Their lightness makes them a perfect match for luscious buttercreams, ganache fillings, Bavarian creams, mousses, and ice creams. By alternating the meringues with the rich fillings, cooks create a great variety of wonderful desserts, from simple ice cream cakes to elaborate gâteaux. Similarly, small meringues, especially those flavored with nuts, can be sandwiched with these fillings to make delightful individual cakes; they are even good on their own as delicate cookies. Meringue can be piped into splendid baskets called *vacherins,* either as large centerpieces (see pages 151–152), or small cases, as in Individual Black Forest Vacherins.

Visitors to pastry shops in France will find meringue cakes with many exotic-sounding names—*succès, progrès, japonais, dacquoise, broyage suisse.* All these exquisite cakes are actually variations of the same basic batter of ground nuts and sugar lightly folded into whipped egg whites. Classic versions make use of almonds, hazelnuts, or a combination of both, but I made meringues with pecans, pistachios, walnuts, and macadamia nuts and found them equally delicious. Because the nuts provide the dominant flavor and the mixture contains much less sugar than plain meringue, nut meringues are less sweet. Cocoa is also a good flavoring for meringue and balances its sweetness.

Meringue batter takes only a few minutes to prepare. With the aid of a pastry bag, it can be quickly and easily formed in many shapes. Circles are most common, but squares, rectangles, hearts, or other shapes can be traced onto a baking sheet and the meringue is then piped to fill them. The pastry bag also helps to give the cakes an even thickness.

Meringues keep well in airtight containers in dry weather or in the freezer. By having some baked meringues on hand, it is very easy to come up with a lovely dessert in no time by simply pairing them with ice cream or with whipped cream and fruit.

Hints

• For better control when piping meringue, hold the pastry bag so that its tip is about 1 inch above the baking sheet.

• When piping meringue, do not allow the mixture to touch the sides of the baking sheet.

• If you are not used to piping meringue in neat spirals, do not worry; any holes can be filled by piping a dot of mixture, and extra mixture can be piped along the edge if the circle is uneven. In addition, any uneven parts can be trimmed after baking.

• The color of baked nut meringues varies somewhat, depending on the color of the nuts. Macadamia nuts and blanched almonds give the lightest-colored meringues, while toasted nuts produce a darker brown meringue.

• When baked meringues are completely cool, put them in airtight containers immediately; do not leave them out, or they will absorb moisture from the air and become sticky.

• Always handle baked meringues carefully because they are fragile. But even if large ones break, the breaks will not be seen when layered with ice cream, buttercream, or other fillings. In addition, the finished cake is usually sprinkled with powdered sugar, which also covers imperfections.

ISLAND MERINGUE LAYER CAKE
Gâteau meringué des îles

In this new gâteau, I incorporated ingredients from Pacific islands. I composed layers of crunchy coconut-macadamia-cocoa meringue and developed a rich macadamia mousseline filling. To complete the theme, I like to serve this cake with slices of kiwi and fresh pineapple.   MAKES 8 SERVINGS

COCONUT-MACADAMIA-COCOA MERINGUE

*3 tablespoons unsweetened
    Dutch-process cocoa powder*
3 tablespoons powdered sugar
2 tablespoons all-purpose flour
*3/4 cup (about 3 1/4 ounces)
    unsalted macadamia nuts (see
    Note)*

2/3 cup granulated sugar
1/4 cup flaked coconut
*5 large egg whites, room
    temperature*
1/4 teaspoon cream of tartar

MACADAMIA MOUSSELINE CREAM

*1/2 cup (about 2 1/4 ounces)
    unsalted macadamia nuts (see
    Note)*
3/4 cup unsalted butter
1 cup milk

1/2 cup heavy cream, well chilled
4 large egg yolks, room temperature
7 tablespoons granulated sugar
3 tablespoons cornstarch
2 tablespoons hazelnut liqueur

*Quick Chocolate Curls (page 389)
    or grated chocolate for garnish*

COCONUT-MACADAMIA-COCOA MERINGUE

Position rack in center of oven and preheat to 250°F. Lightly butter corners of 2 baking sheets and line them with parchment paper or foil. Butter and lightly flour foil, tapping baking sheet to remove excess. Using an 8-inch springform pan rim as a guide, trace a circle onto each baking sheet, drawing it inside the rim. Have ready a rubber spatula for folding and a pastry bag fitted with a ½-inch plain tip.

Sift together cocoa, powdered sugar, and flour into a small bowl. Grind nuts with 6 tablespoons sugar in a food processor until as fine as possible, scraping inward occasionally. Transfer to a medium bowl. Add coconut and stir mixture lightly with a fork.

Whip egg whites with cream of tartar in a large dry bowl with a dry beater at medium speed until soft peaks form. Switch speed to high and gradually beat in remaining sugar at high speed, beating until whites are stiff and shiny. Gently fold in cocoa mixture in 2 batches as quickly as possible until thoroughly blended. Gently fold in nut mixture in 2 batches.

Immediately spoon mixture into pastry bag. Beginning at center of 1 circle marked on a baking sheet, pipe meringue in a tight spiral until circle is completely covered. Repeat with second circle. Pipe any remaining meringue in mounds about 1 inch high and 1½ inches in diameter.

Bake meringues in center of oven about 1½ hours, or until dry and firm to touch. (If baking them on 2 racks in oven, switch their positions halfway through baking time.)

Gently release layers from foil with a large metal spatula. Gently peel off any remaining foil, if necessary. Transfer to a rack and cool completely. (Meringues can be kept in an airtight container up to 5 days in dry weather. Save small meringue mounds for another recipe or as an accompaniment for ice cream.)

MACADAMIA MOUSSELINE CREAM

Preheat oven to 225°F. Toast macadamia nuts in a shallow baking pan in oven 3 to 5 minutes, or until light brown.

Cut half the butter into pieces and keep at room temperature. Refrigerate remaining butter. Bring milk and cream to a boil in a medium, heavy saucepan.

Whisk egg yolks lightly in a medium bowl. Add sugar and whisk until blended. Whisk in cornstarch. Gradually whisk in hot milk mixture. Return mixture to saucepan, whisking. Cook over medium heat, whisking constantly, until mixture comes just to a boil. Remove from heat. Add butter pieces and whisk to blend. Transfer to a shallow bowl and cool completely.

Grind nuts in a food processor until as fine as possible, scraping inward often. Transfer to a medium bowl. Remove butter from refrigerator to soften slightly.

Cream cool butter in a large bowl until smooth and fluffy. Whisk yolk mixture until smooth, then beat it into butter in 6 batches. Beat in liqueur.

Transfer 1 1/4 cups mixture to a medium bowl. Add ground nuts and whisk until smooth. Use this as the filling. Reserve remaining mixture as frosting.

Trim meringues, if necessary, to even rounds. Set 1 meringue on a platter. Spread with nut filling. Top with second meringue. Spread frosting on top and sides of cake. Garnish with chocolate curls or grated chocolate. Refrigerate cake at least 8 hours. (Cake can be kept up to 3 days in refrigerator.)

Serve at cool room temperature. To slice, use a heavy knife and be sure to cut through bottom layer of meringue.

NOTE: Salted macadamia nuts can also be used, but first desalt them (page 389).

NUT MERINGUES WITH CHOCOLATE WHIPPED CREAM AND RASPBERRY SAUCE
Petits succès à la crème au chocolat, coulis de framboises

This is the dessert my husband and I prepared when we cooked dinner for the editor of the Fresh from France series, the editor-in-chief of my publishing house, and the editor of the "Living Section" of *The New York Times.* It combines everything we love in a dessert—it is beautiful, delicious, and fresh-tasting.

MAKES 8 INDIVIDUAL CAKES; 8 SERVINGS

16 individual Hazelnut-Almond
   Meringues (page 381)

CHOCOLATE WHIPPED CREAM

3 ounces semisweet chocolate,   *2 teaspoons granulated sugar*
   chopped   *1 teaspoon pure vanilla extract*
1 cup heavy cream, well chilled

Powdered sugar for sprinkling   *Fresh raspberries (optional)*
   (optional)   *2 cups Raspberry Sauce (page 345)*
3/4 cup heavy cream, well chilled
   (optional)

Bake meringues and cool them. Arrange meringues in pairs of similar size. If necessary, use point of a sharp paring knife with sawing motion to carefully trim uneven edges. (Trimmings can be saved, crushed, and used to sprinkle over ice cream.) Put meringue pairs on a tray, with flat side of 1 meringue facing up (it will be bottom meringue in each "sandwich"); keep its partner nearby, flat side down.

CHOCOLATE WHIPPED CREAM
   Melt chocolate in small bowl set above hot water over low heat, stirring until smooth. Remove from heat but leave chocolate above hot water. Whip cream with sugar and vanilla in a large chilled bowl with chilled beater until stiff. Remove chocolate from above water and let cool 30 seconds. Quickly stir about 1/2 cup whipped cream into

chocolate. As quickly as possible, fold mixture into remaining whipped cream until smooth; work quickly so chocolate does not harden upon contact with cold whipped cream.

Spoon about ¼ cup filling onto center of bottom meringue. Spread it to smooth, even layer about ¾ inch thick, adding more filling if needed. Set top meringue gently on filling, with its flat side down. Smooth sides gently, adding more filling, if necessary.

Set cakes on tray and cover gently. Refrigerate 3 hours to firm up filling. For crunchy meringues, serve within 3 more hours. (Cakes still have good flavor after being refrigerated up to 2 days, but meringues lose their crunchiness.)

Garnish cakes, if desired, just before serving. For a simple garnish, sift powdered sugar lightly over top of each cake. For a more festive garnish, whip cream until stiff. Using a pastry bag and medium star tip, pipe it in ruffles or rows of rosettes on top of each cake, alternating them with rows of fresh raspberries.

To serve, spoon a ribbon of raspberry sauce around each serving.

NOTE: Instead of spreading chocolate filling, it can be piped onto meringue, to give a decorative fluted design. To do this, spoon filling into pastry bag fitted with medium star tip. Pipe a border of filling along edge of bottom meringue so it just shows; then fill in center, using spiraling motion of piping bag. Repeat, making a second layer of filling on top of first. Set top meringue gently on filling, with its flat side down. Do not smooth sides.

ALMOND MERINGUE CAKE WITH COINTREAU CREAM
Gâteau meringué aux amandes à la crème au cointreau

In many professional desserts, part of the interest comes from two different types of cake, such as sponge cake and meringue, put together. An easy way for home cooks to achieve this effect is to use ladyfingers, as in this gâteau, where they are combined with crisp nut meringues and a light Cointreau buttercream. The ladyfingers absorb a Cointreau syrup for added flavor.   MAKES 6 TO 8 SERVINGS

Almond Meringues (page 381)   *¹/₂ cup sliced almonds*

COINTREAU SYRUP
2 tablespoons granulated sugar   *1 tablespoon Cointreau*
2 tablespoons water

COINTREAU MERINGUE BUTTERCREAM
Meringue Buttercream (page 360)   *4 teaspoons Cointreau*

2 to 2¹/₂ ounces packaged split   *Powdered sugar for sprinkling*
    ladyfingers

Bake and cool almond meringues.
    Preheat oven to 350°F. Toast sliced almonds on a small baking sheet in oven for 7 minutes, stirring often, until evenly browned. Transfer to a plate.

COINTREAU SYRUP
    In very small saucepan, melt sugar in water over low heat, stirring. Bring to a boil. Pour into a bowl and cool completely. Stir in Cointreau.

COINTREAU MERINGUE BUTTERCREAM
    Prepare Meringue Buttercream. Gradually beat in Cointreau.

    Trim meringues to even rounds. Set 1 meringue on a platter. Put a dab of buttercream underneath meringue so it doesn't move. Spread meringue gently with ¾ cup buttercream. Cover with a layer of ladyfinger halves, spongy side upward. Trim them if necessary so they fit in one layer but do not stick out beyond edges of meringue. Brush ladyfingers with Cointreau syrup.

Reserve about 1/2 cup buttercream for decorating. Spoon about 1/2 cup buttercream in a few spoonfuls over ladyfingers. Working from center, gently spread smooth. Top with second meringue. Spread remaining buttercream on sides to smooth.

Stick almonds on sides of cake by small handfuls. Using a pastry bag and small or medium star tip, decorate cake by piping either rosettes or a ruffle of reserved buttercream near edge of top layer. Lightly dust center of cake with powdered sugar. If desired, garnish rosettes or ruffle with toasted almond slices. Refrigerate cake about 1 or 2 hours to firm buttercream. (Can be kept 1 day in refrigerator.) Bring to cool room temperature to serve. Cut cake with a serrated knife.

INDIVIDUAL BLACK FOREST VACHERINS
Petits vacherins de la Forêt Noire

Chocolate and cherries characterize the traditional Black Forest cake, my inspiration for these vacherins, which contain chocolate mousse and fresh sweet cherries. Here the easy vacherins are meringue cases piped in one piece, rather than being constructed from many pieces like large vacherins. The chocolate mousse with cherries is also delicious on its own, without meringue shells; in this case it makes about 4 servings.   MAKES 8 SERVINGS

Individual Vacherin Cases (page 160)

CREAMY CHOCOLATE MOUSSE WITH CHERRIES

7 1/2 ounces semisweet chocolate, coarsely chopped
3 tablespoons water
1 tablespoon plus 1 teaspoon kirsch
3 large eggs, separated

3/4 cup heavy cream, well chilled
1/4 pound sweet cherries, pitted and cut in pieces
1 tablespoon sugar

1/2 cup heavy cream, well chilled
1/2 teaspoon sugar

8 pairs of sweet cherries for garnish

Bake vacherin cases and let cool.

CREAMY CHOCOLATE MOUSSE WITH CHERRIES

Melt chocolate with water and 1 tablespoon kirsch in large bowl above hot water over low heat. Stir until smooth. Remove from pan of water. Cool slightly. Beat egg yolks into mixture, 1 at a time. Cool to room temperature.

Whip cream with 1 teaspoon kirsch in chilled bowl with chilled beater until fairly stiff. Fold about one-quarter of cream into chocolate mixture. Gently fold in remaining cream. Fold in cherries.

Whip egg whites until stiff. Add sugar and beat another 30 seconds until shiny. Fold one-quarter of whites into chocolate mixture. Return mixture to remaining whites and fold together gently. Spoon mousse into a shallow bowl and refrigerate 1 hour.

Spoon enough mousse into each meringue case to fill it to the top, using about 2 tablespoons mousse for each. Spoon remaining mousse into a serving dish. Refrigerate filled cases, uncovered, 1 ½ hours, or until mousse sets. (Dessert can be kept, covered, up to 1 day in refrigerator.)

To serve, whip cream with sugar to soft peaks. Top each vacherin with a spoonful of whipped cream and garnish with a pair of cherries. Serve cold. Serve extra mousse in serving dish and any remaining whipped cream separately.

Pastries

Buttery croissants, sparkling tarts with colorful fruit, chocolate éclairs—these are the pastries most of us dream of when we think of French pastry shops. They catch our eye the moment we enter the shop, and we cannot leave until we've had a taste of one of these tempting treats.

The only "secret" to making good pastries at home is to take the time and attention to prepare them carefully, without rushing, and to serve them fresh. Making your own tarts, cream puffs, and savarins can be a relaxing activity, with most enjoyable results.

In this chapter I have concentrated on pastries that can be made quite easily by home cooks and do not require much expertise or special equipment. For example, there are no towering *croquembouches,* or tall pyramids of cream puffs stuck together with hot caramel, as these demand a good deal of practice; instead there are Caramel-

Glazed Cream Puffs, which give the same taste sensation with much less effort.

Each of the basic French pastries is used here to make desserts. There are duchesses, a simple type of éclair, made with choux pastry with a rich chocolate whipped cream filling; a variety of babas, savarins, and other light yeast cakes in new flavors; tarts made from both *pâte brisée* (French tart pastry) and *pâte sucrée* (sweet pastry); and cakes made from puff pastry, brioche, and croissant dough.

Cream Puffs

It's fortunate that one of the best loved of pastries also happens to be the easiest to make. Cream puffs, eclairs, profiteroles, and other delectable desserts are made from *pâte à choux,* a dough that is ready in minutes and requires no chilling before baking and no special equipment. All that is needed is a saucepan, because this dough, unlike others, is cooked before being baked.

The dough can be shaped in a variety of forms, but the most common are rounds for cream puffs and profiteroles and finger shapes for éclairs. These pastries puff attractively in the oven and become hollow, leaving room for filling. For an impressive-looking dessert called Gâteau Paris-Brest, the dough is piped in rings and puffs to form a crown. It is then filled generously with praline cream for its classic version, or, for new variations, with coffee whipped cream, Chantilly cream and berries, or whipped chocolate ganache.

Even the simplest cream puffs filled with vanilla whipped cream are a special treat when freshly made. Pudding-like pastry cream is another frequent choice for a filling, as in Chocolate-Kahlúa Cream Puffs. Modern chefs often make a lighter filling, called simply *crème légère* or light cream, of pastry cream mixed with whipped cream, as in Cream Puffs with Cherries and Kirsch. They also make a richer buttery version called *crème mousseline,* as in Caramel-Glazed Cream Puffs. Ice cream is now the favorite filling for profiteroles, which are coated with a luscious warm chocolate sauce. Buttercream can be piped or spooned into tiny cream puffs for serving as petits fours.

The time-honored flavors of vanilla, coffee, chocolate, and liqueur are still the ones preferred today for fillings; although now fresh fruit is often added, as in Strawberry and Cream Puffs, or it is served alongside these pastries.

Hints

- All pastries made from cream puff dough taste best when baked the same day, but they can be frozen, unfilled. They should be frozen as soon as they cool and should be wrapped well. Ideally, they should be thawed and filled on the day they are to be served.
- Small cream puffs can be frozen before being baked. I noticed that this is now a common procedure in pastry shops, and it is a good trick for home cooks.

CHOCOLATE-KAHLÚA CREAM PUFFS
Choux au chocolat à la liqueur au café

One of the easiest pastries to make, these cream puffs hold a rich chocolate pastry-cream filling accented by coffee liqueur. If you like, substitute Grand Marnier or chocolate liqueur for the Kahlúa.

MAKES ABOUT 24 PUFFS

Cream Puff Pastry (page 383)
1 egg, beaten with a pinch of salt,
*   for glaze*

CHOCOLATE-KAHLÚA PASTRY CREAM

5 ounces semisweet chocolate,
*   chopped*
5 large egg yolks, room temperature
7 tablespoons granulated sugar
2 tablespoons plus 1 teaspoon
*   cornstarch*

1 2/3 cups milk
2 tablespoons plus 2 teaspoons
*   Kahlúa or other coffee liqueur*

Powdered sugar for sprinkling

Position rack in lower third of oven and preheat to 400°F. Lightly butter 2 baking sheets.

Make dough. Using a pastry bag and 1/2-inch plain tip, shape mounds of dough about 1 ¼ inches in diameter, spacing them about 2 inches apart on baking sheets. Brush them with egg glaze, gently pushing down any points.

Bake about 30 minutes, or until dough is puffed and browned; cracks that form during baking should also be brown. Using a serrated knife, carefully cut off top third of each puff and reserve this part as a "hat." Transfer puffs to a rack to cool. (Puffs can be kept up to 1 day in an airtight container, but taste best on day they are baked.)

CHOCOLATE-KAHLÚA PASTRY CREAM

Melt chocolate in a medium bowl above hot water over low heat. Stir until smooth. Remove from pan of water.

Whisk egg yolks lightly in a heatproof medium bowl. Add sugar and whisk until blended. Lightly stir in cornstarch with a whisk.

Bring milk to a boil in a medium, heavy saucepan. Gradually whisk hot milk into yolk mixture. Return to saucepan and cook over medium-low heat, whisking constantly, until mixture is very thick and comes just to a boil. Reduce heat to low and cook, whisking constantly, 1 minute. Do not overcook or yolks will curdle. Remove from heat.

Stir chocolate until smooth and whisk it into pastry cream. Transfer to a bowl and dab surface with a small piece of butter to prevent a skin from forming. Refrigerate 1 hour, or until completely cool. Whisk pastry cream and add Kahlúa. Refrigerate 2 hours. (Filling can be kept, covered, up to 2 days in refrigerator.)

A short time before serving, use a pastry bag and small star tip to pipe filling into cream puffs. Set hats on top at a slant so filling shows. Shake or sift powdered sugar over tops, and serve.

STRAWBERRY AND CREAM PUFFS
Choux aux fraises

These could be considered the French answer to strawberry shortcake—the cream puffs are filled completely with fresh strawberries, then topped generously with Chantilly cream. When I trained briefly in the pastry kitchen of Maxim's in Paris, these puffs, filled with perfect strawberries, were a popular specialty at the restaurant.

MAKES ABOUT 12 PUFFS

Cream Puff Pastry (page 383)   *1 quart strawberries*
1 egg, beaten with a pinch of salt,   *2 tablespoons sugar*
    for glaze

CHANTILLY CREAM
1 1/4 cups heavy cream, well chilled   *1 1/2 teaspoons pure vanilla extract*
2 tablespoons granulated sugar

Powdered sugar for sprinkling

Preheat oven to 400°F. Lightly butter 2 baking sheets.

Prepare dough. Using a pastry bag and medium plain tip, or using 2 tablespoons, shape mounds of dough about 1 1/2 inches in diameter, spacing them about 2 inches apart on baking sheets. Brush them with egg glaze. Using the bottom part of tines of a fork, press tops of puffs very gently.

Bake about 30 minutes, until dough is puffed and browned; cracks that form during baking should also be brown. Using a serrated knife, carefully cut off top third of each puff and reserve this part as a "hat." Transfer puffs to a rack to cool. (They can be baked 1 day ahead and kept in an airtight container, but taste best on day they are baked.)

Hull strawberries, cut them in half, and sprinkle with sugar. Cover and refrigerate for 15 to 30 minutes.

CHANTILLY CREAM

In a large chilled bowl with chilled beater, whip cream with sugar and vanilla until stiff. Refrigerate until ready to use.

A short time before serving, fill cream puffs with strawberries. Using a pastry bag and large star tip, pipe whipped cream generously onto each puff, ending with a large rosette, but allow berries to show slightly from edges. Set hats on top. Shake powdered sugar over them, and serve.

SEE PHOTOGRAPH.

ÉCLAIRS WITH CHOCOLATE WHIPPED CREAM
Duchesses

Lighter and easier to make than traditional éclairs, these pastries are filled with a wonderful chocolate whipped cream and are simply dusted with powdered sugar, rather than being dipped in fondant.

MAKES 6 TO 8 SERVINGS; 12 TO 16 PASTRIES

Cream Puff Pastry (page 383)
1 egg, beaten with a pinch of salt,
    for glaze

RICH CHOCOLATE WHIPPED CREAM

5 ounces bittersweet or semisweet   *2 teaspoons granulated sugar*
    chocolate, chopped   *1 teaspoon pure vanilla extract*
1 cup heavy cream, well chilled

Powdered sugar for sprinkling

Position rack in lower third of oven and preheat to 400°F. Lightly butter 2 baking sheets.

Make dough. Using a pastry bag and ½-inch plain tip, pipe thick fingers of dough about 3 inches long, spacing them about 2 inches apart on baking sheets. Brush them with egg glaze. With a fork dipped in water, lightly mark each pastry with crosswise lines, so they will rise more evenly.

Bake 25 to 30 minutes, or until dough is puffed and browned; cracks that form during baking should also be brown. Using a serrated knife, slit side of each pastry. Transfer them to a rack to cool. (Puffs can be kept up to 1 day in an airtight container, but taste best on day they are baked.)

RICH CHOCOLATE WHIPPED CREAM

Melt chocolate in a medium bowl set above hot water over low heat. Stir until smooth. Remove from heat but leave above water.

Whip cream with sugar and vanilla in chilled bowl with chilled beater until stiff. Cool chocolate 30 seconds. Add about ½ cup whipped cream to chocolate and mix well. Quickly fold chocolate mixture into remaining whipped cream.

Pipe chocolate whipped cream into puffs using a pastry bag and medium star tip, or fill them with a spoon. Refrigerate until ready to serve. (Filled puffs can be kept up to 2 hours.) Sprinkle pastries with powdered sugar just before serving.

CARAMEL-GLAZED CREAM PUFFS
Choux caramelisés à la crème mousseline

Crunchy caramel is a favorite topping for cream puffs in France, because it provides a pleasing contrast of texture to the soft, delectable filling. Known as *crème mousseline,* this filling is a version of pastry cream enriched with butter, so it is smooth and velvety. When raspberries are in season, you can add a few to each puff, as the chef of Olympe restaurant in Paris did the day I dined there.

MAKES 6 TO 8 SERVINGS; 24 SMALL CREAM PUFFS

Cream Puff Pastry (page 383)

SPIRITED MOUSSELINE CREAM

1⅓ cups milk
4 large egg yolks
⅓ cup sugar
¼ cup all-purpose flour
3 tablespoons unsalted butter, room temperature

1 tablespoon plus ½ teaspoon Grand Marnier or clear raspberry brandy (framboise)

CARAMEL GLAZE
1 cup sugar

½ cup water

Position rack in lower third of oven and preheat to 400°F. Lightly butter 2 baking sheets.

Make dough. Using a pastry bag and ½-inch plain tip, shape mounds of dough about 1¼ inches in diameter, spacing them about

2 inches apart on baking sheets. (There is no need to brush these with egg glaze because caramel gives them an attractive color.)

Bake about 30 minutes, or until dough is puffed and browned; cracks that form during baking should also be brown. Transfer puffs to a rack to cool. While they are still warm, cut a slit in their sides with a serrated knife to let steam out; do not let top become detached, or it will be difficult to dip in caramel. (Puffs can be kept up to 1 day in an airtight container, but taste best on day they are baked.)

SPIRITED MOUSSELINE CREAM

Bring milk to a boil in a small heavy saucepan. Whisk yolks and sugar in a bowl until smooth; gently stir in flour with a whisk. Gradually add hot milk to yolks, whisking quickly. Transfer mixture to saucepan and cook over medium-low heat, whisking constantly, until mixture comes just to a boil. Continue cooking over low heat, whisking constantly, for 1 minute. Do not cook too long or yolks will curdle. Remove from heat, transfer to a bowl and dab surface with a small piece of butter to prevent a skin from forming. Refrigerate until completely cool. Whisk in 3 tablespoons butter, about 1 tablespoon at a time. Gradually whisk in spirits.

CARAMEL GLAZE

Do not prepare more than 12 hours before serving. Line a baking sheet with foil. In a small heavy saucepan that does not have a dark bottom, dissolve sugar in water, stirring gently, over low heat. Boil without stirring until syrup becomes light brown (check under bubbles). Remove from heat.

Quickly but very carefully dip top third of each puff in caramel and set on foil-lined baking sheet. *Be very careful not to let caramel drip on your fingers, because it can cause bad burns.* The caramel layer on each puff should be thin. If caramel cools and thickens too much before you have finished dipping all the puffs, reheat it briefly over low heat. Let puffs cool completely.

Fill puffs 2 hours or less before serving. Whisk mousseline cream briefly. With a spoon, fill each puff carefully, so as not to mar glaze. Refrigerate until ready to serve.

PROFITEROLES WITH MINT ICE CREAM AND CHOCOLATE SAUCE
Profiteroles à la menthe et au chocolat

Mint and chocolate have become a popular combination in modern French desserts. The match is especially delicious here in a profiterole, or small cream puff, that is filled with fresh mint ice cream and covered with a warm chocolate sauce. Of course, the traditional filling of vanilla ice cream is also great, and so, for that matter, is coffee or caramel ice cream. I have fond memories of dining in small Parisian restaurants and having a plate of profiteroles that had been generously coated in warm chocolate sauce set in front of me. When the ice cream and pastry puffs are fresh and the sauce is aromatic, this classic dessert is extraordinary. For a lighter, more summery dessert, you can use a fruit sauce instead of the chocolate one; mango, strawberry, or raspberry sauces are good, and can be served cold or slightly heated.

MAKES ABOUT 20 PROFITEROLES

Cream Puff Pastry (page 383)
1 egg, beaten with a pinch of salt, for glaze

1 to 1½ pints Fresh Mint Ice Cream (page 97)

WARM CHOCOLATE SAUCE
8 ounces bittersweet or semisweet chocolate, chopped
⅔ cup heavy cream or water

2 to 4 tablespoons unsalted butter
1 teaspoon pure vanilla extract

Mint sprigs for garnish

Position rack in lower third of oven and preheat to 400°F. Lightly butter 2 baking sheets.

Prepare dough. Using a pastry bag and ½-inch plain tip, shape mounds of dough about 1¼ inches in diameter, spacing them about 2 inches apart on baking sheets. Brush them with egg glaze, gently pushing down any points.

Bake about 30 minutes, or until dough is puffed and browned; cracks that form during baking should also be brown. Using a serrated knife, carefully cut top third of each puff but leave it attached. Transfer puffs to a rack to cool. (Puffs can be kept up to 1 day in an airtight container, but taste best on day they are baked.)

Before serving, soften ice cream in refrigerator. Spoon enough ice cream into each cream puff to fill it generously. Set on a tray, cover, and keep in freezer until ready to serve, preferably not longer than 24 hours.

WARM CHOCOLATE SAUCE

Heat chocolate with cream in a heavy saucepan over low heat, stirring often, until smooth. Remove from heat and stir in butter and vanilla. (Sauce can be kept, covered, 1 week in refrigerator.)

When ready to serve, reheat sauce over low heat, if necessary. Spoon warm sauce over profiteroles, and garnish with mint sprigs.

CREAM PUFFS WITH CHERRIES AND KIRSCH
Choux aux cerises et au kirsch

Although pastry cream has long been the classic filling for cream puffs, today many chefs prefer to lighten it by folding in whipped cream, and often call this type of filling crème légère or light cream. Here sweet cherries mixed with a kirsch-flavored light cream make a fresh, inviting filling for these cream puffs. Be sure to use good-quality imported kirsch, which is a clear cherry brandy.

France produces a variety of these fruit brandies that capture the essence of the fruit. They are sipped after a meal as a digestif, which means a drink to aid digestion. Besides kirsch, other favorites include poire William, made from pears, and framboise, made from raspberries. I like to always keep them on hand in the kitchen cupboard as potent flavorings.   MAKES ABOUT 12 PUFFS

Cream Puff Pastry (page 383)
1 egg, beaten with a pinch of salt,
    for glaze

KIRSCH CREAM WITH CHERRIES

1 cup milk
3 large egg yolks
5 tablespoons granulated sugar
3 tablespoons all-purpose flour

2 cups sweet cherries, pitted and cut
in quarters
3 teaspoons kirsch, or more to taste
1/2 cup heavy cream, well chilled

Powdered sugar for sprinkling

Pairs of cherries for garnish

Preheat oven to 400°F. Lightly butter 2 baking sheets.

Prepare dough. Using a pastry bag and medium plain tip, or using 2 tablespoons, shape mounds of dough about 1 1/2 inches in diameter, spacing them about 2 inches apart on baking sheets. Brush them with egg glaze. Using the bottom part of tines of a fork, press tops of puffs very gently.

Bake about 30 minutes, until dough is puffed and browned; cracks that form during baking should also be brown. Using a serrated knife, carefully cut off top third of each puff and reserve this part as a "hat." Transfer puffs to a rack to cool. (They can be baked 1 day ahead and kept in an airtight container, but taste best on day they are baked.)

KIRSCH CREAM WITH CHERRIES

Bring milk to a boil in a small heavy saucepan. Whisk yolks and 4 tablespoons sugar in a bowl until smooth. Gently stir in flour with a whisk. Gradually add hot milk, whisking quickly. Transfer mixture to saucepan. Cook over medium-low heat, whisking constantly, until mixture comes just to a boil. Continue cooking over low heat, whisking constantly, for 1 to 2 minutes. Do not cook too long or yolks will curdle. Remove from heat, transfer to a bowl, and dab surface with a small piece of butter to prevent a skin from forming. Refrigerate this pastry cream until completely cool.

Sprinkle cherries with 1 teaspoon kirsch and toss. Cover and let stand for 15 to 30 minutes.

When pastry cream is cool, whisk it and add 2 teaspoons kirsch, then the liquid from cherries. Whip cream with sugar in a chilled bowl with chilled beater until stiff. Gently fold whipped cream into pastry cream, then gently fold in cherries. Taste, and add a little more kirsch, if desired.

A short time before serving, fill cream puffs, using a tablespoon. Set the hats on top. Shake powdered sugar over puffs and serve with cherry pairs.

✤ CHOCOLATE-ORANGE GÂTEAU PARIS-BREST
Gâteau Paris-Brest au chocolat et à l'orange

This impressive gâteau is made from choux pastry that is piped in rings and puffs to a lovely crown—or a bicycle tire! It is said to be named for a bicycle race that took place between Paris and Brest. The classic gâteau is filled with praline cream. For this new version, I have substituted an easier but equally delicious filling of orange-scented whipped chocolate ganache.   MAKES 6 TO 8 SERVINGS

Cream Puff Pastry (page 383)   *2 tablespoons sliced almonds for*
1 egg, beaten with a pinch of salt,   *sprinkling*
*   for glaze*

CHOCOLATE-ORANGE WHIPPED GANACHE
3 medium navel oranges   *12 ounces fine-quality semisweet*
1 1/2 cups heavy cream   *chocolate, very finely chopped*

Powdered sugar for sprinkling

Position rack in lower third of oven and preheat to 400°F. Lightly butter a baking sheet. Using an 8-inch cake pan, draw an 8-inch circle on baking sheet; it will be only barely visible.

Prepare dough. Using a pastry bag and large plain tip about 5/8 inch in diameter, evenly pipe dough in an 8-inch ring onto baking sheet, following marked circle. Pipe another ring inside first, touching it. Pipe a third ring on top of crack joining first 2 rings. Brush dough with beaten egg. Gently mark lines on dough by pressing with bottom of a fork lightly dipped in water. Sprinkle sliced almonds on top.

Bake about 35 minutes, or until dough is puffed and browned; cracks that form during baking should also brown.

Using a serrated knife, carefully split cake in half horizontally.

Cool both halves separately on a rack. (Cake can be kept, covered, up to 1 day, but tastes best on day it is baked.)

CHOCOLATE-ORANGE WHIPPED GANACHE

Using a vegetable peeler, pare colored part of orange peels in long strips, without including white pith. Scald cream and strips of orange peel in small heavy saucepan over medium-high heat until bubbling at edges. Remove from heat, cover, and let stand 20 minutes. Strain cream into medium bowl, pressing on orange strips, and return cream to cleaned saucepan.

Put chocolate in heatproof medium bowl. Reheat cream in small heavy saucepan over medium-high heat, stirring with whisk, until it comes to a full boil. Pour cream over chocolate all at once. Stir with whisk until chocolate is completely melted and mixture is smooth. Cool to room temperature, stirring occasionally. Refrigerate, stirring mixture often from sides of bowl to center, until cold and thickened but not set, about 30 minutes.

Whip mixture in mixer at medium speed, or whisk it by hand until it lightens in color, is thick enough to spread, and forms very soft peaks, about 2 minutes. Do not overbeat ganache or it will separate. Use at once, or it will stiffen and become impossible to pipe.

Spoon filling into a pastry bag fitted with large star tip and pipe all of it onto lower half of cake in a ruffle so it shows at edge. Cover with top half. Refrigerate 30 minutes. (Cake can be kept, covered, up to 8 hours in refrigerator.) Sprinkle with powdered sugar before serving. Serve at room temperature.

Tarts

Brilliantly glazed fruit tarts always attract the attention of diners passing the dessert carts of elegant restaurants and grab the attention of shoppers walking by the windows of pâtisseries.

Yet tarts are enjoyed most of all when made at home, both for their wonderful aroma when they bake and because the key to delicious tarts is freshness. Whether the base is of sweet and luscious *pâte sucrée* or of the rich, buttery, unsweetened *pâte brisée;* and whether the tart contains a filling of pastry cream, almond cream, or simply jam-glazed fruit, it is best when baked and filled a short time before serving. At home we have more control and we can spare ourselves the disappointment of biting into a soggy tart, which was filled too far ahead and lost its crispness when the filling soaked into the crust.

In France, berries and other soft fruit are generally used un-cooked for tarts to preserve their fragrance and texture, as in Strawberry Tart with Almond Cream, rather than being baked with the crust. Firm fruit like apples and pears is often baked, as in Traditional French Apple Tart, or is poached in a vanilla syrup and set on a tart filled with pastry cream. The classic finish for tarts filled with red fruit is red currant–jelly glaze, and for other fruits it's apricot-jam glaze. But today some dessert chefs prefer to match the flavor of the jelly glaze to the fruit used in each tart.

All tarts can be made in individual form as tartlets, or in miniature round or boat-shaped molds as petits fours tartlets. When I was training at a Parisian pastry shop, I spent hours brushing each of the three raspberries on hundreds of tiny tartlets with a little bit of red currant glaze—I was required to do this carefully, to avoid knocking any berries off their tartlets! This step appeared tedious, but I learned that the glaze on tartlets has three purposes: it gives tartlets an attractive, shiny appearance, gives the fruit just the touch of sweetness it needs, and helps prevent it from drying out quickly.

Hints

• Sweet pastry softens fast. Roll it out as quickly as possible on a cold surface. Keep the dough moving while rolling it out, and sprinkle the work surface and the dough often with flour. When you need to move the dough, roll it up on the rolling pin.

• Work quickly when rolling out pastry dough, but do not worry if it tears when you fit it in the tart pan. Both French tart pastry and sweet pastry can be easily patched with a piece of dough, and the tart will be fine.

• Chilling is important both before and after shaping a tart—it prevents the pastry from shrinking and being tough. After shaping a tart, do not attempt to skip the step of chilling the pastry before baking it. If the dough is too warm or too soft, it will slide down the sides of the tart pan as it bakes.

• Be sure to use enough pie weights or dried beans when baking an empty tart shell—they should nearly fill the lined tart pan.

• During baking, if a pastry shell breaks or slides down in one place, you can patch it with a piece of raw dough and bake it a few more minutes; it won't look so pretty, but it will prevent a liquid filling from running out.

• Tarts are easiest to handle if baked in tart pans with removable bases, so that all you need to do once the tart is baked, is to set it on an upside down bowl and remove the sides of the pan. The tart can then be slid off its base or left on it.

CITRUS ALMOND TART
Tarte aux agrumes

This lemon-orange tart features a filling that is very easy to make and has a buttery almond flavor. Teri Appleton, a former testing assistant of mine who is now the innovative pastry chef of the stylish Ocean Avenue Seafood restaurant in Santa Monica, uses it as a base for delicious fruit tarts by setting seasonal fruit, such as halved strawberries or mango or peach slices, on top of the baked tart.

MAKES 8 SERVINGS

Citrus-Flavored Sweet Pastry (page 386)

CITRUS FILLING

1/2 cup blanched almonds
3/4 cup sugar
Zest of 1 1/2 lemons, pared in strips
Zest of 1/2 orange, pared in strips
3 large eggs

1/2 cup unsalted butter, melted and cooled
2 tablespoons strained fresh lemon juice
1 tablespoon strained fresh orange juice

Prepare dough and refrigerate. Butter a square 9-inch tart pan with removable bottom. Roll out dough on a cold, lightly floured surface to a square about ¼ inch thick, with about 10½-inch sides. Roll up dough loosely around rolling pin and unroll it over pan. Gently ease dough into pan. Roll rolling pin across pan to cut off dough. Push up sides so they will be slightly higher than edge of pan. Chill 2 hours; or cover with plastic wrap and chill overnight.

Preheat oven to 400°F. and put baking sheet in it to heat. Prick dough all over with a fork. Line dough with parchment paper or aluminum foil and fill with dried beans, making sure that they reach the corners. Bake 5 minutes, reduce heat to 375°F., and bake 10 minutes. Remove paper and beans and bake 5 minutes more, or until base is beginning to brown. Remove tart pan from oven but leave baking sheet in oven. Let tart shell cool. Reduce oven temperature to 350°F.

CITRUS FILLING

Grind almonds with 2 tablespoons sugar in a food processor until very fine and remove. Purée strips of orange and lemon rind with remaining sugar in processor until rinds are in very fine pieces. Beat eggs and rind-flavored sugar until smooth. Stir in ground almonds and melted butter, then stir in the lemon juice and orange juice. Pour mixture into baked tart shell. Bake about 25 to 30 minutes, or until filling is golden brown and set. Serve at room temperature.

TRADITIONAL FRENCH APPLE TART
Tarte aux pommes

Home cooks in France most often make their apple tarts this way, with a double-apple filling: the bottom layer is a compote of butter-cooked apples and is topped with a pinwheel of sliced fresh apples. It is baked in a crust of French tart pastry until the apples are tender, then is brushed lightly with apricot glaze so it shines.

MAKES 6 TO 8 SERVINGS

French Tart Pastry (page 384)

APPLE FILLING

2 1/2 *pounds Golden Delicious*
apples
3 *tablespoons butter*
1/2 *teaspoon strained fresh lemon*
juice

Grated rind of 1/2 *lemon*
1 *vanilla bean*
5 *to* 6 *tablespoons sugar*

APRICOT GLAZE

3 *tablespoons apricot preserves*

2 *teaspoons water*

Prepare dough and refrigerate.

Butter an 8- or 9-inch round tart pan. Let dough soften 1 minute before rolling it. Roll out dough on a lightly floured surface until about 1/4 inch thick. Roll up dough loosely around rolling pin and unroll it over pan. Gently ease dough into pan. Using your thumb, gently push dough down slightly at edge of pan, making top edge of dough thicker than remaining dough. Roll rolling pin across pan to cut off dough. With your finger and thumb, press to push up edge of dough all around pan, so it is slightly higher than rim of pan. Prick dough all over with a fork. Chill for 1 hour; or cover with plastic wrap and chill overnight.

APPLE FILLING

Peel, core, and thinly slice all apples but 1. Melt 2 tablespoons butter in a large saucepan or sauté pan and add apples, lemon juice, lemon rind and vanilla bean. Cover and cook over low heat, stirring occasionally, for about 20 minutes, or until apples are very tender. Continue to cook uncovered, stirring often, about 5 minutes or until any excess liquid has evaporated. Remove the vanilla bean. Add 4 tablespoons sugar. Cook over high heat, stirring constantly, until sugar dissolves and apple mixture is very thick. Taste and add more sugar, if desired. Let cool completely.

Preheat oven to 400°F and put a baking sheet in oven to heat.

Spread cool apple mixture in tart pan. Peel, core, and slice remaining apple in thin wedges. Arrange wedges slightly overlapping on top of apple mixture. Dot with remaining butter. Bake tart on hot baking sheet for 30 minutes. Sprinkle apple slices evenly with 2 teaspoons sugar and continue baking 10 minutes. Reduce heat to 350°F. and continue baking another 20 minutes, or until apple slices are tender. Let tart cool for a few minutes. Remove tart from pan and cool it on a rack to room temperature.

APRICOT GLAZE

Heat preserves and water over low heat, stirring often, until preserves melt. Strain mixture, and brush it over apple slices to glaze. Serve warm or at room temperature.

CHOCOLATE MOUSSE TART
Tarte à la mousse au chocolat

Amaretti cookies and hazelnuts form a nutty crust under the spirited chocolate mousse. Small ones, called *amarettini*, can be used as well. The mousse has quite a punch of amaretto. If you prefer a delicate flavor, use only 2 tablespoons liqueur and substitute water for the rest.   MAKES 8 SERVINGS

HAZELNUT AMARETTI CRUST

1/2 cup hazelnuts (about 2 ounces)   *5 tablespoons unsalted butter,*
5 ounces amaretti cookies   *melted and cooled*

CHOCOLATE MOUSSE WITH AMARETTO

8 ounces semisweet chocolate,   *4 large eggs, separated, room*
*   chopped*   *temperature*
1/4 cup amaretto   *2 teaspoons sugar*
1/4 cup unsalted butter, room
*   temperature, cut in 4 pieces*

1/2 cup heavy cream, well chilled

HAZELNUT AMARETTI CRUST

Preheat oven to 350°F. Toast and skin hazelnuts (see page 388). Cool nuts completely.

Grind nuts in a food processor until finely chopped, leaving a few chunks. Transfer to a medium bowl, reserving 1 tablespoon for garnish.

Grind cookies in food processor until they become fine crumbs; measure 1 cup. Add measured crumbs to bowl of hazelnuts and mix well. Add melted butter gradually and mix lightly with fork. Using fork, lightly pat crumb mixture in even layer in a 9-inch pie pan. Refrigerate about 20 minutes, or until firm.

CHOCOLATE MOUSSE WITH AMARETTO

Melt chocolate in a medium bowl above hot water over low heat, stirring until smooth. Remove from pan of water and stir in amaretto and butter. Add egg yolks, 1 at a time, stirring vigorously after each addition.

Whip egg whites in a medium bowl until soft peaks form. Beat in sugar at high speed and whip until whites are stiff and shiny but not dry. Fold about one-quarter of whites into chocolate mixture. Return chocolate mixture to remaining whites and fold gently until blended. Pour mixture into prepared crust. Cover and refrigerate at least 4 hours, or until set. (Tart can be kept, covered, up to 2 days in refrigerator.)

Whip cream in chilled bowl with chilled beater until stiff. Using a pastry bag and ½-inch plain tip, pipe whipped cream in approximately 16 mounds with 1-inch peaks, touching each other, near edge of tart. Sprinkle mounds lightly with chopped hazelnuts and serve cold.

PEACH TART WITH CINNAMON CREAM
Tarte aux pêches, crème à la cannelle

In classic fresh fruit tarts like this one, the pastry is baked on its own so it remains crisp. The tart is filled with a smooth pastry cream before being topped with the fruit and a sparkling apricot glaze. Poached peaches are the usual choice for a peach tart, but if you have perfectly ripe peaches you can leave them fresh, so they remain juicy and aromatic. In this case, you should serve the tart a short time after setting the peaches on top, so they will not discolor.

Instead of sliced peaches, you can use nectarines, poached apricots, mangoes, papayas, or kiwis, or an attractive arrangement of several fruits. Strawberries are another favorite choice for this type of tart, but they are brushed with heated red currant jelly. Instead of the cinnamon pastry-cream filling, you can use the classic Vanilla Pastry Cream (see recipe), by infusing a vanilla bean in the milk, or by stirring 1 teaspoon vanilla extract into the cool pastry cream; or, if you like, flavor it with peach brandy, kirsch, or grated citrus peel.

MAKES 8 SERVINGS

Sweet Pastry or Rich Sweet Pastry
(page 385, 386)

CINNAMON PASTRY CREAM

1 1/4 cups milk	*1/2 teaspoon cinnamon*
4 large egg yolks	*2 tablespoons cornstarch*
1/3 cup sugar	

APRICOT GLAZE

2/3 cup apricot preserves	*2 tablespoons water*

2 pounds fresh ripe peaches or
*   Poached Peaches (page 372),*
*   or 1 pound peaches and 3 ripe*
*   kiwis*

Make dough and refrigerate. Butter a 9- to 9 1/2-inch tart pan with removable base. Let dough soften 1 minute at room temperature. Set dough on a cold lightly floured surface. Tap it firmly with a heavy rolling pin several times to flatten it. Roll it out, flouring often and working as quickly as possible, to a round about 1/4 inch thick and about 1 1/2 inches in diameter. Roll up dough loosely around rolling pin and unroll it over pan. Gently ease dough into pan. (If dough tears, use a piece of dough hanging over rim of pan to patch it up.)

Using your thumb, gently push dough down slightly at top edge of pan, making top edge of dough thicker than remaining dough. Roll rolling pin across pan to cut off dough at edges. With your finger and thumb, press to push up top edge of dough all around pan so it is about 1/4 inch higher than rim of pan. Refrigerate about 10 minutes. Prick dough all over with a fork. Cover with plastic wrap and refrigerate 1 hour. (Tart shell can be kept, covered, up to 1 day in refrigerator; or it can be frozen.)

CINNAMON PASTRY CREAM

Bring milk to a boil in a small heavy saucepan; remove from heat. Whisk yolks, sugar, and cinnamon in a bowl until smooth. Gently stir in cornstarch with a whisk. Gradually whisk hot milk into yolk mixture. Return mixture to saucepan and cook over medium heat, whisking constantly, until mixture is very thick and comes barely to a boil. Continue cooking over low heat, whisking constantly, for 1 minute. Remove from heat, transfer to a bowl and dab surface with a small piece of butter to prevent a skin from forming. Refrigerate until completely cool. (Pastry cream can be kept, covered, up to 2 days in refrigerator.)

Position rack in lower third of oven and preheat to 425°F. Line tart shell with parchment paper or foil and fill paper with dried beans or pie weights. Set tart shell on a baking sheet and bake 10 minutes, or until side is firm and beginning to brown. Reduce oven temperature to 375°F. Remove paper with beans carefully. Bake tart shell 14 minutes, or until base is firm and just beginning to brown. Set tart shell on flat-bottomed upside-down bowl and remove sides of pan. Transfer tart to a rack and cool to lukewarm. Gently pull out base of pan. Cool shell completely. Transfer to a platter. (Tart shell can be kept, covered, up to 1 day at room temperature.)

APRICOT GLAZE

Heat preserves and water in a small saucepan over low heat, stirring often, until preserves melt. Strain into a small saucepan, pressing on pieces; cover.

Up to a few hours before serving, spread pastry cream in tart. Refrigerate until ready to serve. If possible, serve tart within 4 hours so that pastry remains crisp.

If using fresh peaches, scald them in a pan of boiling water for 30 seconds, transfer to a bowl of cold water, and peel them. If using poached peaches, remove them from syrup and set on paper towels to drain. Cut each peach in 8 slices, inward toward pit. If using kiwis, peel them and slice them ¼ inch thick. Arrange fruit attractively on pastry cream.

Reheat glaze over low heat. Using a pastry brush, gently brush glaze on peaches, brushing each slice individually. If using fresh peaches, serve tart within 30 minutes so peaches retain their color.

SEE PHOTOGRAPH.

AUVERGNE CHEESE TART
Tarte auvergnate au fromage

For cheesecake lovers, serve this easy-to-make tart. It has a light lemon-accented cream cheese filling in a delicately sweetened crust.

MAKES 6 TO 8 SERVINGS

French Tart Pastry (page 384)
6 ounces cream cheese
1/2 cup heavy cream
5 tablespoons sugar

2 large eggs
Grated rind of 1/2 lemon
1/2 teaspoon pure vanilla extract
1 1/2 teaspoons all-purpose flour

Prepare pastry and refrigerate until firm.

Butter an 8-inch tart pan. Let dough soften 1 minute before rolling it. Roll out the dough on a lightly floured surface until about 1/4 inch thick. Roll up dough loosely around rolling pin and unroll it over pan. Gently ease the dough into pan. Using your thumb, gently push dough down slightly at edge of pan, making top edge of dough thicker than remaining dough. Roll rolling pin across pan to cut off dough. With your finger and thumb, press to push up the edge of dough all around pan, so it is slightly higher than rim of pan. Prick the dough all over with a fork. Chill for 1 hour; or cover with plastic wrap and chill overnight.

Set oven at 425°F. and heat a baking sheet in oven. Line dough with parchment paper or aluminum foil and fill it with dried beans or pie weights. Bake for 10 minutes. Remove paper and beans and bake 7 minutes more, or until base is beginning to brown. Remove tart pan from oven but leave baking sheet in oven. Let tart shell cool. Reduce oven temperature to 375°F.

Beat cream cheese with cream at low speed. Gradually beat in sugar. Add eggs, 1 at a time, beating to blend. Stir in lemon rind, vanilla, and flour. Return tart shell, still in its pan, to hot baking sheet.

Pour filling into shell and bake 10 minutes. Reduce oven temperature to 325°F. and continue baking 20 to 25 minutes, or until filling is firm. Let tart cool in oven, with door slightly open. Serve cold. (The tart can be baked 1 day ahead and kept in refrigerator.)

EXOTIC CHOCOLATE TARTLETS
Tartelettes exotiques au chocolat

Serve these tartlets—with their ganache filling that is scented with orange flower water and garnished with pine nuts (or pistachios, as in the variation)—on a petits fours tray. Make them round or, if you like, use small decorative heart- or diamond-shaped tartlet molds.

MAKES SIXTEEN 3-INCH TARTLETS

Rich Sweet Pastry (page 386)
2 tablespoons pine nuts (see Note)
12 1/2 ounces fine-quality semisweet
  chocolate, chopped

1 1/4 cups heavy cream
About 6 tablespoons plus 2
  teaspoons orange flower water
  (see Note)

Wrap pastry in 2 portions and refrigerate at least 4 hours before using it.

Butter 16 round fluted 3-inch tartlet pans. Let 1 portion of dough soften 1 minute at room temperature before rolling it. Set dough on a cold lightly floured surface. Tap it firmly with a heavy rolling pin several times to flatten it. Roll it out, flouring often and working as quickly as possible, until it is slightly less than 1/4 inch thick. Set 4 or 5 tartlet pans next to each other. Roll up dough loosely around rolling pin and unroll it over pans. With a small ball of dough dipped in flour, gently press dough into tartlet pans.

Roll rolling pin across pans to cut off dough at edges. With your finger and thumb, press up edge of dough all around each pan so it extends slightly above rim. Prick dough all over with a fork. Cover lined pans and refrigerate at least 30 minutes. Repeat with second portion of dough. Refrigerate scraps about 1 hour. Roll scraps and line remaining tartlet pans. If you have only 8 tartlet pans, line them, bake them, and repeat. (Tartlet shells can be kept, covered, up to 1 day in refrigerator; or they can be frozen.)

Position rack in center of oven and preheat to 400°F. Line each tartlet shell with parchment paper or foil and fill paper with dried beans or pie weights. Set tartlet shells on a baking sheet and bake about 10 minutes, or until set and beginning to brown. Reduce oven temperature to 375°F. Remove paper and beans and continue baking about 5 minutes, or until light brown. (If you prefer, weight pastry by placing another tartlet pan inside each lined pan, instead of using paper and pie weights; remove inside tartlet pan after first baking period.) Cool slightly on a rack, remove shells carefully from pans, and cool completely on rack.

Toast pine nuts in a shallow baking pan in oven 3 minutes. Transfer to a plate and cool.

Put chocolate in a large heatproof bowl. Bring cream to a full boil in a medium, heavy saucepan. Pour cream over chocolate all at once and stir with a whisk until chocolate is completely melted and mixture is smooth.

Cool to room temperature. Whisk in 5 tablespoons orange flower water. Taste and add remaining orange flower water, if desired.

Spoon about 2 tablespoons ganache into each tartlet. Put 3 or 4 lightly toasted pine nuts in center of each. Refrigerate about 30 minutes, or until filling sets. (Tartlets can be kept, covered, up to 2 days in refrigerator.) Serve at room temperature.

NOTE: Substitute pure vanilla extract for orange flower water. Chopped unsalted pistachios can be substituted for pine nuts.

ALSATIAN APPLE-APRICOT TART
Tarte alsacienne aux pommes et aux abricots

Cooks in Alsace love to bake their wonderful fruit—especially cherries, apricots, pears, and apples—into tarts, with a shell made from either a yeast dough or a rich pie dough. Unlike fruit tarts in the rest of France, here the fruit is moistened with a light, creamy custard before the tart is baked.   MAKES 6 TO 8 SERVINGS

French Tart Pastry (page 384)

FRUIT FILLING

1 1/4 pounds Golden Delicious
    apples
2 tablespoons butter
1 tablespoon sugar

8 to 10 ounces ripe fresh apricots
    or Poached Apricots (page
    372)

CUSTARD

2 large eggs plus 1 large yolk
7 tablespoons sugar
2/3 cup heavy cream, half-and-half,
    or milk

1 teaspoon pure vanilla extract

Prepare pastry and refrigerate until firm.

Lightly butter a 9 1/2- to 10-inch tart pan. Let dough soften 1 minute before rolling it. Roll out the dough on a lightly floured surface until about 1/4 inch thick. Roll up dough loosely around rolling pin and unroll it over pan. Gently ease the dough into pan. Using your thumb, gently push dough down slightly at edges of pan, making top edge of dough thicker than remaining dough. Roll rolling pin across pan to cut off dough. With your finger and thumb, press to push up the edge of dough all around pan, so it is slightly higher than rim of pan. Prick the dough all over with a fork. Refrigerate 30 minutes, or freeze 15 minutes, or cover with plastic wrap and refrigerate overnight.

FRUIT FILLING

Peel and core apples and cut in eighths. Melt butter in skillet. Add apples and sauté over medium heat until softened, about 7 minutes. Sprinkle with sugar and sauté 2 minutes, turning them from time to time. Let cool. Cut fresh apricots in half and remove pits. Drain poached apricots on paper towels.

Preheat oven to 400°F. Heat baking sheet in oven.

CUSTARD

Beat eggs and yolk with sugar until blended. Add cream and vanilla and mix well.

Put apricots, cut side up, in center of tart. Arrange apple pieces attractively around them. Carefully set tart pan on hot baking sheet in oven. Pour custard over fruit. Bake 30 to 40 minutes, or until custard sets and fruit is tender. (Tart can be kept overnight in refrigerator or can be frozen, but tastes best on day it is baked.) If it was frozen, heat before serving. Serve at room tempature.

NOTE: If you like, brush cooled tart lightly with 4 or 5 tablespoons apricot glaze, as in Pear Tart with Almond Cream (page 266).

STRAWBERRY TART WITH ALMOND CREAM
Tarte aux fraises à la crème d'amandes

A luscious almond cream bakes in this tart, which has a crust of sweet French pastry. It is then topped with fresh soft fruit such as strawberries or kiwis and brushed with a jam glaze that makes them glisten. For the pear variation, a favorite throughout France, the fruit is baked with the cream and becomes embedded in it. When I worked at a Parisian restaurant called La Ciboulette, I learned to make a version of this tart with a puff pastry shell, which can be easily prepared at home with purchased puff pastry.

MAKES 6 TO 8 SERVINGS

Sweet Pastry (page 385)

ALMOND CREAM

2/3 cup whole blanched almonds
1/2 cup sugar
6 tablespoons unsalted butter
1 large egg plus 1 large yolk

1 tablespoon kirsch or amaretto
*   liqueur, or 2 teaspoons rum*
2 tablespoons all-purpose flour

3/4 cup strawberry preserves or red
*   currant jelly*

1 1/4 pounds fairly small
*   strawberries, hulled*

Prepare dough and refrigerate until firm.
Butter a 9-inch square or 10-inch round tart pan with removable

bottom. Let dough soften 1 minute before rolling it. Roll out the dough on a cold lightly floured surface to a square or round about 1/4 inch thick and about 2 inches larger than pan. Roll up dough loosely around rolling pin and unroll it over pan. Gently ease dough into pan. Using your thumb, gently push dough down slightly at top edge of the pan, making top edge of dough thicker than remaining dough. Roll rolling pin across pan to cut off dough. With your finger and thumb, press to push up the top edge of dough all around pan, so it is about 1/4 inch higher than rim of the pan. Prick dough all over with a fork. Chill for 1 hour; or cover with plastic wrap and chill overnight or freeze.

Position a rack in lower third of oven and preheat to 425°F. Heat a baking sheet on rack in oven.

ALMOND CREAM

In a food processor, grind almonds with 2 tablespoons sugar to a fine powder. Beat butter in a bowl until soft. Add remaining sugar to butter and continue to beat until the mixture is smooth. In a small bowl, beat egg and yolk. Gradually beat egg mixture into butter mixture. Add liqueur, then stir in almond mixture and flour.

Spread almond cream in lined tart pan. (It will seem like a small amount but it puffs.) Bake tart on hot baking sheet for 10 minutes. Reduce temperature to 350°F. and bake another 30 minutes, or until almond cream is set and golden brown. Transfer to a rack to cool.

Heat preserves or jelly over low heat, stirring often, until melted. Strain preserves, pressing on pieces; there is no need to strain jelly. Brush preserves or jelly on tart. Arrange whole strawberries on top, pointing up. Brush jelly over berries. Serve at room temperature.

KIWI TART WITH ALMOND CREAM

Substitute 6 ripe kiwis for the strawberries. Peel kiwis and slice them 1/4 inch thick. Arrange slices on tart in circles, starting at outer edge and overlapping them.

Instead of jelly, prepare apricot glaze: heat 1/3 cup apricot preserves and 4 teaspoons kirsch or water over low heat, stirring often, until preserves melt. Strain the mixture, then brush over kiwi slices.

PEAR TART WITH ALMOND CREAM

Substitute 3 ripe pears, each about 8 ounces, for the strawberries. After spreading almond cream in tart pan, peel, halve, and core pears. Cut them in thin slices crosswise, keeping each half together. Using a metal spatula, set a pear half on almond cream at each corner of pan, with narrow end of pear pointing toward center of tart. Cut remaining sliced pear halves in half again lengthwise, and arrange these pear quarters on tart. Remove a few slices, if necessary, so slices are not too crowded. Press slightly to flatten slices on tart. Bake tart on hot baking sheet in preheated 425°F. oven for about 5 minutes. Reduce temperature to 400°F. and bake 5 minutes more, or until pastry begins to brown. Reduce temperature to 350°F. and bake for another 30 minutes, or until pears are soft and almond cream is set and golden brown. Transfer to a rack to cool.

Instead of jelly, prepare apricot glaze: heat ⅓ cup apricot preserves and 4 teaspoons amaretto liqueur, rum, or water over low heat, stirring often, until preserves melt. Strain mixture, and brush over pear slices and almond cream.

Puff Pastry Desserts

Puff pastry seems magical. It rises to majestic heights, even though it does not contain yeast or baking powder. Because of this pastry's unique structure of many fine layers of dough alternating with layers of butter, the steam created from the water in the dough during baking pushes the fine layers apart and causes the pastry to puff.

Good puff pastry is tender, buttery, and flaky and is terrific in cakes and in tarts. It can also be made into square or diamond-shaped cases called *feuilletés* that are baked and filled with creamy mixtures like whipped cream and fruit, pastry cream, or chocolate mousse. The most famous puff pastry dessert is the Napoleon, made with layers of cream and fruit. The French call it *millefeuille,* or "a thousand leaves," referring to the multilayered character of the puff pastry. Puff pastry is also good for making cookies, such as Coconut Palm-Leaf Cookies.

Making puff pastry at home is time-consuming. The actual working time is not long, but the dough requires several resting periods to prevent it from being tough.

Fortunately, puff pastry can be purchased from good pastry shops or bakeries and can be of excellent quality, especially if it is made with butter. It can also be found frozen at many supermarkets. Whether you prefer to make your own pastry or to buy it, with good homemade fillings like the wonderful apple compote in Latticed Apple-Cinnamon Puff Pastry Cake or the Chantilly cream and fresh nectarines in Nectarine Napoleon, you will create mouth-watering puff pastry desserts.

Hints

• Fresh puff pastry can often be purchased at pastry shops. Frozen puff pastry sheets can be purchased at fine supermarkets.

• Fresh puff pastry is hard to roll as thin as prerolled dough sheets, and so more is needed to make a sheet of the same dimensions.

• Always roll out puff pastry on a well-chilled surface, whether homemade or purchased from a bakery. Use a marble slab that you can chill in the freezer or refrigerator; or fill a roasting pan with ice cubes and put it on your regular work surface until it is cold, then dry the surface thoroughly.

• Try to roll puff pastry quickly and to handle it as little as possible, because it softens rapidly, especially if homemade.

• If puff pastry softens too much during rolling or shaping, as often happens on a warm day, chill it a few minutes before continuing.

• Chilling the pastry several times keeps the butter from melting and helps prevent the pastry from being tough. Be sure to chill puff pastry after shaping, or it will shrink badly during baking.

• When brushing puff pastry with egg glaze, do not let the glaze drip over the sides of the pastry and onto the baking sheet, because it could cause the dough to stick to the sheet and prevent it from rising well.

• Puff pastry freezes best when cut into shapes but unbaked. The dough itself can also be frozen.

- Freshness is essential for good puff pastry desserts. Try to serve all puff pastry desserts on the day they are baked.

CHOCOLATE MOUSSE FEUILLETÉS
Feuilletés à la mousse au chocolat

This modern dessert is made of *feuilletés,* or puff pastry cases, filled with chocolate mousse and served with white chocolate sauce and fresh berries. Chocolate with berries has been a popular match in America for some time, but in France this taste combination has caught on only recently. Although the dessert has several components that are brought together at the last moment, all of them can be easily prepared ahead.   MAKES 15 SERVINGS

FEUILLETÉS
14 ounces fresh puff pastry, or half a 17-ounce package frozen puff pastry sheets

1 egg, beaten with a pinch of salt, for glaze

CHOCOLATE MOUSSE
12 ounces fine-quality semisweet chocolate, chopped
6 tablespoons heavy cream
2 tablespoons unsalted butter, room temperature

6 large egg yolks, room temperature
3 large egg whites, room temperature
1 1/2 teaspoons sugar

WHITE CHOCOLATE SAUCE
3 cups heavy cream
1 vanilla bean

4 ounces fine-quality white chocolate, finely chopped

Fresh strawberries or raspberries for garnish

FEUILLETÉS
Sprinkle a large baking sheet lightly with water.

If using fresh puff pastry, roll it on a cold lightly floured surface to rectangle approximately 12 inches × 9 inches. Work as quickly as possible. Keep edges of dough as straight as possible and flour often. Cut pastry in 3-×-2-inch rectangles.

If using a frozen pastry sheet, thaw it 20 minutes and unfold it. Cut dough lengthwise in 3 strips, and each strip in 3-×-2-inch rectangles.

Transfer pastry rectangles to prepared baking sheet and refrigerate 30 minutes. Preheat oven to 450°F.

Brush pastries with egg glaze. Using the point of a sharp knife, mark a crisscross design on top, cutting through only top few layers of pastry. Bake pastries 5 minutes. Reduce heat to 400°F and bake 15 minutes more, or until pastries are puffed and browned. Transfer to racks and cool to room temperature. (Cases can be kept 1 day in an airtight container or can be frozen.)

CHOCOLATE MOUSSE

Heat chocolate in cream in a double boiler or heatproof medium bowl over hot, not simmering, water over low heat until melted, stirring occasionally. Stir until smooth and remove from pan of water. Whisk in butter, then whisk in egg yolks, 1 at a time.

Whip egg whites in a small bowl until soft peaks form. Beat in sugar and continue whipping at high speed until whites are stiff and shiny but not dry. Fold one-quarter of whites into chocolate mixture until blended. Return chocolate mixture to remaining whites and fold gently just until blended. Spoon mousse into a bowl and refrigerate at least 1 hour, or up to 3 hours before serving.

WHITE CHOCOLATE SAUCE

Bring 2 cups heavy cream to a boil with vanilla bean in a medium, heavy saucepan. Cover and let stand 15 minutes.

Uncover and return to a boil. Simmer over medium-high heat until thick enough to coat a spoon and reduced to 1 cup. Remove vanilla bean and cool to room temperature.

Melt chocolate in a small bowl above hot water over low heat. Whisk until smooth. Remove from pan of water and let cool. Whisk white chocolate into cream mixture and cool to room temperature. Gradually whisk in remaining 1 cup heavy cream.

To serve, carefully cut each pastry case in half horizontally, using a serrated knife. Put bottom half of each case on a plate. Using a pastry bag and medium star tip, pipe mousse onto case in crosswise loops so it shows at edges. Set top half on at an angle, allowing mousse to show. Spoon sauce on plate around pastry case, and set a few fresh berries on sauce.

NECTARINE NAPOLEON
Millefeuille aux brugnons

The charm of a Napoleon is in the contrast of the crisp, flaky pastry and creamy filling, and thus is best when assembled a short time before serving. This summer version features fresh nectarines and Chantilly cream layered with the pastry, and is especially simple to make if you purchase the puff pastry. You can also make it with sliced strawberries or peeled sliced peaches.   MAKES 8 SERVINGS

1 frozen puff pastry sheet (half a
   17-ounce package), or 14 to
   16 ounces fresh puff pastry
1 1/4 cups heavy cream
2 tablespoons plus 1 1/2 teaspoons
   powdered sugar

1 teaspoon pure vanilla extract
1 pound small ripe nectarines
2/3 cup apricot preserves
1 tablespoon water
About 1 teaspoon powdered sugar
   for sprinkling

If using a sheet of frozen dough, thaw dough 20 minutes and unfold sheet.

Sprinkle water lightly on an 11-×-17-inch baking sheet. Roll dough quickly on a cold lightly floured surface to a rectangle approximately 11 inches × 17 inches; if using a packaged sheet, enlarge it mainly in lengthwise direction. Keep dough as straight as possible and flour often. Roll dough around rolling pin and unroll onto prepared baking sheet. Trim edges, if necessary. Prick dough all over with fork at close intervals. Refrigerate 30 minutes. Meanwhile, position rack in center of oven and preheat to 400°F.

Bake dough 12 minutes, or until it begins to brown. Reduce oven temperature to 350°F. and bake 5 minutes, or until golden brown and crisp. Set a large rack over baking sheet and turn pastry over onto rack; sheet will be very thin. Cool on rack.

Slide pastry sheet onto a large cutting board. Using a small sharp knife and cutting with its point, trim edges of pastry straight. Cut it lengthwise in 3 equal strips; each will be slightly more than 3 inches wide.

Whip cream with sugar and vanilla in chilled bowl with chilled beater until stiff. Put cream in pastry bag with medium star tip. Cut nectarines in thin wedges, 1/2 inch thick at widest point.

Heat apricot preserves with water over low heat until melted. Strain into a small bowl. Brush apricot glaze on bottom pastry layer. Arrange layer of nectarines on top. Pipe 3 rows of whipped cream over them but not quite to edge of pastry, because it would come out. Set a second layer of pastry on top. Brush with apricot glaze. Set a layer of nectarines on top. Pipe another layer of whipped cream over them.

Cut remaining pastry layer in 8 equal pieces (to make serving easier). Set them in place on top of Napoleon, side by side. Dust lightly with powdered sugar. Top each piece with a nectarine wedge and brush wedge lightly with glaze. Pipe rosettes of whipped cream for garnish.

Serve at once; or refrigerate up to 2 hours. To serve, use a serrated knife to carefully cut Napoleon in portions. Be especially careful cutting through middle layer.

SEE PHOTOGRAPH.

⚘ LATTICED APPLE-CINNAMON PUFF PASTRY CAKE
Jalousie aux pommes à la cannelle

Jam is the usual filling for *jalousie,* or latticed puff pastry cake, but I prefer this cinnamon-accented apple compote because it has a more natural fruit taste and is not overly sweet.

             MAKES 2 CAKES, EACH 3 TO 4 SERVINGS

1 ½ pounds fresh homemade Puff
    Pastry (page 386), or
    purchased or frozen sheets (see
    Note)

APPLE FILLING
2 pounds tart apples, such as   *1 teaspoon ground cinnamon*
    Pippin or Granny Smith   *3 tablespoons raspberry preserves*
2 tablespoons butter   *4 tablespoons sugar*

2 egg yolks, beaten, for glaze

Cut dough in 2 pieces. Refrigerate at least 1 hour before rolling.

APPLE FILLING
    Peel apples and cut in half. Core them and cut in thin slices. Melt butter in a sauté pan and add apples and cinnamon. Cover and cook over medium-low heat, stirring occasionally, about 20 minutes, or until apples are very tender and falling apart. Uncover and cook, stirring often, about 5 minutes, or until any excess liquid has evaporated. Add preserves and sugar and heat, stirring, to dissolve sugar. If necessary, cook over medium-high heat, stirring, until filling is very thick. Let cool completely. (Filling can be kept, covered, 1 day in refrigerator.)

    Lightly sprinkle water on a baking sheet. Roll half the dough on a cold, lightly floured surface to a 9-×-12-inch rectangle about ⅛ inch thick. With a sharp knife, cut in 2 pieces lengthwise, one slightly wider than other. (Chill if pastry is becoming too soft at this point.) Turn smaller piece over and set on baking sheet. Spoon 1 cup apple filling down center of dough on baking sheet. Let it come to 1 inch of edges. Brush edges lightly with water.

Fold second dough strip in half lengthwise. Using a sharp knife, cut slits in folded side of dough nearly to other side (about ¾ inch from end), spacing slits about ½ inch apart. Unfold dough and set on bottom dough layer, so that slits are above filling. Gently press to seal dough at edges and prevent filling from coming out. Refrigerate. Shape a second cake using remaining dough and filling. Refrigerate cakes 1 hour.

Preheat oven to 425°F. Trim edges of dough, if necessary. Make a decorative fluted edge on pastry by using back of a small knife and bringing it slightly inward at about ½-inch intervals. Brush carefully with egg glaze, brushing each center strip individually so glaze doesn't stick them together. With thin knife outline slits above filling to be sure they're not stuck together.

Bake 15 minutes. Reduce oven temperature to 375°F. and bake another 15 to 20 minutes, or until crisp and golden brown; cake tastes best when baked thoroughly. Transfer to a rack to cool. Serve warm or at room temperature. (Cake can be kept overnight, covered, but tastes best on day it was baked.)

NOTE: If desired, substitute two 17-ounce packages frozen puff pastry sheets for fresh puff pastry. Defrost dough of 1 package 20 minutes and unfold sheet. Cut off one-third of each sheet lengthwise, along 1 fold. Reserve it for other uses. Set 1 sheet on baking sheet sprinkled with water. Spread with 1 cup filling. Fold second dough sheet in half lengthwise and follow instructions above to finish shaping cake. Repeat with second package of pastry sheets. Refrigerate cakes 30 minutes to 1 hour. Preheat oven to 400°F. Brush cakes with glaze and bake 15 minutes. Reduce oven temperature to 350°F. and bake another 10 to 15 minutes.

✺ FEUILLETÉS WITH BERRIES AND CHANTILLY CREAM
Feuilletés aux Baies Fraîches à la Crème Chantilly

For this festive dessert, puff pastry cases are split and filled with Chantilly cream that has been spiked with raspberry brandy, then topped with blackberries, blueberries, and strawberries. A smooth berry sauce is the perfect accompaniment for this dessert. Puff pastry cases are also great with vanilla ice cream and warm caramel sauce (page 65), and garnished with either berries, peaches, or nectarines.

MAKES 15 SERVINGS

Feuilletés (page 268)
1 quart strawberries, hulled
2 cups blueberries
2 cups blackberries or raspberries
2½ cups heavy cream, well chilled
2 tablespoons sugar

3 tablespoons plus 1 teaspoon clear raspberry brandy (framboise) (see Note)
4 cups Raspberry, Strawberry or Blackberry Sauce (pages 345, 346, 347)

Bake *feuilletés* and let cool.

Cut strawberries in quarters, and mix lightly with other berries.

Carefully cut each pastry case in half horizontally with a serrated knife.

In a large chilled bowl with chilled beater, whip cream with sugar until soft peaks form. And brandy and whip until stiff. Using a pastry bag with a medium star tip, pipe cream decoratively on bottom half of each *feuilleté.* Transfer to serving plates. Top each pastry with berries, putting some on plate also. Set top half of each case in place at an angle.

Either pour some sauce on each plate next to pastry; or serve sauce separately. If any cream or berries are left, serve them separately.

NOTE: If desired, substitute 2½ teaspoons pure vanilla extract for the raspberry brandy.

Savarins and Other Yeast-Leavened Cakes

Like many other culinary creations, the idea for the French cakes called *babas* come about by chance. The eighteenth-century duke of the French province of Lorraine thought of moistening his dry, day-old kugelhopf with rum and garnishing it with Chantilly cream.

Over the years the recipe was refined, and a syrup was added to balance the sharpness of the rum. A whole group of yeast-leavened cakes was subsequently developed using this principle. The most elegant is the ring-shaped savarin, named for the famous French gastronome Brillat-Savarin, author of *Physiology of Taste.*

The original kugelhopf was not forgotten either. This beautiful fluted cake, garnished with almonds and studded with raisins, remains the quintessential coffee cake in France, and it is usually served as a breakfast treat rather than for dessert. It is well loved by the Alsatians, the Austrians, and the Germans.

Unlike kugelhopf and other yeast cakes, which resemble breads in their slightly chewy texture and are best served at coffee time or teatime, savarins and their relatives are light, moist, delicate cakes, perfect as an ending for a festive dinner.

These cakes are made from a soft batterlike dough that is easy to make. In order to encourage the cakes to absorb syrup easily, the batter is quite rich in eggs and yeast so that it becomes very bubbly and acquires a spongy texture after baking. The dough has little sugar because the syrup gives it enough sweetness.

Like most fine yeast doughs, the dough for these cakes rises twice. The first time, it rises without any butter mixed into it, so that it is very light and can rise quickly. Instead the butter is put in pieces on the dough, so that it slowly comes to the same temperature as the dough and is easy to beat in after the first rising. After the dough is transferred to the molds, it is left to rise to the top. During baking, it expands even more.

In addition to the cylindrical babas and the ring-shaped savarins, the basic batter can be baked in a variety of other forms, from boat-shaped barquettes to simple round layers to cupcakes. It can be flavored with raisins, citrus peel, and even candied ginger.

It is the syrup and spirits added after baking that makes these yeast cakes unique. In addition to rum, the classic flavoring for babas and savarins, other popular spirits for these cakes are Grand Marnier and curaçao. I made these light cakes using different fruit liqueurs and brandies and enjoyed all the new versions, especially when the spirits matched the other flavors in the cake. Kirsch, for example, is great in Individual Cherry Savarins.

Special techniques are used to moisten these cakes. The hot syrup is ladled over large cakes, but small ones are dipped directly into it.

Chefs sprinkle the cakes with rum or other spirits by pouring them directly from the bottle and regulating the amount by holding their thumb over the neck of the bottle. It takes some practice to do this evenly, and is often more convenient at home to slowly spoon the spirits over the cakes in order to have a clear idea of the quantity being used.

These cakes are either served plain or brushed with apricot glaze, which makes them shiny and helps to prevent the liqueur from evaporating. While the classic embellishment of colorful candied fruit and nuts is still popular for babas, fresh fruit is the preferred garnish for cakes of other shapes. An individual or large savarin filled with whipped cream and seasonal fruit in the ring's center is a beautiful sight.

French cooks also use yeast doughs to make tarts, as in Sweet Citrus "Pizza," a round pastry made of a rich yeast-leavened dough with a sweet buttery lemon topping. This type of dough can also be covered with apples, pears, plums, apricots, or other fruit and baked as a country-style tart.

The most famous French pastry is, of course, the croissant. Made from a yeast-leavened dough, it is layered with butterlike puff pastry but is easier to make. Homemade croissants are buttery, flaky, and fabulous. The dough is also perfect for preparing filled pastries, such as Chocolate-Hazelnut Croissant Rolls.

Hints

YEAST-RISEN DOUGHS IN GENERAL

• If using fresh yeast, substitute one ⅗-ounce cake of fresh yeast for one ¼-ounce envelope (about 2½ teaspoons) of dry yeast. Crumble the fresh yeast over the water and let stand about 10 minutes, or until foamy. Stir the yeast mixture until smooth before adding it to the remaining ingredients.

• For baking yeast doughs, thoroughly butter all molds, including any rings, flutes, or crevaces.

• When letting a yeast dough rise in small pans, set a sheet of plastic wrap or a slightly dampened towel over them to cover several pans.

• Remove the plastic wrap or towel before the yeast dough has risen to the top of the pans to prevent it from sticking to the covering.

SAVARIN-TYPE CAKES

• If you would like to bake savarin dough in pans or molds other than those specified in the recipes, use enough dough to fill them by one-third to one-half.

• To measure savarin dough by tablespoons, take the desired amount between your thumb and forefinger and pinch it off from rest of dough.

• Savarins and other large cakes can absorb the syrup only *gradually.* Moisten the cake *very* slowly and evenly by ladling syrup over cake in a thin stream, over all of the surface of the cake. If too much syrup is added to one part at a time, that part of the cake can become soggy. Liqueur or other spirits should also be sprinkled gradually over cake.

• The syrup is reheated several times because the cakes absorb hot syrup most easily.

• After being moistened with syrup, babas and savarin-type cakes can be kept, covered, 1 day in the refrigerator.

• If syrup comes out of a cake onto the platter, pat the platter dry before serving.

• Glazing cakes with strained preserves helps to seal in the liqueur. Serve unglazed cakes as soon as possible after sprinkling them with liqueur, to prevent it from evaporating.

SAVARIN DOUGH
Pâte à savarin

Use this dough for a variety of light cakes moistened with syrup, including large and individual ring-shaped savarins, spirited babas, and Nectarine Gâteau with Peach Brandy.

MAKES 12 TO 18 SERVINGS, DEPENDING ON SIZE OF MOLDS;
ABOUT 2½ CUPS DOUGH

1 envelope dry yeast (¼ ounce)
¼ cup warm water (105°F. to 115°F.)
1 tablespoon plus 1 teaspoon sugar
7 tablespoons unsalted butter, cut in 14 pieces

2 cups unbleached all-purpose flour
4 large eggs
1 teaspoon salt

Sprinkle yeast over water in small bowl, add 1 teaspoon of sugar and let stand 10 minutes. Let butter stand at room temperature. Follow one of the following three methods to make the dough.

TO MAKE DOUGH IN MIXER

Sift flour into bowl of heavy-duty mixer fitted with dough hook. Add 2 eggs, salt and remaining 1 tablespoon sugar. Mix at low speed until a few tablespoons of flour are drawn into egg mixture, about 15 seconds. Add yeast mixture and remaining 2 eggs and mix at low speed until dough is soft and smooth, scraping dough down occasionally from hook and sides of bowl, about 10 minutes. Continue to beat dough at medium speed, scraping down occasionally, until dough is very smooth and most of it comes away from sides of bowl and wraps around hook, about 12 minutes. Dough will be soft and very sticky. Lightly oil medium bowl. Transfer dough to oiled bowl and put butter pieces, side by side, on top of dough. Cover with plastic wrap or with a lightly dampened towel and let dough rise in warm draft-free area until doubled in volume, about 1 hour. Transfer dough to clean mixer bowl. Beat in butter with dough hook at low speed, scraping down often, until blended, about 3 minutes.

TO MAKE DOUGH IN FOOD PROCESSOR

Put yeast mixture, remaining 1 tablespoon sugar and eggs in food processor fitted with plastic or metal blade and process until blended, about 5 seconds. Sift in flour and salt and process 30 seconds without stopping machine. (If machine is stopped and restarted at this point, sticky dough can prevent blade from turning well.) If dough is not entirely smooth, transfer to medium bowl and slap dough a few times in bowl by hand. Lightly oil medium bowl. Transfer dough to oiled bowl and put butter pieces, side by side, on top of dough. Cover with plastic wrap or with a lightly dampened towel and let dough rise in warm draft-free area until doubled in volume, about 1 hour. Stir in butter with cutting and folding motion of a wooden spoon. Gently slap dough a few times in bowl until butter is completely blended in.

TO MAKE DOUGH BY HAND

Sift flour into large bowl and make a well in center. Add 2 eggs, salt, and remaining 1 tablespoon sugar to well and mix them with wooden spoon, gradually drawing in 2 or 3 tablespoons of flour. Add remaining 2 eggs and yeast mixture to well and stir to a soft dough. Dough will be very sticky. With cupped hand under dough, slap dough against bowl for about 1 minute. Lightly oil medium bowl. Transfer dough to oiled bowl and put butter pieces, side by side, on top of dough. Cover with plastic wrap or with a lightly dampened towel and let dough rise in warm draft-free area until doubled in volume, about 1 hour. Stir in butter with a cutting and folding motion of a wooden spoon. Gently slap dough a few times in bowl until butter is completely blended in.

❧ CLASSIC RUM BABAS
Babas au rhum

These cakes are baked in special bucket-shaped baba molds, also called dariole molds, but popover pans or cupcake pans can be used instead. The amount of rum sprinkled on each baba depends on how spirited you like them; 1 ½ teaspoons for each baba gives a delicate rum flavor, while 2 or 2 ½ teaspoons give quite a punch.

MAKES 12 BABAS

⅔ cup dark raisins	*Savarin Dough (see previous recipe)*
1 tablespoon rum	

BABA SYRUP
1 ¼ cups sugar	*2 cups water*

1 cup apricot preserves	*36 almond slices for garnish*
2 tablespoons water	*Chantilly Cream (see recipe)*
7 to 9 tablespoons rum	*(optional)*
6 red candied cherries, cut in half,	
for garnish	

Rinse raisins, drain, and put them in a small jar. Add 1 tablespoon rum, cover tightly, and shake. Let stand while making dough.

After mixing butter into dough, drain raisins. Stir raisins into dough, with a cutting and folding motion of wooden spoon.

Generously butter twelve ½-cup baba molds. Spoon 3 tablespoons dough into each. Set individual molds on baking sheet. Cover with plastic wrap and let rise in warm, draft-free place for 25 minutes. Remove covering and continue to let rise to top of molds, about 15 to 30 minutes more.

Position rack in center of oven and preheat to 400°F. Bake babas on their baking sheet about 15 minutes, or until dough comes away from sides of pan, top is browned, and cake tester inserted into centers comes out clean. Unmold onto rack and cool completely.

BABA SYRUP

Heat sugar and water in medium, heavy saucepan over low heat, stirring gently until dissolved. Raise heat to high and bring to a boil. Remove from heat. (Syrup can be made 1 day ahead and refrigerated.) Reheat to a simmer before using and remove from heat.

Set cake rack above deep tray. Put 1 baba in hot syrup, rounded side facing down, and leave a few seconds. Ladle syrup over baba several times until it is moist but not soggy. Roll cake quickly around in syrup to encourage it to absorb more syrup. Cake should absorb a generous amount of syrup so that no part of cake remains dry; but if left in syrup too long, it may fall apart. Lift cake with a broad slotted skimmer. Check to be sure cake is well moistened and softened throughout by touching; if there are any firm parts, ladle syrup over the cake a few more times. Remove carefully with skimmer and drain on its side on prepared cake rack. Repeat with other babas, reheating syrup occasionally. If any syrup remains, slowly spoon it over cakes. Drain cakes 30 minutes on rack.

Heat preserves and water over low heat in medium saucepan, stirring, until preserves are completely melted. Strain into another saucepan, pressing on pieces.

Put babas on plates or on a tray. A short time before serving, spoon rum very slowly over each baba, rolling baba so it absorbs rum evenly; it is easiest to spoon 1 teaspoon rum over each baba, then to spoon ½ to 1 teaspoon additional rum over each.

Set babas on rack on their sides. Reheat strained preserves until just beginning to bubble. Stir in 1 tablespoon rum. Brush on all sides of babas.

Arrange babas on their sides on platter. Decorate each baba with a candied cherry half, and with 3 almond slices around cherry. Brush each cherry lightly with apricot glaze. Cool 10 minutes. (Babas can be kept, covered, for 1 day in refrigerator.) Serve at room temperature with Chantilly cream on the side, if desired.

BABA CUPCAKES

Substitute about 16 cupcake or muffin pans for baba molds. Use about 2 tablespoons dough for each. Bake about 12 minutes. To moisten them with rum, set them spongy side up. Before brushing them with glaze, set them on rack, rounded side up.

❧ GINGERED SAVARIN WITH PINEAPPLE
Savarin au gingembre à l'ananas

Instead of using spirits in the syrup for a savarin, you can flavor it with a vanilla bean, citrus zest and juice, or with fresh ginger, as in this dessert. Diced candied ginger in the cake batter complements the syrup. The cake is also sublime with slices of exotic fruit, such as guava, fresh figs, mango, or papaya.   MAKES 12 SERVINGS

Savarin Dough (page 278)
¼ cup finely diced crystallized
*   ginger (see Note)*

GINGER SYRUP
One 3-inch piece fresh ginger, peeled   *1½ cups sugar*
*   and cut in thin slices*   *2 cups water*

½ small fresh pineapple   *1 tablespoon water*
½ cup apricot preserves   *Chantilly Cream (page 355)*

Prepare dough. Stir in crystallized ginger with a cutting and folding motion of a wooden spoon. Generously butter a 5-cup ring mold. Transfer dough to mold and, using a rubber spatula, smooth dough to an even layer. Cover with plastic wrap and let rise in warm, draft-free place for 25 minutes. Remove covering and continue to let rise to top of molds, about 15 to 30 minutes more.

Position rack in center of oven and preheat to 400°F. Bake about 23 minutes, or until dough comes away from sides of pan, top is browned, and cake tester inserted into cake comes out clean. Unmold onto rack. Cool completely. (Cake can be baked ahead and kept up to 3 days in an airtight container; or it can be frozen.)

GINGER SYRUP
Heat fresh ginger, sugar, and water in medium, heavy saucepan over low heat, stirring gently until dissolved. Raise heat to high and bring to a boil. Reduce heat to very low, cover, and cook 20 minutes. Remove ginger with a slotted spoon. Syrup can be made 1 day ahead

and refrigerated. Reheat to a simmer before using and remove from heat.

Set cake rack above deep tray. Put cake on prepared rack, with firm crust side facing down. Slowly and evenly ladle hot syrup over cake until it has absorbed as much syrup as possible. Let stand about 2 minutes. Return syrup that dripped onto tray to saucepan. Reheat to a simmer over medium-high heat. Repeat moistening of cake. Continue reheating syrup and moistening cake a few more times, until most of syrup is absorbed; do not overheat syrup or it will caramelize. If sides of cake appear dry, gently brush syrup over them. Drain cake 30 minutes on rack. Carefully transfer cake to a platter with 2 wide slotted metal spatulas.

Peel pineapple and cut in round ¼-inch-thick slices. Remove cores. Cut pineapple slices in half to form wedges. Pat pieces dry with paper towels and reserve 8 wedges for garnish.

Heat preserves and water in small saucepan over low heat, stirring, until preserves are completely melted. Strain, pressing on pieces. Brush strained preserves over cake. Garnish with reserved pineapple wedges, and brush them with preserves.

Arrange pineapple slices in center of ring. Using a pastry bag and medium star tip, pipe large rosettes of Chantilly cream over slices in center, covering them. (Cake can be refrigerated up to 4 hours.) Serve cold and serve any remaining cream separately.

NOTE: To dice crystallized ginger, cut it in very thin slices, then in thin sticks, then in tiny cubes.

ORANGE BABAS WITH GRAND MARNIER
Babas à l'orange au grand marnier

Like the rum sprinkled on classic babas, the amount of Grand Marnier sprinkled on each of these depends on your taste.

MAKES 12 BABAS

ORANGE SAVARIN DOUGH
1/4 cup chopped candied orange peel
2 tablespoons Grand Marnier

Savarin Dough (page 278)
2 teaspoons grated orange peel

Baba Syrup (page 280, 281)
1 cup apricot preserves
2 tablespoons water
7 to 9 tablespoons Grand Marnier

About 1/4 cup sliced almonds for
   garnish
16 pieces diced candied orange peel
   for garnish

ORANGE SAVARIN DOUGH

Put chopped candied peel in small jar. Add 2 tablespoons Grand Marnier, cover tightly, and shake. Let stand while making dough.

After mixing butter into dough, drain candied peel, reserving any Grand Marnier that was not absorbed. Stir candied peel and grated peel into dough, with a cutting and folding motion of a wooden spoon.

Follow instructions on page 277 for spooning dough into molds, baking, preparing syrup, and dipping cakes in syrup.

Heat preserves and water over low heat in a medium saucepan, stirring, until preserves are completely melted. Strain into another saucepan, pressing on pieces.

Put babas on plates or on a tray. A short time before serving, slowly sprinkle each cake with 1 teaspoon Grand Marnier, then with another 1/2 to 1 teaspoon more Grand Marnier.

Set babas on rack on their sides. Reheat strained preserves until just beginning to bubble. Measure Grand Marnier reserved from candied peel and add more Grand Marnier, if necessary, to obtain 1 tablespoon. Stir liqueur into preserves. Brush mixture all over babas. Garnish each by making a flower with 5 almond slices as petals and a center of diced candied peel. (Babas can be kept, covered, for 1 day in refrigerator.) Serve at room temperature.

NOTE: These can also be baked as cupcakes, as in Baba Cupcakes, page 281.

NECTARINE GÂTEAU WITH PEACH BRANDY
Gâteau aux brugnons à l'eau de vie de pêches

For this modern gâteau filled with fresh nectarine slices and peach brandy whipped cream, savarin dough is baked in a round cake pan instead of the usual ring mold, then split in two layers. Chef Fernand Chambrette, my culinary mentor, came up with the idea for this cake when we were experimenting with savarin cakes with fruit fillings.

MAKES 12 SERVINGS

Savarin Dough (page 278)   *2 tablespoons peach brandy*
Savarin Syrup (pages 288, 289)

PEACH BRANDY WHIPPED CREAM
1 cup heavy cream, well chilled   *2 tablespoons peach brandy*
2 teaspoons sugar

3/4 pound nectarines   *2 tablespoons peach brandy*

Prepare dough. Generously butter a 9-inch layer cake pan. Transfer dough to pan and, using a rubber spatula, smooth dough to an even layer. Cover with plastic wrap and let rise in warm, draft-free place 25 minutes. Remove covering and continue to let rise nearly to top of pan, about 15 to 30 minutes more. Position rack in center of oven and preheat to 400°F. Bake about 15 minutes, or until dough comes away from sides of pan, top is browned, and cake tester inserted into cake comes out clean. Unmold onto rack. (Cake can be kept up to 3 days in an airtight container; or it can be frozen.)

Prepare savarin syrup. Set cake rack above deep tray. Put cake on prepared rack, with firm crust side facing down. Slowly and evenly ladle hot syrup over cake until it has absorbed as much syrup as possible. Let stand about 2 minutes. Return syrup that dripped onto tray to saucepan and reheat to a simmer over medium-high heat. Repeat moistening of cake. Continue reheating syrup and moistening cake a few more times, until most of syrup is absorbed; do not over-heat syrup or it will caramelize. If sides of cake appear dry, gently brush syrup over them. Drain cake 30 minutes on rack.

Carefully transfer cake to a platter with 2 wide slotted metal spatulas. Carefully cut cake in half horizontally with a long serrated knife. Slide top of cake gently onto a springform base without turning cake layer over. Be careful because cake is very moist. Sprinkle 2 tablespoons peach brandy on bottom cake layer.

PEACH BRANDY WHIPPED CREAM

Beat cream with sugar in chilled bowl with chilled beater until soft peaks form. Add brandy and beat until fairly stiff.

Slice all but 1 nectarine inward toward pit. Sprinkle slices with 1 tablespoon peach brandy.

On bottom cake layer spread half the whipped cream. Top with nectarine slices, arranging those at outer edge so that they point inward. Carefully slide top layer onto cake and sprinkle it slowly and evenly with remaining 1 tablespoon peach brandy.

Spread top layer with remaining cream. (Cake can be refrigerated up to 4 hours.) Just before serving, slice remaining nectarine in very thin wedges and arrange them in a circle, pointing inward, on top outer edge of cake. Serve cold.

INDIVIDUAL CHERRY SAVARINS
Savarins aux cerises

Savarins baked in small ring molds make glamorous individual desserts, especially when garnished with fresh fruit and whipped cream. Use imported kirsch in this dessert for the best flavor. Choose small savarin pans or ring molds, each holding 1/4 to 1/3 cup; the center of the ring can be closed or open.

MAKES 16 TO 18 SERVINGS

Savarin Dough (page 278)   *1 pound sweet cherries*
Baba Syrup (pages 280, 281)

KIRSCH WHIPPED CREAM
1 cup heavy cream, well chilled   *4 teaspoons kirsch*
2 teaspoons sugar

5 to 6 tablespoons kirsch

Prepare dough. Generously butter 16 to 18 individual savarin pans. Set them on baking sheet. To fill pans, use a piping bag and medium plain tip (about ½ inch in diameter). Pipe in enough dough to fill rings by about a third to a half, piping it into a smooth ring shape following form of mold. To finish each ring, cut off dough from tip with a knife. Use oiled fingers to pat dough smooth. Cover with plastic wrap and let rise in warm, draft-free place for 25 minutes. Remove covering and continue to let rise to top of molds, about 15 to 30 minutes more.

Position rack in center of oven and preheat to 400°F. Bake about 12 minutes, or until dough comes away from sides of pans, tops are browned, and cake tester inserted into cakes comes out clean. Unmold onto rack. (Cakes can be baked ahead and kept up to 3 days in an airtight container; or they can be frozen.)

Prepare baba syrup. Set cake rack above deep tray. Put 1 cake into hot syrup, with firm crust side facing down, and leave a few seconds. Ladle syrup over cake several times until it is moist but not soggy. Cake should absorb a generous amount of syrup so that no part of cake remains dry, but if left in syrup too long, it may fall apart. Lift cake with a broad slotted skimmer. Check by touching to be sure cake is well moistened and softened throughout; if there are any firm parts, ladle syrup over it a few more times. Remove carefully with skimmer and drain on prepared cake rack, with firm crust side facing down. Repeat with other savarins. Reheat syrup occasionally. If any syrup remains, slowly spoon it over cakes. Drain cakes 30 minutes on rack.

Halve and pit all but 16 to 18 cherries. Leave stems on whole cherries. Put cakes on serving platter.

KIRSCH WHIPPED CREAM

Beat cream with sugar in chilled bowl with chilled beater until soft peaks form. Add 4 teaspoons kirsch and beat until stiff.

As close as possible to serving time, put about 1 tablespoon cherry halves into center of each ring. Sprinkle each ring slowly and evenly with 1 teaspoon kirsch. Using a pastry bag and medium star tip, pipe a large rosette of flavored whipped cream in center of each ring, covering cherries. Top rosette with a whole cherry. To serve, slide wide metal spatula under each cake and filling.

SUMMER FRUIT SAVARIN
Savarin aux fruits d'été

A mélange of the season's berries provides the filling for this great party cake, while the intensely perfumed French raspberry brandy known as *eau de vie de framboise* flavors the accompanying whipped cream.   MAKES 12 SERVINGS

Savarin Dough (page 278)

SAVARIN SYRUP

1 ½ cups sugar	*2 cups water*

BERRY SALAD

1 ½ cups small strawberries, hulled
¾ cup raspberries
¾ cup blackberries or blueberries
1 tablespoon plus 1 ½ teaspoons sugar

1 tablespoon plus 1 ½ teaspoons clear raspberry brandy (framboise)

FRAMBOISE WHIPPED CREAM

1 cup heavy cream, well chilled
2 teaspoons sugar

2 tablespoons clear raspberry brandy

4 teaspoons clear raspberry brandy

3 cups Raspberry Sauce (page 345) (optional)

Prepare dough. Generously butter a 5-cup ring mold. Transfer dough to mold and use a rubber spatula to smooth dough to an even layer. Cover with plastic wrap and let rise in warm, draft-free place for 25 minutes. Remove covering and continue to let rise to top of mold, about 15 to 30 minutes more.

Position rack in center of oven and preheat to 400°F. Bake about 23 minutes, or until dough comes away from sides of pan, top is browned, and cake tester inserted into cake comes out clean. Unmold onto rack and cool completely. (Cake can be baked ahead and kept up to 3 days in an airtight container; or it can be frozen.)

SAVARIN SYRUP

Heat sugar and water in medium, heavy saucepan over low heat, stirring gently until dissolved. Raise heat to high and bring to a boil. Remove from heat. (Syrup can be made 1 day ahead and refrigerated.) Reheat to a simmer and remove from heat before using.

Set cake rack above deep tray. Put cake on prepared rack, with firm crust side facing down. Slowly and evenly ladle hot syrup over cake until it has absorbed as much syrup as possible. Let stand about 2 minutes. Return syrup that dripped onto tray to saucepan. Reheat to a simmer over medium-high heat. Repeat moistening of cake. Continue reheating syrup and moistening cake a few more times, until most of syrup is absorbed; do not overheat syrup or it will caramelize. If sides of cake appear dry, gently brush syrup over them. Drain cake 30 minutes on rack. Carefully transfer cake to a platter with 2 wide slotted metal spatulas.

BERRY SALAD

Cut strawberries in halves or quarters lengthwise. Combine berries in bowl. Sprinkle berries with sugar and with framboise and mix gently with a rubber spatula. Cover and refrigerate 15 minutes. Spoon salad into center of ring. (Cake can be kept, covered, for 1 hour in refrigerator.)

FRAMBOISE WHIPPED CREAM

Beat cream with sugar in chilled bowl with chilled beater until soft peaks form. Add 4 teaspoons brandy and beat until stiff. Refrigerate until ready to use.

As close as possible to serving time, slowly spoon 2 tablespoons raspberry brandy over cake, moving spoon over surface of cake several times. Using pastry bag and medium star tip, pipe flavored whipped cream around edge of fruit mixture and around base of cake. Serve cake on plate of raspberry sauce or serve sauce and remaining cream separately.

SEE JACKET PHOTOGRAPH.

ALSATIAN COFFEE CAKE WITH RAISINS AND ALMONDS
Kugelhopf

Alsatian cooks are famous for their cakes, especially those that make use of yeast for rising. The best known is kugelhopf, a ridged, turban-shaped cake with an almond imbedded in each ridge. If you visit the region, you can't miss this classic coffee cake. Even at outdoor markets you can find them in several sizes, not to mention in every pastry shop. Beautiful ceramic fluted kugelhopf pans are favorite souvenirs of Alsace.

The dough is easy to make and requires no kneading, just thorough beating with a mixer. The Alsatians use kirsch to give it a special flavor. The alcohol evaporates during the baking, though, so there is no need to worry that the cake might make you tipsy at breakfast!

MAKES 12 TO 16 SERVINGS

1 cup dark raisins
3 tablespoons kirsch
1 cup milk
2 envelopes dry yeast (1/4 ounce each)
2/3 cup granulated sugar
3 1/2 cups all-purpose flour
1 1/2 teaspoons salt
3 large eggs
1 cup unsalted butter, room temperature
16 to 18 whole blanched almonds
Powdered sugar for sprinkling

Put raisins in a small bowl, pour kirsch over them, and mix well. Cover and let stand at least 4 hours, or overnight.

Heat milk to lukewarm. Sprinkle yeast over 1/2 cup of milk and add ¼ teaspoon sugar. Let stand for 10 minutes until foamy. Put ½ cup flour in a medium bowl and stir in ¼ cup milk and yeast mixture. Cover with a damp towel and leave for about 10 to 15 minutes.

Meanwhile, spoon remaining 3 cups flour into bowl of a mixer and make a well in center. Add salt, remaining sugar, and remaining milk. Mix central ingredients briefly with a wooden spoon. Add eggs to well. Cut half the butter into 8 pieces and add them. Using the dough hook of mixer, mix to a smooth dough at a low speed. Gradually add remaining butter, about 1 tablespoon at a time. Last, beat in yeast mixture. Scrape down mixture and continue to beat with the dough hook on medium speed until mixture is very smooth, about 10 to 12 minutes. Cover with a damp towel and let rise for 30 minutes. It will become lighter but will not double in bulk.

Heavily butter a 9½-inch kugelhopf mold or fluted tube pan; be sure to butter tube and each fluted section. Put an almond in base of each flute in design. Stir raisins and kirsch into risen batter and carefully transfer it to mold, taking care not to move almonds. Smooth the top. Cover with a damp towel and let rise for 1 hour, or until mixture nearly reaches top of mold.

Preheat oven to 400°F. Bake kugelhopf for 10 minutes. Reduce oven temperature to 350°F. and continue baking about 45 minutes more, or until a cake tester inserted in kugelhopf comes out clean. If kugelhopf browns too much on top, cover it with foil.

Cool cake in pan on a rack for about 10 minutes, then turn out onto a rack and let cool. Sprinkle with powdered sugar just before serving.

SWEET CITRUS "PIZZA"
Galette pérougienne

Like pizza, this country-style cake features a yeast-leavened dough baked with a topping, in this case a sweet buttery one. Served warm, it is a great dessert for winter. If you have never made yeast dough, this is a very simple one to start with, and one I have often taught in my basic pastry classes.

When my husband and I traveled through the provinces of France, we found relatives of this cake everywhere. They were especially abundant in the Jura area, near the Alps, where they often had a sugar-and-butter topping like this one, or were topped with apricots, cherries, or other seasonal fruit. In northeastern France, in the Lorraine region, we tasted this cake at a pâtisserie in Vittel, the town in the Vosges Mountains where they make the famous bottled water. Called gâteau lorrain, this version was made from the basic dough that was simply sprinkled with sliced almonds; the finished cake was split and filled with pastry cream. At the southern end of France, in St. Tropez, we sampled a similar cake, filled with lemon pastry cream and called—what else?—gâteau de St. Tropez!

MAKES 2 CAKES, EACH 4 TO 6 SERVINGS

YEAST DOUGH

1 envelope dry yeast (¼ ounce)	1 teaspoon salt
¾ cup lukewarm water (105° to 115°F.)	2 large eggs
1 tablespoon sugar	6 tablespoons butter, room temperature
3 cups all-purpose flour	

TOPPING

6 tablespoons butter, cold	Rind of 1 large lemon, orange, or tangerine (see Note)
½ cup sugar	

YEAST DOUGH

Sprinkle yeast over ¼ cup lukewarm water in cup or small bowl, add 1 teaspoon sugar and leave for 10 minutes. In a food processor, process flour, salt, and remaining 2 teaspoons sugar briefly to mix them. Add eggs. With blades of processor turning, gradually pour in yeast mixture and remaining water. Process 1 minute to knead dough. Add butter and process just until absorbed. Dough will be soft and sticky. Transfer dough to a lightly oiled bowl and turn dough over to oil its entire surface. Cover with a damp towel and let rise in a warm place 1 hour, or until doubled in bulk.

Lightly butter 2 baking sheets. Divide dough in 2 equal parts, and place each on a baking sheet and pat with lightly floured hands to a 10-inch circle.

TOPPING

Cut butter into very thin slices and put them in one layer on cakes, leaving a ¾-inch border uncovered to make a rim. Sprinkle with ½ cup sugar, still leaving a border, and grate on citrus rind. Let rise 15 minutes. Preheat oven to 425°F.

Bake 15 to 20 minutes, or until dough browns and sugar melts. If there is too much melted butter in center, brush it on rim of dough. Serve warm. Serve the cake on the day it was baked; or freeze it and reheat before serving.

NOTES

• For a variation, replace grated rind with 1 teaspoon cinnamon.
• To make dough by hand, begin by sprinkling yeast over ¼ cup lukewarm water in cup or small bowl; add 1 teaspoon sugar and leave for 10 minutes. Then sift flour into a bowl and make a well in center. Add yeast mixture, remaining water, eggs, remaining 2 teaspoons sugar and salt to well. Mix ingredients in middle of well. Stir in flour and mix well. Knead dough vigorously, slapping it on working surface, until it is smooth and elastic. Pound butter with your fist to soften it thoroughly. Set it on top of dough and knead it until butter is blended in. If dough is very sticky, flour it occasionally while kneading.

CHOCOLATE-HAZELNUT CROISSANT ROLLS
Pains au chocolat aux noisettes

Closely related to the irresistible *pains au chocolat* made of croissant dough filled with whole squares of chocolate that are found at every French pâtisserie, these pastries contain an easy hazelnut filling as well.

MAKES 12 PASTRIES

CROISSANT DOUGH

1 envelope dry yeast (¼ ounce)
½ cup plus 2 tablespoons warm water (110°F.)
2 tablespoons sugar

¼ cup warm milk
2 cups all-purpose flour
1½ teaspoons salt
½ cup unsalted butter, well chilled

CHOCOLATE-HAZELNUT FILLING

1 large egg
Pinch of salt
1 cup hazelnuts
2 tablespoons sugar
2 tablespoons milk

1 tablespoon unsalted butter, melted and cooled
Two 3½-ounce bars semisweet chocolate

CROISSANT DOUGH

Sprinkle yeast over ¼ cup warm water in a small bowl, add 1 teaspoon sugar, and let stand 10 minutes. Stir with a fork, then mix with remaining warm water and milk.

Sift flour into a large bowl and make a well in center. Add salt, remaining 1⅔ tablespoons sugar and yeast mixture to well. Mix in flour gently with a wooden spoon. Continue mixing gently with your fingers until mixture forms a dough. Turn dough over several times but do not knead. If it is very soft, roll it gently in a little flour.

Lightly oil a medium bowl. Place dough in oiled bowl and turn it over to oil surface. Cover with plastic wrap and let dough rise in a warm, draft-free place about 45 minutes. It will become lighter but does not need to double.

Remove dough and work it by gathering it up and letting it fall into bowl twice, touching it lightly. Cover with plastic wrap and refrigerate at least 4 hours or overnight.

Lightly flour butter. Put butter on a cool floured surface or between 2 pieces of wax paper and tap it with a rolling pin to flatten it to a rectangle. Fold 2 sides of butter inward to form a rough square. Continue pounding butter and folding it until it becomes more flexible. Shape it in a 4-inch square. Refrigerate 5 minutes.

Roll dough on a cold floured surface to a 7-inch circle, leaving center of circle slightly thicker than edges. Put square of butter on center of circle. Pull dough in from two opposite sides to cover butter and meet in center of square. Press edges together to seal. Repeat with other two sides so that butter is completely enclosed. Use side of your fist to pound point where dough meets to seal it.

Turn dough over so that seal faces down. Pound lightly 4 or 5 times with rolling pin to begin to flatten butter inside dough. Roll dough quickly to a 12-×-7-inch rectangle. Fold rectangle in three, like a business letter, folding third closest to you upward and third farthest from you downward. Put dough on a plate, cover and refrigerate 15 minutes.

Return dough to lightly floured work surface with fold to your right. Roll again to a rectangle, fold in three, and refrigerate 15 minutes. Repeat rolling and folding once more. Refrigerate 30 minutes, or up to 8 hours.

CHOCOLATE-HAZELNUT FILLING

Preheat oven to 350°F. Butter a baking sheet. Beat egg with a pinch of salt in a small bowl and reserve as glaze. Toast and skin hazelnuts (see page 388). Cool nuts completely.

Grind nuts with sugar in a food processor until as fine as possible, scraping inward occasionally. Transfer to a medium bowl and stir in milk and melted butter.

Using a sharp heavy knife, cut chocolate bars into sticks about 3 inches long and ¾ inch wide; if chocolate breaks a little, keep pieces together.

Roll half the dough on a cold, lightly floured surface to an 11-×-10-inch rectangle. Keep remaining dough chilled. Trim edges of rectangle so they are straight.

Put 1 tablespoon hazelnut filling on dough about 2 inches from a long edge. Spread filling to about size of a chocolate stick. Top with a chocolate stick. Put 2 tablespoons more filling in a row on dough, spacing them about ½ inch apart. Top each with a piece of chocolate.

Brush dough on other side of chocolate (not side near edge of dough) with a strip of egg glaze about 1½ inches wide. Fold dough from edge so that it covers chocolate. You will now have a cylinder at edge of dough, with filling inside. Once again fold dough over in order to stick it to egg glaze. Cut along fold to release cylinder of dough from rest of dough sheet. Cut dough in spaces between chocolate, into cylinders with open ends. Put on prepared baking sheet. Repeat with remaining dough and remaining filling.

Let pastries rise, uncovered, in a draft-free area about 45 minutes, or until doubled in bulk. After 20 minutes, preheat oven to 425°F.

Brush pastries lightly with egg glaze. Bake 7 minutes. Reduce oven temperature to 375°F. and bake about 12 minutes, or until browned. Transfer to a rack and cool slightly. (Pastries can be kept up to 1 day in an airtight container, but are best on day they were baked. They can instead be wrapped tightly and frozen; defrost and warm them slightly before serving.) Serve warm or at room temperature.

PLAIN CROISSANTS

Omit filling. Roll dough to a rectangle about ⅛ inch thick. Cut it in 4-inch squares, and cut each square in 2 triangles. Roll each triangle up, beginning at the longest side. Transfer to a buttered baking sheet and curve the ends to a crescent shape. Let rise as above. Brush gently with egg glaze. Bake at 425°F. 5 minutes, reduce oven temperature to 375°F., and bake about 10 minutes, or until browned.

BRIOCHE RAISIN ROLLS WITH VANILLA CREAM
Pains aux raisins

These time-honored temptations appear in many French pastry shops and make a delightful breakfast treat. Brioche made and kneaded by hand the traditional way requires quite a bit of time, energy, and skill. For these rolls I prefer to use an easy version of brioche that can be made quickly in the mixer. The dough is rolled out, spread with vanilla pastry cream, sprinkled with raisins, and rolled up in a cylinder. Then it is cut into rolls and baked.

MAKES 15 PASTRIES

EASY BRIOCHE DOUGH

1 envelope dry yeast (¼ ounce)
2 tablespoons warm water (110°F.)
1 tablespoon sugar
2 cups all-purpose flour

1¼ teaspoons salt
3 large eggs plus 1 large yolk
½ cup unsalted butter, room temperature

Vanilla Pastry Cream (page 45)
1 cup raisins

1 egg, beaten with a pinch of salt, for glaze

EASY BRIOCHE DOUGH

Sprinkle yeast over water in a small deep bowl or cup, add ¼ teaspoon sugar and let stand 10 minutes. Stir yeast mixture.

Put flour into bowl of mixer and make a well in center. Add salt, remaining sugar, and whole eggs. Mix central ingredients briefly with dough hook of mixer. Add yeast mixture. Using dough hook, mix at low speed until mixture comes together to a dough, pushing in flour occasionally. Scrape down mixture. Add egg yolk and beat with dough hook until blended. Continue to beat with dough hook on medium speed about 12 minutes, or until mixture is very smooth.

Cut butter into 16 pieces. Add butter to dough and beat on low speed, scraping dough down often, just until butter is blended in. Dough will be soft.

Place dough in a lightly oiled medium bowl and turn it over to oil surface. Cover with plastic wrap and let dough rise in a warm draft-free place about 1½ hours, or until nearly doubled in bulk. Gently turn dough over several times to knock out air. Return dough to bowl, cover, and refrigerate at least 4 hours, or overnight.

Prepare pastry cream and refrigerate. Roll out dough on cool floured surface to a 15-×-10-inch rectangle, flouring often. Whisk pastry cream and spread it over dough, leaving a 1-inch border on 1 long side. Sprinkle dough evenly with raisins. Brush plain border with beaten egg. Roll dough up from opposite long side, like a jelly roll. Press roll of dough along egg-brushed border to seal.

Trim ends. Cut a 1-inch slice of rolled dough. Using a rubber spatula, set slice on a baking sheet, with its more narrow side (side that was pressed with knife) facing down. Continue slicing dough and transferring slices to baking sheet, spacing them about 2 inches apart. Let rise, uncovered, in a draft-free area about 30 minutes. Meanwhile, position rack in center of oven and preheat to 400°F.

Bake rolls 15 minutes. (If there is room for only 1 baking sheet on central rack, bake them in 2 batches.) Reduce oven temperature to 375°F. and bake another 7 minutes, or until rolls are golden brown. Transfer to a rack and cool slightly. (Pastries can be kept up to 1 day in an airtight container, but are best on day they are baked. They can instead be wrapped tightly and frozen; defrost and warm them slightly before serving.) Serve warm or at room temperature.

Cookies, Petits Fours, and Chocolates

An assortment of tempting treats—delicate cookies, petits fours, and smooth, rich chocolates—await the diner at the end of a dinner at a grand restaurant. At home it is more practical to make a smaller number of petits fours to conclude a festive meal, but they can be just as delicious.

The French use the term *petits fours* to cover a broad range of small cakes, cookies, pastries, and chocolates usually served at party buffets or, in the style of fine restaurants, with the after-dinner espresso or to accompany ice cream. There are two main types of petits fours. The first is *petits fours secs,* literally dry petits fours, meaning those that are crisp, and correspond roughly to our cookies. These include macaroons and elegant cookies like Rolled Cigarettes and Delicate Lemon Cookies. The second type, *petits fours frais,* or fresh petits fours, usually are made of cake or pastry and a creamy filling, such as Chocolate-Chestnut Petits Fours.

298

Buttery French cookies and luscious homemade chocolates make delightful presents. Favorites are the curved Almond Tile Cookies, airy nut meringues, or the moist coconut "mountains" that decorate the windows of fine pâtisseries. A selection of a few types of cookies and chocolate truffles, arranged attractively in a gift box or basket, is always a welcome offering for the holidays.

Cookies

French pâtissiers and home cooks prepare delectable butter cookies made from a rich sweet dough similar to the sweet pie pastry used for tarts, which is rolled out and cut into shapes. They can be frosted, like the orange butter cookies in this section, but most often they are eaten plain.

For serving with desserts, the most popular cookies are those made from a batter, which is either piped or spooned onto a baking sheet, flattened, and baked until set. These cookies, like Buttery Walnut Wafers, Rolled Cigarettes, and Almond Tile Cookies, are thin, delicate, and crisp. From a similar batter, Tulip Cookie Cups are made, which are buttery cookies that are used as charming containers for serving ice creams, sorbets, mousses, and fresh fruit with whipped cream. These cookies are a fashionable element of contemporary desserts.

Depending on their size, cookies in France play different roles. Smaller cookies are presented as accompaniments for ice creams and other desserts, or as after-dinner sweets with coffee, while larger ones are served as snacks. The French do not prepare enormous "monster" cookies.

Hints

• When rolling out cookie dough, treat it like sweet pastry (see Hints page 267). Roll it quickly on a cool surface.

- Bake batter cookies just until set and lightly browned. If baked until crisp, they will be too firm when cool.
- Never put dough or batter on a warm baking sheet. If necessary, before baking additional batches of cookies, cool the baking sheets by running cool water on the underside of the sheet.

～ FROSTED ORANGE BUTTER COOKIES
Sablés niçois

These festive cookies from Nice are dotted with colorful diced candied peel. For an extra touch, frost them with the Orange Royal Icing. Or frost only half of them and, when serving, alternate the frosted ones with the plain ones, so the candied peel in the cookies can be seen.   MAKES ABOUT 20 COOKIES

COOKIE DOUGH

1/2 cup plus 1 tablespoon unsalted butter, cold
1 large egg plus 1 large yolk
1/2 cup granulated sugar
Pinch of salt
Grated rind 1 orange

2 tablespoons finely chopped candied citrus peel
1 3/4 cups all-purpose flour
1/4 cup cake flour
1 to 2 tablespoons strained fresh orange juice (optional)

ORANGE ROYAL ICING

1 large egg white
3/4 cup powdered sugar
1 tablespoon flour

1 tablespoon strained fresh orange juice

About 2 tablespoons diced candied citrus peel for garnish

COOKIE DOUGH

Cut butter into approximately 1/2 tablespoon–size cubes. Combine egg, egg yolk, sugar, salt, grated rind, candied peel, and butter in food processor fitted with metal blade. Mix using ten on/off turns; then process 5 seconds. Small pieces of butter will remain. Add both types flour and process about 2 seconds; scrape down with rubber spatula and process again about 3 seconds, or until dough begins to form sticky crumbs but does not come together in a ball. If crumbs are dry, add orange juice. Put dough in a plastic bag or in plastic wrap, press into a ball, then flatten into a disc.

Refrigerate dough at least 4 hours. (The dough can be kept up to 3 days in the refrigerator.)

Preheat oven to 375°F. Lightly butter 2 baking sheets. Roll out half the dough on a cool lightly floured surface until ¼ inch thick. Using a 2½- or 3-inch cutter, cut dough in circles and transfer them to baking sheets. Repeat with remaining dough. Press trimmings gently together and chill them. Roll them out and cut more circles. Refrigerate cookies for 30 minutes, or chill them in the freezer for 15 minutes.

ORANGE ROYAL ICING

Using a wooden spoon, beat egg white with powdered sugar until mixture is very smooth and white. Add flour and mix thoroughly. Stir in the orange juice.

Spread a thin layer of icing on each cookie. Set a small piece of candied citrus peel in center. Bake 12 to 15 minutes, or until cookies and icing brown lightly.

NOTE: To make cookie dough by hand: Sift both types flour onto a work surface and make a well in center. Put egg, egg yolks, salt, sugar, grated orange rind, and candied peel in well and mix briefly, using your fingers. Cut butter in about 10 pieces and pound to soften them slightly. Separate butter again in pieces and add them to well. Using your fingers, mix and crush ingredients in center of well until mixed but still not smooth. Draw in flour and crumble ingredients through your fingers, raising them in the air, until dough begins to come together. Blend dough by pushing portions of it away from you and smearing it on work surface, then gathering it up together again. Repeat twice more until dough is nearly smooth. Press it into a ball and dust it with flour. Wrap in plastic wrap or in a plastic bag.

🌿 BRETON BUTTER COOKIES
Sablés bretons

Cookies of this type are popular throughout France, whether made at home or in pastry shops or purchased in tins from Brittany. They are known in France as *sablés,* or "sand cookies," because of their crumbly texture, and are delicious because they include a generous proportion of butter. The dough is similar to the sweet pastry used for fruit tarts but is slightly richer. Like tart shells, these cookies are best when freshly baked.   MAKES ABOUT 12 TO 18 COOKIES

½ cup unsalted butter, cold
4 large egg yolks
¼ teaspoon salt
½ cup sugar
1 ½ cups all-purpose flour

1 teaspoon pure vanilla extract, or
   2 teaspoons grated lemon or
   orange zest
1 egg, beaten with a pinch of salt,
   for glaze

Cut butter into approximately ½ tablespoon–size cubes. Combine yolks, salt, sugar, and butter in food processor fitted with metal blade. Mix using ten on/off turns; then process 5 seconds. Small pieces of butter will remain. Add flour and vanilla extract or grated zest and process about 2 seconds; scrape down with rubber spatula and process again about 3 seconds, or until dough begins to form sticky crumbs but does not come together in a ball. If dough is dry, sprinkle with 1 teaspoon water and briefly process again. Transfer to work surface.

Blend dough by pushing portions of it away from you and smearing it on the work surface, then gathering it up together again. Repeat twice more until the dough is nearly smooth. Press it into a ball. Wrap in plastic wrap or in a plastic bag. Refrigerate dough at least 3 hours before using it. (The dough can be kept up to 3 days in refrigerator.)

Preheat oven to 375°F. Lightly butter 2 baking sheets. Roll out dough on a cool lightly floured surface until ¼ inch thick. Using a 2½- or 3-inch cutter, cut dough in circles and transfer them to baking sheets. Press trimmings gently together and chill them. Roll them out and cut more circles.

Brush cookies with beaten egg. With tines of a fork, mark a triangle or other design on each cookie. Refrigerate 15 minutes. Bake

10 to 12 minutes, or until lightly browned. Cool cookies on a rack. (The cookies can be kept up to 1 week in an airtight container; or they can be frozen.)

NOTE: To make pastry by hand: Sift flour onto a work surface and make a well in the center. Put egg yolks, salt, sugar, and vanilla or grated peel in well and mix briefly, using your fingers. Cut butter in about 10 pieces and pound to soften them slightly. Separate butter again in pieces, add them to well, and quickly mix with other ingredients in well until partially mixed. Gradually draw in flour to make coarse crumbs. Toss mixture, rubbing it between your fingers, until crumbs begin to stick together. If dough is dry, add 1 teaspoon water, and continue to crumble dough through your fingers.

DELICATE LEMON COOKIES
Petites galettes au citron

These cookies are very quick and easy to make. They are shaped by pushing the batter from a spoon, like many American cookies, but then are flattened by tapping the baking sheet vigorously several times on the work surface so that they will be crisp. Serve them with any ice cream or sorbet. MAKES ABOUT 40 COOKIES

7 tablespoons unsalted butter
2/3 cup sugar
2 large eggs

Grated zest of 2 lemons
3/4 cup all-purpose flour

Preheat oven to 425°F. Lightly butter 2 baking sheets.

Beat butter until soft and smooth. Add sugar and beat until smooth. Add 1 egg and beat until blended. Beat second egg in a small bowl, then gradually beat it into mixture. Stir in lemon zest. Sift flour over mixture and stir it in with a wooden spoon. Let batter stand 15 minutes at room temperature.

To shape cookies, take 1/2 teaspoon of batter and use another teaspoon to push batter onto baking sheet. Space cookies about 3 inches apart. Tap baking sheet vigorously several times on work surface to flatten cookies.

Bake 6 to 7 minutes, or until edges of cookies are brown and centers light beige. Transfer to a rack to cool. (If cookies harden and become difficult to remove, return them to oven for 30 seconds to soften.) Cool baking sheets and bake remaining cookies. (The cookies can be kept about 1 week in an airtight container; or they can be frozen.)

COCONUT PALM-LEAF COOKIES
Palmiers à la noix de coco

Palmiers, or palm-leaf cookies, are made of puff pastry rolled with sugar. I like to sprinkle grated coconut on the dough at the same time as the sugar, to add extra flavor. These are fast and simple to prepare with purchased puff pastry.   MAKES ABOUT 20 COOKIES

1 frozen pastry sheet (half a 17-ounce package), or 10 to 12 ounces fresh puff pastry or trimmings
6 tablespoons sugar

1 egg, beaten with a pinch of salt, for glaze
1/2 cup finely shredded unsweetened coconut

If using a sheet of frozen dough, thaw dough 20 minutes and unfold sheet. If using puff pastry trimmings, pile them and press them so they adhere. Refrigerate fresh pastry or trimmings for 1 hour.

Sprinkle work surface with sugar instead of flour. Set dough on sugar and sprinkle it with more sugar. Roll out dough on sugar to a rectangle about 1/4 inch thick. Fold it in three. Then roll out again to a rectangle. Refrigerate 20 to 30 minutes uncovered.

Set dough on work surface sprinkled with sugar, and sprinkle dough with more sugar. Roll out dough to a rectangle about 12 inches × 10 inches. Let it rest a few times when rolling, if necessary. Brush with egg, sprinkle it with coconut, and pat it so coconut adheres.

Trim edges of dough. Fold one long edge over twice to reach center of dough. Repeat with other long edge. Press folded dough lightly with a rolling pin to seal. Fold one folded section of dough on top of other and firmly press together.

Use a sharp knife to cut dough into 1/4-inch slices. Place cookies on a nonstick baking sheet about 2 inches apart. Open bottom of slices slightly to round them. Refrigerate 30 minutes. Preheat oven to 400°F. Bake 8 minutes, or until undersides begin to brown. Reduce oven temperature to 350°F. Turn cookies over with a metal spatula and bake 5 minutes longer, until golden. Watch carefully; these cookies burn easily. Cool on racks. (Cookies can be kept 2 days in an airtight container, or they can be frozen. If they were frozen, thaw and reheat briefly in oven to crisp.)

TULIP COOKIE CUPS
Tulipes

The best known of modern French cookies, these are made from a batter similar to that used for "cigarettes," but are placed on a glass or mold and given a fluted cuplike shape. They are used as delicious containers for ice creams, sorbets, or mousses garnished with colorful fruit slices and accompanied by fruit sauces. Simple preparations, such as plain fruit salad with a little whipped cream, become glamorous when served in a tulip. MAKES 8 OR 9 LARGE COOKIES

7 tablespoons unsalted butter, room temperature
¾ cup powdered sugar

3 large egg whites, lightly beaten
⅔ cup all-purpose flour
½ teaspoon pure vanilla extract

Thoroughly butter 2 heavy baking sheets. Preheat oven to 350°F. Have ready a metal spatula for removing cookies and 2 glasses or cups with about 2-inch bottoms for shaping them, and 2 small ramekins that fit over upside-down glasses.

Beat butter until very soft. Add powdered sugar and beat until mixture is very smooth. Gradually add egg whites, beating well after each addition. After most of the whites are added, add 1 or 2 tablespoons of flour to prevent the batter from separating. Sift remaining flour into mixture and stir gently with a wooden spoon just until mixture is smooth. Stir in vanilla. (Batter may look slightly separated, but that is okay.)

Take 2 tablespoons of mixture and push it onto baking sheet with another spoon. Spread batter as thin as possible. Hold spatula flat (use an offset spatula, if available, for easy spreading) and press firmly while spreading. Spread to about a 5-inch circle. Shape another cookie; bake only 2 at a time, rebuttering sheets for each new batch.

Bake cookies about 8 minutes, or until they brown at edges. Do not overbake them or they will become brittle and can't be shaped. Using a spatula, free the cookies from baking sheet but do not remove them. Remove 1 cookie and set it on a glass, and cover with a ramekin. Press gently to give it a cuplike shape. Repeat with other cookie. When cool, remove ramekin and cool cookies completely on a rack. (Cookies can be kept 3 days in an airtight container.)

ALMOND TILE COOKIES
Tuiles aux amandes

A classic French cookie and one of the easiest to make, tiles are made of a large amount of sliced almonds held together with a small amount of light batter. The batter is stirred together in a few minutes, then baked a few minutes more. You can set them on a curved surface or in a ring mold to give them their traditional curved shape, so that they resemble tiles often found on the roofs of country houses; but they also are fine served flat. Restaurants often make a large quantity of the batter, and bake 1 or 2 sheets of cookies as they need them, so they are very crisp and fresh.

MAKES ABOUT 14 LARGE COOKIES

2 tablespoons unsalted butter	2 tablespoons all-purpose flour
1 cup sliced almonds (about 3 1/3 ounces)	1 large egg plus 1 large white
	1 teaspoon finely grated lemon rind
1/2 cup sugar	

Thoroughly butter 2 heavy baking sheets. Preheat oven to 400°F. Have ready a metal spatula for removing cookies from oven and a small ring mold or small rolling pin for giving them their curved shape.

Melt butter in a small saucepan over low heat and let it cool but do not let it congeal.

In a medium bowl, combine almonds, sugar, and flour and mix

well. Add egg, egg white, and lemon rind. Mix well with a wooden spoon. Gradually add melted butter and stir until blended.

Take 1 tablespoon of mixture and, using a teaspoon, push mixture onto the baking sheet. Continue with remaining mixture, spacing cookies about 2 inches apart and putting 6 cookies on each baking sheet. Dip a fork in water. Holding fork flat, flatten cookies as much as possible with bottom of fork; dip fork in water after every 2 cookies.

Bake 1 baking sheet of cookies about 5 or 6 minutes, or until edges are golden brown and centers brown very lightly. Using metal spatula, free cookies from baking sheet by carefully sliding spatula under each but leave them on baking sheet. Remove them 1 at a time and turn them over into ring mold or onto rolling pin. The soft cookies will curve into their characteristic shape. Work quickly because they cool fast. (If they harden, return them to oven for a few seconds to soften.) When they are set, transfer them to a rack to cool completely.

Stir batter before baking each new batch. Spoon batter onto cool cookie sheets. Bake and shape remaining cookies, rebuttering sheets for each new batch. Let them cool. (They can be kept for a week in a closed container, or they can be frozen.) To serve cookies, arrange them on a platter, overlapping, with their curved side up.

BUTTERY WALNUT WAFERS
Langues de chat aux noix

The light batter flavored with ground walnuts is piped in sticks; it then spreads in the oven to crisp finger shapes. These are a delightful accompaniment to any ice cream or sorbet.

MAKES 40 TO 50 COOKIES

1/4 cup walnuts   *3/4 cup powdered sugar*
2/3 cup all-purpose flour   *2 large egg whites*
7 tablespoons unsalted butter

Preheat oven to 425°F. Lightly butter 2 baking sheets.

Grind walnuts to fine powder in a food processor or in a nut grinder until very fine. Sift flour and mix it with nuts.

Beat butter until very soft and smooth. Sift in powdered sugar, mix briefly, and beat until mixture is very smooth.

Beat egg whites lightly with a fork, then gradually add them to butter mixture, beating thoroughly with a mixer at high speed after each addition. (If mixture begins to separate, add 1 teaspoon of flour mixture, mix well, then continue adding whites.) Lightly stir in flour-nut mixture with a wooden spoon.

Using a pastry bag and small plain tip, pipe thin "pencils" of batter about 2½ inches long on baking sheet, spacing them about 2 inches apart. Tap baking sheet vigorously several times on work surface to flatten cookies.

Bake 6 to 7 minutes, or until edges of cookies are golden brown. Transfer cookies to a rack to cool. (Cookies can be kept in an airtight container for about 2 weeks; or they can be frozen.)

ROLLED CIGARETTES
Cigarettes russes

These thin, crisp, buttery rolled cookies are the most popular French accompaniment for ice cream. Widely imitated industrially, there is no substitute for the fresh original. As soon as the cookies are removed from the oven, they must be rolled into their desired shape. For this reason, they are baked only a few at a time; their baking time is brief, however. Since the cookies need to be rolled quickly while they are still hot, they require a little practice. If you like, you can omit the step of rolling. The cookies taste just as good when flat.

MAKES 20 TO 25 COOKIES

7 tablespoons unsalted butter, room temperature

¾ cup powdered sugar

3 large egg whites, lightly beaten

½ cup plus 1 to 2 tablespoons all-purpose flour

½ teaspoon pure vanilla extract

1 teaspoon melted butter (optional)

Thoroughly butter 2 heavy baking sheets. Preheat oven to 350°F. Have ready a metal spatula for removing cookies and 4 chopsticks or pencils for rolling them.

Beat butter until very soft. Add powdered sugar and beat until mixture is very smooth. Gradually add about half the egg whites, beating well after each addition. Stir in 1 tablespoon flour. Beat in remaining whites. Sift ½ cup flour into mixture and stir gently with a wooden spoon just until mixture is smooth. Beat in vanilla.

Bake 1 cookie ahead as a test (because humidity in air and dryness of flour affect this recipe). Take about 1 ½ teaspoons of batter with a spoon and push it off with another spoon onto 1 baking sheet.

Spread batter in a round, as thin as possible, and about 3 ½ inches in diameter, but not so thin that you see the baking sheet. Bake about 6 or 7 minutes, or until cookie browns at edges. Do not overbake or it will become brittle and won't roll. Using a spatula, remove cookie onto a working surface near oven.

Put chopstick or handle of wooden spoon at one end of cookie and roll cookie quite firmly around it, giving cookie a cigarette shape. When finished, press cookie with chopstick against working surface to seal end, so cookie won't unroll.

If cookie is not crisp enough, add 1 teaspoon melted butter to batter so it will spread more. If cookie is too dry and brittle, add 1 tablespoon flour to batter, so it will not spread so thin.

To shape more cookies, spoon 3 mounds of about 1 ½ teaspoons of batter onto 1 baking sheet, spacing them about 2 inches apart. Try to use same amount of batter for each. Spread, bake, and roll as for test cookie.

As soon as you have rolled 1 cookie, continue with next cookie, using another chopstick. Work quickly because cookies harden quickly as they cool and then cannot be rolled. If cookies harden, return them for a few seconds to oven; when hot, they'll become flexible and can be rolled. Let rolled cookies cool briefly before removing chopstick. Cool cookies on a rack.

Continue with remaining batter. Let cookies cool completely. (They can be kept 3 days in an airtight container or they can be frozen.) Handle them gently because they are fragile.

Macaroons and Meringues

Unlike many other cookies, macaroons and meringues contain neither butter nor flour. Meringues are made of two ingredients—egg whites and sugar—while macaroons are composed of the same ingredients, with the addition of ground nuts. Although meringues may contain nuts, macaroons have a completely different texture from that of nut-flavored meringues because the proportion of nuts in macaroons is always much greater. In addition, macaroons are baked for a much shorter time and at a higher temperature than meringues, so their texture is moist and slightly chewy, rather than dry and crumbly like that of meringues. Vanilla, chocolate, or citrus peel can be added to either one for an extra touch.

Almonds are the most common nut used in macaroons in France, followed by coconut and hazelnuts. I experimented with macadamia nuts and pecans and found that they make terrific macaroons as well.

At one time, preparing macaroons was quite tedious because the nuts had to be pounded in a mortar with a pestle in order to make them fine enough. With the aid of modern kitchen appliances like the food processor and electric nut grinder, these cookies have become easy to make. The nuts are ground as fine as possible, almost to a powder, so the macaroon batter will be smooth.

The proportions of nuts, sugar, and egg whites vary from one pâtisserie to another and produce very different results. Equal weights of nuts and sugar make the finest macaroons, but some bakeries use up to three times as much sugar as nuts for reasons of economy.

How much egg white to add to the mixture of nuts and sugar depends on how the cookies will be shaped. Macaroons to be rolled into balls require just enough egg white to hold the ingredients together in a firm batter. Those to be piped from a pastry bag need slightly more, so the batter is softer and can be pressed easily. Sometimes the egg whites are added in the form of glossy Italian meringue (egg whites whipped with hot sugar syrup), to make the cookies smoother and more delicate. Whatever the shaping method, macaroons are made relatively thick, so they don't dry out in the oven.

Careful baking is the crucial step in meringue and macaroon preparation, so that neither is too sticky. Meringues should be set and should feel dry but should not brown. Macaroons should brown only lightly, and should be just firm enough to be removed from the baking sheet but still soft in the center. When hot, macaroons might appear too soft, but it is amazing how much they harden as they cool. If the texture of a macaroon seems perfect when it is hot, it will be too hard, dry, and brittle when cool.

Macaroons are removed from the baking sheet in an unusual way. The paper on which they were baked is lifted, and water is poured onto the baking sheet under the paper. Upon contact with the hot baking sheet, the water sizzles vigorously and releases the macaroons. The steam it creates also helps keep the cookies moist. Coconut macaroons and filled Mirror Cookies don't need this special treatment.

Serve meringues and macaroons at the end of a meal or for a snack with coffee, tea, or milk. They are delicious with ice cream and make a pleasant accompaniment for poached fruit or for creamy desserts such as Bavarian creams and mousses. For an elegant finale to a dinner, serve a variety of macaroons and meringues on a platter together with or after dessert, as in many of France's best restaurants.

Hints

• Meringues and macaroons are a good way to use leftover egg whites.

• Egg whites can be frozen. If you do not remember how many you froze, you can measure the thawed egg whites: a scant ⅔ cup egg whites equals 4 large egg whites.

• It is best not to bake meringues or macaroons on very humid days, because they might be sticky.

• Meringues and macaroons should be put into airtight containers as soon as they are cool; if left out, they absorb moisture easily from the air and become too sticky and soft.

• For additional hints on making meringues, see page 230.

• Since nuts are the main flavor in macaroons, use the freshest ones possible. Blanch and peel almonds yourself for the best flavor (see page 388).

• Most types of macaroon batter are easiest to make in a food processor, because the nuts can be ground in it, then the remaining ingredients added to the ground nuts and mixed in the processor.

• See also hints on grinding nuts, page 191.

FRENCH ALMOND MACAROONS
Macarons moëlleux

These sweet, rich cookies are absolutely delicious and are easy to make. The fresh almond flavor will come through best if you blanch and peel the almonds yourself. Serve the macaroons with coffee, with ice cream, or as recommended at Lenôtre's famous Parisian pastry shop, with chocolate mousse.   MAKES ABOUT 30 MACAROONS

2 1/4 cups blanched almonds (about
    10 ounces)
1 1/2 cups granulated sugar

3 large egg whites
1 1/2 teaspoons pure vanilla extract
2 tablespoons powdered sugar

Position rack in upper third of oven and preheat to 350°F. Line 2 baking sheets with parchment paper or wax paper; butter paper lightly.

Grind almonds with 6 tablespoons sugar in food processor fitted with steel blade by processing continuously until mixture forms fine, even crumbs. Add egg whites and vanilla and process until smooth, about 20 seconds. Add remaining sugar in 2 additions and process about 10 seconds after each, or until smooth.

With moistened hands, roll about 1 tablespoon mixture into a smooth ball between your palms. Put on prepared baking sheet. Continue with remaining mixture, spacing cookies about 1 inch apart on baking sheets.

Press each macaroon to flatten slightly so it is about 1/2 inch high. Brush entire surface of each with water. Sift powdered sugar over each. Bake until very lightly but evenly browned, 18 to 20 minutes;

centers should still be soft. Remove from oven.

Lift one end of paper and pour about 2 tablespoons water under it, onto baking sheet; water will boil on contact with hot baking sheet. Lift other end of paper and pour about 2 tablespoons water under it. When water stops boiling, remove macaroons from paper, either by carefully pulling them off, or with the aid of a metal spatula. Transfer to a rack to cool. (Macaroons can be prepared 1 week ahead and kept in airtight containers.)

HONEY MACAROONS
Replace vanilla with 1 ½ tablespoons mild honey.

MIRROR COOKIES
Miroirs

The shiny jam-glazed almond-cream centers piped inside these macaroon rings give the cookies their name.

MAKES 35 TO 40 COOKIES

ALMOND CREAM

½ cup blanched almonds (about 2 ounces)
3 tablespoons sugar

3 tablespoons unsalted butter
1 large egg yolk
½ teaspoon dark rum or brandy

MACAROON MIXTURE

1 cup blanched almonds (about 4 ounces)
¾ cup sugar

2 large egg whites
2 tablespoons finely chopped blanched almonds

APRICOT GLAZE

3 tablespoons apricot preserves

1 teaspoon water

ALMOND CREAM

Grind almonds with 1 tablespoon sugar in food processor fitted with steel blade until mixture forms very fine, even crumbs. Cream butter in a small bowl, beat in remaining 2 tablespoons sugar, and continue beating until very smooth. Beat in egg yolk, then rum. Stir in ground almond mixture.

MACAROON MIXTURE

Position a rack in bottom third of oven and preheat to 300°F. Line 2 baking sheets with foil. Butter and flour foil, shaking off excess.

Grind whole almonds with 2 tablespoons sugar in food processor fitted with steel blade until mixture forms fine, even crumbs. Reserve 2 tablespoons sugar for beating into egg white, and add remaining sugar to almond mixture. Process until mixture is very fine. Add 1 egg white and process about 10 seconds. Scrape mixture down from sides and inward from center and process a few more seconds until smooth. Transfer to a bowl.

Whip remaining egg white in small bowl until stiff. Add reserved 2 tablespoons sugar and continue beating about 30 seconds until glossy. Stir one-third of whites into almond mixture; mixture will be difficult to stir. Gently fold remaining whites in 2 batches into almond mixture. Mixture will be difficult to fold; use a folding and cutting motion and continue until mixture is smooth.

Using a pastry bag fitted with a medium star tip (1/4 to 5/16 inch, # 3 B), pipe mixture onto prepared baking sheets in rings of about 1 1/4 inches in diameter, spacing them about 1 inch apart. Press to end each ring in a small rosette. Sprinkle rings with chopped almonds.

Spoon almond cream into pastry bag. Pipe almond cream into center of each ring, to fill it. Almond cream should touch edges of ring.

Bake until rings are firm and edges are lightly browned, about 20 minutes. Let cool on baking sheet for 1 minute. Use a metal spatula to very carefully free cookies from paper, sliding spatula under almond cream center so it doesn't fall out. Transfer cookies to a rack and let cool completely.

APRICOT GLAZE

Heat preserves and water in a small saucepan over low heat, stirring often, until preserves melt and come nearly to a boil. Strain mixture, pressing so as much mixture as possible goes through strainer. Return to saucepan and simmer 1 minute over low heat.

Using a small pastry brush, brush glaze over almond cream center of each cookie but not over rim. Leave to cool and set. (Cookies can be kept up to 5 days on a plate covered with plastic wrap at room temperature, or in an airtight container; be sure jam has set before putting cookies into container so they won't stick to each other.)

NOTE: If both baking sheets don't fit together on rack, bake cookies in 2 batches, rather than one above other, to ensure even cooking. Piped mixture can wait on baking sheets while first batch bakes.

MACADAMIA MACAROONS
Macarons aux noix de macadam

Macaroons are one of the oldest types of cookies known in the history of food, and remain one of the most popular throughout Europe, notably in France and Italy. Macadamia nuts make deluxe, new macaroons. I devised these rich little treasures in the French style and featured them in *Gourmet* magazine. They make great accompaniments for vanilla ice cream or fruit sorbet.

MAKES ABOUT 30 MACAROONS

2 1/2 cups raw or roasted (unsalted or salted) macadamia nuts (about 11 1/2 ounces)
30 macadamia nut halves (about 1 ounce) for garnish

1 1/2 cups sugar
3 large egg whites
1 1/2 teaspoons pure vanilla extract

If using raw nuts, toast 2 1/2 cups needed for macaroon mixture; there is no need to toast those needed for garnish. If using salted nuts, desalt both those for cookies and nut halves for garnish (see page 389).

Preheat oven to 350°F. Butter 2 baking sheets and line with parchment or wax paper that extends slightly beyond edges of baking sheets; then butter paper.

In a food processor, grind 2 1/2 cups nuts with 6 tablespoons sugar until fine. Add egg whites and vanilla and process for 20 seconds, or until the mixture is smooth. Add remaining sugar in 2 batches and process after each addition for about 10 seconds, or until mixture is very smooth.

With moistened hands, roll tablespoons of mixture into smooth balls between your palms and put them on prepared baking sheets, spacing the cookies about 1 inch apart.

Brush each macaroon with water. Press to flatten each macaroon slightly so it is about 1/2 inch high. Set a macadamia nut half on center of each macaroon and press lightly so it adheres. Bake macaroons in upper third of oven for about 18 minutes, or until they are very lightly but evenly browned and their centers are still soft. Remove from oven. Lift one end of the paper lining each baking sheet and pour about 2 tablespoons water under it, onto baking sheet; water will boil on contact with hot baking sheet. Lift other end of paper and pour about 2 tablespoons water under it. When water stops boiling, remove macaroons from paper with aid of a metal spatula, transfer them to a rack, and let them cool completely. (Macaroons can be kept 5 days in an airtight container.)

COCONUT AND SOUR CREAM PEAKS
Congolais

Although these cookies bear a certain resemblance to coconut macaroons, the sour cream makes them much moister. They are white, but their peaks and bases are golden.   MAKES 20 TO 24 COOKIES

8 tablespoons sugar
2 tablespoons all-purpose flour
1 large egg
2/3 cup sour cream

1 teaspoon pure vanilla extract
2 1/2 cups unsweetened coconut
3 large egg whites

Thoroughly butter 2 baking sheets. Preheat oven to 250°F. Thoroughly mix 6 tablespoons sugar with flour.

Beat egg in a large bowl. Whisk in sour cream and vanilla, then add coconut and mix well.

Beat egg whites until very stiff. Add remaining 2 tablespoons sugar and continue beating at high speed for 30 seconds, or until whites are very shiny.

Gently stir about one-third of egg whites into coconut mixture; then fold in about one-third of sugar-flour mixture. Fold in another third of egg whites, then a third of sugar-flour mixture; then remaining whites and remaining sugar-flour mixture. Fold quickly but gently.

Put about 1 tablespoon of mixture on baking sheet. Use your

fingers to shape it in a mountain shape, about 1 ½ inches high. Continue making "mountains" with remaining mixture. Bake about 1 hour, or until cookies are firm and brown lightly on their peaks and their bases. Gently remove from baking sheet and cool on a rack. (The cookies can be kept for about 2 weeks in an airtight container; or they can be frozen.)

WHITE-AND-CHOCOLATE MERINGUE SANDWICHES
Meringues au chocolat et chantilly

These pretty cookie sandwiches are made of two colors of baked meringue and of whipped cream filling—each in chocolate and white. They are easy to make because only one batch of meringue and one of whipped cream is prepared, and half of each is simply flavored with chocolate. MAKES 8 SANDWICHES

MERINGUES

2 tablespoons cocoa powder   *¼ teaspoon cream of tartar*
4 tablespoons powdered sugar   *1 cup granulated sugar*
4 large egg whites

WHIPPED CREAM FILLINGS

2½ ounces bittersweet or semisweet   *1 tablespoon granulated sugar*
   chocolate, chopped   *1 teaspoon vanilla*
1 cup heavy cream, well chilled

MERINGUES

Lightly grease the corners of 2 baking sheets. Line sheets with foil or parchment paper. Butter and flour foil or paper, shaking off the excess. Preheat oven to 275°F.

Sift cocoa with 2 tablespoons powdered sugar. Beat egg whites and cream of tartar in the large bowl of a mixer at medium speed until stiff. Switch speed to high. Pour 2 tablespoons sugar into whites in a thin stream, beating constantly at high speed until meringue is very shiny. Gently fold in remaining sugar in 2 batches, working as quickly as possible.

Spoon half the meringue into a pastry bag fitted with a large (about ½-inch) plain tip. Pipe meringue in egg shapes. Try to pipe them all the same length. If desired, instead of piping, take a tablespoonful of meringue and transfer it to baking sheet with another spoon; again try to make them fairly even in size. Sift remaining powdered sugar over meringues.

Fold cocoa mixture into remaining meringue. Use it to shape more meringues, like the first ones. Bake meringues about 1 hour, or until firm; if they begin to brown during baking, reduce oven temperature to 250°F. Remove from oven and let cool. (They can be kept 1 week in an airtight container in a dry place.)

WHIPPED CREAM FILLINGS

Melt chocolate in a small heatproof bowl over hot water over low heat, stirring occasionally. Stir until smooth. Remove from heat but leave chocolate above hot water.

Whip cream with sugar and vanilla in a chilled bowl with chilled beater until stiff. Transfer half the cream to another bowl and reserve in refrigerator; this cream will remain white.

Remove chocolate from above water and cool for 30 seconds. Quickly stir about ⅓ cup whipped cream into chocolate. Quickly fold mixture into remaining whipped cream until smooth. Fold quickly so that chocolate does not harden upon contact with cold whipped cream. Refrigerate until ready to use.

Assemble a short time before serving. Arrange meringues in pairs in cupcake papers, putting 1 chocolate and 1 white meringue together with their flat sides facing each other but not quite touching. Using a pastry bag and large star tip, pipe a ruffle of white whipped cream on the flat side of each chocolate meringue. Then spoon the chocolate whipped cream into the pastry bag and pipe chocolate whipped cream on the flat side of each white meringue.

Instead of piping cream, you can spread white whipped cream on each chocolate meringue, and chocolate whipped cream on each white meringue.

Put meringues together so they form "sandwiches" with chocolate filling next to white filling. Refrigerate, uncovered, until ready to serve. (Meringue sandwiches can also be frozen.)

WALNUT MERINGUES
Meringues aux noix

For something sweet to serve with coffee, these are just perfect. Instead of walnuts, you can use pecans or sliced almonds, or substitute raisins for half of the nuts.   MAKES ABOUT 24 MERINGUES

*4 large egg whites, room
    temperature*
¼ teaspoon cream of tartar

1 cup plus 2 tablespoons sugar
¾ cup coarsely chopped walnuts
About ½ cup walnut halves

Line 2 baking sheets with foil. Lightly grease corners of baking sheets so the foil adheres; butter and flour foil, shaking off excess. Preheat oven to 275°F.

Beat egg whites and cream of tartar in large bowl of a mixer at medium speed until stiff. Switch speed to high and pour ½ cup sugar into whites in a thin stream, beating constantly at high speed until meringue is very shiny. Gently fold in remaining sugar in 2 batches, then chopped walnuts, working as quickly as possible.

Spoon mixture in irregular mounds onto prepared baking sheets, using 1 mounded tablespoon for each and spacing them about 1½ inches apart. Set a walnut half on each meringue. Bake 30 minutes; lower oven temperature to 250°F. and continue baking another 30 minutes, or until meringues are firm on outside and dry at base, so they can be easily removed from foil; they will be a beige color. Transfer them to a rack and let cool. (Meringues can keep for weeks in airtight containers.)

Fresh Petits Fours

The term *petit four* often evokes an image of a cube of white cake coated with a sweet fondant icing. In France, however, *petits fours frais,*

or fresh petits fours, refers to a broad range of enticing small sweets. Fresh petits fours are those that are served fairly soon after they are made, either because they are made from a delicate cake or because they contain a fresh filling.

Diminutive versions of pastries make lovely petits fours, and because of their smaller size, their fillings are often richer than usual. Jewellike fruit tartlets are popular petits fours, and so are tiny cream puffs with a buttercream or mousseline cream filling. The possibilities for making such miniature marvels are limited only by imagination. At Maxim's, I learned how to make rich almond petits fours by cutting a large square tart baked with almond cream into squares. At Faugeron, another famous Parisian restaurant, they made petits fours from butter cookies (similar to Breton Butter Cookies; see recipe), by topping them with wild strawberries and rosettes of whipped cream—a simple idea with a wonderful result.

Other petits fours are actually portion-size cakes that are individually baked. Almond and Brown Butter Petits Fours baked in small square or round molds, or filled cakes cut into shapes after baking, such as Strawberry Petits Fours, illustrate this method. One- or two-bite shapes of a variety of cakes are also popular petits fours. These can be cubes of fresh cake, such as Cocoa and Coconut Génoise Squares, homemade French Pound Cake or "Genoa" Almond Cake (see recipes), perhaps dusted with a little powdered sugar or spread with a simple glaze.

Although professional bakers like to use fondant coating and intricate decorations on petits fours, I find fondant impractical for home cooks. It is not easily available, is time-consuming to make, and demands practice in order to obtain a coating that is smooth, shiny, and not too thick. Fondant is also very sweet, which is not a virtue in modern desserts. Instead I prefer toppings that are tastier and simpler, such as the Chestnut Frosting in Chocolate-Chestnut Petits Fours, or a buttercream and a decoration of fresh strawberries, as in Strawberry Petits Fours.

Hints

• Most of the cakes in the cake chapter can be made into petits fours. Rich cakes can be left plain and simply cut in cubes, while lighter cakes like génoise can be filled with buttercream or ganache.

Simply bake the cakes in square or rectangular molds, split them in 2 layers, fill them, and cut them in shapes. Because petits fours are small, the layers should be thin.

• Squares are the most economical shapes for cutting petits fours because there is no waste, but for variety you might like to cut hearts, rounds, diamonds, or other attractive shapes.

ALMOND AND BROWN BUTTER PETITS FOURS
Visitandines

These are my favorite petits fours. *Beurre noisette,* or brown butter, and a generous amount of ground almonds, give them their luscious flavor and rich texture. In pastry shops, they are usually baked in boat-shaped or small rectangular molds, which give them a slightly crisp crust, as more of their surface is exposed to direct heat. Sometimes small round molds resembling mini-muffin pans are used instead. Cupcake pans also work well, but then the petits fours are larger and more cakelike. For an ultra-rich treat, some chefs spread or pipe dark chocolate ganache on them.

MAKES 24 TO 30 SMALL CAKES, OR 12 CUPCAKES

1 1/3 cups slivered almonds	*8 large egg whites, room*
1 1/4 cups sugar	*temperature*
3/4 cup all-purpose flour	*1 cup unsalted butter*

Generously butter 30 small boat-shaped molds or small square molds (each holding about 2 tablespoons) or 24 mini-muffin pans or 12 nonstick cupcake pans with soft butter. Preheat oven to 400°F. for small molds, or 375°F. for mini-muffins or cupcakes.

In a food processor, grind almonds with 1/4 cup sugar to a fine powder. Transfer to a heavy saucepan. Add remaining sugar. Sift in flour and mix well. Add whites to almond mixture and mix very well, using a whisk.

In a small saucepan, melt butter over medium-low heat until it starts to brown in dots (look under bubbles) and has a nutty smell. This can take 10 minutes or more, but should be watched carefully. Transfer butter to a glass measuring cup, for easy pouring.

Heat almond mixture over low heat, whisking constantly, until just warm to touch; be careful because mixture burns easily. Remove from heat. Gradually whisk in melted butter. Transfer batter to a measuring cup and let stand 5 minutes; then stir batter.

Pour enough batter into molds to fill them by about two-thirds. Set boat molds, small square molds, or tartlet pans on a sturdy baking sheet. Bake small molds or mini-muffins about 15 minutes, cupcakes about 20 minutes, or until top is set and light beige, and edges are golden brown. Unmold immediately onto rack and cool. (They can be kept 1 week in airtight container, but are best on day they are baked.)

CHOCOLATE-CHESTNUT PETITS FOURS
Petits fours au chocolat et aux marrons

Ground chocolate delicately flavors the hazelnut base of these petits fours, while melted chocolate adds richness to the generous layer of chestnut frosting.   MAKES 32 PETITS FOURS

CHOCOLATE-FLECKED HAZELNUT CAKE

2½ cups hazelnuts (about 10½ ounces)

4 ounces semisweet chocolate, coarsely chopped

¾ cup plus 2 tablespoons sugar

¼ cup all-purpose flour

4 large eggs, separated, room temperature

¼ teaspoon cream of tartar

2 tablespoons kirsch

¼ cup unsalted butter, melted and cooled

CHESTNUT FROSTING

One 8¾-ounce can sweetened chestnut purée (¾ cup)

3 large egg yolks

½ cup unsalted butter, room temperature

1 tablespoon unsweetened cocoa powder, sifted

1 tablespoon kirsch

CHOCOLATE-FLECKED HAZELNUT CAKE

Position rack in center of oven and preheat to 350°F. Toast and skin hazelnuts (see page 388). Cool nuts completely.

Line bases of two 8-inch square baking pans with foil. Butter and flour foil, tapping to remove excess flour. Chop chocolate in a food processor until as fine as possible. Transfer to a medium bowl.

Grind cooled nuts with ¼ cup sugar in food processor until as fine as possible, scraping inward occasionally. Transfer to a large bowl. Sift flour onto nut mixture and stir to blend.

Beat egg yolks lightly in a large bowl. Beat in 6 tablespoons sugar and continue beating at high speed about 5 minutes, or until mixture is pale and very thick.

Whip egg whites with cream of tartar in a large bowl until soft peaks form. Gradually beat in remaining ¼ cup sugar at high speed and beat until whites are stiff and shiny but not dry.

Stir kirsch into yolk mixture. Gently fold in about one-third of whites until nearly incorporated. Sprinkle about one-third of nut mixture over yolk mixture and fold in gently. Repeat with remaining whites and nut mixture in 2 batches. When batter is nearly blended, gradually fold in chocolate. Last, pour in cool melted butter while folding. Continue folding lightly but quickly, just until batter is blended.

Transfer batter to prepared pans and spread evenly. Bake about 20 minutes, or until a cake tester inserted in centers of mixture comes out clean. Invert onto racks and cool.

CHESTNUT FROSTING

Combine chestnut purée and egg yolks in a small heavy saucepan and whisk until blended. Cook over low heat, stirring constantly, about 2 minutes, or until mixture thickens and is lukewarm. Remove from heat and whisk until cool.

Cream butter in a medium or large bowl until smooth and fluffy. Gradually beat in cooled chestnut mixture and cocoa. Add kirsch and beat until smooth. Refrigerate 30 minutes.

Spread frosting over cakes. Refrigerate about 3 hours, or until set. Trim edges. Using a sharp knife, cut cakes in to 1½-inch squares. (Petits fours can be kept, covered, up to 3 days in refrigerator.) Serve cold.

NOTE:

On a warm day, chill food processor container about 15 minutes before chopping chocolate.

🌿 STRAWBERRY PETITS FOURS
Petits fours aux fraises

Fresh petits fours can be made from any cake batter. These are made from a white almond cake made with egg whites. Rather than splitting a cake in layers, these are made by an easier method—the batter is baked on a baking sheet and cut in 2 pieces to form the layers. The layers are filled with strawberry buttercream and topped with fresh strawberry slices, but you can use any buttercream flavor you like (see pages 190–191).   MAKES 24 PETITS FOURS

LIGHT ALMOND CAKE

1 cup blanched almonds (about
  4 1/2 ounces)
3/4 cup plus 2 tablespoons sugar
6 tablespoons all-purpose flour

8 large egg whites, room
  temperature
1/3 cup milk

STRAWBERRY BUTTERCREAM

Buttercream (page 356)

2 cups ripe strawberries, hulled

24 round strawberry slices for
  garnish

LIGHT ALMOND CAKE

Position rack in center of oven and preheat to 375°F. Line an 11-×-17-inch baking sheet with parchment paper or foil; butter paper or foil.

Grind almonds with 1/2 cup plus 2 tablespoons sugar in a food processor until as fine as possible, scraping inward occasionally. Transfer to a medium bowl. Sift flour onto almond mixture and stir until blended.

Whip egg whites in a large bowl until soft peaks form. Gradually beat in remaining 1/4 cup sugar at high speed and beat until whites are stiff and shiny but not dry.

With a wooden spoon, stir milk into almond mixture. Stir in about one-quarter of whites. Gently fold remaining whites into almond mixture in 3 batches. Fold lightly but quickly, just until batter is blended.

Spread batter evenly on prepared baking sheet. Bake 15 minutes, or until cake is light brown on top and golden brown at edges. Cool in pan on a rack.

STRAWBERRY BUTTERCREAM

Prepare buttercream. Purée 2 cups strawberries in food processor until very smooth. Measure ⅔ cup purée, and using a wooden spoon, very gradually beat purée into buttercream.

Cut cake in half crosswise with a sharp knife; each piece will be about 8 inches wide. Carefully remove 1 piece from paper and set on a platter; cake will feel slightly sticky.

Spread about half the buttercream in a thin layer on cake on platter. Top with second piece of cake, positioning it so cut sides of layers are even with each other. Refrigerate 10 minutes.

Spread remaining buttercream over top cake layer. Arrange strawberry slices on top, about 1½ inches apart. Refrigerate about 1 hour, or until frosting is set. Trim edges of cake and cut cake in 1½-inch squares. (Petits fours can be kept, covered, up to 1 day in refrigerator.)

❧ COCOA AND COCONUT GÉNOISE SQUARES
Petits fours au cacao et à la noix de coco

An easy chocolate glaze and a sprinkling of coconut give these petits fours an enticing look. Although shaped like brownies, they are much lighter, because they are made of génoise.

MAKES 16 PETITS FOURS

COCOA AND COCONUT GÉNOISE
1/4 cup unsalted butter

7 tablespoons all-purpose flour

3 tablespoons plus 1 teaspoon unsweetened cocoa, preferably Dutch process

1 teaspoon baking powder

6 tablespoons unsweetened coconut

4 large eggs

2/3 cup sugar

CHOCOLATE GLAZE AND GARNISH
3 ounces semisweet chocolate, chopped

2 tablespoons unsalted butter

2 tablespoons unsweetened coconut

COCOA AND COCONUT GÉNOISE
Butter an 8-inch square cake pan, line base with parchment paper or foil, and butter paper or foil. Flour paper and sides of pan and tap to remove excess. Preheat oven to 350°F. Melt butter in a small saucepan over low heat and let cool completely. Sift together flour, cocoa, and baking powder. Stir in coconut until thoroughly blended.

Beat eggs lightly with a mixer. Beat in sugar and beat mixture at high speed about 8 minutes, or until very thick.

Sprinkle one-third of cocoa mixture over batter and fold it in as gently as possible. Add remaining cocoa mixture in 2 more batches, in same way. When last portion is nearly folded in, begin adding melted butter in a thin stream and folding it in.

Transfer batter to pan and bake about 25 minutes, or until cake shrinks slightly from sides of pan and top springs back when lightly pressed with your fingertip; a cake tester inserted into center of cake should come out clean. Run a thin-bladed flexible knife carefully around edges of cake, and turn it out onto a rack to cool.

CHOCOLATE GLAZE AND GARNISH

Melt chocolate in a small bowl above hot water over low heat. Stir until smooth. Stir in butter until absorbed. Remove from pan of water.

Spread glaze over top of cake. Sprinkle with coconut. Refrigerate about 1 hour, or until set. Cut cake into 16 squares.

Chocolates

The French learned to love chocolate from the Spanish, who brought it from the New World. For a while, the nobles kept the prized flavoring for themselves and served it only as a drink. It was in the seventeenth century, when Marie-Thérèse, daughter of the King of Spain, became the French queen by marrying Louis XIV, that chocolate became popular in France because, according to French writers, this queen was a real chocoholic. Over the years chocolate, especially the dark bittersweet kind, has become the favorite dessert flavoring in France.

French chocolate truffles, the most luxurious of candies, are made from a smooth, easy-to-make mixture called ganache. A creamy mixture with a deep chocolate flavor, ganache typifies the French love of pure tastes and the modern preference for desserts that are not overly sweet. Ganache is made in minutes by simply pouring hot cream over chopped chocolate and stirring the mixture until it is smooth. Semisweet, bittersweet, white, and milk chocolates can all be made into ganache.

There is a growing variety of excellent chocolates on the market, and truffles deserve to be made with the best. Because these candies contain so few ingredients, the flavor of the chocolate truly comes through. The finest chocolate will, therefore, produce the most luscious truffles. With each type of chocolate used, the color, taste, and texture of the truffles will be different.

Although chocolate is the dominant taste in ganache, it can be

accented with other dessert flavorings. Some ingredients, such as orange peel, cinnamon sticks, and coffee beans, are gently infused in the
cream and then strained out, so the ganache remains silky-smooth.
Others, such as candied ginger, can be chopped and stirred into the
ganache.

Some cooks do not prepare dipped chocolates because many
recipes require tempering, a procedure that ensures crisp, shiny chocolate coatings and involves melting chocolate, lowering its temperature, and heating it again to a specific temperature.

In most of the chocolates in this chapter, I have avoided this step.
In Classic Chocolate Truffles, the dipped candies are rolled in cocoa,
so that the chocolate coating is covered anyway. An even easier
method, which has the advantage of being quick too, is to prepare
undipped truffles, as in Easy Chocolate-Orange Truffles. Instead of
being coated in chocolate, the ganache centers are simply rolled in
chopped toasted nuts, which provide a crunchy texture to complement
the intense chocolate interior.

Besides round truffles, ganache can be made into chocolates of
other shapes, such as Honey Ganache Squares. And Whipped Ganache (see recipe), like buttercream, can be used as a filling for
chocolate candy cups, for a beautiful and festive chocolate.

You may have seen some candy makers who take pride in their
giant truffles. But believe me, you will find truffles much more enjoyable if you follow the French example—make them small! Their flavor
is so intense, one is enough for most people. And, of course, you can
always have another!

Hints

• Use *couverture,* or special dipping chocolate with a high cocoa-
butter content, for dipping, because it is more fluid when warm so it
is easier to use and gives a thin, delicate coating. In addition, *couverture*
is high-quality chocolate, and so the coating tastes better.

• For dipping chocolates, a relatively large amount of chocolate is
needed so the layer of chocolate in the bowl will be deep enough to
immerse the candy. The leftover chocolate can be poured onto a
piece of foil, allowed to harden, and reused for flavoring desserts.
It will probably contain streaks but these will disappear when it is
remelted.

EASY CHOCOLATE-ORANGE TRUFFLES
Truffes au chocolat à l'orange

A coating of chopped nuts provides a crunchy texture to complement the flavorful chocolate interior of these truffles. These rich truffles are a snap to make because no dipping is required. They can be
made ahead, and taste even better on the second day.

MAKES ABOUT TWENTY 1-INCH TRUFFLES

2 medium navel oranges
3/4 cup heavy cream
8 ounces fine-quality semisweet or
bittersweet chocolate, very finely
chopped

2/3 cup finely chopped pecans,
walnuts, unsalted macadamia
nuts, or toasted almonds (see
Note)

Using a vegetable peeler, pare colored part of peel from oranges in
long strips, without including white pith. Scald cream and strips of
orange peel in small heavy saucepan over medium-high heat until
bubbling at edges. Remove from heat, cover, and let stand 20 minutes. Strain cream into medium bowl, pressing on orange strips, and
return to cleaned saucepan.

Put chocolate in heatproof medium bowl. Heat orange-flavored
cream over medium-high heat, stirring with a whisk, until it comes to
full boil. Pour cream over chocolate all at once. Stir with whisk until
chocolate is completely melted and mixture is smooth. Cool to room
temperature, occasionally stirring gently.

Cover bowl of chocolate mixture and refrigerate, stirring mixture
occasionally from sides of bowl to center, until it is very thick and firm
enough to spoon out in mounds but not hard, about 45 minutes.

Line a tray with foil. Using 2 teaspoons, spoon mixture in 3/4-inch
mounds onto foil, using about 2 teaspoons mixture for each. Cover
and refrigerate until firm enough to handle, about 15 minutes.

Press each mound into a rough ball and return to tray. Roll each
between your palms to smooth ball, and return to tray. Work quickly
so they do not soften too much. If truffles become very soft, refrigerate
or freeze to slightly firm them before continuing to roll them into
balls.

For rolling in nuts, truffles should be somewhat soft so that nuts stick. If they are very soft and difficult to handle, refrigerate briefly. Line tray with foil. Put nuts in shallow bowl. Roll each truffle in nuts, pressing so nuts adhere and truffle is well coated. Place on foil-lined tray. Cover and refrigerate until firm, about 2 hours. (Truffles can be kept in airtight container up to 5 days in refrigerator; or they can be frozen.) Serve cold or at cool room temperature, in candy papers.

NOTE: Nuts should be chopped to fine pieces, but not to a powder.

CLASSIC CHOCOLATE TRUFFLES
Truffes au chocolat classiques

French truffles prepared the classic way are dipped in melted chocolate, then rolled in cocoa. In form, they are inspired by the black truffles so loved in classic French cuisine. Their crisp bittersweet chocolate shell encasing the creamy chocolate center make them the chocolate lover's favorite sweet. Although professional chocolatiers temper the chocolate to ensure that the shell sets quickly, evenly, and without any streaks of cocoa butter, this step can be skipped at home—under the cocoa coating, nobody would notice whether the chocolate shell is shiny anyway! Dutch-process cocoa is best for rolling because it has a more delicate flavor than regular cocoa.

MAKES ABOUT 30 TRUFFLES

GANACHE CENTERS
2/3 cup heavy cream　　　　　　　*8 ounces fine-quality semisweet*
1 large or 2 small vanilla beans,　　　*chocolate, very finely chopped*
　split lengthwise

COATING
1 cup unsweetened Dutch-process　　*12 ounces fine-quality semisweet*
　cocoa powder　　　　　　　　　　*chocolate, preferably*
　　　　　　　　　　　　　　　　　couverture, chopped

GANACHE CENTERS
Scald cream with vanilla beans in small heavy saucepan over medium-high heat until bubbling at edges. Remove from heat, cover,

and let stand 30 minutes. Remove vanilla beans. Scrape any cream and loose seeds from vanilla beans back into pan of cream.

Put chocolate in a medium bowl. Bring cream to a full boil in a small heavy saucepan over medium-high heat. Pour cream over chocolate all at once. Stir with a whisk until chocolate is completely melted and mixture is smooth. Cool to room temperature. Scrape down mixture with a rubber spatula. Cover with a paper towel and plastic wrap and refrigerate, occasionally stirring gently, about 1 hour, or until just thick enough to spoon out in mounds but not hard.

Line 2 trays with foil. Spoon ganache in ¾-inch mounds onto prepared trays, spacing them about 1 inch apart for easy handling. Cover with a paper towel and plastic wrap and refrigerate about 30 to 45 minutes, or until firm.

Remove a mound carefully, keeping second tray in refrigerator while working with first. Press mound to a ball and return to tray. Repeat with remaining mounds on tray.

Roll each ball between your palms until smooth. Work quickly so they do not soften too much; rinse and dry your hands often. If truffles begin to soften too much during rolling, refrigerate them about 5 minutes and continue. Refrigerate prepared truffle centers while shaping those on second tray. Cover with paper towels and plastic wrap and refrigerate all truffles at least 3 hours, or until very firm. (They can be kept, covered, up to 3 days in refrigerator; or they can be frozen.)

COATING

Spread cocoa in a small tray or shallow bowl so that it is about ½ inch deep. Line 2 trays with foil.

Melt chocolate in a double boiler or heatproof medium bowl over hot, not simmering, water over low heat, stirring very often with a rubber spatula. Stir until smooth. Remove from pan of water.

Either temper chocolate (page 389) for a professional finish; or cool melted chocolate, stirring often, until it reaches 88°F., or slightly cooler than body temperature.

Set container of chocolate in a bowl of warm water off heat, making sure it sits squarely in bowl and does not move around.

Set 1 ganache center in melted chocolate. Turn it over with 2 fingers or a looped-shaped dipping utensil until completely coated. Lift out and shake gently a few times, so that excess chocolate drips back into bowl. Wipe truffle gently against rim of bowl to remove excess chocolate. Set truffle in tray of cocoa and spoon enough cocoa over it to cover it. Repeat dipping and coating with 4 or 5 more centers. Shake tray of cocoa gently to be sure truffles are coated with cocoa. Transfer truffles very gently to foil-lined tray.

Continue coating remaining truffles, placing them in cocoa and transferring them to tray. Replace warm water in bowl occasionally. If chocolate gets thick, set bowl of chocolate over pan of hot, not simmering, water over low heat for 2 or 3 minutes to soften it.

If truffles do not set at room temperature within 10 minutes, refrigerate them about 10 minutes, or until set. Transfer truffles gently to a rack. Gently brush off excess cocoa with a pastry brush.

Refrigerate truffles 1 hour. (Truffles can be kept in an airtight container up to 1 week in refrigerator; or they can be frozen.) Serve at room temperature in white or gold candy papers.

NOTES

• This recipe calls for large amounts of chocolate and cocoa, because these quantities are needed for convenient dipping and rolling. The extra chocolate can be poured into a foil-lined dish, left to harden, and reused in desserts (although not for dipping). The extra cocoa can be sifted and reused.

• If you prefer a very light cocoa coating, set truffles on foil-lined trays after dipping in chocolate and refrigerate about 15 minutes, or until just set; then roll them in cocoa.

LEMON–WHITE CHOCOLATE TRUFFLES WITH PISTACHIOS
Truffes au chocolat blanc au citron et aux pistaches

Because white chocolate truffles are very sweet, I like to flavor them with lemon, to balance their flavor. For a pretty presentation, roll some of the truffles in coconut instead of pistachios, so they are pure white, and serve them alongside the pistachio-coated truffles.

MAKES ABOUT TWENTY 1-INCH TRUFFLES

1 large lemon

3/4 cup heavy cream

12 ounces fine-quality white
chocolate, very finely chopped

2/3 cup finely chopped unsalted
pistachio nuts

Using a vegetable peeler, pare colored part of peel from lemon in long strips, without including white pith. Scald cream and strips of lemon peel in small heavy saucepan over medium-high heat until bubbling at edges. Remove from heat, cover, and let stand 30 minutes. Strain cream into medium bowl, pressing on lemon strips, and return to cleaned saucepan.

Put chocolate in heatproof medium bowl. Heat lemon-flavored cream over medium-high heat, stirring with whisk, until it comes to a full boil. Pour cream over chocolate all at once. Stir with a whisk until chocolate is completely melted and mixture is smooth. If white chocolate does not melt completely or is not uniform in color, set bowl of mixture above pan of hot water over low heat and stir gently with whisk until chocolate is completely melted and mixture is smooth. Cool to room temperature, occasionally stirring gently.

Cover bowl of mixture and refrigerate, stirring mixture occasionally from sides of bowl to center, until very thick and firm enough to spoon out in mounds but not hard, about 2 hours.

Line tray with foil. Using 2 teaspoons, spoon mixture in 3/4-inch mounds onto foil, using about 2 teaspoons mixture for each. Cover and refrigerate until firm enough to be pressed into balls, about 1 1/2 hours.

Press each mound to a rough ball and return to tray; use rubber spatula if necessary to help lift mounds off paper. Roll each between your palms to smooth ball and return to tray. Work quickly so they do not soften too much. If truffles become very soft, refrigerate or freeze to slightly firm them before continuing to roll them into balls.

For rolling in nuts, truffles should be somewhat soft so that nuts stick. If they are very soft and difficult to handle, refrigerate briefly. Line tray with foil. Put nuts in shallow bowl. Roll each truffle in nuts, pressing so nuts adhere and truffle is well coated. Place on foil-lined tray. Cover and refrigerate until firm, about 2 hours. (Truffles can be kept in airtight container up to 5 days in refrigerator; or they can be frozen.) Serve cold, in candy papers.

SEE JACKET PHOTOGRAPH.

❧ MILK CHOCOLATE TRUFFLES
Truffes au chocolat au lait

If you roll these truffles in cocoa, the touch of bitterness acts as a foil for the sweet milk chocolate. If you prefer sweet truffles, roll them in toasted chopped almonds instead. And if you want both cocoa and crunchiness, roll them in both!

MAKES ABOUT TWENTY 1-INCH TRUFFLES

11 ounces fine-quality milk chocolate, very finely chopped
³/4 cup heavy cream

²/3 cup finely chopped toasted almonds, or ¹/3 cup Dutch-process cocoa

Put chocolate in heatproof medium bowl. Heat cream in small heavy saucepan over medium-high heat, stirring with a whisk, until it comes to a full boil. Pour cream over chocolate all at once. Stir with whisk until chocolate is completely melted and mixture is smooth. If chocolate does not melt completely or is not uniform in color, set bowl of mixture above pan of hot water over low heat and stir gently with whisk until chocolate is completely melted and mixture is smooth. Cool to room temperature, occasionally stirring gently.

Cover bowl of chocolate mixture and refrigerate, stirring mixture occasionally from sides of bowl to center, until very thick and firm enough to spoon out in mounds but not hard, about 1 ¹/2 hours.

Line tray with foil. Using 2 teaspoons, spoon mixture in ³/4-inch mounds onto foil, using about 2 teaspoons mixture for each. Cover and refrigerate until firm enough to be pressed into balls, about 1 ¹/2 hours.

Press each mound to a rough ball and return to tray. Roll each ball between your palms to smooth ball, and return to tray. Work quickly so they do not soften too much. If truffles become very soft, refrigerate or freeze to slightly firm them before continuing to roll them to balls.

To roll truffles in almonds, truffles should be somewhat soft so that nuts stick. If they are very soft and difficult to handle, refrigerate briefly. Line tray with foil. Put nuts in shallow bowl. Roll each truffle in nuts, pressing so nuts adhere and truffle is well coated. Place on foil-lined tray.

To roll truffles in cocoa, refrigerate at least 2 hours before rolling so they are firm. Line tray with foil. Put cocoa in shallow bowl. Roll firm truffles 1 at a time lightly in cocoa until coated, gently shaking off excess cocoa. Place on foil-lined tray.

Cover truffles and refrigerate until firm, about 2 hours. (Truffles can be kept in airtight container up to 5 days in refrigerator; or they can be frozen.) Serve cold, in candy papers.

NOTE: If desired, roll truffles in cocoa, then in almonds.

SEE JACKET PHOTOGRAPH.

HONEY GANACHE SQUARES
Carrés à la ganache au miel

For these elegant chocolates, honey ganache is cut in squares, dipped in bittersweet chocolate, and set on a bed of chopped walnuts. The walnuts stick to the chocolate, adding crunch to the candies and preventing "feet," or chocolate drips.

MAKES ABOUT 50 TO 60 CHOCOLATES

HONEY GANACHE

10 ounces fine-quality bittersweet chocolate, very finely chopped

½ cup heavy cream
¼ cup liquid honey

COATING AND GARNISH

1½ cups finely chopped walnuts (about 6 ounces)
12 ounces fine-quality bittersweet chocolate, preferably couverture, *chopped*

About 1½ cups walnut halves (about 7 ounces), if desired, for garnish

HONEY GANACHE

Put chocolate in a heatproof medium bowl. Bring cream to a full boil in a small heavy saucepan over medium-high heat. Pour cream over chocolate all at once. Stir with a whisk until chocolate is completely melted and mixture is smooth. Whisk in honey.

Line base and sides of a 7 1/2- to 8-inch square baking pan with a single piece of wax paper. Pour ganache into prepared pan, cover with a paper towel and plastic wrap, and refrigerate about 2 hours, or until firm.

Line 3 trays with foil or wax paper. Turn out ganache onto a cutting board. Cut into 1-inch squares with a sharp knife.

Put squares on prepared trays. Cover with a paper towel and plastic wrap and refrigerate at least 3 hours. (Mixture can be kept, covered, 3 days in refrigerator.)

COATING AND GARNISH

Line 3 trays with foil. Put finely chopped walnuts on 1 tray. Melt chocolate in a double boiler or heatproof medium bowl over hot, not simmering, water over low heat, stirring very often with a rubber spatula. Stir until smooth. Remove from pan of water.

Either temper chocolate (page 389) for a professional finish; or cool melted chocolate, stirring often, until it reaches 88°F., or slightly cooler than body temperature.

Set container of chocolate in a bowl of warm water off heat, making sure it sits squarely in bowl and does not move around.

Keep 2 trays of ganache squares in refrigerator. Take 1 ganache square and set it in melted chocolate mixture. Turn it over with a fork until completely coated. Lift it out and gently shake it a few times to remove excess chocolate. Set it on bed of walnuts, removing it from fork with a knife. Set a walnut half on top, if desired.

Continue dipping remaining candies. When tray of walnuts becomes crowded, remove candies carefully to a clean foil-lined tray. Let stand at room temperature until set. If coating does not set within 10 minutes, refrigerate about 10 minutes, or until set. Remove carefully from foil. (Candies can be kept in an airtight container up to 1 week in refrigerator.) Serve in candy papers.

❧ CHOCOLATE CUPS WITH RASPBERRY BUTTERCREAM
Caissettes de chocolat à la crème aux framboises

Tiny chocolate cups are a treat, especially when made at home with fine chocolate and filled with a smooth buttercream flavored with raspberries. For a fresh touch, each can be garnished with a fresh raspberry a short time before serving. Other flavors of buttercream can be used instead in the chocolate cups. A filling of coffee buttercream can be garnished with chocolate coffee beans, and orange buttercream with candied orange peel. Whipped Ganache (see recipe) also makes a delicious filling for these cups.

MAKES ABOUT 28 CANDIES

6 ounces fine-quality bittersweet or semisweet chocolate, preferably couverture, *chopped*
Raspberry Buttercream (page 359)

Candied violets in small pieces, grated chocolate, silver balls, or other small candies for garnish

Use very small foil or paper candy cups, of 1-inch top diameter. Arrange cups on a tray, setting them in a double layer to reinforce them. Melt 3 ounces chocolate in very small heatproof bowl over hot, not simmering, water over low heat, stirring very often with a rubber spatula. Remove from pan of water. Cool to slightly less than body temperature. Using a very small brush of about ¼ inch in diameter (see Note), brush thin layer of melted chocolate into candy cups, covering base and sides without leaving any holes and without dripping chocolate onto outside of cup. Set on tray and refrigerate about 15 minutes, or freeze 7 minutes or until set.

Melt remaining 3 ounces chocolate as above. Cool to slightly less than body temperature. Remove cups from refrigerator or freezer and repeat coating. Handle them as little as possible. Refrigerate about 15 minutes, or freeze 7 minutes or until set.

Bring buttercream to cool room temperature. Using a pastry bag and medium star tip, fill each chocolate cup with buttercream, ending with fairly large rosette. Set a piece of candied violet or other candy on center of rosette. Refrigerate until set, about 1 hour. (Candies can be kept in airtight container up to 4 days in refrigerator.) Just before serving, gently peel off paper or foil candy cups.

NOTE: Small brushes are available in art-supply stores.

Basics

Perhaps the primary lesson in my training in French dessert making was the importance of mastering the basics. If you know how to make the basic cakes, fillings, sauces, and a few techniques, you can make any dessert. Chef Albert Jorant, the head pastry chef at La Varenne, put it best: "There are only about fifty dessert recipes," he often said; "all the rest are variations."

Knowledge of the basics also helps organize the information in your mind, so that when you learn about or taste a new dessert, there is a great likelihood that you will have a good idea of how it is made. It enables you to make sense out of the thousands of recipes that come to us from books, from friends, and even from the backs of packages. Eventually, it becomes easy to look at a recipe and recognize what basic elements are being used, even if the writer has not labeled them as such.

French pâtisserie is constructed in a logical fashion. All the fillings and frostings and many desserts are related to each other, and can even be expressed as formulas. Here are some examples:

Ice cream = crème anglaise

Parfait = crème anglaise + whipped cream

Bavarian cream = crème anglaise + gelatin + whipped cream

Buttercream = bombe mixture (syrup + egg yolks) + butter

Bombe mousse = bombe mixture + whipped cream; *or* Italian meringue + whipped cream

Meringue buttercream = Italian meringue + butter

Mousseline cream = pastry cream + butter

Diplomate cream = pastry cream + gelatin + whipped cream

Soufflé mixture = pastry cream + whipped egg whites

In this chapter are the basic recipes that are used very often, but there are many more recipes that can be used as "basics," or elements that can be mixed and matched, throughout the book. Bavarian creams, mousses, ice creams, and parfaits, for instance, which are delicious desserts on their own, can also be layered with génoise, baked nut meringues, and other cakes to create new sophisticated desserts.

Sauces

A fresh fruit sauce, a rich chocolate sauce, or a luscious crème anglaise can turn fruit, ice cream, or a simple cake into a festive dessert. Sauces have always been central to French cooking, but in modern desserts their importance has soared.

Custard sauce or *crème anglaise* is the most widely used sauce among dessert chefs. From it are made ice creams and Bavarian creams, and when poured over sliced fresh or poached fruit, it makes a lovely dessert.

Cool, refreshing, fruit sauces will no doubt be the major dessert sauces of the nineties. On the finest of tables, desserts ranging from a simple scoop of ice cream to an elaborate charlotte are now often served surrounded by a ribbon of sauce of a brilliant hue, which adds natural beauty and fresh flavor.

French fruit sauces highlight the essence of the fruit. They are relatively low in calories, are ready in minutes, and many do not require any cooking at all.

These light sauces, made from purées of fruit, are often called *coulis* in French, a term that is being used more and more in English as well. They are an ideal accompaniment for a great variety of desserts, including cakes, puddings, soufflés, crêpes, pastries, Bavarian creams, and sliced fruit. The sauce is chosen to complement both the color and the flavor of the dessert.

Two basic techniques are used to prepare fruit sauces. Soft fruits are simply puréed and sweetened with powdered sugar. Firmer fruits are first poached in a simple syrup flavored with lemon juice and a vanilla bean, and then are puréed. These procedures produce a sauce of a much more natural flavor than did the former practice of making sauces from fruit preserves or jam.

Using these simple principles, there is a rainbow of colors and a multitude of flavors available. From the soft green of kiwi sauce, to the bright red of strawberry sauce, to the deep orange of apricot sauce, to the dark blue-purple of blackberry sauce—all add great excitement to contemporary desserts.

With these quick vibrant sauces, sensational desserts can be made in no time. Swirl some nectarine sauce on a plate, top with a scoop of vanilla ice cream, and garnish with a few blueberries, and you will have a lively sundae. Top a slice of cake with peaches mixed with whipped cream, and encircle with a ribbon of fresh berry sauce. Prepare a colorful fruit salad of kiwi slices, strawberries, bananas, and fresh figs and accompany it with an exotic mango sauce. Spoon two sauces of contrasting colors side by side on the same plate, and top with ice cream and fruit, as in Apricot and Raspberry Coupe (see recipe), for an elegant, cooling dessert.

The flavor of fruit sauces can be enhanced with a liqueur or brandy made of the same fruit. For example, peach liqueur is lovely in peach sauce, while pear brandy perks up pear sauce. Spirits can even be mixed and matched with sauces made from different fruits. Crème de cassis contributes a pleasing nuance to blackberry sauce, while kirsch adds a nice touch to apricot sauce.

Hints

CUSTARD SAUCE

• Have ready all utensils—a whisk, wooden spoon, strainer, and mixing bowl—before beginning to make custard sauce.

• Use a good-quality heavy enameled or stainless-steel saucepan. To make stirring easier, choose a pan with a rounded rather than a straight bottom.

• Stir and scrape the bottom of the saucepan, to prevent the sauce from sticking. Be sure to reach the pan's entire surface.

FRUIT SAUCES

• The amount of powdered sugar needed in fruit sauces depends on the natural sweetness of the fruit, which in turn depends on the fruit's variety and ripeness. Even at the height of its season, the same fruit will vary in sweetness from year to year.

• How sweet to make a sauce is a matter of personal taste and depends on what the sauce will accompany. The sauce should taste slightly sweet but should have the refreshing natural tanginess and flavor of the fruit. When serving the sauce with a relatively sweet ice cream, sweeten the sauce enough so that it will not taste unnaturally tart with the ice cream. If in doubt, taste it with a little of the ice cream before serving.

• Depending on the fruit, the thickness of fruit sauces varies. If a sauce is too thick to be poured, whisk in lemon juice, liqueur, water, or poaching syrup by teaspoons until the sauce reaches the desired consistency.

• Many fruit sauces thicken on standing. Before serving a sauce that was made ahead, whisk it until smooth and, if necessary, thin it as above.

• The texture of fruit sauces is different from that of custard or cream sauces. In most cases, fruit sauces are most attractive if spooned around or topped by the food they will accompany, rather than being spooned over it. Raspberry, blackberry, and strawberry sauces are the smoothest and can be used to coat foods, especially fruit.

• Fruit sauces have the freshest flavor if they are served on the day they are made.

- Add liqueur or brandy to a sauce just before serving. Relatively more brandy or liqueur is needed if the sauce will be served with ice cream than with other foods.

VANILLA CUSTARD SAUCE
Crème anglaise

Called in France *crème anglaise* or "English cream," this is the most popular dessert sauce in the French kitchen. It is served with all sorts of cakes—from light cakes like génoise to richer cakes like "Genoa" Almond Cake (see recipe) to dense chocolate cakes to pound cakes. You can also use it as a topping for fresh berries or other fresh or poached fruit, or to accompany charlottes or puddings. Although vanilla is the classic flavoring, the sauce is delicious in its other versions as well—lemon, orange, coffee, and any strong-flavored fruit brandy or liqueur.

MAKES ABOUT 1¾ CUPS SAUCE; ABOUT 6 TO 8 SERVINGS

1 vanilla bean, split lengthwise	*5 or 6 large egg yolks*
1½ cups milk	*¼ cup sugar*

Scrape seeds from split vanilla bean into milk. Bring milk and vanilla bean to a boil in a medium, heavy saucepan. Remove from heat, cover, and let stand 15 minutes.

Reheat milk to a boil. Whisk egg yolks lightly in a large bowl. Add sugar and whisk until smooth. Gradually whisk in hot milk. Return mixture to saucepan, whisking. Cook over medium-low heat, stirring mixture and scraping bottom of pan constantly with a wooden spoon, until sauce thickens slightly. After cooking sauce for 5 minutes, remove from heat and check if it is ready: it should reach 170°F. on an instant-read thermometer; or, dip a metal spoon in sauce and draw your finger across back of spoon—your finger should leave a clear trail in mixture that clings to spoon. If necessary, cook briefly and check again. Do not overcook sauce or it will curdle.

Strain sauce immediately into a bowl and stir for about 30 seconds to cool. Cool completely. Refrigerate at least 30 minutes before serving. (Sauce can be kept, covered, up to 2 days in refrigerator.)

NOTES

- Sauce will be slightly thicker with 6 egg yolks than with 5.
- If vanilla bean is not available, add 1½ teaspoons pure vanilla extract to the cooled sauce.

LIQUEUR

Omit vanilla bean, or use it but do not scrape out seeds. If omitting bean, bring milk to a boil and proceed to next step. Just before serving, stir 4 to 6 teaspoons liqueur into sauce—Grand Marnier, raspberry brandy, kirsch, apricot brandy, peach brandy, hazelnut liqueur, or rum.

COFFEE

Omit vanilla bean. Bring milk to a boil, remove from heat, and whisk in 4 teaspoons instant coffee granules. Proceed with next step.

LEMON

Pare zest of 1 lemon and cut it in thin strips. Substitute it for vanilla bean.

ORANGE

Pare zest of 2 oranges and cut it in thin strips. Substitute it for vanilla bean.

PRALINE

Stir 6 or 7 tablespoons Praline powder (page 374) into finished sauce.

CHOCOLATE SAUCE
Sauce au chocolat

Serve this rich sauce warm with vanilla or mint ice cream. Or use it to prepare the classic pears Belle Hélène, by topping vanilla ice cream with poached pear halves (page 373), then pouring this sauce over the pears.   MAKES 6 TO 8 SERVINGS

8 ounces semisweet or bittersweet
  chocolate, chopped
²/₃ cup heavy cream

3 to 4 tablespoons butter, room
  temperature
2 teaspoons pure vanilla extract

Heat chocolate in cream in a small heavy saucepan over low heat, stirring often, until smooth. If thicker sauce is desired, continue simmering, stirring often, until thickened. Remove from heat and stir in butter and vanilla. The sauce can be refrigerated and reheated over low heat.

SPIRITED CHOCOLATE SAUCE
Substitute 1 to 2 tablespoons Cognac or rum for the vanilla.

DARK CHOCOLATE SAUCE
Replace cream with water, coffee, or ⅓ cup water mixed with ⅓ cup Grand Marnier.

RASPBERRY SAUCE
Coulis de framboises

Also known as Melba sauce, this sauce is bursting with fresh flavor and brilliant color. It's hard to think of a more wonderful summer dessert than a scoop of homemade vanilla ice cream with this sauce and a garnish of more berries.

MAKES ABOUT 1 CUP SAUCE; ABOUT 4 SERVINGS

3 cups fresh raspberries (about 12
  ounces)
10 to 12 tablespoons powdered
  sugar, sifted
1 to 2 teaspoons clear raspberry
  brandy (framboise) or kirsch,
  or 1 tablespoon raspberry
  liqueur (optional)

1 to 2 teaspoons strained fresh
  lemon or lime juice (optional)

Purée berries in food processor or blender. Add 10 tablespoons powdered sugar. Process until very smooth. Strain into a bowl, pressing on pulp in strainer; use rubber spatula to scrape mixture from under-side of strainer.

Taste sauce and whisk in more powdered sugar if needed. Whisk sauce thoroughly so that sugar is completely blended in. If lumps of powdered sugar remain, strain sauce again. Cover and refrigerate 30 minutes. (Sauce can be kept, covered, 1 day in refrigerator.) Stir before serving and add spirits or lemon juice, if desired. Serve cold.

NOTE: If desired, substitute a 10- to 12-ounce package frozen un-sweetened or lightly sweetened berries for the fresh ones.

BLACKBERRY SAUCE
Coulis de mûres

Poached summer fruit and ice cream benefit from the intense flavor of this sauce. Its color varies, depending on whether reddish or darker blackberries are used.

MAKES ABOUT 1 CUP SAUCE; ABOUT 4 SERVINGS

3 cups fresh blackberries (about 12 ounces)

9 to 10 tablespoons powdered sugar, sifted

1 to 2 tablespoons blackberry brandy, crème de cassis, or black raspberry liqueur, or 1 to 2 teaspoons kirsch (optional)

1 to 2 teaspoons strained fresh lemon or lime juice (optional)

Purée berries in food processor or blender. Add 9 tablespoons pow-dered sugar. Process until very smooth. Strain into a bowl, pressing on pulp in strainer; use rubber spatula to scrape mixture from under-side of strainer.

Taste sauce and whisk in more powdered sugar, if needed. Whisk sauce thoroughly so that sugar is completely blended in. If lumps of powdered sugar remain, strain sauce again. Cover and re-frigerate 30 minutes. (Sauce can be kept, covered, 1 day in refriger-

ator.) Stir before serving and add spirits or lemon juice, if desired.
Serve cold.

NOTE: If desired, substitute a 10- to 12-ounce package frozen unsweetened or lightly sweetened berries for the fresh ones.

STRAWBERRY SAUCE
Coulis de fraises

This sauce is a great accompaniment for desserts like charlottes,
Bavarian creams, and cream puffs. I also like to toss it with sliced fresh
fruit to make a festive fruit salad.

MAKES ABOUT 1 CUP SAUCE; ABOUT 4 SERVINGS

*3 cups fresh strawberries (about 12
ounces)*
*9 to 10 tablespoons powdered
sugar, sifted*
*2 teaspoons strawberry liqueur,
kirsch, or Grand Marnier
(optional)*

*1 to 2 teaspoons strained fresh
lemon or lime juice (optional)*

Hull berries and purée them in food processor or blender. Add 9
tablespoons powdered sugar and process until very smooth. Strain
into a bowl, pressing on pulp in strainer; use rubber spatula to scrape
mixture from underside of strainer.

Taste sauce and whisk in more powdered sugar, if needed. Whisk
sauce thoroughly so that sugar is completely blended in. If lumps of
powdered sugar remain, strain sauce again. Cover and refrigerate 30
minutes. (Sauce can be kept, covered, 2 days in refrigerator.) Stir
before serving and add spirits or lemon juice, if desired. Serve cold.

NOTE:

• Sauce can be left unstrained, if desired, and in this case will make
1½ cups, but will be slightly smoother if strained.
• If desired, substitute a 10- to 12-ounce package frozen unsweetened or lightly sweetened berries for the fresh ones.

◈ BLUEBERRY SAUCE
Coulis de bluets

Blueberries are almost never seen in France, except in a few stores that specialize in exotic fruit, but the French have smaller, somewhat similar berries called *myrtilles*. North American blueberries do make a good French-style fruit sauce, especially when flavored with crème de cassis. Serve it with vanilla or mint ice cream, and sprinkle the dessert with fresh blueberries.

MAKES ABOUT 1 CUP SAUCE; ABOUT 4 SERVINGS

3 cups fresh blueberries (about 12 ounces)
9 to 10 tablespoons powdered sugar, sifted

1 tablespoon crème de cassis, or 1 to 2 teaspoons Cognac (optional)
1 to 2 teaspoons strained fresh lemon or lime juice (optional)

Purée berries in food processor or blender. Add 9 tablespoons powdered sugar and process until very smooth. Strain into a bowl, pressing gently on pulp in strainer to avoid pushing through too much of skins; use rubber spatula to scrape mixture from underside of strainer.

Taste sauce and whisk in more powdered sugar if needed. Whisk sauce thoroughly so that sugar is completely blended in. If lumps of powdered sugar remain, strain sauce again. Cover and refrigerate 30 minutes. (Sauce can be kept, covered, 2 days in refrigerator.) Stir before serving and add spirits or lemon juice, if desired.

NOTE: If desired, substitute a 10- to 12-ounce package frozen unsweetened or lightly sweetened berries for the fresh ones.

◈ MELON SAUCE
Coulis de melon

Use cantaloupe, honeydew, or another of the many sweet melons that are now becoming available. If you like, accent the sauce with a little melon liqueur.

MAKES ABOUT 1¼ CUPS SAUCE; ABOUT 5 SERVINGS

1 1/4 to 1 1/2 pounds cantaloupe or
 honeydew melon
4 to 5 tablespoons powdered sugar,
 sifted

2 teaspoons strained fresh lemon or
 lime juice
4 to 5 teaspoons Midori melon
 liqueur (optional)

Remove melon seeds with a spoon. Cut off rind and discard. Cut flesh in cubes, and purée fruit in food processor or blender. Add 4 tablespoons powdered sugar. Process until very smooth. Strain into a bowl, pressing on pulp in strainer. Use rubber spatula to scrape mixture from underside of strainer.

Taste sauce and whisk in more powdered sugar if needed. Whisk sauce thoroughly so that sugar is completely blended in. If lumps of powdered sugar remain, strain sauce again. Cover and refrigerate 30 minutes. (Sauce can be kept, covered, 1 day in refrigerator.) Just before serving stir in lemon juice and add liqueur, if desired. Serve cold.

NOTE: Instead of juice or liqueur above, sauce made from cantaloupe or other orange melons can be flavored with 2 tablespoons strained fresh orange juice.

KIWI SAUCE
Coulis de kiwis

For a simple dessert, serve this cool, refreshing pale green sauce with a slice of angel food cake, génoise, or sponge cake, and garnish with sliced kiwis and strawberries.

MAKES ABOUT 1 CUP SAUCE; ABOUT 4 SERVINGS

4 kiwis (about 1 1/4 pounds)
About 3/4 cup powdered sugar,
 sifted

1 to 2 teaspoons strained fresh
 lemon or lime juice (optional)
1 to 2 teaspoons kirsch (optional)

Peel kiwis with a paring knife. Cut flesh in chunks, and purée fruit in food processor or blender. Add 3/4 cup powdered sugar. Process until very smooth. Strain into a bowl, without pressing on pulp in strainer. Use rubber spatula to scrape mixture from underside of strainer.

Taste sauce and whisk in more powdered sugar if needed. Whisk sauce thoroughly so that sugar is completely blended in. If lumps of powdered sugar remain, strain sauce again. Cover and refrigerate 30 minutes. (Sauce can be kept, covered, 1 day in refrigerator.) Stir before serving and add lemon juice or kirsch, if desired. Serve cold.

NOTE: Sauce can be left unstrained if you prefer it with seeds. In this case, there will be 1 ½ cups.

MANGO SAUCE
Coulis de mangues

I love to serve this flavorful sauce with homemade lemon or kiwi sorbet or mint ice cream or with fruit salad.

MAKES ABOUT 1 CUP SAUCE; ABOUT 4 SERVINGS

1 ½ to 1 ¾ pounds ripe mango
5 to 6 tablespoons powdered sugar, sifted

1 to 2 teaspoons strained fresh lemon or lime juice (optional)
1 to 2 teaspoons rum (optional)

Peel mango with a paring knife. Cut flesh from pit, and purée fruit in food processor or blender. Add 5 tablespoons powdered sugar. Process until very smooth. Strain into a bowl, pressing on pulp in strainer. Use rubber spatula to scrape mixture from underside of strainer.

Taste sauce and whisk in more powdered sugar if needed. Whisk sauce thoroughly so that sugar is completely blended in. If lumps of powdered sugar remain, strain sauce again. Cover and refrigerate 30 minutes. (Sauce can be kept, covered, 1 day in refrigerator.) Stir before serving and add lemon juice or rum, if desired. Serve cold.

PEACH SAUCE
Coulis de pêches

Made from poached peaches, this sauce is great with fresh peach ice cream or vanilla ice cream, accompanied by a few berries. The variation is even easier to prepare, as there is no need to peel the nectarines.   MAKES ABOUT 1 ⅔ CUPS SAUCE; ABOUT 6 SERVINGS

Poached Peaches in their syrup
   (page 372)
4 or 5 tablespoons powdered sugar,
   sifted
2 to 3 teaspoons strained fresh
   lemon or lime juice (optional)

3 to 4 tablespoons peach brandy, or
   2 to 3 teaspoons kirsch
   (optional)

Refrigerate peaches in their syrup at least 30 minutes. Remove any pits and purée peaches with 4 tablespoons of poaching syrup in food processor or blender. Add 4 tablespoons powdered sugar and purée until smooth. Strain into a bowl, pressing on pulp in strainer. Use rubber spatula to scrape mixture from underside of strainer.

Whisk sauce until smooth. Gradually whisk in up to 3 tablespoons more syrup, if a thinner sauce is desired. Taste and add more powdered sugar if needed. Whisk sauce thoroughly so that sugar is completely blended in. If lumps of powdered sugar remain, strain sauce again. Cover and refrigerate 30 minutes. (Sauce can be kept, covered, 1 day in refrigerator.) Stir before serving, and add lemon juice or spirits, if desired. Serve cold.

NECTARINE SAUCE
Substitute nectarines for peaches.

APRICOT SAUCE
Coulis d'abricots

Apricot sauce can be made all year from dried apricots, as in
Apricot and White Chocolate Cold Soufflé (see recipe), but this version is for the brief season when they are fresh. Serve the sauce with
peach, vanilla, or mint ice cream or strawberry sorbet, and garnish the
dessert with fresh sliced apricots.

MAKES ABOUT 1⅔ CUPS SAUCE; ABOUT 6 SERVINGS

Poached Apricots in their syrup
  (page 372)
4 or 5 tablespoons powdered sugar,
  sifted
1 to 2 teaspoons strained fresh
lemon or lime juice (optional)

2 tablespoons apricot or peach
  brandy, or 1 to 2 teaspoons
  kirsch, rum, or Grand
  Marnier (optional)

Refrigerate apricots in their syrup at least 30 minutes. Purée apricots
with 2 tablespoons poaching syrup in food processor or blender. Add
3 tablespoons powdered sugar and purée until smooth. Strain into a
bowl, pressing on pulp in strainer. Use rubber spatula to scrape mixture from underside of strainer.

Whisk sauce until smooth. Gradually whisk in up to 2 tablespoons
more syrup, if a thinner sauce is desired. Taste and add more powdered sugar, if needed. Whisk sauce thoroughly so that sugar is completely blended in. If lumps of powdered sugar remain, strain sauce
again. Cover and refrigerate 30 minutes. (Sauce can be kept, covered,
1 day in refrigerator.) Stir before serving, and add lemon juice or
spirits, if desired. Serve cold.

RED WINE AND PEAR SAUCE
Coulis de poires au vin rouge

This sauce of rosy wine color tastes best with plain cake and ice
cream. The more delicately flavored pear sauce variation, made with-

out wine, has a light beige color and looks best when spooned onto a plate and topped by ice cream and colorful fruit.

MAKES ABOUT 1 CUP SAUCE; ABOUT 4 SERVINGS

PEARS IN RED WINE

½ cup granulated sugar   *1 vanilla bean*
2 cups dry red wine   *¾ pound ripe pears*

2 tablespoons powdered sugar, sifted   *Pinch of ground cinnamon or*
1 to 2 teaspoons strained fresh   *ginger (optional)*
*   lemon or lime juice (optional)*

PEARS IN RED WINE

Combine sugar, wine, and vanilla bean in medium, heavy saucepan and heat over low heat, stirring gently, until sugar dissolves. Raise heat to high and bring to a boil. Keep warm over very low heat.

Peel pears, cut in half, and core them. Bring syrup to a boil and add pears. Cover with a lid slightly smaller than diameter of saucepan to keep fruit submerged. Reduce heat to low and cook fruit until tender when pierced with sharp knife; cooking time can vary from 30 minutes to 1 hour. Cool fruit in syrup, still covered with small lid, to room temperature. Refrigerate 8 hours. (Fruit can be kept in syrup for 2 days in refrigerator.)

Purée fruit with 4 tablespoons of poaching syrup in food processor or blender. Add 2 tablespoons powdered sugar and purée until smooth. Strain into a bowl, pressing on pulp in strainer. Use rubber spatula to scrape mixture from underside of strainer.

Whisk sauce until smooth. Gradually whisk in up to 2 tablespoons more syrup, if a thinner sauce is desired. Taste and add more powdered sugar, if needed. Whisk sauce thoroughly so that sugar is completely blended in. If lumps of powdered sugar remain, strain sauce again. Cover and refrigerate 30 minutes. (Sauce can be kept, covered, 1 day in refrigerator.) Stir before serving, and add lemon juice or spice, if desired. Serve cold.

PEAR SAUCE

Replace wine in syrup with water. Cut a lemon in half. Peel pears and rub them well with cut lemon. Cut pears in half and core them. Add them to simmering syrup with 1 tablespoon lemon juice. Poach about 12 minutes, or until tender. After chilling pears in syrup at least 30 minutes, purée them with 4 tablespoons syrup and 2 tablespoons powdered sugar. Flavor finished sauce with 1 teaspoon strained fresh lemon juice and, if desired, with 2 or 3 teaspoons pear brandy. Omit the spice.

PLUM SAUCE
Coulis de prunes

For a lovely color, use red-fleshed plums for this sauce. Serve it with vanilla ice cream and sliced summer fruit.

MAKES ABOUT 1 ⅓ CUPS SAUCE; ABOUT 5 SERVINGS

Poached Plums in their syrup (page 373)	1 to 2 teaspoons strained fresh lemon or lime juice (optional)
5 or 6 tablespoons powdered sugar, sifted	1 to 2 teaspoons plum brandy or crème de cassis (optional)

Refrigerate plums in their syrup at least 30 minutes. Remove any pits and purée plums with 5 tablespoons of poaching syrup in food processor or blender. Add 5 tablespoons powdered sugar and purée until smooth. Strain into a bowl, pressing gently on pulp in strainer. Use rubber spatula to scrape mixture from underside of strainer.

Whisk sauce until smooth. Gradually whisk in 1 tablespoon more syrup, if a thinner sauce is desired. Taste and add more powdered sugar if needed. Whisk sauce thoroughly so that sugar is completely blended in. If lumps of powdered sugar remain, strain sauce again. Cover and refrigerate 30 minutes. (Sauce can be kept, covered, 1 day in refrigerator.) Stir before serving, and add lemon juice or spirits, if desired. Serve cold.

Fillings and Frostings

Three basic fillings—Chantilly cream, buttercream, and pastry cream—are those used most often in French baking. All can be spiced with a variety of sweet flavorings.

Chantilly cream, or sweetened whipped cream, is the most versatile of them all. It serves as a filling for pastries, as a filling and frosting for cakes, and as a garnish or accompaniment for an endless number of desserts.

Buttercream is the most widely used filling and frosting for cakes in France. It can also be piped into miniature chocolate cups (as on page 337) or onto very small cookie bases to make a wonderfully rich confection. Pastry cream, as its name suggests, is paired most often with pastries, especially as a filling for cream puffs and fruit tarts. Sometimes it is used to fill cakes, but not to frost them.

Ganache is today's most popular chocolate frosting, filling, and candy base, and is quick and simple to make.

For more information on using each of these mixtures, see their recipes and the chapters on cakes, pastries, and chocolates.

CHANTILLY CREAM OR SWEETENED WHIPPED CREAM
Crème chantilly

The favorite accompaniment to almost all desserts, Chantilly cream, or lightly sweetened whipped cream, is very easy to prepare in just a few minutes. Vanilla extract is the usual flavoring, but I also love the coffee, chocolate, and liqueur versions. Remember that only a small amount of liqueur can be added, because too much liquid will make the whipped cream lose its body.   MAKES ABOUT 2 CUPS

1 cup heavy cream, well chilled   *1 teaspoon pure vanilla extract*
2 to 3 teaspoons sugar

Chill mixer bowl and beater for about 20 minutes. Beat cream with sugar in chilled bowl with chilled beater until soft peaks form. Add flavoring and beat until stiff.

SPIRITED WHIPPED CREAM

Replace vanilla with 4 teaspoons clear raspberry brandy (framboise), kirsch, or Grand Marnier; or with 2 tablespoons peach brandy, coffee liqueur, or hazelnut liqueur (Frangelico). (If using cream for piping, it is best not to add more than 2 teaspoons liqueur, so the cream will hold a shape well.)

COFFEE WHIPPED CREAM

Omit vanilla. Add 1 teaspoon coffee extract or instant coffee powder along with sugar.

CHOCOLATE WHIPPED CREAM

Melt 2 ounces semisweet chocolate in a double boiler or small heat-proof bowl over hot, not simmering, water over low heat, stirring occasionally. Stir until smooth. Remove from heat but leave chocolate above hot water.

Whip cream with 4 teaspoons sugar in chilled bowl with chilled beater until stiff.

Remove chocolate from above water and cool for 30 seconds. Quickly stir about ⅓ cup whipped cream into chocolate. Quickly fold mixture into remaining whipped cream until smooth. Fold quickly so that chocolate does not harden upon contact with cold whipped cream. Use immediately for spreading on cake.

SOFTLY WHIPPED CREAM

For use as an accompaniment, but not for piping, whip cream with any of the above flavorings just until soft peaks form.

BUTTERCREAM
Crème au beurre

Most French gâteaux are filled and frosted with this silky buttercream, which is very easy to spread and pipe and freezes well. Unlike old-fashioned American frostings, French buttercream is not overly sweet. Because it is rich, it is best on light cakes such as génoise, sponge cake, and meringue, and should be spread in a thin layer. Buttercream can be flavored with any sweet flavoring, but any liquids should be added in small quantities because too much will cause the buttercream to separate. For additional buttercream flavors, see index.

MAKES 2½ TO 2⅓ CUPS, ENOUGH TO FILL AND FROST
AN 8-INCH 3-LAYER CAKE OR A 9-INCH 2-LAYER CAKE

5 large egg yolks, room temperature   *1 ¼ cups unsalted butter, cool but*
½ cup plus 2 tablespoons sugar   *not hard*
⅓ cup water   *Flavoring (see below)*

Beat egg yolks in bowl of mixer until well blended. Have ready a 2-cup measure with ice water.

Combine sugar and ⅓ cup water in small heavy saucepan, preferably one with lip for pouring. Cook over low heat, stirring very gently from time to time, until sugar dissolves. Increase heat to medium-high and bring to a boil. Boil without stirring, but brushing down sugar crystals from side of pan occasionally with pastry brush dipped in water, until mixture reaches soft-ball stage, about 4 minutes. To test, remove pan from heat; using a teaspoon, take about ½ teaspoon hot syrup and dip spoon into cup of ice water, keeping spoon level. With your hands in ice water, remove syrup from spoon. *Caution: Do not touch syrup unless your hands are in iced water.* If syrup is ready, it will form a soft ball. If syrup dissolves into water, continue cooking 30 seconds and test again; if syrup was overcooked and forms a firm ball, add 2 or 3 tablespoons water to saucepan of syrup to bring down its temperature, return to heat and cook, without stirring, until it reaches soft-ball stage. If you prefer to use a candy thermometer, cook syrup until thermometer registers 238°F., taking account that thermometer must be immersed in 2 inches of liquid to give an accurate reading.

As soon as syrup is ready, gradually beat it in a thin stream into egg yolks; try to pour it between whip and sides of bowl so not too much gets caught in whip. Beat mixture at high speed until it is completely cool and thick, scraping down sides once or twice. Transfer to another bowl.

Cut butter in 10 pieces. Using a paddle beater (creaming beater), if available, cream butter in large bowl until smooth and fluffy. Add egg yolk mixture in 4 batches, beating thoroughly after each addition.

Buttercream can now be flavored and used. (Buttercream can be kept in covered container up to 1 week in refrigerator or it can be frozen. Before using, let it come to room temperature, about 30 minutes, and beat until smooth.)

Use a wooden spoon or paddle beater, not a whisk, to stir in flavoring, adding it gradually. (Cakes frosted and filled with buttercream can be kept, covered, for 3 to 5 days in refrigerator, depending on type of cake.)

NOTES

• Some cooks prefer to hand-whisk hot syrup into egg yolks instead of using a mixer, so that less syrup sticks to sides of bowl. With this method, as soon as all the syrup has been added, mixture should be beaten at high speed of mixer.

• If liquid is added to buttercream too quickly, or too much is added, the buttercream will separate. If this happens, refrigerate the buttercream for about 30 minutes. Then set the bowl of buttercream above a warm water bath for a few seconds until just a few tablespoons of the buttercream melt. Remove from above the water and beat the buttercream well with a wooden spoon until it is smooth. If necessary, repeat the brief heating procedure again. If the buttercream is not smooth yet, melt 2 or 3 tablespoons butter and gradually beat it into the buttercream.

• The buttercream recipe can easily be doubled, and the extra kept for frosting and filling another cake. When making buttercream ahead, it is best to keep it unflavored; most flavorings will retain their taste better if added just before the buttercream is spread on the cake.

• Buttercream is best spread in a thin layer. About ½ cup is enough for use as a filling between 8-inch cake layers and about ⅔ to ¾ cup between 9-inch layers.

VANILLA
Using a wooden spoon, gradually beat 2½ teaspoons pure vanilla extract into the Buttercream.

COFFEE
Dissolve 2 tablespoons instant coffee granules in 2 tablespoons hot water and let cool. Using a wooden spoon, gradually beat into the Buttercream.

LEMON
Using a wooden spoon, stir 4 teaspoons finely grated lemon peel into the Buttercream. Gradually stir in 2 teaspoons strained fresh lemon juice.

ORANGE
Using a wooden spoon, stir 4 teaspoons finely grated orange peel into the Buttercream. Gradually stir in 4 teaspoons strained fresh orange juice.

CINNAMON
Using a wooden spoon, stir 2 teaspoons ground cinnamon into the Buttercream.

BITTERSWEET OR SEMISWEET CHOCOLATE
Melt 10 ounces chopped bittersweet or semisweet chocolate in double boiler or heatproof medium bowl over hot, not simmering, water over low heat, stirring occasionally. Remove from pan of water and let cool to body temperature. Using a wooden spoon, gradually beat chocolate into the Buttercream.

WHITE OR MILK CHOCOLATE
Melt 8 ounces chopped fine-quality white chocolate or milk chocolate in double boiler or heatproof medium bowl over hot, not simmering, water over low heat, stirring occasionally. Remove from pan of water and let cool to body temperature. Using a wooden spoon, gradually beat chocolate into the Buttercream.

SPIRITS
Measure 3 tablespoons Grand Marnier, clear raspberry brandy (framboise), kirsch, pear brandy, or rum into small cup. Using a wooden spoon, very gradually beat liqueur into the Buttercream. If liquid is added too quickly, Buttercream may separate.

RASPBERRY
Purée 10 ounces fresh raspberries (about 3 cups) or 8 ounces thawed frozen raspberries in food processor or blender until very smooth. Strain purée into medium bowl, pressing on pulp in strainer. Use

rubber spatula to scrape mixture from underside of strainer. Measure
2/3 cup purée. Using a wooden spoon, very gradually beat purée into
Buttercream.

ALMONDS OR HAZELNUTS
Preheat oven to 350°F. Toast 1 cup whole unblanched almonds or
hazelnuts on a baking sheet until lightly browned, about 7 minutes.
If using hazelnuts, transfer them to a large strainer and rub with a
towel to remove most of skins. Cool completely. Grind nuts in food
processor with pulsing motion until very fine. Using a wooden spoon,
gradually stir nuts into the Buttercream.

WALNUTS OR PECANS
Preheat oven to 350°F. Toast 1 1/3 cups walnuts or pecans on baking
sheet until lightly browned, about 5 minutes. Cool completely. Grind
nuts in food processor with pulsing motion until very fine. Using a
wooden spoon, gradually stir nuts into the Buttercream.

MERINGUE BUTTERCREAM
Crème au beurre à la meringue

In France, this is the favorite summer buttercream. Lighter than
the classic version, it uses egg whites rather than yolks. The whites are
beaten with hot syrup to make Italian meringue, then combined with
the butter. The same flavorings used in traditional buttercream (pages
190–191) can be used in meringue buttercream, except for fruit
purées.   MAKES 2 TO 2 1/2 CUPS

ITALIAN MERINGUE
3/4 cup plus 2 tablespoons sugar   3 large egg whites
1/3 cup water

1 1/4 cups unsalted butter   Flavoring (see below)

ITALIAN MERINGUE
Combine sugar and water in small heavy saucepan. Place over
low heat and swirl pan gently until sugar dissolves. Increase heat and

bring to a boil. Boil, without stirring, 3 minutes, skimming off foam occasionally. Meanwhile, whip egg whites until stiff but not dry.

Continue boiling syrup until candy thermometer registers about 245°F. (hard-ball stage), about 4 minutes. (To test without a thermometer, take a little of the hot syrup on a teaspoon and dip spoon into a cup of ice water, keeping spoon level. With your hands in ice water, remove syrup from teaspoon; if syrup is ready, it will form a firm ball. *Caution: Do not touch syrup unless your hands are in the water, because it is extremely hot.*) Remove syrup immediately from heat.

Gradually beat hot syrup into center of whites, with mixer at high speed; then continue beating until resulting meringue is cool and shiny.

Cream butter in large bowl until very soft and smooth. Gradually beat in meringue, about ¼ cup at a time. Gradually beat in flavoring.

SPIRITS
Gradually beat in 4 teaspoons Grand Marnier, Cointreau, clear raspberry brandy (framboise), kirsch, pear brandy, or rum.

COFFEE
Add 2 tablespoons instant coffee powder to meringue while it is still warm.

MERINGUE BUTTERCREAM WITH 2 EGG WHITES
MAKES ABOUT 1½ TO 1¾ CUPS, FOR FROSTING BUT NOT FILLING A 9-INCH CAKE

⅔ cup sugar	2 egg whites
⅓ cup water	1 cup unsalted butter

Prepare Meringue Buttercream as above, using these quantities. When using flavorings, add about two-thirds as much as for larger quantity above.

GANACHE (CHOCOLATE CREAM FROSTING)
Ganache

Made of just chocolate and cream, ganache is a wonderfully versatile mixture. It can be spread as a fudgy frosting or filling for a cake and is the classic center for chocolate truffles. As an icing for petits fours, ganache has many advantages over the traditional fondant—it is richer, tastes better, and is so much easier to prepare and to work with. It also makes a sinful topping for brownies or filling for sandwich cookies and can even be a base for preparing chocolate mousse. Rosettes of ganache make a striking garnish of a very deep chocolate color.   MAKES 1 GENEROUS CUP

8 ounces fine-quality semisweet or   3/4 cup heavy cream
*   bittersweet (see Note) chocolate,*
*   very finely chopped*

Put chocolate in heatproof medium bowl. Heat cream in small heavy saucepan over medium-high heat, stirring with whisk, until it comes to full boil. Pour cream over chocolate all at once. Stir with whisk until chocolate is completely melted and mixture is smooth. Cool to room temperature, occasionally stirring gently. (Ganache can be prepared 3 days ahead and refrigerated, covered. Before using as frosting or filling, set bowl of ganache above a pan of hot water over low heat to soften, stirring often; then cool to desired consistency for spreading.)

NOTES

• If using bittersweet chocolate, choose a type that tastes sweet enough on its own, as no sugar is added.
• The amount above is enough to frost an 8-inch cake or to fill a 9-inch 2-layer cake; or to fill and frost an 8-inch 2-layer cake in a thin layer; or to frost about 20 to 24 small or medium petits fours.

MILK CHOCOLATE GANACHE
Use 9 ounces fine-quality milk chocolate. If milk chocolate does not melt completely or is not uniform in color, set bowl of ganache mix-

ture above pan of hot water over low heat and stir gently with a whisk until chocolate is completely melted and mixture is smooth and well blended.

WHITE CHOCOLATE GANACHE

Use 10 ounces fine-quality white chocolate. If white chocolate does not melt completely or is not uniform in color, set bowl of ganache mixture above pan of hot water over low heat and stir gently with whisk until chocolate is completely melted and mixture is smooth and well blended.

TO USE GANACHE AS FILLING OR FROSTING

When using ganache made with semisweet or bittersweet chocolate, cool ganache, preferably at room temperature, until thick enough to spread. On a warm day or to save time, cool ganache by setting bowl of mixture in larger bowl of ice water or in refrigerator, gently stirring often from sides of bowl to center. Depending on type of chocolate, semisweet or bittersweet ganache can take as little as 20 to 30 minutes to cool in refrigerator.

Milk chocolate and white chocolate ganache take longer to thicken than dark chocolate ganache. Refrigerate them after they have cooled to room temperature; they will require 1 to 1½ hours to thicken in refrigerator.

Ganache is ready to spread when it has thickened and drops or flows slowly, rather than running from spoon. Do not let it get too thick or it will be difficult to spread. Spread ganache quickly so it does not thicken too much on standing. (If ganache becomes too thick, set bowl of mixture briefly above saucepan of hot water to soften it.)

When ganache is thick enough to spread, it can also be piped in rosettes or other decorative designs.

On a cool day, a cake frosted with semisweet or bittersweet ganache can be kept at room temperature so frosting becomes slightly firmer but is still shiny. On a warm day, refrigerate cake so that frosting sets. Refrigerate cakes frosted with milk chocolate or white chocolate ganache.

If a ganache-frosted cake has been refrigerated longer than 1 hour, let it stand at room temperature about 30 minutes before serving, so that ganache softens.

GANACHE FLAVORING VARIATIONS
VANILLA (FOR ANY TYPE CHOCOLATE)
Scald cream with 1 large (Tahitian) or 2 small vanilla beans, split lengthwise, in small heavy saucepan over medium-high heat until bubbling at edges. Remove from heat, cover, and let stand 30 minutes. Remove vanilla bean. Scrape any cream and loose seeds from vanilla bean back into pan of cream. Reheat vanilla-flavored cream and continue with recipe.

COFFEE (FOR SEMISWEET OR BITTERSWEET CHOCOLATE)
Place ⅓ cup (about 1 ounce) coffee beans, preferably Mocha Java, in a plastic bag on a board and coarsely crush them with a rolling pin. Scald cream with crushed coffee beans in small heavy saucepan over medium-high heat until bubbling at edges. Remove from heat, cover, and let stand 30 minutes. Strain cream through double layer of cheesecloth. Squeeze hard on cheesecloth to extract as much of cream as possible. Measure strained cream and add enough additional cream to obtain ¾ cup. Reheat cream and continue with recipe.

ORANGE (FOR SEMISWEET, BITTERSWEET, OR WHITE CHOCOLATE)
Using a vegetable peeler, pare colored part of peel of 2 medium navel oranges in long strips, without including white pith. Scald cream with strips of orange peel in small heavy saucepan over medium-high heat until bubbling at edges. Remove from heat, cover, and let stand 20 minutes. Strain cream into medium bowl, pressing on orange strips, and return to cleaned saucepan. Reheat orange-flavored cream and continue with recipe.

LEMON (FOR WHITE CHOCOLATE)
Using a vegetable peeler, pare colored part of peel of 1 large lemon in long strips, without including white pith. Scald cream with strips of lemon peel in small heavy saucepan over medium-high heat until bubbling at edges. Remove from heat, cover, and let stand 30 minutes. Strain cream into medium bowl, pressing on lemon strips, and return to cleaned saucepan. Reheat lemon-flavored cream and continue with recipe.

CINNAMON (FOR SEMISWEET OR BITTERSWEET CHOCOLATE)

Use two or three 3-inch cinnamon sticks, depending on whether you prefer a delicate or more pronounced cinnamon flavor. Scald cream with cinnamon sticks in small heavy saucepan over medium-high heat until bubbling at edges. Remove from heat, cover, and let stand 30 minutes. Remove cinnamon sticks. Reheat cinnamon-flavored cream and continue with recipe.

SPIRITS (FOR SEMISWEET OR BITTERSWEET CHOCOLATE)

Use only ⅔ cup cream to prepare ganache. When mixture is well blended, use whisk to gradually stir in 5 to 6 teaspoons rum, Cognac, Grand Marnier, or other spirits, to taste.

GANACHE BUTTERCREAM
Ganache beurrée

Adding butter to ganache produces ganache buttercream. This superb frosting has a creamier texture than basic ganache and is easier to use as a frosting for large cakes. Ganache buttercream is replacing ordinary chocolate buttercream as the most popular chocolate frosting in many modern pâtisseries; it tastes more chocolaty and is quicker and simpler to make, yet is equally easy to use for spreading and piping. A variety of cakes, from génoise to nut cakes to *bûche de noël,* benefit from this fabulous filling and frosting. It can be made from any of the ganache variations. White chocolate ganache buttercream is a perfect partner for fresh berries and other fruit—it complements their bright colors and gives them just the right touch of sweetness.

MAKES ABOUT 2 CUPS, ENOUGH TO FILL AND FROST
AN 8- OR 9-INCH 2-LAYER CAKE

Ganache (made with bittersweet or semisweet chocolate) (previous recipe)

½ cup unsalted butter, cut in pieces

Prepare ganache and cool to room temperature. Whisk ganache briefly until smooth. Cream butter in a large bowl with a paddle beater, if available, until very soft and smooth. Add ganache in 3 batches, beating constantly at low speed of mixer until mixture is smooth.

NOTE: After spreading ganache buttercream on a cake, refrigerate until it sets, about 1 hour. If cake has been refrigerated for more than 1 hour, let it stand at room temperature about 30 minutes before serving, so that buttercream softens.

MILK CHOCOLATE GANACHE BUTTERCREAM
Prepare Milk Chocolate Ganache (page 362) and cool to room temperature. Refrigerate, stirring occasionally, until cold and thickened but not set, about 30 minutes. Continue as above.

WHITE CHOCOLATE GANACHE BUTTERCREAM
Prepare White Chocolate Ganache (page 363) and cool to room temperature. Refrigerate, stirring occasionally, until cold and beginning to thicken, about 45 minutes. Continue as above.

WHIPPED GANACHE
Ganache montée

For a lighter effect, ganache can be whipped. Generally this type of ganache is made with a slightly higher proportion of cream. In its whipped form, ganache is paler in color and more airy in texture. Whipped ganache can be spread as a frosting and filling on all types of cakes, especially sponge cakes and other light cakes, and, like buttercream, can be used as a filling for tiny chocolate cups (see page 337).   MAKES 1 3/4 TO 2 CUPS, ENOUGH TO FILL AND FROST AN 8- OR 9-INCH 2-LAYER CAKE

8 ounces fine-quality semisweet or   *1 cup heavy cream*
   bittersweet (see Note) chocolate,
   very finely chopped

Put chocolate in heatproof medium bowl. Heat cream in small heavy saucepan over medium-high heat, stirring with whisk, until it comes to a full boil. Pour cream over chocolate all at once. Stir with a whisk until chocolate is completely melted and mixture is smooth. Cool to room temperature, stirring occasionally. Refrigerate, stirring mixture often from sides of bowl to center, until cold and thickened but not set, about 30 minutes.

Whip mixture in bowl of mixer at medium speed, or whisk it by hand until it lightens in color, is thick enough to spread, and forms very soft peaks, about 1 1/2 minutes. Do not overbeat ganache or it will separate. Whipped ganache must be used immediately or it will harden. (If whipped ganache separates or hardens, set bowl of mixture above a pan of hot water over low heat and let stand, stirring often, until it is hot to touch and smooth. Refrigerate again until it begins to thicken and whisk again until just spreadable.)

NOTES

• If using bittersweet chocolate, choose a type that tastes sweet enough on its own.
• To use, spread quickly on a cake. Refrigerate cake until frosting becomes slightly firm, about 15 minutes. If cake has been refrigerated for more than 1 hour, let stand at room temperature about 30 minutes before serving so that frosting softens.

WHIPPED MILK CHOCOLATE GANACHE
Use 9 ounces fine-quality milk chocolate. After cooling ganache to room temperature, refrigerate about 1 hour. Whisk ganache by hand until just thick enough to spread but not to form peaks, about 1 1/2 minutes. Do not overbeat; mixture separates easily. Use immediately.

WHIPPED WHITE CHOCOLATE GANACHE
Use 10 ounces fine-quality white chocolate. After cooling ganache to room temperature, refrigerate about 1 hour and 15 minutes. Whisk ganache by hand until just thick enough to spread but not to form peaks, about 3 minutes. Do not overbeat; mixture separates easily. Use immediately.

VANILLA PASTRY CREAM
Crème pâtissière

A rich, puddinglike mixture, pastry cream is spread on the bottom of fruit tarts and is the filling for cream puffs and some cakes. It also is the basis for sweet soufflés. To find pastry creams in other flavors, see index.   MAKES ABOUT 1 3/4 CUPS

1 1/2 *cups milk*
1 *vanilla bean, split*
5 *large egg yolks, room temperature*

6 *tablespoons sugar*
2 *tablespoons plus 2 teaspoons*
  cornstarch

Bring milk and vanilla bean to a boil in a medium, heavy saucepan. Remove from heat, cover, and let stand 15 minutes.

Whisk egg yolks lightly in a heatproof medium bowl. Add sugar and whisk until blended. Lightly stir in cornstarch with a whisk.

Reheat milk to a boil in a medium, heavy saucepan. Gradually whisk hot milk into yolk mixture. Return to saucepan and cook over medium-low heat, whisking constantly, until mixture is very thick and comes just to a boil. Reduce heat to low and cook, whisking constantly, 1 minute. Remove from heat.

Transfer to a bowl. If not using immediately, dab surface of the pastry cream with a small piece of butter to prevent a skin from forming, or cover with a piece of plastic wrap directly on the surface of the cream. Refrigerate until completely cool. (Pastry cream can be kept, covered tightly, up to 2 days in refrigerator.) Whisk pastry cream before using.

Flavorings

In this section are a few fundamental flavorings that can be prepared ahead: poached fruit, lightly candied orange peel julienne, and praline.

Poached fruit is a colorful topping for ice creams, cake layers, and tarts. The fruit is gently poached in a vanilla-and-lemon-scented sugar syrup until it is tender. Both the fruit and the syrup gain flavor from each other, and both are used in recipes for Bavarian creams, charlottes, and fruit sauces.

Candied orange peel julienne is prepared in a similar way to poached fruit and is sprinkled on a variety of desserts, especially ice cream.

Pairing toasted nuts with bittersweet caramelized sugar produces a mouth-watering preparation—praline. It contributes a distinctive taste to desserts ranging from soufflés and baked custards to Bavarian creams, ice cream, charlottes, and custard sauces. Cake and pastry fillings, from pastry cream and buttercream to whipped cream and mousses, are enhanced by its rich taste, as in Hazelnut Praline Cake and Macadamia Mousse Cake (see recipes). When coarsely chopped, praline makes a marvelously crunchy topping for ice cream, cake, or fresh fruit. As a flavoring it is intense enough to stand alone, yet it harmonizes well with vanilla, coffee, and chocolate (see Chocolate-Praline Ice Cream). Candy makers often add praline to ganache and utilize the mixture to make praline truffles. Praline is so popular among the French that they even have a verb, *praliner,* meaning to add praline to a sweet mixture.

Praline is said to have been invented in France in the seventeenth century by the chef of the Duke of Plessis-Praslin. It began as a simple candy—an almond coated in caramelized sugar. *Pralines,* as these almond candies are called, are still loved as sweets and are used whole in some cakes.

It was only when someone thought of grinding these almond candies that praline could be used widely as a flavoring in desserts. Later pastry chefs began to make it with hazelnuts, too. I have experimented with other nuts as well—Brazil nuts, pecans, walnuts, and macadamia nuts—and found they make wonderful new variations.

The taste of praline depends on the nuts chosen and on how dark the caramel is. Some chefs like to use a combination of almonds and hazelnuts, but most prefer to keep each nut separate so its character remains distinct. The usual proportions are equal amounts of nuts and sugar by weight. A somewhat similar mixture called *nougatine* or *nougat* is made from almonds that are not grilled before being mixed with light caramel.

Unlined copper saucepans are excellent for cooking caramel and making praline because they conduct heat efficiently, but they have to be cleaned thoroughly before each use (see Hints below). A heavy, stainless-steel saucepan also works very well.

The traditional method for preparing praline calls for heating dry sugar and raw almonds together until the sugar melts and caramelizes and the almonds become grilled. Since the mixture must be stirred constantly, this procedure is tiring and time-consuming. In addition, the sugar often caramelizes too quickly and burns before the almonds are toasted through.

Now many cooks prefer to toast the nuts separately in the oven, add them to golden brown caramel made from sugar syrup, and then heat them together just until they are thoroughly mixed. This is the easiest way to obtain good results, because the nuts are well toasted and the caramel is cooked exactly to the desired stage.

When the nut and caramel mixture cools it hardens, and is then crushed or ground. The texture of the final praline can be varied—it can remain chunky or be ground to a powder or a paste. Chunks are good for garnishing and powder for flavoring desserts.

Hints

POACHED FRUIT

- Syrup left from poaching fruit can be reused to poach more fruit.
- Poaching fruit in a syrup containing wine usually takes more time than in a syrup made only with water.
- Freshly poached fruit tastes best, but for recipes in which cooked fruit is needed as one of several elements, good-quality canned fruit can be substituted.
- Vanilla beans can be reused. Rinse them gently and let dry completely. Store in an airtight container. For poaching fruit, it is not necessary to use a new vanilla bean.

PRALINE

- Use a heavy saucepan when making praline. Flimsy pans will burn from the high temperature of the caramel. Avoid using a saucepan with a black interior because it is difficult to see the color of the caramel.

• If using an unlined copper sugar pan to make the caramel, always clean it inside before use by rubbing it with coarse salt and vinegar, then rinsing it with water.

• Use perfectly clean dry measuring cups, spoons, and saucepan when making praline.

• It is important to dissolve the sugar completely before the caramel mixture boils or it may crystallize inside and cause the praline to crystallize. Use a brush dipped in water to wash down any sugar crystals that jump up to the sides of the pan while the syrup for caramel is boiling; otherwise these crystals could cause the caramel to crystallize.

• Caramel can cause bad burns. Be careful not to let any drip or splash on your fingers. Do not touch the hot praline.

• If the praline mixture crystallizes when the nuts are added, keep heating it over medium-low heat, without stirring, until the sugar melts again. Be very careful not to let the mixture burn.

• To clean the saucepan and spoon after making caramel, fill the pan with cold water and put the spoon inside. Heat over low heat; the caramel will dissolve into the water.

• If praline is hard to break into chunks, use a hammer or rolling pin. Put the mixture in a plastic bag first so it does not scatter all over the kitchen.

• When grinding praline coarsely, some of the mixture becomes finely ground. The coarse pieces can be separated from the fine ones by putting all the praline in a coarse strainer and pushing the smaller pieces through it. Coarsely chopped praline can be ground again until it is fine.

• Do not leave chopped or ground praline standing unwrapped; it absorbs moisture from the air quickly and becomes sticky. Measure it just before using it.

POACHED FRUIT
Fruits pochés

Poaching makes firm fruit tender and helps it to keep longer. Gently poached fruit in a vanilla-scented syrup makes a lovely dessert on its own, or served with Chantilly cream or crème anglaise. It is also used to make tarts and as the filling and garnish for cakes. The poaching syrup can be reused to poach other fruit. Remember that relatively strong-flavored fruits like apricots and plums will flavor the syrup, and many types of plums will turn it red. For instructions on poaching other fruit and on other types of syrup, see index.

MAKES 4 TO 6 SERVINGS

3/4 cup sugar
3 cups water
1 vanilla bean (optional)
Pared zest of 1 lemon or 1 orange
   (optional)

1 to 1 1/4 pounds ripe fruit (see below)
1 tablespoon strained fresh lemon juice

Combine sugar, water, vanilla bean, and lemon or orange zest in medium, heavy saucepan and heat over low heat, stirring gently, until sugar dissolves. Raise heat to high and bring to a boil. Remove from heat.

Prepare fruit as specified below.

Bring syrup to a boil. Add fruit and lemon juice. Cover with a lid slightly smaller than the diameter of saucepan to keep fruit submerged. Reduce heat to low and cook fruit until tender when pierced with sharp knife (see cooking times below). Cool fruit in syrup, still covered with small lid, to room temperature. Refrigerate 30 minutes. (Fruit can be kept in syrup for 2 days in refrigerator.)

PEACHES

To prepare: Cut peaches in half by cutting around pits and pulling halves apart; if this is difficult, quarter them. Remove pits.
Poaching time: About 8 minutes. When peaches have cooled to lukewarm, peel with a paring knife and return to syrup.

NECTARINES

To prepare: Cut nectarines in half by cutting around pits and pulling halves apart. Remove pits.
Poaching time: About 8 minutes.

APRICOTS

To prepare: Cut apricots in half and remove pits.
Poaching time: About 6 minutes.

PEARS
Use 1 1/2 pounds ripe but fairly firm pears.
To prepare: Cut a lemon in half. Peel pears, and rub them well with cut side of lemon. Cut pears in half lengthwise. With the point of a peeler, remove flower end and core of each pear, including long stringy section that continues to stem.
Poaching time: About 12 minutes.

PLUMS
To prepare: Cut plums in half and remove pits.
Poaching time: About 12 minutes.

CHERRIES
To prepare: Pit cherries, if desired.
Poaching time: About 8 minutes.

KUMQUATS
To prepare: Leave kumquats whole.
Poaching time: About 10 minutes.

PINEAPPLE
Use a 4-pound pineapple. Increase sugar to 1 cup and water to 3 1/3 cups.
To prepare: Peel pineapple. Cut crosswise in 1/2-inch-thick slices.
Poaching time: About 8 minutes. To check if slices are tender, pierce side of a slice, not tough core.

LIGHTLY CANDIED ORANGE ZEST
Zestes d'oranges légèrement confites

This is a quick version of candied citrus peel, and makes a lively garnish for fruit desserts and ice creams.

MAKES GARNISH FOR 6 TO 8 SERVINGS

1 large orange
1/4 cup sugar

1 cup water

Using a vegetable peeler, pare colored part of orange peel in long strips, without including white pith. Cut zest in very thin strips, about 1/8 inch wide, with a large sharp knife.

Put strips of zest in a small saucepan and cover with water. Bring to a boil and boil 3 minutes. Drain, rinse with cold water, and drain well.

Combine sugar and 1 cup water in a small heavy saucepan. Heat mixture over low heat until sugar dissolves, gently stirring occasionally. Increase heat to high and bring to a boil. Add strips of zest to syrup and shake pan gently so zest is submerged. Poach zest, uncovered, over medium heat for 20 minutes, or until it is very tender and syrup thickens. Cool zest completely in syrup. (Candied zest can be kept in its syrup up to 1 week in refrigerator.)

Drain orange zest on paper towels. Use as long strands or cut in smaller pieces, to garnish desserts.

PRALINE
Pralin

Made from toasted nuts blended with caramel, praline is one of the best-loved French flavorings for soufflés, cake fillings, and all types of desserts. Commercial praline used by pastry chefs is ground repeatedly between rollers so that the final product is a very fine paste, much smoother than can be prepared at home. Homemade praline has a different texture but is equally delicious. Generally almonds, hazelnuts, or a mixture of the two are used in France, but I have made delicious praline from macadamia nuts, pecans, and other nuts, as in the variations. Praline is also great to keep on hand for sprinkling on ice cream or on fruit and whipped cream desserts.

MAKES 1 1/3 TO 1 1/2 CUPS

3/4 cup blanched or unblanched almonds (see Note), hazelnuts, or Brazil nuts; or 1 cup pecans, walnuts, or macadamia nuts

8 or 9 tablespoons sugar
1/4 cup water

Toast nuts as specified below for each type.

Remove nuts from oven but leave them in baking pan used to toast them so they keep warm. Lightly oil a baking sheet.

In small heavy saucepan that does not have black interior, put 8 tablespoons sugar (9 tablespoons if using macadamia nuts). Pour ¼ cup water over sugar. Heat mixture over low heat until sugar dissolves, gently stirring occasionally. Then boil over high heat without stirring, occasionally brushing down any sugar crystals from sides of pan with a wet pastry brush, until mixture begins to brown. Reduce heat to medium-low and cook, swirling pan gently, until mixture turns a rich-brown caramel color and a trace of smoke begins to rise from pan. Do not let caramel get too dark or it will burn and praline will be bitter; but if caramel is too light, praline will be too sweet. Remove caramel immediately from heat and stir in nuts, being careful not to get splashed, until they are well coated with caramel. Stir over low heat for 1 ½ to 2 minutes, to coat nuts with caramel. Transfer mixture immediately to oiled baking sheet and let cool completely. Break praline into small chunks.

To coarsely chop praline, transfer to food processor and use on/off turns.

To grind praline to a powder, process in food processor, scraping mixture inward occasionally, until finely ground.

Transfer praline immediately to an airtight container. (Praline can be stored in airtight container 3 weeks at cool room temperature; or it can be frozen for several months. It may lose its crunchiness after a few weeks, but will still taste good.)

NOTE: Almond praline made from blanched almonds is lighter-colored and more delicate in flavor than that made from unblanched ones.

ALMONDS
Preheat oven to 400°F. Toast almonds in a shallow baking pan in oven until lightly browned, about 8 minutes.

HAZELNUTS OR BRAZIL NUTS
Preheat oven to 350°F. Toast nuts in shallow baking pan in oven, 8 minutes for hazelnuts or 10 minutes for Brazil nuts. Transfer to a large

strainer. Rub nuts against strainer with a towel to remove skins; some of skins will remain. Return nuts to baking pan to keep warm.

PECANS OR WALNUTS

Preheat oven to 350°F. Toast nuts in shallow baking pan in oven 7 minutes.

MACADAMIA NUTS

Preheat oven to 350°F. If using raw macadamia nuts, toast them in shallow baking pan, shaking the pan occasionally, for 7 minutes, or until very lightly browned. If they are already toasted, heat them in oven for 3 minutes.

❧ CHOCOLATE-DIPPED ORANGE SECTIONS

These are a welcome simple treat on their own, and make a colorful accompaniment or garnish for cakes and ice cream.

4 TO 6 SERVINGS

2 small oranges
4 ounces fine-quality bittersweet or
*   semisweet chocolate, chopped*

Use a serrated knife to cut skin and white pith from oranges. Separate sections, discarding membrane. Put orange sections on a rack lined with paper towels and let dry about 1 hour, turning them over occasionally and patting often with paper towels; a small amount of moisture can make chocolate solidify during dipping.

Line a tray or plate with waxed paper. Melt chocolate in a small deep bowl set in a pan of water over low heat. Stir until smooth. Remove from heat and cool to slightly less than body temperature.

Dip half of each orange piece in chocolate, letting excess chocolate drip into bowl, and transfer orange section to waxed paper. Let dipped orange sections stand at cool room temperature or refrigerate 30 minutes until chocolate sets. (They can be kept uncovered up to 4 hours in refrigerator.)

Cakes and Pastries

The basic cakes and pastries in this section are those used most often by French pastry chefs. All apprentices in pastry shops are required to learn to make them and to use them. It is worthwhile to get to know these recipes at home, because they come up over and over in the making of desserts. All but puff pastry are simple to master, and they become even easier to make with a little experience.

Génoise cake can be served on its own or with fruit as a simple dessert. Ladyfingers and nut meringues are most often elements of other desserts, but can also play the role of accompaniments. The pastries are nearly always served with fillings.

For information on how to use these cakes and pastries, see the earlier chapters on these subjects.

GÉNOISE (FRENCH SPONGE CAKE)
Génoise

Most of the French gâteaux in the windows of pastry shops are made with this cake as a base. Although the cake itself can be flavored with vanilla, citrus rind, and other flavorings, usually it is by varying the frostings and the syrups used to moisten the layers that pastry chefs achieve a dizzying array of splendid cakes. MAKES A 9-INCH CAKE

1/4 cup unsalted butter
3/4 cup plus 2 tablespoons cake
  flour

4 extra-large eggs
2/3 cup sugar
1/2 teaspoon pure vanilla extract

Preheat oven to 350°F. Butter a round 9-inch cake pan, about 2 inches deep, or a 9-inch springform pan. Line base with a round of parchment paper or foil and butter paper or foil. Flour paper and sides of pan and tap to remove excess.

Melt butter in small saucepan over low heat and let cool completely. Sift flour.

Whisk eggs in mixer bowl. Beat in sugar. Set bowl of egg mixture in shallow pan of hot water over low heat and whisk 3 minutes. Remove from water. Using a mixer, beat at high speed about 7 minutes, or until mixture is very thick. Beat in vanilla. Sift one-third of flour over batter and fold it in as gently as possible. Add remaining flour in 2 more portions, in same way. When last portion is nearly folded in, begin adding butter in a thin stream and folding it in.

Pour batter into pan and bake until cake shrinks slightly from sides of pan and top springs back when lightly pressed with your fingertip, about 30 to 35 minutes. Run thin-bladed flexible knife carefully around edges of cake, and turn out onto rack to cool.

COCOA GÉNOISE
Instead of amount of cake flour above, sift ⅔ cup cake flour with ¼ cup Dutch-process cocoa and ½ teaspoon baking powder. Increase sugar to ¾ cup.

GÉNOISE LAYERS
MAKES THREE 8-INCH OR TWO 9-INCH LAYERS

6 tablespoons unsalted butter	*1 cup sugar*
1⅓ cups cake flour	*¾ teaspoon pure vanilla extract*
6 extra-large eggs	

Preheat oven to 350°F. Prepare three 8-inch or two 9-inch layer cake pans as in Génoise, above.

Prepare batter as above, using amounts listed here. Divide batter among prepared pans. Bake until cakes shrink slightly from sides of pans and tops spring back when lightly pressed with your fingertip, about 18 minutes for 8-inch pans or about 30 minutes for 9-inch pans. Run a thin-bladed flexible knife carefully around edges of cakes, and turn out onto racks to cool.

❧ LADYFINGERS
Biscuits à la cuiller

The French name for ladyfingers means "spoon cookies," because the batter used to be spooned into molds, whereas now it is piped onto baking sheets. Use ladyfingers to accompany mousses, ice creams, sorbets, or fruit desserts, or to make frames for charlottes, such as Strawberry-Banana Charlotte (see recipe).

MAKES ABOUT 48 LADYFINGERS; ABOUT 10 OUNCES

4 large eggs, separated, room
    temperature
2/3 cup granulated sugar
3/4 teaspoon pure vanilla extract

1/4 teaspoon cream of tartar
3/4 cup all-purpose flour
1 tablespoon plus 1 teaspoon
    powdered sugar

Position rack in center of oven and preheat to 350°F. Butter and lightly flour 2 nonstick baking sheets, tapping pans to remove excess flour. With your finger, mark crosswise lines on baking sheets 3 inches apart, to mark length of ladyfingers.

Have a rubber spatula ready for folding and a pastry bag with a large plain tip of 5/8-inch diameter. Using a clothespin or paper clip, close end of bag just above tip, so mixture will not run out while bag is being filled.

Beat egg yolks lightly in a large bowl, beat in 6 tablespoons sugar, and continue beating at high speed about 5 minutes, or until mixture is pale and very thick. Beat in vanilla.

Whip egg whites with cream of tartar in a large bowl until soft peaks form. Gradually beat in remaining sugar at high speed and beat until whites are stiff and shiny but not dry, about 15 seconds.

Sift about one-quarter of flour over yolk mixture and fold gently until nearly incorporated. Gently fold in about one-quarter of whites. Repeat with remaining flour and whites, each in 3 batches, adding each batch when previous one is nearly blended in. Continue folding lightly but quickly, just until batter is blended.

Spoon batter immediately into prepared pastry bag. Pipe 3- × 1 1/4-inch ladyfingers onto baking sheets, spacing them about 1 inch apart. Sift powdered sugar lightly but evenly over ladyfingers.

Bake in center of oven about 12 minutes, or until they are just firm on outside and spring back when pressed very lightly, but are slightly soft inside. Transfer to a rack and let cool. (Ladyfingers can be kept up to 1 day in an airtight container in 1 layer; or they can be frozen in layers separated with wax paper.)

NUT MERINGUES
Fonds de succès

Pair any of the nut meringues below with whipped cream, butter-cream, or mousses to make fabulous desserts. Or serve small ones on their own as delicate cookies.

MAKES TWO 8-INCH ROUNDS; ABOUT 8 SERVINGS

3/4 to 1 cup nuts (see variations below)
2/3 cup sugar
1 tablespoon cornstarch

4 large egg whites, room temperature
1/8 teaspoon cream of tartar

Prepare nuts as specified below.

Position rack in center of oven and preheat to 300°F. Butter and lightly flour 2 nonstick medium baking sheets, tapping each to remove excess flour. If using regular baking sheets, lightly butter corners and line sheets with foil; butter and lightly flour foil. Using 8-inch spring-form pan rim as a guide, trace circle onto each baking sheet, drawing it around outside of springform rim. Have ready rubber spatula for folding and pastry bag fitted with 1/2-inch plain tip.

Grind nuts with 1/2 cup sugar in food processor until as fine as possible, scraping inward occasionally. Transfer to a medium bowl. Sift cornstarch over nut mixture, and, using a fork, stir mixture lightly until blended.

Beat egg whites with cream of tartar in large bowl, beginning at medium speed and increasing to medium-high, until they form soft peaks. With mixer at high speed, gradually beat in remaining sugar and continue beating until whites are just stiff and shiny but not dry, about 15 seconds.

Sprinkle about one-third of nut mixture over whites while folding gently; continue sprinkling and folding as gently and as quickly as possible until just blended.

Immediately transfer mixture to pastry bag with the rubber spatula. Beginning at center of circle marked on baking sheet, pipe meringue in a tight spiral until circle is completely covered. Use uniform pressure so rounds have even thickness. If there are holes in spiral, pipe a small dot of meringue in each hole. Pipe another spiral on second baking sheet. Pipe any remaining meringue in mounds about 1 inch in diameter and ¾ inch high, giving them rounded tops.

Bake meringues 30 minutes. (If both baking sheets do not fit on central rack, bake them on 2 racks and switch their positions after baking them about 15 minutes.) Reduce oven temperature to 275°F. Continue baking until meringues are light brown, dry, and just firm but not hard, about 10 to 15 minutes; to check, touch center of each meringue very lightly—your finger should not leave an impression in mixture. Meringues burn easily if overbaked, but remain sticky if underbaked. They will become firmer as they cool.

Immediately release meringues gently from baking sheets or foil with a large metal spatula; peel off foil, if necessary. If meringues are sticky on bottom, return to oven until dry, about 5 minutes more. Transfer to a rack and let cool completely. (Meringues can be kept up to 5 days in airtight container in dry weather; or they can be frozen.)

ALMOND MERINGUES
Use ¾ cup (about 4 ounces) whole blanched almonds or slivered almonds.

HAZELNUT MERINGUES
Use 1 cup (about 4 ounces) hazelnuts (also called filberts). Preheat oven to 350°F. Toast hazelnuts in shallow baking pan in oven until skins begin to split, about 8 minutes. Transfer to large strainer and rub hot nuts against strainer with terrycloth towel to remove most of skins. Cool nuts completely.

HAZELNUT-ALMOND MERINGUES
Use ½ cup hazelnuts and ⅓ cup unblanched almonds. Preheat oven to 350°F. Put hazelnuts and almonds in 2 separate small baking pans. Toast both types in oven 8 minutes. Transfer hazelnuts to large strainer. Rub hot hazelnuts against strainer with terrycloth towel to

remove most of skins. Cool both almonds and hazelnuts completely. Combine nuts in bowl.

PECAN MERINGUES

Use 1 cup (about 3¾ ounces) pecans.

WALNUT MERINGUES

Use 1 cup (about 3½ ounces) walnuts.

MACADAMIA NUT MERINGUES

Use 1 cup (about 4½ ounces) unsalted macadamia nuts.

PISTACHIO MERINGUES

Use 1 cup (about 4 ounces) shelled unsalted pistachios; if buying them unshelled, you will need 8 ounces.

COCOA-PECAN DACQUOISE

Use ½ cup pecans. Replace cornstarch with 2 tablespoons Dutch-process cocoa sifted with 2 tablespoons flour. Increase sugar to ¾ cup; use 6 tablespoons for grinding with nuts, and beat the rest into egg whites.

INDIVIDUAL NUT MERINGUES

MAKES ABOUT 16 ROUNDS OR COOKIES

Instead of 8-inch circles, mark smaller rounds as follows: Using a 3-inch plain cookie cutter, mark 16 to 18 circles, spacing them about ½ inch apart, on buttered and floured baking sheets. Have ready pastry bag fitted with either ½-inch or ⅜-inch plain tip; larger tip is easier to use, while smaller tip produces thinner, more delicate meringue rounds.

Preheat oven and prepare nut meringue as above. Beginning at center of 1 circle marked on baking sheet, pipe meringue in tight spiral until circle is completely covered. Continue with remaining circles.

If meringues are piped with smaller tip, bake them about 28 minutes. If they are piped with larger tip, bake them 30 minutes; then reduce oven temperature to 275°F. and continue baking until done, about 5 to 10 minutes more. Check for doneness as with large meringues. Remove 1 and look at bottom—it should be golden brown; do not let it get darker or meringue will have burnt taste.

CREAM PUFF PASTRY OR CHOUX PASTRY
Pâte à choux

This is the quickest and easiest pastry to make, and the only one that is cooked on top of the stove before being baked. Use it to prepare cream puffs, éclairs, and profiteroles.

MAKES ABOUT 20 SMALL CREAM PUFFS

1/2 cup water
1/4 teaspoon salt
1/4 cup unsalted butter, cut in pieces

1/2 cup plus 1 tablespoon all-purpose flour, sifted
3 large eggs

Heat water, salt, and butter in a small heavy saucepan until butter melts. Bring to a boil and remove from heat. Add flour immediately and stir quickly with a wooden spoon until mixture is smooth. Set pan over low heat and beat the mixture for about 30 seconds. Remove and let cool for a few minutes.

Add 1 egg and beat it thoroughly into mixture. Beat in second egg until mixture is smooth. In a small bowl, beat third egg with a fork. Gradually beat enough of this egg into the dough until dough becomes very shiny and is soft enough so it just falls from the spoon. Shape dough while warm, according to recipes.

FRENCH TART PASTRY
Pâte brisée

Unlike American pie pastry, French tart pastry or *pâte brisée* contains egg yolks and uses all butter rather than other shortenings. It is either unsweetened or lightly sweetened and is perfect for sweet fruit fillings, as in Traditional French Apple Tart (see recipe).

MAKES A 9- TO 10-INCH SHELL

2 large egg yolks
2 tablespoons ice water, or more as
  needed
1 1/2 cups all-purpose flour
3/8 teaspoon salt

2 tablespoons powdered sugar
  (optional)
1/2 cup unsalted butter, cold, cut
  into bits

TO MAKE DOUGH IN FOOD PROCESSOR

Beat egg yolks with ice water. Combine flour, salt, and sugar in a food processor fitted with a metal blade. Process briefly to blend. Scatter butter pieces over mixture. Mix using on/off turns until mixture resembles coarse meal. Pour egg yolk mixture evenly over mixture in processor. Process with on/off turns, scraping down occasionally, until dough forms sticky crumbs that can be easily pressed together but does not come together in a ball. If crumbs are dry, sprinkle with 1/2 teaspoon water and process with on/off turns until dough forms sticky crumbs. Add more water in same way, 1/2 teaspoon at a time, if crumbs are still dry. Using a rubber spatula, transfer dough to a sheet of plastic wrap, wrap it, and push it together. Shape dough in a flat disk.

TO MAKE DOUGH BY HAND

Beat egg yolks with ice water. In a large bowl, combine flour, salt, and sugar; add butter and blend until mixture forms fine crumbs. Add egg yolk mixture and toss until liquid is incorporated, adding more ice water by 1/2 teaspoons, if necessary, to form dough into a ball. Knead dough lightly with heel of hand against a smooth surface for just a few seconds and press it gently into a ball. Dust dough with flour and wrap it in wax paper. Shape dough in a flat disk.

Refrigerate dough 1 hour. (Dough can be kept up to 2 days in refrigerator.)

SWEET PASTRY
Pâte sucrée

This cookielike dough is delicious and sweet, and is my favorite type for fruit tarts, especially those with creamy fillings.

MAKES A 9-INCH SQUARE OR 10-INCH ROUND TART

1 1/4 cups all-purpose flour
1/4 cup cake flour
7 tablespoons sugar
1/4 teaspoon salt

1/2 cup unsalted butter, very cold,
*   cut into bits*
1 large egg, lightly beaten

TO MAKE PASTRY IN FOOD PROCESSOR

Combine both types flour, sugar, and salt in a food processor fitted with a metal blade. Process briefly to blend. Scatter butter pieces over mixture. Mix using on/off turns until mixture resembles coarse meal. Pour egg evenly over mixture in processor. Process with on/off turns, scraping down occasionally, until dough forms sticky crumbs that can easily be pressed together but does not come together in a ball. Transfer dough to a work surface.

TO MAKE PASTRY BY HAND

Sift both types flour onto a work surface and make a well in center. Add egg, sugar, and salt and mix them using your fingertips. Pound butter to soften it and cut it in pieces. Add it to well and quickly mix with other ingredients in well until partially mixed. Gradually draw in flour to make coarse crumbs. Toss mixture, rubbing it between your fingers, until crumbs begin to stick together.

Blend dough further by pushing about one-quarter of it away from you and smearing it with heel of your hand against work surface. Repeat with remaining dough in 3 batches. Repeat with each batch, if dough is not yet well blended.

Using a rubber spatula, transfer dough to a sheet of plastic wrap,

wrap it, and push it together. Shape dough in a flat disk or square, according to shape of your tart pan. Refrigerate dough 4 hours. (Dough can be kept up to 2 days in refrigerator.)

CITRUS-FLAVORED SWEET PASTRY

Using either method above, add grated zest of ½ orange and grated zest of ½ lemon along with sugar.

RICH SWEET PASTRY

Substitute 3 large egg yolks for the whole egg. Reduce sugar to 6 tablespoons. Substitute 1½ cups all-purpose flour for combination of flours. If dough is too dry to come together, sprinkle with ice water, ½ teaspoon at a time, until dough is moist enough to form sticky crumbs.

✍ PUFF PASTRY
Pâte feuilletée

Puff pastry takes time to prepare because it requires several resting periods, but the amount of work itself is not great. Mastering puff pastry takes some practice; it may not rise well on the first attempt, but it will always taste good. Our chefs at La Varenne recommended we turn our first batches into Napoleons (page 270) or palm-leaf cookies (page 304), because these do not need to rise much for the pastry's rich buttery flavor to be enjoyed.   MAKES ABOUT 1½ POUNDS

2 cups all-purpose flour	*1 cup plus 5 tablespoons unsalted*
⅔ cup cake flour	*butter, well chilled*
1¼ teaspoons salt	*¾ to 1 cup ice water*

Combine both types of flour and salt in a food processor fitted with metal blade, and mix with a few on/off turns. Cut 4 tablespoons butter into small pieces, and add to processor. (Keep remaining butter in refrigerator.) Process with on/off turns until mixture resembles meal. With motor running, add ¾ cup ice water and process just until dough begins to hold together. If dough is dry, add more water, 1 teaspoon at a time, until dough begins to hold together. Transfer dough to work surface. Knead very lightly by passing dough from one hand to the other and turning it over. Dust dough lightly with flour, flatten to a disk, cut a deep cross in middle. Pat until smooth, wrap in wax paper, and refrigerate 30 minutes, until firm but not hard. Clean and chill work surface. (Use a marble slab that you can chill in the freezer or refrigerator.)

Lightly flour remaining butter on both sides on wax paper and cover with another sheet of wax paper. Pound butter with a rolling pin to soften and flatten it. Fold it in three, return it to paper, and pound again. Repeat two or three times until butter becomes flexible. Shape it in a square with about 6-inch sides. Keep butter cold while doing this. Return butter to refrigerator for a few minutes to cool it but do not let it harden.

Roll dough on a cold floured surface to a circle slightly larger than square of butter (about 10 inches in diameter), and with a slight hump in center. Set butter on dough. Pull dough from two opposite sides and bring them together over butter, and press them to seal edges. Repeat with two other opposite sides so butter is completely enclosed. Pound with side of your fist to seal dough.

Turn dough over so it is seam side down. Pound lightly 3 or 4 times with rolling pin to begin flattening butter. Roll quickly to a 20-×-8-inch rectangle; do not roll over long ends. Fold in three like a business letter (bottom third up and top third down). This is first "turn." Rotate dough 90° so a fold is to your right. Roll again to a 20-×-8-inch rectangle. This is second turn. Wrap dough in wax paper. Make 2 indentations with your fingers as a reminder of how many turns were done. Cover and refrigerate 20 to 30 minutes. Meanwhile clean surface.

Put dough with a fold to your right and do two more turns. Mark with 4 fingers, and refrigerate 20 to 30 minutes. (At this point dough can be kept, covered, 3 or 4 days in refrigerator; or it can be frozen.)

On day you are using dough, do two more turns. Refrigerate at least 1 hour or up to 12 hours before using.

NOTE: To prepare dough by hand, soften 3 tablespoons butter by pounding with a rolling pin. Keep remaining butter in refrigerator. Sift flour into a bowl and make a well inside. Put salt, softened 3 tablespoons butter, and ¾ cup water in well. Mix ingredients in well, and gradually add flour by incorporating it with your fingertips. Transfer dough to a cold work surface. If there are dry crumbs, sprinkle them with a bit more water. Add to remaining dough. Dough will not yet be mixed. Do not knead it, but rather cut it with spatula in 4 or 5 pieces, gather together and cut again in other direction. Gently turn dough over from one hand to the other to make it smoother, but do not worry if it's not entirely smooth. Then dust with flour, flatten to a disk, wrap in wax paper, refrigerate 30 minutes, and proceed with recipe.

Techniques

To Blanch Almonds

Boil enough water to generously cover almonds. Add almonds, return to a boil, and boil about 15 seconds. Remove an almond with a slotted spoon. Squeeze one end of almond with your thumb and index finger; almond will come out of its skin. If it doesn't, boil them a few more seconds and try again. When almonds can be peeled easily, drain them and peel the rest. Spread blanched almonds in one layer on shallow trays or dishes lined with paper towels, and put paper towels on top of almonds as well. Pat them dry. Almonds should always be thoroughly dried before they are ground.

To Toast and Skin Hazelnuts

Preheat oven to 350°F. Toast nuts in shallow baking pan in oven about 8 minutes, or until skins begin to split. Transfer to a large strainer. Rub nuts vigorously against strainer with a towel to remove skins; some of skins will remain.

To Toast Raw Macadamia Nuts

Toast raw macadamia nuts on a baking sheet or in a baking dish in a preheated 350°F. oven, shaking the pan occasionally, for 7 minutes, or until they are very lightly browned. Transfer them to a plate and let them cool completely.

To Desalt Salted Macadamia Nuts

Put the nuts in a large strainer and rinse them with warm water for about 10 seconds, tossing them often. Drain for 5 minutes in the strainer, tossing them occasionally. Transfer nuts to a baking sheet. Dry them in a preheated 250°F. oven for 5 minutes, shaking the baking sheet occasionally. Transfer to a plate and let cool completely.

To Make Quick Chocolate Curls

Use a large piece or a bar of dark or white chocolate. Let chocolate come to warm room temperature by leaving it in a warm place in kitchen, but do not let it melt. Use a swivel-type vegetable peeler to peel curls from smooth side of bar, pressing firmly. Let curls fall directly onto dessert or onto wax paper. Refrigerate until ready to use. Do not touch curls, as they will melt from the warmth of your hands. To move them, use a fork, or let them fall from wax paper onto dessert.

To Temper Chocolate

Tempering is a special procedure for melting fine chocolate for coating candies. It basically involves melting chocolate, letting it cool completely, and then heating it very slightly until it reaches the ideal temperature for dipping. Tempering makes chocolate set quickly, helps prevent streaks, and gives it a shinier, crisper finish. Always temper chocolate in a cool room and use the finest *couverture* chocolate. Do not use chocolate that you have already melted for other purposes.

Melt chopped chocolate in a double boiler or heatproof medium bowl over hot, not simmering, water over low heat, stirring very often with a rubber spatula, until it reaches about 115°F. on an instant-read thermometer. Stir until smooth. Remove from pan of water.

Dry base of container of chocolate. Pour about half the chocolate onto a marble slab. Spread it and scrape it back and forth with a scraper or metal spatula until it just begins to set and reaches about 80°F.

Scrape chocolate from marble and return it immediately to remaining chocolate. Mix thoroughly. Return it to water bath and heat it, stirring constantly, until it reaches the ideal dipping temperature: 88°F. for semisweet or bittersweet chocolate; 84°F. for white or milk chocolate. It is now ready for dipping.

Index

391

ABOUT THE AUTHOR

Award-winning author Faye Levy has written cookbooks on French cooking in three languages for publishers on three continents.

Her cookbook series, *FRESH FROM FRANCE,* has been highly acclaimed. The first volume in the series, **Vegetable Creations,** won an International Association of Cooking Professionals/Seagram cookbook award and was chosen by *Publishers Weekly* for their honor list of "The Best Books of the Year." The second volume, **Dinner Inspirations,** was proclaimed by M. F. K. Fisher "excellent in every way" and by Jacques Pépin as representing "the very best of contemporary French restaurant and home cooking."

In 1986 two of Faye's books won Tastemaker awards. **Faye Levy's Chocolate Sensations** was voted the Best Dessert and Baking Book of the Year by the International Association of Cooking Professionals/Seagram Awards; and **Classic Cooking Techniques** won as the best Basic/General Cookbook of the Year.

Faye Levy is the only American to have written a book on French cooking for the French. **La Cuisine du Poisson,** the cookbook she authored with Fernand Chambrette, was published by Flammarion. Faye is the first woman to be included in Flammarion's cookbook series, "les grands chefs," that includes Escoffier, Bocuse, and Lenôtre. Faye has also written two books on French desserts in Hebrew.

For six years Faye wrote a column, "The Basics," for *Bon Appétit* magazine, and during that time two of her innovative articles on French desserts were featured as cover stories of the magazines. Faye Levy has also developed creative dessert recipes for her articles in *Gourmet* and *Chocolatier* magazines.

A frequent culinary contributor to prestigious newspapers, Faye is respected for her clear, reliable, well-tested recipes. Her articles on the recent bicentennial of the French Revolution were published as front-page stories of the food sections of the *Boston Globe,* the *Philadelphia Inquirer,* the *Detroit News,* the *Portland Oregonian,* the *St. Louis Post-Dispatch,* the *Cleveland Plain Dealer,* the *Los Angeles Herald Examiner,* the *Orange County Register,* and the *Fort Lauderdale News.*

In her books and articles, Faye's focus has been on the home cook. Yet chefs, caterers, and other cooking professionals have demonstrated great enthusiasm for her work, and this has led to her becoming a monthly columnist of *Western Chef* magazine, where her articles are often featured as the cover story.

Faye holds the "Grand Diplôme" of the first graduating class of the famous Parisian cooking school La Varenne, where she spent over five years. Faye also studied at Lenôtre's school for professional pastry chefs near Paris.

Faye is the author of **The La Varenne Tour Book,** the school's first cookbook. As La Varenne's cookbook and recipe editor, she planned the school's curriculum and developed and drafted the recipes for the award-winning cookbooks, **Basic French Cookery, French Regional Cooking,** and **The La Varenne Cooking Course.** She was also a major contributor to **La Varenne Pratique.**

Faye Levy lived in Israel seven years and is an honor graduate of Tel Aviv University. She recently became a regular food columnist of the *Jerusalem Post* and for the last three years has been the monthly cooking columnist of Israel's foremost women's magazine, *"At."*

Faye and her husband/associate Yakir Levy live in Santa Monica, California.